Managing
Business
Risk

Managing Business Risk

An Organization-Wide Approach to Risk Management

Peter C. Young
Steven C. Tippins

AMACOM
American Management Association

New York • Atlanta • Boston • Chicago • Kansas City • San Francisco • Washington, D. C.
Brussels • Mexico City • Tokyo • Toronto

Library of Congress Cataloging-in-Publication Data

Young, Peter C.
    Managing business risk: an organization-wide approach to risk management / Peter C. Young, Steven C. Tippins.
       p. cm.
    Includes index.
    ISBN 0-8144-0461-8
    1. Risk management.   I. Tippins, Steven C.   II. Title.

HD61.Y68   2000
658.15'5—dc21

                                    00-042014

Printing number

10   9   8   7   6   5   4   3   2   1

Contents

Preface

Without a doubt, risk management has become a subject of enormous interest over the past ten years. The reasons are varied, ranging from emerging capabilities in the management of financial risks, to heightened awareness of catastrophic risks, to evolving exposures in legal liability, to concerns over financing human asset risks such as disability, poor health, retirement, and even investments in productivity.

We concede that a degree of faddishness exists regarding the current interest in risk management. Despite the real and tangible need for organizations to assess and manage risks, there remains a certain sense that a roving spotlight has been trained on the field of risk management and that it eventually will sweep away to focus on other management concerns. Thus, we see some urgency to clarify and explain the subject of risk management to a broader audience and to assert its more immutable characteristics while the opportunity exists to do so.

This observation explains one of the two motivations for the writing of this book. Risk management is an important subject, and it has a real contributory value to the overall purposes of an organization. Yet risk management historically has received scant attention from managers not specifically engaged in its practice—that is, of course, until recently. Therefore, a general introduction to the subject of risk management is needed to provide a basic treatment of both the concepts and the practices that define the field.

Our second motivation is the desire to organize the current

discussion about risk management practices. As the book reveals, there are several competing ideas about risk management—ideas that have been framed in such a way that they may actually inhibit the development of risk management. As just one example, the rapid emergence of financial risk management within the treasury function of many large companies has produced an environment in which risk management is characterized as being "not an insurance matter but a financial management matter." While we don't dispute the importance of financial aspects of risk management, the result is that behavioral psychology, governance, operations and strategy, stakeholder management, and other critical risk management issues tend to be relegated to a secondary role. In our judgment, risk management is not a technical management issue but rather a general management concern and thus requires an integrated interdisciplinary approach.

In an effort to respond to this concern, we develop a concept known as Organization Risk Management (ORM), which attempts to provide a broad and general context for understanding risk management. The ORM idea is a loose-jointed model that allows readers to explore actual risk management practices but also to consider how current trends and issues may transform risk management. It is our hope that in presenting both a conceptual idea of risk management as well as a description of current practices, readers will have a richer appreciation of risk management form and function than would be possible through a conventional introduction to the subject.

These two motivations, naturally enough, inform the structure and content of this book. To appreciate how risk management's present and future compare, readers must have a perspective on the history of risk management, on the broad and general structure of risk management practices, and on the controversies and issues that confront risk managers today. Such a wide ranging task will require an "organizing idea"—that is, a framework for understanding risk management that allows readers to appreciate the implications of the distinctions and differences that exist when we look at risk management across industries. The ORM model serves as such a framework because it is defined and explained as an organization-wide approach to the management of risk.

The discussion of ORM in the ensuing chapters, and the contrast it will provide with traditional risk management practices, raises a question that will receive some attention in the final chapter of the book. As a conceptual framework for understanding risk management, ORM is compelling and (we hope) logical—but it is not widely seen in organizations today. Readers reasonably will wonder why this is so, and the book will attempt to offer an explanation.

Chapter 1 presents an overview history of risk management, which will provide context for readers to appreciate current practices and the relationship that traditional practice has with the Organization Risk Management idea. Of course, the chapter will include a broad discussion of ORM.

Chapters 2 through 7 are structured to accomplish the following three objectives:

1. To give readers an understanding of the technical substance of risk management
2. To allow readers to appreciate the distinctions that arise when technical aspects of risk management are applied in traditional and in ORM-based environments
3. To help readers see how the nature of an organization's particular business or industry influences the specific functional aspects of risk management

To these ends, Chapter 2 focuses on the process of risk assessment; then chapters 3–5 look at risk control. Chapters 6 and 7 present a discussion on risk financing, with a particular emphasis on the subject of insurance.

Chapter 8 offers an extended discussion of the implementation of a risk management program. Beyond a presentation of general practices and challenges, however, the chapter includes an investigation of the limitations of the ORM idea in practice.

Finally, we should say a word about our intended audience. As noted at the outset, risk management is a subject that is receiving attention from all types of managers. This observation correctly implies that the book is written for the manager who is not directly involved in the risk management function or, perhaps, who is new to it. Longtime risk managers will find much of the discussion to be well known and understood by practitioners, although parts of the ORM discussion may be unfamiliar. We further presume that while the book will be of interest to managers in all types of organizations, it is likely to resonate with managers in organizations that currently do not have a highly developed risk management function. Organizations with experienced risk managers already in place most likely have been exposed to many of the concepts, principles, and practices presented in this book.

Readers will note throughout an extensive use of supplemental articles, cases, and illustrations. We have chosen to do so in order to make a persuasive case that most—if not all—the ideas presented within the book have real world manifestations. All these supplements are drawn from *Business Insurance* and *Risk Management,* the two most influential publications in the risk management world today. We would particularly commend readers to the *Read More About It* articles at the end of each chapter, which are intended not only to illustrate chapter themes but to enable our most interested readers to delve more deeply into key topics.

Acknowledgments

We would like to thank several people in the development of this book. Our editor, Ray O'Connell, was the victim of an eighteen-month stress test in overseeing our effort, and we want him to know that we appreciate his patience and humor. We also thank Christina McLaughlin and Karen Brogno—particularly for their 11th hour heroics in getting this book into print. Stan Nyquist and Ted Fredrickson, University of St. Thomas MBA program director and Graduate School of Business dean, respectively, have been constantly supportive and deserve a special general acknowledgment.

We have long enjoyed an association with a number of risk managers, underwriters, brokers, and other industry experts. In various ways—some obvious and some not so obvious—they all have contributed to our thinking and the development of this book. The risk in "naming names" is that the named persons expect it and the unnamed never forget it—so with apologies to the unnamed, we would like to thank the following individuals:

Fiona Gilvey and Malcolm McCaig (Deloitte & Touche); Paul Winston (Business Insurance); Mavis Allen (Risk Management); Martin Fone and Rich Vincelette (Munich American Risk Partners); Brad Johnson (Marsh); Jean Kennedy (Medtronic); Taud Hoopingarner (Dakota County); Denise Kapler (Ramsey County); Ron Guilfoile (City of St. Paul); K. C. Kidder and Jill Coombs (Wells Fargo); J. C. Beckstrand (E. W. Blanch); Gerry Dickinson and Chris Parsons (City University–London); Martin Hudson (St. Paul Companies); Alan Punter (Aon); Mike Smith (the Ohio State

University); Terry Webb (Lloyd's); Tom Hugdahl (3M); Mike Anderson (NSP); David Randle (Apex); Pam Rogers (Sears); Dick Heydinger (Hallmark); Anne Zug (Jefferson Health Services); Judy Lindenmeyer (FMR Corp.); Chris Duncan (Delta Airlines); David Adler (Portman Risk Management); William Kelly (J. P. Morgan); Jeff Cassidy (ACE); and David Mair (U.S. Olympic Committee).

We dedicate this book to the most important people in our lives—Prudence and Nicholas, and Sian, Hannah, and Mallory. Thanks, gang.

Managing Business Risk

1

An Introduction to the Subject of Risk Management

Our current model of risk management is "integrated risk management," which has a couple meanings. We have expanded our risk management services department to include risk control and risk financing functions under one roof. So our strategies for dealing with risks, once identified and measured, are balanced (or integrated) between control and financing strategies. Additionally, we have integrated the risk management process into the business decision-making processes for many of our internal customers. When that occurs, risk management issues are integrated right into the business decision-making process.

Director of Risk Management
International Consumer Products Firm

Perspectives

Qualities of a Risk Manager

Lee Fletcher
Reprinted with permission from *Business Insurance,* May 15, 2000. © Crain Communications Inc. All rights reserved.

Finding success as a risk manager obviously involves many qualities, but according to two industry experts, one must be a true generalist with the ability to take on many roles and be a strong proponent of teamwork and communication.

The Risk & Insurance Management Society Inc.'s "Skill Sets for a Successful Risk Management Career" provides a base of information for those considering a risk management career, those already in a risk management career, and those looking to move on.

"There is nothing different about building a career in risk management than from building a successful management career in any other industry," according to Pamela G. Rogers, director of risk management for Sears, Roebuck & Co. in Hoffman Estates, Illinois. Rogers emphasizes the need to have excellent rapport and communication skills with all types of employees. "Don't alienate the gatekeeper (secretary or administrative assistant)—be able to talk to anyone at any level."

It is important that a risk manager be able to admit that he or she doesn't know everything, and even more important to know how to find out who does, according to Rogers. [I]t's a good idea to get out and circulate with all levels of employees to learn what they do on a daily basis. "Rolling up your sleeves" and joining others onsite can provide a world of information, she adds.

She also emphasizes that others are often extremely eager to help. "Let other people teach you, especially young people. Speak with recruiters; they are invaluable resources. Learn about the skills they look for," Rogers says.

Tim East, manager of the risk management business process for The Walt Disney Co. based in Glendale, California, also emphasizes that successful risk managers be able to communicate well. He says communicating well is the ability to communicate face-to-face and in terms that others can understand.

East says that people call him when they have a claim—after the fact and not before. He emphasizes aiming to reverse that order. "Build the relationships before we need them, otherwise it's difficult to get honest answers," East says.

He says that focusing on win-win situations is an important way to work with other employees: for example, delivering good news and avoiding conflict with other staff or operating units. Through the development of relationships, a risk manager can observe how others do their jobs. According to East, risk management is accomplished by others, not by oneself.

Risk managers, according to Rogers, are other employees too, and "if they're not good at their jobs, there will be no risk management position." Almost all risk managers work with some other company departments, for example, risk management (both domestic and international), insurance management (both domestic and international), claims management, risk management information systems, safety and loss control, and human resources, according to Rogers. She emphasizes the importance of prioritizing and delegating tasks to others who are involved.

East says that sometimes change may be necessary for improvement, but [warns managers] to pick battles cautiously. He said the best way to create change is to provide the information in such a manner that everyone comes to the same "logical" conclusion.

Both East and Rogers say that part of a risk management career, like any career, may involve moving on to a different job. When considering a move, East says to consider relations with one's boss and staff, relations with other departments, and the amount of room for professional growth. Additionally, evaluate if any major errors or mistakes have been blamed on you and ask these questions: Do you have management's trust? Is there freedom and flexibility in your working environment; and most importantly, are you happy and satisfied?

If a number of questions are answered in the negative, East suggests either making a commitment to improve one's present situation or moving on.

Introduction

The purpose of Chapter 1 is to provide readers with a context for understanding the present state of business risk management principles and practices. The chapter opens with an extended discussion of the historical foundations and development of the field. This presentation includes some treatment of the various competing strands of risk management that can be found in organizations today.

The second section attempts to isolate and describe current practices in business risk management. This section includes an exposition of key trends and issues that seem to be affecting the future of risk management.

The final section of Chapter 1 introduces the concept of Organization Risk Management (ORM). ORM is shown to be a model that describes some current practices, but its principal purpose is to serve as an organizing idea for considering and evaluating both present and future developments in the field.

A Brief History of Risk Management

If we define risk management as any measure taken to evaluate risk and to control its potential impact, then it is safe to say that risk management has been practiced since the dawn of time. Certainly ancient civilizations took steps to protect themselves against foreign invasion, drought, and flood, and even the mischief making of the gods. However, we principally are concerned with risk management as a conscious organizational management practice. In that much narrower context, risk management has a history that extends only to the middle of the twentieth century.

Risk management appears to be one of a cluster of management sciences that emerged from or was greatly influenced by the Second World War. The prosecution of such a global enterprise required extraordinary efforts in logistics, material management, strategy and tactics, operations, and even applied statistics. Although many of these areas were advancing as topics of study well before WWII, it is still largely true that these emerging fields were literally battle-tested and shown to have real value in overall management practice. The explosion of activity in American universities after the war fed upon this trend, and it is not surprising to learn that strategic management, operations management, logistics and material management, and operations theory all took great leaps forward in the 1940s and 1950s.

It would be inaccurate to argue that this story applies directly to the field of risk management. However, the dramatic increase in interest in the science of management spilled over into most areas of business education. One indirectly influenced area was the study of insurance, risk, and uncertainty.

In the early post-war period, many university business schools offered courses and programs in insurance and actuarial science, and it was natural that some emphasis should be placed on the buyer or demand side of the subject. Academic journals of the time reflect this activity, and there are several articles from that era that asserted the value to organizations of pursuing a broad approach to managing (mainly) insurable risks as well as the purchase of the corresponding insurance coverages. Evidence from practitioner publications of this era reveals the emergence of a new and more dynamic role for the corporate "insurance buyer." The general thrust of this expanding role is interesting to reflect on briefly.

Although the insurance buyers' role was most importantly affected by the particular issues relevant to their organization, it is nevertheless possible to describe the function's general sequence of development as follows:

1. Corporate insurance buyers began with general responsibilities for purchasing the property and liability insurance coverages necessary for their organization. Sometimes employee benefit responsibilities were present as well.

2. Due to internal and market dynamics, insurance buyers were expected to exert some influence on the risks that were insured. As a result, initiatives in health and safety, engineering risk control, and policies and procedures began to emerge as part of the duties of an insurance buyer.

3. Related to the slow extension of insurance buyer duties, many larger organizations began considering whether they might

not be better off forgoing insurance and paying directly for certain risks and losses. Sometimes this decision was prompted by the absence of affordable insurance (or the absence of insurance altogether), and sometimes by the belief that the corporation had a better appreciation of its own risks than did the insurer. In any event, the use of deductibles and other "retention" tools began to emerge. Management of the financing of these retained risks fell under the responsibility of the insurance buyer.

4. As corporations became more conscious of risk and the means of managing risks, there was a slow extension of risk management principles beyond insurable risks into general business risks. In a sense, the field of risk management could be described as being at this developmental point today.

The term *risk management* (used in its roughly modern sense) emerged in the mid-1950s. It is not clear whether this term arose first from the academic or the practitioner worlds, but the concept of the risk manager seemed to capture the development of the insurance buyer function at that time. Interestingly, the term *insurance buyer* still is used extensively (more so outside the United States), though for many who hold that title the job description is indistinguishable from that of a risk manager.

For purposes of introduction, we might refer to the preceding history as the story of traditional risk management, and it is the principal form of risk management practiced today. Traditional risk management can be defined as an interdisciplinary function that is concerned with the management of (largely) insurable risks. Insurable risks are, almost by definition, confined to pure risks—that is, those risks where there is only a chance of loss and no chance of gain (e.g., fires, liability suits, and accidents). The sidebar of risk management terminology defines a few other key concepts and terms related to risk and uncertainty.

There are several other notable strands of the risk management story that occasionally are related to the traditional version though sometimes are independent of it. For example, current risk management practices have strong connections with the industrial safety

Risk Management Terminology

Risk is defined as the "variation in outcomes around an expectation." In other words, we expect certain things to occur or not occur, and "risk" refers to how life differs from what we expect. This definition has a number of embedded ideas. First, risk has to do with variability. Second, risk has to do with our expectations (or attitude toward risk, if you will). Third, risk has to do with the relationship between the things we expect to happen and the things that actually do occur.

Uncertainty is defined as "doubt about our ability to know." This suggests that uncertainty is a state of mind whereas risk—at least in one dimension—is a state of nature.

Uncertainty often results from the absence of information, but it also may be due to *attitudes toward risk,* which will differ among individuals. Scholars from many disciplines study how humans behave under conditions of risk and uncertainty. For instance, economists tend to focus on the impact of risk on the individual's quest to maximize utility (i.e., satisfaction). Psychologists argue that economic rationality is but one factor governing attitudes toward risk, and so they focus more on personality, family upbringing, personal history, and other behavioral characteristics. Although the psychological research is rich and complex, one can detect patterns that are related to knowledge and understanding of a risk, and the degree to which fear or dread governs the individual's perspective. By contrast, anthropologists place considerable credence in the notion that culture influences greatly attitudes toward risk largely by imposing "filters" through which individuals broadly judge risks as being important or unimportant. Even medical researchers are actively involved in risk-related research and have uncovered gene-based influences in attitudes toward risk.

Categories or typologies of risk have been developed. While all have uses, the most commonly cited construction is based on pure risk and speculative risk. *Pure risks* are those risks with a two-outcome domain: Either nothing will happen or a loss will occur. One's house either will burn or will not burn.

Speculative risks have a three-outcome domain: Nothing happens (or a neutral outcome occurs), a loss occurs, or a gain occurs. When playing cards one could win, lose, or break even.

The pure risk/speculative risk distinction is somewhat arbitrary and may be a little harmful. It is true that psychologists have demonstrated that individuals react differently to pure and speculative risks (basically, relative to pure risks, people tend to be less risk-averse in speculative risk situations), and thus risk managers should recognize that reaction to risk will be different depending on the type of risk involved. However, in most respects risks are risks, and this book's general concern with risk centers on its impact on a business mission. Thus, there probably is merit in looking at risk in a comprehensive and integrated way, because segmenting risks (and responsibility for managing those risks) probably has been more hindrance than help to the cause of effective, comprehensive risk management.

Risk arises from *sources of risk*. A source of risk is an "environment" from which hazards or risk factors emerge. *Hazards* are characteristics of a risk source that elevate the chance for loss (or potential severity of loss), whereas *risk factors* are those characteristics that elevate the chance or magnitude of loss or gain. For example, icy roads would be a hazard arising from the physical environment source of risk. Voter unrest or uncertainty would be an example of a risk factor arising from the social or political environmental source of risk.

Hazards may produce *perils,* which are actual causes of loss; the hazardous condition of an improperly maintained heater may result in the peril of fire. One does not say, commonly, that perils arise from risk factors because this would require us to employ a very elastic definition of peril ("a cause of gain"?) that English speakers would likely reject. In this book, the term *opportunity* serves as a speculative risk analog to "peril." Usage of that term is open to some debate, but the book will develop the concept of "opportunities arising from risk factors."

Finally, though this discussion is based on the notion of risk "arising from sources of risk," the imagery is somewhat imprecise. Risk also requires *exposure,* which does not arise from

> sources of risk. An icy road cannot produce a loss to a driver who does not drive on that road. Likewise, an investor who does not invest does not face market risks. One may argue that, like the tree falling unheard in the forest, an icy road exists physically as a hazardous condition whether anyone experiences the icy road or not. This is a fair point, but in the context of organizations managing risks, it is exposure to risk that provides the primary motivation to act.

and safety engineering fields. There are similar connections with employee benefits and human resources management, operations and systems management, information technology (IT) security, and legal counsel (especially in the areas of contracts and litigation management). Perhaps the most recent version of risk management has arisen in the financial management world—what is called financial risk management.

Financial risk management is directly, and importantly, the result of the emergence of financial tools for controlling interest rate, price, currency, credit, and other financial risks. Corporations (particularly, financial institutions) have long had exposure to such risks, but the rise of exchanges and capital market innovation in the 1970s, 1980s, and 1990s have contributed to the expansion of many financial risk management tools such as forwards, futures, options, and other types of derivatives.

Given the dynamism present in both the investment world and in corporate financial management circles, it shouldn't be too surprising to learn that the financial risk manager presently is in the ascendancy and has some chance of claiming the ultimate title of "corporate risk manager." Indeed, much of the academic research and higher-level practitioner literature today reflects an assumption that all organizational risk management derives from financial risk management.

We will temporarily suspend commentary on the relative merits of one view of risk management or the other—but we will observe that, taken as a whole, these various strands of risk management do suggest that organizations confront risks every-

Insights

Targeting Behavioral Risks Key to Improved Loss Control

Judy Greenwald
Reprinted with permission from *Business Insurance,* May 15, 2000. © Crain Communications Inc. All rights reserved.

An approach that emphasizes employee behavior over the traditional focus on working conditions can result in dramatically improved loss control, says one risk manager.

St. Louis–based Earthgrains Co., for instance, reduced its injury rates by 50 percent the first year after it introduced its behavioral risk improvement [BRI] program, says Kevin Coyne, director, risk management for Earthgrains, the nation's second-largest producer of baked breads.

Robert D. Schneller, VP risk control strategies at Marsh Risk Consulting in Houston, said one of the fundamentals of BRI is focusing on employees' work activities. In contrast, most companies' safety programs focus on workplace conditions, despite studies that show that as many as 80–90 percent of all accidents are caused by workers engaging in risky behaviors, Schneller says. And typical attempts at solutions, such as worker punishment and education, are comparatively ineffective. "We see people perform at risk" even after these types of efforts are made, he says. But "a strong culture will influence what people" do and can encourage them to do things the appropriate way.

Observing that behavior, culture, and attitude are all interrelated, Schneller says it is much easier to start with behavior, rather than culture, in encouraging safe practices. As a way of demonstrating how behavior can be changed, Schneller observes that most drivers today automatically click on their safety belts, which was not the case twenty-five years ago. After a few weeks, such behavior "becomes automatic," he says. Behavior-based approaches, Schneller says, use positive reinforcement measures "to improve the way that we do our work and continue to excel."

Discussing the experiences of Earthgrains, which began to introduce BRI at its 700-worker plant in Paris, Texas, in 1998, Coyne says that "BRI, for us, has been a gradual process." Although such programs can't be introduced in a day, "it's something that will really help over time," he says.

For example, Coyne says, feedback to employees on their behavior initially was supplied solely in writing. Only now is the company beginning to provide direct verbal feedback. "We are beginning that part of the process. . . . Dramatic improvements are possible," says Coyne. He notes that Earthgrains is now expanding its observations by supervisors—a key element in the BRI approach—to others of its facilities.

For now, the company plans to introduce the program only at facilities that employ at least 250 workers. Coyne says he is not sure how successful BRI would [be] at Earthgrains' smaller facilities, in part because the program requires a lot of administrative support. Among the advice he offers to others considering implementing BRI:

- Be sure facilities are prepared to administer the program. "The people and the plant have to be ready to be involved in that process," says Coyne.
- "Be sure you're prepared to make this an ongoing program," not just a "flavor of the month," he says. "That just doesn't work."
- Use consultants to guide your program.
- Bring the union into the process early on. "You can't skip the union piece," warns Coyne. If you don't get the union's cooperation up front, you won't get a consistent effort.
- Implement the process step by step. "That's a very important part of the process," Coyne says.

where, and the form of risk management adopted by a particular organization will be influenced by the nature of its risks and the relative importance it assigns to these risks.

The Practice of Risk Management Today

While the preceding section provides a tidy explanation of the evolution of risk management over the past fifty years, readers would be misled if they assumed that the present world of corporate risk management offered a uniform picture. The current evidence of risk management practices is very mixed. Some studies have found that the presence of a full-time risk manager is related to the size of the organization—that is, larger organizations are more likely to have a risk manager than are small organizations. The logic of this finding is obvious. Small organizations commonly cannot afford to have a full-time position allocated to risk management.

What is less clear from these studies is the overall quality of risk management practices. To put it plainly, a full-time risk manager could be incompetent while a part-timer may be extraordinarily gifted. No studies have attempted to look at the issue of risk management competence, and so we are left to rely on objective measures such as the presence of a full-time risk manager, as well as the size of a risk management department and its budget, scope of authority, and perhaps salaries as evidence of risk management effectiveness. Readers are warned, therefore, to avoid overinterpreting the following discussion, since several of the points raised are drawn from inference or from limited data.

A long-standing alternative view to the "organizational size" theory of risk management is based on studies conducted in the 1970s. At that time, there was evidence to suggest that the presence of a full-time risk manager was related to the "riskiness" of the organization. In other words, corporations that were in high-risk businesses were more likely to have full-time risk managers than were organizations with low-risk businesses.

There is some intuitive logic to this view. Organizations with a high susceptibility to, say, worker injury or product liability suits may be more likely to attend to the management of such risks. It has been argued that the evidence for this view actually is quite weak, and indeed it would be incorrect to believe that these competing views have an equal weight of evidence to support them. However, we should not wish to dismiss this view completely as it casts some light on a theme of this book, which is that the nature of an organization's business will influence the forms risk management adopts.

Although this book is focused on risk management in private sector organizations, we must note that risk management practices are evident in nonprofit organizations and in public entities as well. Findings from studies in these areas are limited, though there is some evidence to suggest that:

- Public sector risk management practices are advancing rather swiftly in medium-size organizations (e.g., governments with populations over 50,000); furthermore, the emergence of self-insurance pools is extending risk management practices into smaller local governments.
- Nonprofit risk management is generating great interest, as demonstrated by the creation of several nonprofit risk management associations—notably, the Nonprofit Risk Management Center, the University Risk Management and Insurance Association, and The American Society of Healthcare Risk Management.

The Risk Manager's Job

Let us set aside controversial issues and briefly look at practicing risk managers. If we were to ask what traditional full-time risk managers do, what would we find?

The answer, unsurprisingly, would be that most traditional risk managers today still focus on the management of insurable risks. However, in accordance with the history described previously, those duties would have evolved to some degree beyond the insurable risk limitation. Taken as a general representation, then, the following list of activities describes the average traditional risk manager's duties:

- Buying and managing insurance coverages
- Implementing loss prevention and control programs
- Reviewing contracts and documents for risk management purposes
- Providing training and education on safety-related issues
- Assuring compliance with governmental mandates, such as the Occupational Safety and Health Act and the Americans with Disabilities Act
- Arranging noninsurance financing schemes (e.g., self-insurance plans or captive insurance subsidiaries)
- Supervising claims management and coordinating with legal counsel to manage litigation
- Designing and coordinating employee benefit programs
- Leading the development and maintenance of catastrophe management plans
- Assisting in review of mergers and acquisitions activities
- Assisting in public relations issues where necessary
- Coordinating activities with the treasury function to address core business risks (e.g., raw materials sourcing and price risks), where appropriate

Other duties could be mentioned, but this represents a fairly complete listing of the traditional risk manager's job.

The Placement of the Traditional Risk Management Function

Most all risk managers and risk management departments are found within the finance or treasury function of their respective organizations. When this is not the case, the risk manager may be located within either the purchasing, internal audit, legal, or—occasionally—human resources department. In rare instances, the risk manager is a direct report to the chief executive; more commonly, the risk manager reports to the chief financial officer (CFO). Recently, some risk managers have achieved vice president–level positioning within their organizations, but this development probably cannot be considered a trend.

There are some issues and problems that attach to the placement of the risk management function. Most notably, if it can be argued that organizations are becoming generally more attentive to a wide range of corporate risks, then it is likely that traditional risk managers are not well positioned to address this expanding range. We may reasonably wonder whether the mismatch between the present, more general view of risk management and its historic and current practice is not partly responsible for the blossoming of other risk management practices throughout the organization. We may also wonder whether placement puts traditional risk managers at something of a disadvantage in asserting any responsibility for managing or coordinating organization-wide risk management efforts. Speculation on these points is more directly provided in Chapter 8.

Organization Risk Management

In the private sector, there are significant changes occurring in the practice of risk management—changes that, taken as a whole, are redefining risk management as the management of all organization risks on an integrated basis. While the number of organizations practicing this holistic form of risk management is limited, most observers predict that this new definition eventually will prevail. Why?

The explanation varies a bit from industry to industry, but in general the trend seems to be driven by several factors; for example:

- The restructuring of organizations has tended to broaden the responsibilities of all managers

- Increasing competition has forced organizations to scrutinize cost structures, leading to insights into the reduction of the cost of risk
- Just-in-time processes, total quality improvement practices, and other modern developments all stress the need to control risk and to do so in an integrated fashion
- Consolidation in the financial industry has resulted in an increasing integration of insurance, banking, and other financial services—which in turn has led to broader-based thinking about risk financing
- The absence of coordinated risk management practices (or, occasionally, the demonstrated effectiveness of the same) has been a feature of many sensational and highly publicized events (e.g., recent tobacco trials, the Barings Bank financial collapse, Y2K preparedness, and recent earthquakes in Taiwan, to name a few)

As a consequence, there is some evidence of a move toward a more organization-wide approach to risk management. In recent years we have even seen the emergence of the chief risk officer (CRO) concept and heightened evidence of "boardroom risk management."

Anticipating the ultimate destination of this emerging trend is difficult and controversial, as is evidenced in the basic confusion over the naming of this trend. For example, the term *enterprise risk management* is sometimes used, as is *global risk management, holistic risk management,* and *strategic risk management.* They all convey a similar idea, but closer examination reveals some notable differences. For instance, the enterprise and strategic risk management ideas are heavily influenced by financial risk management theory and practice, whereas the global and holistic risk management views belie a strong traditional insurance management influence. We choose a different terminology—not as an act of one-upmanship, but to provide a distinct label to ORM's more "general management" orientation, which can incorporate both financial and traditional (and other) influences.

Insights

Risk Managers Advised to Join Forces with CFOs

Michael Bradford
Reprinted with permission from *Business Insurance,* May 15, 2000. © Crain Communications Inc. All rights reserved.

A risk manager can get a chief financial officer's attention in many ways, but the best might be the direct approach.

"You want to get to the CFO? Go there," says David Mair, associate director of risk management with the United States Olympic Committee in Colorado Springs, Colorado. "Go to the land of the CFO, go down to the office with the glass doors, and sit down and talk."

Mair, who reports to the U.S. Olympic Committee's CFO, advises risk managers to learn their CFOs' schedules and to wisely choose times to hold discussions. "I know, for example, that my CFO does not leave the office any day before 5:45. He simply does not go. I also know that from 5:00 to 5:45, I can get some time every day." At the same time, "I know that you don't go bother him at lunch," Mair says. "He works through the lunch hour because that's his concentrating time—while everybody else is at lunch and he's not being bothered."

Michael R. Vogler, a principal with PricewaterhouseCoopers in Atlanta, points out that the best way to approach a company's CFO depends on its culture. In his previous job in risk management with RJR Nabisco Inc., Vogler says it was necessary to make an appointment, sometimes several weeks ahead of time, to meet with the CFO. That lasted until the company suffered a large loss. After that, getting on the boss's calendar was not as difficult. In a similar position he held with a restaurant company—a smaller organization than RJR Nabisco—"it was a matter of just walking up and knocking on the door," Vogler recalls.

Whatever the approach, it is important that once the meeting takes place, both sides understand the language used, Vogler stresses. Not only should the risk manager use terms understood by the CFO, but he or she also should understand what the CFO is saying.

As a consultant, Vogler has attended client meetings at which upper management did not want to invite the risk manager because of a perception that the risk manager would not understand what was being discussed. Vogler encouraged the participation of the risk manager despite those misgivings.

"When they get off on accounting issues and start talking about FASBs" and other financial terms, "you better know what they're talking about," Vogler [tells] risk managers.

Mair, for his part, urged risk managers to "speak English" in discussions. The CFO, he says, "doesn't care about deductibles, retentions, or what the exclusions are. What he wants to know is: Is it covered? Is it not covered? Is it insured at all? Or what could be the impact to the bottom line?"

One of the "principal reasons that risk managers and CFOs have problems is that they don't share a common language," says Diane Askwyth, senior consultant with Pricewaterhouse-Coopers in Florham Park, New Jersey. Paul F. Buckley, treasury director–risk management at Lucent Technologies Inc., based in Murray Hill, New Jersey, agrees. Sometimes, he says, the risk manager and CFO have a "fly-by" in which "you think you said something the CFO understood and he understood completely different. We both had good intentions but flew straight by each other." And if there is a miscommunication, "you're the one in trouble, not him," he said.

Mair encourages risk managers to "ask questions. . . . At the end of the day, we are, fundamentally, problem-solvers. The CFO has problems. Let's go in and listen and see where we can help."

He also says it is important to "know the CFO's people. There will be some days when you simply won't be able to get to the senior person in finance or treasury. But know the people that you can get to. Know the controller, know the accountant."

[Lucent's] Buckley emphasizes that a risk manager who is not versed in the financial aspects of business can find his or her credibility damaged. He refers to one case in which a risk manager touted a move he made as having saved his company $60 million. Financial managers at the company calculated that the savings were closer to $12 million and that the risk manager had misunderstood some of the accounting aspects of the move. "And that really hurt that risk manager," Buckley says. "He did a great thing, but he just didn't understand how to communicate about it to the CFO."

Askwyth of PricewaterhouseCoopers had a chance to review a report presented by a risk manager who had been fired from a large company. She was astonished at the number of finance-related mistakes in the report. Without considering such fundamentals as "the time value of money and how long it would take losses to come home to roost," the risk manager recommended a guaranteed-cost insurance program for the employer, she says.

Buckley says such a mistake is an example of "that loss of credibility" an unprepared risk manager can suffer, the consequences of which can be disastrous. "Once you've lost it, it's time to move on."

The ORM Model

Organization Risk Management (ORM) is a general management function that seeks to assess and address the causes and effects of uncertainty and risk on an organization. In principle, the purpose of ORM is to enable an organization to progress toward its goals in the most direct, economical, and effective path.

To appreciate the relationship between risk management and other functional aspects of management within an organization, it is useful to think about the central purposes of management. One construction would be to describe management as entailing strategic management, operations management, and risk management components (see Exhibit 1-1). Specifically:

- *Strategic management* consists of activities that involve the determination of an organization's or functional unit's mis-

Exhibit 1-1. Strategy, operations, and risk management model

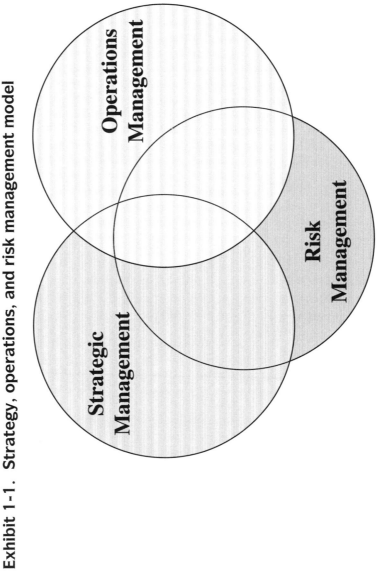

sion, goals, and objectives and, of course, the creation of strategy and the management of progress toward strategy fulfillment.

- *Operations management* consists of those actions and decisions that enable the organization or functional unit to "do what it does."
- *Risk management* consists of those decisions and actions that facilitate the most direct achievement of organization objectives via its operations.

Readers must realize that the ORM model applies to the organization as a whole, but it equally applies to each position within that organization. In other words, risk management is central to the overall management of an organization, but it occupies a segment of the specific responsibilities of each manager and employee. As an example, the director of operations within a manufacturing firm would have strategic responsibilities with respect to budget and the identification of specific goals and objectives, as well as advocacy to the board of directors. Additionally, the manager would have operational responsibilities, ranging from workforce management, task supervision, allocation of department resources, and general reporting activities. But equally, that manager would have responsibilities that entail an assessment and appreciation of relevant risks and the application of risk management measures to control those risks. This would be true of managers and employees within the department. For example, a shop floor supervisor may identify actions and make decisions each day that would be characterized as risk management.

Strategic, operational, and risk management activities are not mutually exclusive. Indeed, overlap (see Exhibit 1-1) is an important element of the ORM idea because it demonstrates the centrality of risk management. Risk management, in this conceptualization, is not a peripheral technical function but rather a core management function; something each employee does within the scope of his or her duties, but also something the organization does to itself.

The Elements of ORM

Even though the practice of risk management will vary from organization to organization, the ORM idea incorporates five distinct elements into its structure:

1. Mission identification
2. Risk and uncertainty assessment
3. Risk control
4. Risk financing
5. Program administration

Throughout this book, the distinctions between these elements will be subject to a degree of fuzziness. Some tools and techniques will be used both for "control" and "financing," for instance. Thus, readers should appreciate that there always is a certain level of arbitrariness in labeling management practices. Nevertheless, for introductory purposes, these element categories allow newcomers to the risk management field to better understand the overall purpose and practice of risk management. Each element is defined as follows:

1. *Mission identification.* A risk manager has a responsibility to assure that risk management goals and objectives (indeed, the "mission" of the risk management function) align with the overall purposes of the organization. In this sense, ORM is described as mission-driven, which means that the practice of risk management is measured by the degree to which it supports the central purposes of the organization. These central purposes serve as the yardstick against which success or failure is measured, but they also provide the basis for the philosophy that supports risk management activities.

2. *Risk and uncertainty assessment.* Risk and uncertainty assessment involves three overlapping activities:

- *Risk and uncertainty identification.* Identification involves the systematic process of discovering an organization's risks and exposures to risk. It is a continuous process.

■ *Risk analysis.* Analysis involves the examination of risks in an effort to determine how hazardous conditions lead to actual losses. Increasingly, analysis also involves the study of risks with upside potential—that is, situations where risk factors can give rise to opportunities.

■ *Risk measurement.* Measurement entails the assessment of the impact of risk on an organization. This invariably will be undertaken in different ways. For example, measurement might be highly quantitative or quite subjective. Measurement also may focus on the impact of risk on specific objects or on the organization as a whole.

3. *Risk control.* Entailing activities that focus on avoiding, preventing, reducing, transferring, and neutralizing risks and uncertainties, risk control can range from simple measures, such as making sure workers wear hard hats, to complex measures such catastrophe management plans.

4. *Risk financing.* These activities enable an organization to reimburse losses that occur and to fund programs to reduce uncertainty and risk, or to enhance positive outcomes. The financing of losses can include measures such as the purchase of insurance, the establishment of a letter of credit, or participation in a captive insurance company.

5. *Program administration.* The administration of a risk management program involves a range of technical and general management activities—from the buying of insurance, to claims administration, to the development of a hedging arrangement, to safety training and the instituting of loss control programs. Risk management requires a technical competence, but equally, a risk manager must have solid general management capabilities.

ORM in Practice

The ORM idea leads to an organizational scheme that differs from traditional risk management practices. Most traditional risk managers are located within a finance department (or an affiliated department). If a separate risk management department exists (or if a distinct risk management unit exists within a finance department), the risk management unit typically consists of one to three individuals. Typically, a medium-size organization would have a risk manager, a secretary, and perhaps an insurance manager. Larger organizations may have as many as a dozen employees, but this large number commonly would be indicative of in-house claims management personnel.

Contrasted with the traditional approach, the ORM idea suggests that the risk manager—or as is seen with some frequency, the risk management team—is proximate to the executive function. Overall direction should be provided by the executive level, especially because the scope of ORM is organization-wide. In addition, the ORM idea is not particularly conducive to a "risk management department" model per se. Rather, many or most risk management activities would be practiced throughout the organization, so the ORM risk manager (or team) would serve more as a linking pin coordinating and organizing risk management efforts. Risk management responsibilities would be written into every employee's job description, and the risk manager would coordinate these responsibilities and facilitate implementation. Under this idea, the risk manager is idealized as the chief risk officer, connoting the elevated position within the organization and also the broadened scope of responsibilities.

The fact that the ORM model is rarely seen in organizations today does not diminish its importance—especially for an introductory book. Like all good models, it serves as a frame of reference for current practices and promotes critical examination to explain and justify the differences. To be sure, many differences from the ideal are warranted and desirable. Conversely, examination of these inconsistencies may reveal that the old way of doing things is no longer the best way.

Having said that, readers will still wonder why the ORM approach has not been more widely adopted. Chapters 2 through 7 will explore the underlying reasons that have limited broader acceptance of the ORM idea, but the final chapter (Chapter 8) will explicitly consider the practical limitations of the Organization Risk Management approach.

Contracts, Obligations, Commitments, and Agreements: Units of Analysis

Before concluding this introductory chapter, it is useful to discuss briefly a concept that will serve an important analytical role throughout the book. Although it stands alone as an organizing idea, it does relate in very significant ways to the practice of Organization Risk Management. The concept is known as the COCA organization.

Throughout this chapter we have proposed the idea that the management of risk is a central or general management function in organizations. But how is this core role of risk management adequately conveyed—especially when risk management historically has been viewed as a rather narrow technical or specialized function?

The answer can be found by recognizing that organizations are collections of contracts, obligations, commitments, and agreements between managers (and/or owners) and resource holders. These contracts, obligations, commitments, and agreements (COCAs) are assembled, or in any event accumulated, in the service of the overall purposes or objectives of the organization. The concept of a resource holder is similar to that of a stakeholder, but the emphasis on possession of an asset or claim (i.e., a resource) that serves the purposes of the organization probably is more useful in a risk management setting. For purposes of this book, the significance of COCAs can be summarized as follows:

- COCAs create an organization's exposure to risk. Some risks are created by the COCAs, while some risks "pass through" the COCAs.
- Risks are fundamental characteristics of COCAs.
- COCAs are expressly or impliedly multiparty; meaning that

only rarely are entities in a position where only their interests are served.

■ Formation of COCAs is a key moment in risk management because it is the first and best opportunity to manage and distribute risk.

The COCA concept is developed in Chapter 2 as a foundation for risk assessment and in Chapter 3 as a means of risk control.

Judging Attitudes toward Risk

Perhaps one of the greatest difficulties risk managers encounter is understanding their organization's attitude. Of course, organizations do not have an "attitude toward risk" per se, but certainly their leaders and key managers do, and their attitudes greatly influence how the organization behaves under conditions of risk and uncertainty.

Indeed, one could persuasively argue that attitudes toward risk—or subjective risk—are the critical aspect of risk to manage. One could have very accurate objective data on business risks and still face considerable obstacles in getting directors, officers, and managers to act—or even come to some consensus on a view of those risks.

Although Chapters 2 through 7 provide numerous insights on the management of subjective risk, it is appropriate here to think about the specific objective of managing subjective risk and how a risk manager might set about doing it.

First, the objective. Risk management is not just about reducing or eliminating risk. Rather, risk management is governed by the overall purposes of the organization, such that risk taking may become a central element of the risk management program. In other words, risk management involves striving for a balanced portfolio of risks that supports the organization's overall objectives. But what about the specific issue of subjective risk?

To begin, dispense with the idea that there is one true attitude toward a given risk or set of risks. Yes, there may be a scientifically objective description of a risk, but to say that there is an absolute value for subjective risk is nonsensical. Certainly, as later chapters argue, information management can reduce uncertainty and help managers better understand the objective characteristics of a risk— and this is a desirable outcome—but this is not the same thing as managers having an identical attitude toward that better-understood risk.

This observation will not strike managers as remarkable, for these comments could apply to any matter of business concern. People's attitudes about any policy—capital investment initiatives, operational considerations, human resources allocations—will not be identical even if the outcomes are known with certainty. Decision making in all but the most autocratic organizations is driven by compromise and consensus building, which means that unity of purpose and perfection of outcome is unattainable. The same is true with the management of subjective risk within organizations. The risk manager's role in managing subjectivity is to champion a process by which convergence or consensus might occur. Like all management challenges, this means that tending to the "process" is important, too.

There are numerous books on organization behavior and management that can provide insight into the challenge of consensus building, and it is rather futile for a book such as this one to spend much time on that subject. However, with respect to building consensus on an organization's attitude toward risk, the following technical matters may be useful.

Top directors and officers have very different perspectives— and certainly this observation extends to include attitudes toward risk. Their perspectives are going to be influenced by deeply personal factors but also by the context of their positions. Cynics may observe that the overarching objective is to avoid getting sued, but even if that is true, it requires a degree of responsiveness to the needs of the stakeholders being served. Thus, in an important sense, the directors and officers represent a means by which stock-holder (and stakeholder) attitudes toward risk are processed and converted into a policy form. The point is that while risk managers often lament that top managers do not have the same view of a particular risk, it actually would be more surprising if they did. Executive attitudes toward risk exist in a strategic or governance realm mainly and only occasionally in a managerial or operational realm.

This suggests that when risk management matters are presented to the governing body of an organization that either 1) the matter needs to anticipate the governance realm of the risk or 2) the issue of subjective risk needs to be explicitly raised and discussed.

Equally, managers within an organization have a distinctive perspective, and this influences attitude toward risk as well. While one would assume that such individuals generally have the best interest of the owners in mind, their responsibilities present a host of pressures, incentives, and disincentives that tend to focus their attention on their specific operating unit.

Applying these lessons to the concepts covered throughout Chapter 1, we have these recommendations to risk managers:

- Risk managers have an obligation to engage both directors and officers in a discussion of risk and attitudes toward risk. The objective is to create a basic awareness of attitudes toward risk, why they exist, and how they differ.
- Risk management education is a duty of every risk manager. Risk is a complicated subject, and effective communication is a serious challenge. However, the development of a culture of risk management begins with education.
- The process of educating managers, directors, and officers on risk management can serve as a springboard for establishing the risk management mission, obtaining top-level buy-in, setting a more participatory environment for the practice of risk management, and creating a better appreciation for the differing attitudes toward risk and how consensus may be obtained.

Read More About It

Risk Roundtable: Risk Managers Take on the Future

A distinguished group of practitioners [give] their opinions on a series of subjects that seem likely to shape the risk manager of the new millennium.

Mary Daniels, ARM, is director of risk management and employee benefits for World Wide Facilities Inc. in Garden City, New York.

Charles Dougherty, ARM, is manager, risk management and insurance, for the Union Carbide Corporation in Danbury, Connecticut.

Louis Drapeau, ARM, is manager, risk management, for the Budd Company in Troy, Michigan, and a former president of RIMS.

Jackie Hair, ARM, is the corporate risk manager for Cisco Systems in San Jose, California.

Harvey Lermack is an independent consultant and trainer in Philadelphia, specializing in risk management and professional skills consulting and training.

Christopher Mandel, ARM, CPCU, is senior director, risk management department, for Tricon Global Restaurants in Louisville, Kentucky, and RIMS vice president, external affairs.

Susan Meltzer, CRM, FCIP, is assistant vice president, Insurance and Risk Management, for Sun Life Assurance Co. of Canada in Toronto, and the current president of RIMS.

Risk Management Magazine: How have your responsibilities changed over the last five years or so, and what has driven those changes?

Meltzer: My responsibilities encompass more risks than in the past. We are establishing a more global approach to risk management and I am part of the team looking at how to manage our risks more effectively.

Daniels: In my previous organization I had asked to be given responsibility for employee benefits in addition to risk management because I felt that there was tremendous risk there. When my present firm found out that I had employee benefits experience they eventually said, ''Let's put it all in her hands.''

Mandel: My responsibilities have grown geographically, and broader in terms of additional subsidiary growth, but have narrowed functionally.

Drapeau: My responsibilities have become much more global in nature. The driver in my case was a large merger by our German parent.

Hair: We have completely changed our responsibilities over the last few years, specifically because we're high-tech. In traditional companies, risk management has the reputation of being the control mechanism—the people who say no to everything. That's not our philosophy. We believe that risk is an opportunity. So we help the business units find ways to exploit those opportunities.

Dougherty: I do not think that basic responsibilities have changed much over the last few years, but the bar has been raised in terms of measurement of performance. It has become a requirement that not only will we identify, measure, and finance risks, but we will find ways to contribute to the overall financial performance of the corporation. I believe that this has been driven by the expectations of our shareholders and the financial community.

RMM: How has technology changed the way you do your job, and in what ways can it improve?

Daniels: Technology does a tremendous job for me, particularly for claims handling. I am very happy with what I have. It can improve in the amount of time it takes to get into the system. It's a question of dependability.

Meltzer: Our department is in the midst of selecting a risk management information system [RMIS], so we have not yet maximized the role of technology internally. However, the advent of e-mail has been a huge boon to me, personally. I am more efficient and effective in my communications. When I am away from the office, messages and mail do not pile up because I can deal with them remotely.

Mandel: A sophisticated RMIS is central to getting our jobs done. The Web is increasingly a source of information and expertise as well as sharing among practitioners. We need much work in terms of risk management Internet capabilities and organization, though.

Drapeau: Technology has the potential to make great changes in the way we do our jobs. The problem, as I see it, is that we are not taking advantage of the technology available to us. The chain is only as strong as its weakest link.

Lermack: I don't think I could manage a job like this without having the information available to me on the Internet. When you're dealing with, for example, environmental issues, you can get to the EPA; you can deal with those groups that impact you. I need to have updated information on environmental health, safety, and training technologies. That's an enormous amount of information. By having this information available, once we learn how to sort and prioritize it, it will allow us to expand our perspective. I've made some contacts in Europe, and their perspective is obviously a lot different on some of these issues than ours. So technology is not only allowing me to get more information; it's also allowing me to tackle a wider perspective.

There are two other issues: computer-based training technologies and the ability to share real-time information. I might have two hundred people out providing training materials; if I get feedback that there's a problem, I can immediately broadcast it. That's been extraordinarily valuable up and down the line.

Hair: I couldn't live without technology. We're such a small department—three people to serve 18,000 employees in over 400 locations on a worldwide basis—that it's not physically possible for me to travel to all those locations to spread the word. I have to have more efficient ways of doing things. By putting everything on our intranet, I can reach all 18,000 employees. Employees who have problems with repetitive stress–type injuries can go to websites that we're linked to and determine how to deal with their injury. If it's a workers compensation claim, they can find out how to go about filing a claim and how to manage their recovery. Let's say you have a hundred employees that are suffering symptoms. How could I possibly have a hundred conversations with all those people and do them justice and walk them through the process? It's not possible. So we put everything on the Web. It's effective and it's key to our being able to manage the functions of such a large organization with such a small staff.

The other part of technology that is critical is being able to do research. All the information that you need on any particular topic, you should be able to get off the Internet.

How can it be improved? There's so much information out there that it now comes down to the point where I no longer have the time to go out and look for it. So I would like to see the information I'm most interested in come to me. I would like to see information on the Internet catalogued so you can drill down to specific areas rather than just broad, general areas.

Dougherty: The single most important technology helping me to do my job is e-mail. It is far easier to communicate with people within the company and with our vendors. We now have the ability to share a wealth of information with e-mail attachments and access to internal server sites.

RMM: Enterprise and holistic risk are terms that have been bandied about quite a lot recently. What do these terms mean to you, and do they have application in your jobs?

Meltzer: These terms to me are just a 1990s ways of saying risk management. The only difference is that these concepts have assisted the risk manager by having the corporation recognize the array of risks that face them. Unfortunately, a lot of the material on enterprise risk management emphasizes identification, assessment, reporting, and monitoring of risks. It does not focus on risk solutions.

In my industry, we have learned about financial risk management, and in our case, it is primarily credit and market risk. What the financial services industry has not been adept at is the application of operational risk management: transaction risk, product design, and product distribution are a few examples. If you look carefully at this, the solution is traditional risk management.

Daniels: Those terms really mean "putting everything in one basket." It's just new terminology people use to make it sound sophisticated. As far as I'm concerned, it's all risk management. It's not that new.

However, I do think the risk manager has to be more encompassing of finance, taxes, and accounting, and understand how they function within the corporation, because you're not getting the whole picture if you don't understand that process. Risk management is a lot more than just insurance today. It's a lot more than slips and falls and D&O. You have to understand finances and taxes. You need to be able to talk that language with the CFO and treasurer. If you don't understand the language, you can't be as convincing in describing the risks.

Mandel: To me, enterprisewide means looking at all risks to the balance sheet or the ongoing concern of an organization. Holistic has been viewed similarly, but in my opinion, it includes leveraging opportunities as well as mitigating risks, for instance, making a captive a profit center.

Drapeau: Enterprise risk is an interesting concept, but it has to overcome many obstacles in most organizations. Ultimately, managing pure risk is one thing, but eliminating speculative risk also eliminates the entire reason for being a success or failure in your line of business.

Lermack: I believe in a risk management focus regardless of the function, and of integrating that into people's daily work. Risk management will be successful when there are no risk management training courses. When people are trained how to do their work properly, they learn how to assess and manage all the risks associated with their work.

When we looked at risk management at Conrail, we tried

to take a holistic approach. So we looked at environmental, health, safety, damage prevention, and hazardous materials, all with as little a line between them as possible. Traditionally, environmental in our case meant anything that the railroad does that has an impact on the community, our customers, or our employees. So that, for example, hazardous waste is generally thought of as an environmental issue, but it also has a real safety application. You don't want to be handling hazardous waste incorrectly. So what we have been trying to do is move all those issues together, to get people to take a look at the risks involved in their job. In learning the hazardous waste rules, we might say, "All right, you've got this material here, what can happen with that material to impact your health, to leak out into the community and impact the community, to have an impact on the environment as specified by the EPA?"

Hair: Those terms meant a lot to me in my prior position. We could go about mapping out what risks the organization faced and organize them and quantify them, and do something with the information that we collected. In a company like Cisco, we're changing so rapidly that by the time I could identify all the various risks the organization faces, they would have changed and the information would be meaningless. If we were to stand still that long, we would no longer be what we are. This may be unique to high-tech companies. When I think about enterprise and holistic risk management, they don't mean the same things to me now that they did five years ago.

Also, we do twelve to sixteen acquisitions per year—that's one a month. So within thirty days, any information that I had would be out of date.

RMM: How do you deal with these acquisitions?

Hair: I look at them as opportunities to be exploited. If I tried to insert risk management into the process on a preacquisition basis, I would be doing a disservice to the organization. There may be driving forces out there or competitors trying to bid on the same company, and you have to make quick decisions. If I said, "Wait, we've got to look at all their liabilities and we've got to look at all the risks that we're assuming, etc.," we wouldn't make the decision on a timely basis, and we might miss a key opportunity for access to a key market.

Now, that doesn't mean I don't take steps to make the process a more beneficial one. Internally I'm very close to the business development people. When we acquire a company, we talk about some of the things we could have looked more closely at. So the next time around, they will look more closely. I try to help them make better-informed decisions. And I think that's really the key that we can bring to the table. If their decisions are better and more informed, then the impact on the organization is going to be all the greater.

RMM: Chris, how does the enterprise risk concept apply in your company?

Mandel: We are slowly leveraging both concepts. We have been treating reputational and employment-related risks along with traditional p/c [property/casualty] risks for a few years. These have been identified through an environmental committee that looks at all the issues that affect our core operating environment. We have just set up a captive that is being used largely to offset capital gains from our selling of stores while also providing traditional risk financing arrangements for standard risks.

Dougherty: Enterprise risk to me is the overall measurement of the success or failure of a business or operation; in effect, whether or not you should have started the operation. Holistic risk management is somewhat different in that the focus is on risks that can be quantified and managed as a group. This group breaches the historical separation between insurance, foreign exchange, human resources, and others. They really apply to any type of operation. We are just getting started in this work. This is an area where technology should be of value in allowing the detailed and sophisticated calculations to be made quickly and at low cost.

RMM: Recently there was a major development in the risk financing arena. A Japanese company issued two catastrophe bonds for its earthquake risk. This was reportedly the first such deal transacted by a noninsurance company. What effect will this type of deal have on the industry, and would you consider such a deal?

Hair: I think it's a very interesting concept. We've had conversations with the capital markets and we're keeping our options open. As more and more companies find that they need to be more flexible with how they do business, the capital markets will support that flexibility. The capital markets are going to wind up driving insurance carriers to look at how they do business and change their business model. In the short term, I think it's going to drive them toward more of a middle-market mentality, where they can dictate the terms. It is becoming very clear that larger companies want the flexibility to do business that they see as in their best interest. And then they want to partner with somebody who's going to let them get there. In a company like Cisco, where we embrace risk and the opportunity to do business differently, our interests are going to be best served by working with a partner that shares that philosophy.

Dougherty: We would certainly consider the alternative approach for large event loss potentials.

Drapeau: We would do it if the right pure risk situation presented itself.

RMM: How do you think the increasing use of alternative risk financing, securitization, and the like will affect traditional insurers?

Meltzer: There are some insurers in our business who have a distinct advantage in this area. Not only do they have the expertise in underwriting catastrophe, but they have the financial understanding and wherewithal to compete with the capital markets. The capital markets are used to a substantial rate of return, unlike insurers. I don't know that they would be interested in this business subsequent to one catastrophe. Insurers have a higher threshold.

Mandel: If we were to structure such a deal, we would look to our banking partners today, but hopefully our insurance company partners equally so in the future.

Drapeau: Insurers are theoretically the best positioned to assume such risk.

Hair: For insurers to stay in the business they have to be more flexible and more competitive. Already you're starting to see some changes. I think they're starting to embrace technology and they are changing their products so that they are not as constrained as they have been in the past.

Dougherty: If risk managers access the capital markets, insurers will likely become less assumers and spreaders of risk and more transaction and service companies—if they are able to make the transformation.

RMM: It seems likely that the government will deregulate commercial lines. How do you think this will affect the alternatives open to you?

Mandel: H.R.10 should facilitate the integration of insurance and banking, blurring the lines between them and making more choice available to finance a broader array of risks.

Dougherty: H.R.10 removes barriers that prevent affiliation among insurance companies and other financial providers such as banks, and [should] open up significantly more choices. The potential combination of some of these companies could spawn new products that better meet our needs and get us closer to holistic risk management.

RMM: How important is education to your success as a risk manager, now and in the future?

Dougherty: Formal education is absolutely vital, as you must have at least the basic knowledge to understand the risks that you deal with and the traditional tools that are available. The process of education also gives you practice in using skills that are part of everyday business life, such as problem solving, research, and communication. Just as important is the feedback that you receive on your efforts. We must also be experts in educating ourselves on a nonformal basis, particularly about our employer's operations, because if we do not understand them well, we cannot hope to effectively manage the risks that they present.

Hair: I'm a strong proponent of education and career development. I have an MBA and I do think that makes a difference in your credibility. It also allows you to talk the same language with your CFO, with your treasurer, with all the key finance people throughout the organization. It also keeps you on top of what's going on technology-wise, and what's available in the marketplace.

If you've done the same thing for the last twenty years and you've done nothing to really improve your education, then I think that you are going to be left behind. And as we talk about the capital markets, the people that deal in this world are extremely bright and they are extremely quick. They talk the talk; they have the buzzwords. If you're not able to keep up, it reflects not only poorly on you, but it also reflects poorly on your organization. So it's really critical. And I don't think, in all honesty, I would be as effective at my job if I wasn't willing to keep up the education side as well.

Lermack: Education is very important to me from a couple of standpoints. First of all, I'm an MBA and strategic management, strategic planning teacher, and I want to find ways to specifically and explicitly bring those kinds of issues into my courses. I think that it's critical that we are more active in doing that. I'm a member of the RIMS education committee and I hope that we can find a way to link that better.

RMM: Do you think there would ever be a place for a risk management requirement along the lines of what lawyers and doctors have?

Meltzer: Absolutely not! RIMS is an organization of corporations with internal risk managers. We believe very strongly in the efficiency of internal risk management. This is not a third-party practice. As a matter of fact, if a corporation wishes to hire an internal lawyer, he or she would not have to be admitted to the bar or the law society. They wouldn't even necessarily have to have an LLB. We cannot impose discipline or requirements on internal corporate functions. In addition, risk management is very different depending upon the corporation. One corporation may require significant expertise in financial risk management, another in chemical loss control, another in defense of claims which could require an MBA, an engineer, or a lawyer. How do you standardize that?

Daniels: I would love to see a requirement for practicing, but I think it's too late to make that kind of demand. I don't think it would ever happen. How would you tell a firm that they have to hire someone with a designation?

Mandel: The FRM [Fellow in Risk Management] program is the beginning of such a move, though frankly the CPCU never really developed the discipline to the point of becoming a profession, even as the CPA did for accountants. Nevertheless, we need more standardized education that broadens the discipline to the enterprise scope and gives treasurers and CFOs the ability to understand more clearly what they need, who they should hire, and how they should develop wannabes.

RMM: If you were able to take a full-semester course, what subject would you study?

Meltzer: Strategic leadership and planning.

Daniels: If I were to take a semester-long course it would be in finance, because I think that's the wave of the future. And human resources—if you don't have the ability to work with people and get them to perform, you're not going to be very good. You may not get accurate information and people who want to respond to you in timely fashion. I could not do the job I do here if I did not have the support of many of the brokers and many of the insurance companies, who help me tremendously.

Mandel: I would choose an enterprisewide risk financing course as well as advanced finance generally. This is the biggest area of opportunity for most risk managers.

Drapeau: Finance.

Lermack: If there's any one course at a university or college that I think would be critical to any risk manager, it's business strategic planning. It strikes me that anybody who is in a staff position needs to better understand the strategic planning processes of business and the new business realities. By that I mean such things as globalization and the global impact of technology on the way that we do business, and the changes in the workforce. The workforce is not stagnant anymore; it's totally mobile and outsourced. I think many risk managers don't think through those issues the way they could if they had a better understanding of the overall business strategy.

They need to understand the direction and the strategy of the company as a whole and, specifically, external forces that are really causing change in the business. Because if you're building a risk management strategy or focus on the way the business is established now, if your business is not thinking through appropriately or on the cutting edge, well, you're going to be building a poor strategy at best. At worst, you're going to be left in the dust. I think it's really critical that risk managers are out in front both from a personal career standpoint, as well as from an application standpoint for their businesses.

Hair: Finance is one of the critical things that risk managers should understand well. If nobody does anything more for their education than take a semester-long class in finance, it would be to their advantage. They need to understand thoroughly how decisions impact their organization.

Dougherty: I would take a course that simulated the running of a business. This would broaden my ability to see the risks that I have not yet identified and how we could impact a business in a positive sense.

RMM: Does anyone have any thoughts on the direction of the market, and what affect a hardening might have?

Meltzer: I am not sure if the market is going to harden anytime in the near future, primarily due to the overcapitalization of the property/casualty insurance market specifically and the capital markets in general. We have used the soft market to formalize long-term insurance programs and do not expect to be overly impacted by a swing in the market. I don't know if it will drive innovation, as usually hard markets are a short-term spike in the cycle and don't last long enough to drive innovation.

Daniels: I've been saying for the last year that it's going to harden a little bit. I haven't seen that, really. But it has to. The loss ratio is too high. So eventually it's going to harden.

Mandel: I think there are viable arguments for both sides. I do feel that year 2000 implications could facilitate a change [and lead to a] move to integrate more quickly with treasury views and the use of capital markets. . . .

Drapeau: A downturn in the economy may trigger a turn in the insurance marketplace, and then risk managers will have to avail themselves of alternative market solutions.

Hair: I think it's starting to harden a little bit, mainly on the property side. There's [been] a lot of concern on the insurers' part about . . . year 2000, regardless of this new legislation that just passed. [I]nsurance carriers [have been] concerned that they're going to be sued for a lot of expenses that they didn't count on paying for.

Dougherty: There are weak signs of the market hardening . . . [as] [was] seen in the resolve [of] many insurers [to impose] year 2000 restrictions. I do not believe, however, that we will see a significant rise in premiums; I think that we are at or near bottom. Broad-scale hardening will likely be a result of overall trouble in the economy, especially in the stock markets, and this will overshadow the higher premiums that may occur.

Daniels: If the market hardens, there will be more people looking into captives, rent-a-captives, self-insurance. Otherwise, there's going to have to be some real safety and loss control. But safety and loss control takes a year or two before it has an effect on premiums. You really need to be looking at that all the time.

RMM: Assuming you've done a good job, you've paid attention to the things that need attention, are there still issues out there that keep you up at night, things that can appear out of your control?

Dougherty: Mass tort litigation. As we have seen all too often, allegations of a product harming many people can be very costly even when there is no scientific basis for the allegation. We have to trust and support our efforts in product stewardship, which is the process of thoroughly understanding how and where our products are being used to assure that they are being used responsibly and with proper hazard communication.

Meltzer: What keeps me awake is the necessity to identify more risks in an ever-increasing risk environment. There are risks facing the corporation today that have not been identified and/or assessed, or even imagined in the past. The best approach I know is to keep working with the business and operations units to ensure that I am made aware of emerging risks so that we can construct risk management techniques to handle them.

Mandel: The speed of change in organizations, structures, functions, and the implications that the Internet may turn most things on their heads—these are challenges. I have no solutions, but only strive to learn and understand as much as possible to keep up with the changes. I try to look ahead to see how these issues will impact my day-to-day position and my future, ten years out.

Drapeau: New exposures that are created by our rapidly changing world that we haven't thought of yet—hopefully we will recognize them before the plaintiff attorneys do.

Lermack: The possibility that someone is injured or worse, and that there was something that I could have done to help—to identify that risk or help them identify, assess, and manage that risk.

RMM: Is that a thought that drives what you do?

Lermack: Absolutely, every minute of every day. And it's a frustrating thing being located at headquarters and putting together programs that are delivered by 200 people, and trying to know what the hot issues are. The critical thing I always try to tell people is: Don't teach them safety rules, teach them how to understand and assess the risks for themselves. So that if there's a rule that we missed or something we didn't identify—and there always will be—they'll be able to draw on that education. That's really strong in my mind. Every time somebody gets injured or worse, it's always something we hadn't thought of, it's always something different.

Hair: What I'm concerned most about is that we can scale with the organization. We need to partner with the business units to be a part of the solution rather than a part of the problem. Making sure that the approach we take is the appropriate approach for the right reasons and not falling back into the more traditional risk management, which is to say no just because something's risky.

RMM: Any thoughts on where the next decade will lead us in risk management?

Dougherty: Risk management [had] its first challenge the moment the year 2000 arrived; hopefully our preparations [met] the test. I see risk managers developing their skills to more precisely identify and measure all types of risks to the point that the traditional ones that can currently be covered by insurance will become a minor part of the portfolio.

Meltzer: Risk management is becoming more of a core issue for corporations and as such is becoming recognized as a strategic business practice within the organization. Risk management will become a conduit for identification and reporting of risks, and risk managers will become technical advisers to business units on efficient manners of managing risks. These will include innovative risk control programs as well as risk financing.

Drapeau: We are constantly changing toward what we have always argued risk management is: big picture management of risk as opposed to insurance buying. It's only taken us thirty years to get there.

Daniels: I think workplace violence is going to be a big problem. It's going on now, but people don't talk about it.

Mandel: I've come to believe that only the most well-rounded and broad thinkers will survive the new order. That means those who are willing to take risks and step out, rather than hide and hope for the best. Risk management departments will increasingly be integrated into treasury and finance operations, and be expected to do more with less. FRM will become as close to the CPA of risk management as we make and market it. Quality in education will rule the day, and the risk manager's ability to talk equally well with bankers as with insurers and brokers will be the defining threshold for moving ahead.

Lermack: I would just reiterate that we have to learn how to help people understand how to assess and manage risks on the ground, because that's where things are happening. And you can't do it by rules, and you can't teach it by memorization. You have to teach it using the latest and best educational techniques to reinforce that among people.

Hair: The old-world way of doing business is not going to provide the means necessary to sustain a company's competitive advantage. Risk management must become the driving force internally to encourage managers to exploit opportunities more quickly and efficiently. Using technology, understanding technology, and embracing technology is going to be critical for the risk management function to be able to serve that role going forward.

Read More About It

Enterprising Solutions

Elizabeth Eiss
Reprinted with permission from *Risk Management* magazine, August 1999. Copyright 1999 by Risk Management Society Publishing. All rights reserved. For more information call 212.286.9364. www.rims.org/rmmag

Integrated risk has a number of interpretations. Most people have an intuitive feel for its meaning, but in the risk management discipline, is intuition on the mark?

By common definition, risk refers to a dangerous element, or possibility of loss or injury, while to integrate means to coordinate or blend into a functioning unit.

For business, then, integrated risk refers to the unified risk of the whole enterprise. The objective of integrated risk programs is to provide the broadest possible risk solution to eliminate or mitigate the financial impact of risk to the company's capital base. Risk management, from this perspective, is ultimately capital management.

This definition can encompass more than the exposures normally part of an insurance program. Although insurance addresses certain risks, businesses face many other types of risk as well, including operational, human, market, or reputational risk. Integrated risk programs treat multiple types of risk within one capital management program. Once risk is identified and analyzed, its effect can be stabilized through insurance and financial engineering. An effective program combines risk assumption, transfer, financing, and other knowledge-based solutions that improve control of enterprise risk and, consequently, result in more effective capital management. (Some types of risk are typically not included in integrated programs, either due to legal restrictions or simply because good management is the best risk solution.)

The goal of this article is to provide a common foundation for evaluating the options offered under the banner of integrated risk solutions, and a perspective on the benefits, the process, the challenges, and the potential of integrated risk solutions.

What Are the Benefits?

According to industry estimates, only 20 percent of business exposures are insured today. If this is accurate, companies assume or manage the other 80 percent in some other manner. Some risk is knowingly assumed, and various independent mechanisms have been developed to hedge these exposures. Insurance or options in the financial and commodity markets are examples. Some risk is assumed knowingly, but only because there is no more viable or efficient alternative. Risk control is crucial in these cases, as are business advisers with the expertise to be sure all options have been identified and explored. Risk is also assumed unknowingly, when lack of knowledge or information sharing results in poor risk management. Lastly, emerging risk from an ever-evolving business environment may not be adequately recognized.

Within the context of multiyear, multi-line integrated programs, a wider variety of risk solutions addressing expected and suspected exposures is possible. Although earnings are not insured per se, events that threaten components driving earnings performance can be addressed. These are not off-the-shelf programs. The solutions are customized—crafted around the exposures and goals of the individual company. Standard property and casualty event risk tends to form the backbone of an integrated program, which can then be tailored to treat other types of risk that have not traditionally been covered by insurance programs. Commodity, interest rate, and foreign exchange rate risks are examples of noninsurance risk that may be included by making traditional techniques adjustable—a retention triggered, for example, by a change in the price of key commodities. Weather conditions could be another trigger. In addition, there are many financial exposures that can be considered within or alongside integrated programs, such as loss portfolio transfers, liability accruals and contingent liabilities, risk from acquisitions and divestitures, self-insured loss funding, environmental risk, and uninsured risks. These are all treatable exposures through finite structures—which simply means capping an exposure and funding it over time.

There are three primary benefits of integrated programs: efficiency, flexibility, and savings. Integrated programs can also lead to administrative simplicity. These attributes are characterized in multiple ways:

■ *Stabilization and predictability of capital resources*. Financial volatility can be reduced through the portfolio approach used in integrated programs. Unusual swings in p/c losses and other business drivers, such as raw material prices, can be linked to smooth the impact on earnings.

■ *Sharing the benefit of risk dispersion*. Integrated risk programs can potentially combine uncorrelated or negatively correlated risks into one portfolio or basket of exposures. The probability that all risks in the basket will not experience adverse events at the same time allows more favorable pricing for the basket of risks. An integrated program takes advantage of natural hedges in the portfolio of risk as opposed to hedging each individually.

■ *Efficiency in limit purchasing*. Since it is unlikely that multiple events will exhaust individual towers of cover in any one year, it is more efficient to stretch one limit across multiple covers and multiple years. Reinstatement options are generally available to restore the limit in event of a loss. Individual towers can be purchased in addition to the block of capacity if additional limits are needed for a certain exposure. Since the programs are multiyear, predictable underwriting capacity is available.

■ *Efficient tax and accounting treatment.* Including other financial exposures in an integrated program may enable accounting and tax efficiencies that can only be achieved with insurance.

■ *Flexibility and customization.* Each program is tailored to the specific client's risk exposures and consequently addresses unique business drivers.

■ *Security of insure or counterparty.* More risks are placed with a highly rated insurance carrier in a highly regulated industry.

■ *Administrative cost reduction.* Integrated programs are often simpler to administer and thus less costly. Frictional costs associated with multiple risk partners are reduced by using fewer carriers. Reporting provisions are also simplified.

■ *More time and energy for risk control vs. risk financing.* Since these are multi-line, multiyear contracts with simplified administration, risk managers have more time to focus on actual risk and loss cost reduction.

■ *Revenue growth.* This may be the biggest benefit of integrated risk programs. A successful integrated program frees up time to focus on the core business and improve returns.

Who Benefits?

Most companies would benefit from the advantages of an integrated risk program. At the same time, it is not for everyone. Here are some of the elements you should consider in making the decision to go forward with such a program:

■ *Orientation*. Risk exposures and optimal solutions often overlap. Companies managing risk collectively with an enterprise perspective will find these programs attractive. Companies seeking a better way to buy capacity may also appreciate integrated programs, choosing to integrate the p/c first and including other financial risk later. The impact of integrated programs on the total cost of risk and capital optimization is the best gauge of its value. Those companies focused on pure price relief may find these programs less appropriate.

■ *Size*. Most programs have been built for companies with annual risk costs in excess of $1 million. However, growing companies can share the benefits, too. Some risk solution providers are working to bring integrated risk programs to individual companies with lower risk cost expenditures. Integrated risk programs have also been conceived for homogeneous risk pools or purchasing groups. Interest in integrated risk is driven more by organizational objectives, needs, and capital preservation requirements than by company size.

■ *Industry*. Companies can benefit no matter what industry they belong to.

■ *Public or private*. Both company forms benefit from the stability afforded by integrated programs. For a public company, market capitalization is less vulnerable because quarterly events, which might cause adverse earnings fluctuations, can be smoothed over time. Private company capitalization is less stressed for the same reason, even if [private companies] are not subject to the intense scrutiny of Wall Street, because adverse events will not force the company to draw upon lines of credit or other short-term financing.

■ *Risk exposures*. Nearly all traditional property and casualty insurance risk can be considered as long as adequate cover is available. For example, D&O Side A is generally not included since companies want the Side A limit to apply separately to each director and officer as opposed to sharing the limit. Many business risk exposures can be contemplated as well by making traditional mechanisms variable with key business drivers.

■ *Excess vs. primary.* Many integrated programs are excess programs attaching above the working layers to focus on severity exposures. The ideal integrated excess program is written in concert with the working layer solution—either through client self-insured retentions, a primary risk partner, or a captive.

Challenges

Inertia in a soft market is an obstacle. Given the currently low prices for monoline insurance risk treatments, the value of an integrated program may not be compelling enough to motivate restructuring an insurance program if the total cost of risk and risk volatility is not considered.

Organizational rigidity that segments risk management is also a challenge. Many companies have begun the transition to reduce silo risk management while still choosing to buy traditional insurance programs because of current economics, or just integrating the p/c elements of their risk program. This can still pave the way to an integrated program; moving from silo to enterprise risk management does take time and the support of a broader set of stakeholders.

Because the limit purchased is stretched over multiple risks and years, there might be less cover available in the event that multiple events occur. However, reinstatement provisions can offset this downside. The use of capital that would otherwise go toward individual and often unused towers is another positive offset.

Traditional insurance programs are treated as expense items on the income statement and are not "off–balance sheet." Thus, including other financial exposures in an insurance-based integrated program may enable accounting and tax efficiencies. It is crucial that accounting and tax advisers carefully evaluate integrated programs that include financial risk.

The United States' domestic insurance marketplace is highly regulated and standardized in terms of form, rate, and rule—and each state regulates differently. Customized, multiline and multiyear risk solutions are more difficult to achieve in this type of environment. Greater flexibility is available through excess and surplus lines as opposed to admitted paper, so most integrated programs will probably be written that way. The federal and state commercial lines deregulation that is currently under consideration may make these kinds of customized business risk solutions more possible.

Knowledge-based Solutions

Anyone can create risk within a business and everyone can help control risk—if there is proper knowledge and motivation. Risk management has always contemplated risk control as well as risk transfer and post-loss cost containment. The challenge for most businesses is making people aware of risk and how it can be controlled. Integrated risk solutions can be broader than contractual promises to pay when adverse economic events occur. Technology can play an important role in helping companies create knowledge and awareness of risk by enabling more employees to access information online simply and easily when they need it. The most innovative integrated risk solution providers will seek to supply their clients with knowledge tools as well as solid financial backing.

Potential

There are clear benefits to an enterprisewide view and treatment of risk: efficiency, flexibility, savings, and administrative simplicity. The solutions are different and better matched to a full range of business risk, not just insurance risk. However, like other examples of integration, such as a manufacturer acquiring suppliers and distributors, the idea and the economics must make sense. This equation will be different for each company depending on the risks faced and the corresponding management objectives.

Risk management is capital management. Integrated risk providers can enable and provide a more complete set of risk and capital solutions. Study the alternatives, and then find a partner that will help turn your business risk into return.

How to Go Integrated

The process is relatively simple and can take advantage of many processes already in place. There are five basic phases:

1. *Concept*. Identify and quantify the risks that could affect your business. Define your company's risk appetite and establish clear risk management objectives. Risk partners can be a resource to explore how various types of risk can be integrated into an effective capital management program.

2. *Analysis and strategy*. Convert concepts to real proposals based on a thorough analysis of critical data. Determine the feasibility and cost-savings benefits of aggregating risks into one basket.

3. *Commitment*. Successful integrated solutions are based on long-term strategic partnerships. All stakeholders should be involved in every phase of the process. Confirmation of commitment is a critical step.

4. *Implementation*. A transition plan is crucial to ensure continuity of key functions and minimize front-end changes to operations. Processes, communication channels, and checkpoints should be established to ensure that the program meets business needs.

5. *Evolution*. A well-constructed integrated risk program should evolve with the business. It should add stability and strategic value through quality relationships and continuous adjustments to match the company's business environment and risk needs.

Read More About It

The Paradox of Bureaucratic Risk Control

Erik Bax
Reprinted with permission from *Risk Management* magazine, February 2000. Copyright 2000 by Risk Management Society Publishing. All rights reserved. For more information call 212.286.9364. www.rims.org/rmmag; full notes and references are available from the author at e.h.bax@bdk.rug.nl.

Rules clearly play an integral role in maintaining the safety of an industrial workplace; but are formal rules and procedures an effective means of controlling behavior in all dangerous situations, or are there environments in which they can back-fire?

How do the complexity of the production process, the risk of the work, and corporate culture shape the effectiveness of formal safety regulations?

Theory

As early as the 1930s, it was acknowledged that human beings will break even the most sophisticated technological safety and security systems. This insight inspired psychologists to research the origins of human error. Bhopal, Chernobyl, and Piper Alpha have forced recognition that the interaction between man and technology is a major source of risk in today's society. But human errors can only be understood if studied in context. This holds not only for the interaction between man and technology, but also for the ways in which social interaction comes into play and how the relevant social relationships are shaped by management. This draws attention to the organization as the context from which risk originates and within which risk management must develop.

In *Normal Accidents,* Charles Perrow lays the foundations of a theory of risk in organizations by relating the degree of a social system's risk proneness to the complexity of interactions within that system and the degree of coupling—[or] the extent to which there is slack between a system's parts, units, and sub-systems. Depending on the values that these two variables take in a specific situation, risks should be managed either by centralization or by decentralization of authority.

In another model, the Resident Pathogen Metaphor suggested by J. Reason, the organization is compared to the human body, in which latent pathogens can be triggered to overcome the immune system and cause disease. One of the general assertions about accident causation deduced from this view is that "the more complex and opaque the system, the more pathogens it will contain."

From the works of Max Weber and Karl Mannheim we can see that the modernization and rationalization of Western society created an increase of instrumental rationality and, consequently, a relative growth of complexity. Notably, Mannheim shows that this rise of instrumental rationality also leads to a decrease of substantial rationality ("an act of thought that reveals intelligent insight into the interrelations of events in a given situation"). The effect is that "a few people can see things more and more clearly over an ever-widening field, while the average man's capacity for rational judgement steadily declines."

So we are confronted with a paradox in the development of Western society. The increase of instrumental means to end rationality is striven for in order to promote control; but the effect is not only a growth of complexity, but also a relative decrease of insight into the interrelations that make up that complexity, and thus a loss of control.

This shift in rationality is the very core of the process of bureaucratization of society, based on rational thought, technology, and empirical science. It implicitly regards man as a threat because of the supposed irrational character of human behavior. Control can only be reached by building into machines as many human functions as possible; what is left should be submitted to rules and procedures.

Among the unintended effects of bureaucratic control are such phenomena as goal displacement, ritualism, and the so-called vicious circle of bureaucracy, which leads to the paradox of bureaucratic regulation. In order to control complexity, measures and procedures are introduced that add to this very complexity. It is doubtful whether, from the perspective of risk management, bureaucratic regulation leads to effective control, as it makes the organization ever more diffuse, thus enhancing the chances of ambiguous information and communication. In its extremes, bureaucratic regulation may lead to contradictions within the organization and can reduce the possibility of those to whom the rules apply understanding those regulations.

The above does not imply that centralization of authority—a core feature of bureaucratic control—is always to be avoided in risk management. In some cases, centralization is preferable. Likewise, even in crisis management the effectiveness of centralization as an instrument of control depends strongly on the characteristics of the system.

The TYRAD Study

In 1994 we conducted a case study in the chemical process industry with the TYRAD Company. In terms of Perrow's analysis, this industry could be described as complex and tightly coupled. Therefore, one would expect a decentralized approach to risk management. We found, however, a perfect example of bureaucratic control.

TYRAD's safety policy can be characterized as top-down bureaucratic control. Many of its rules and procedures are developed through scenario planning, where a team of safety engineers elaborates rules and procedures aimed at controlling an imagined installation breakdown, emergency situation or disaster. These rules and procedures are made official company policy and are sent to TYRAD's departments.

Thus, operators on the shop floor are confronted with an ever-growing number of rules and regulations. This is dysfunctional and counterproductive for two reasons. First, many operators no longer know what rules should be applied in what situation and who should apply them. Second, most rules and procedures are developed in TYRAD's headquarters. Many operators complain not only that there are too many too detailed rules, but also that these are not congruent with everyday shop floor reality.

This is a clear example of the dynamic we are addressing: The more a situation is considered to be dangerous, the more likely it is that management will try to control it with formal rules and procedures—and the more likely these rules and procedures will not be effective in controlling the potential risks. Since the human brain has a limited capacity to process information, it follows that the more risk prone and complex work settings are, the less suitable formal rules will be as means of controlling those situations and the more workers will rely on their own informal rules.

The fact that TYRAD has a rather good safety record, despite the presence of an abundance of formal rules, is explained by the sophistication of workers' informal organization. Precisely because operators considered formal rules and procedures dysfunctional, they set up an alternative and informal set of rules.

Testing the Hypotheses

In order to test whether these findings were specific to TYRAD or whether they had a more general application, we investigated the extent to which employees perceive their work situations as being controlled by rules officially issued by the organization. Formal control of such rules translates into control by appointed personnel such as supervisors, managers, and the like, and the application of formally approved sanctions. We also examined the relationship between the degree of risk workers are exposed to on the job and the nature of the rules to control these risks.

We split our sample into two categories. The first, high-risk workers, consists of workers who say that mistakes in their work could endanger their own life or the lives of colleagues and those outside the organization. The second category, low-risk workers, consists of people whose mistakes would, in the worst case, only affect the functioning of the production process and not endanger any lives.

We discovered that people who work in high-risk situations are confronted with more formal rules and experience more inspection of their conformity to those rules than people who work in more stable environments. However, although high-risk workers do not perceive the formal rules by which they work as necessarily insufficient, irrespective of the risky nature of the work, it is the job complexity that shapes their perception of whether or not formal rules are sufficient to prevent accidents.

That is, the more complex the work, the less workers view formal rules as effective.

In congruence with our hypothesis, we also discovered that more dangerous or risk-intense workplaces encourage the development of informal rules. A combination of both these and formal regulations are perceived to be vital in preventing accidents in such volatile environments.

TYRAD Revisited

How are formal and informal rules related to such issues as the technological outline of production processes, production organization, and human resource policies? We returned to the TYRAD Company and studied the shutdown of a gas installation to get a better idea of the factors that could explain the effectiveness of risk control by formal rules and procedures. The shutdown is temporarily needed to enable maintenance and is considered to be potentially very dangerous. The gas stream to the installation is cut off and the gas and residues are removed to allow for repairs, new electric wiring, painting, and substitution of parts. The actual shutdown process takes a couple of weeks and is executed by a highly specialized crew of TYRAD engineers and specialists of subcontractors. These field workers cooperate as a team and work according to well-defined procedures and a very detailed work plan provided by the TYRAD office.

Balancing Acts

Safety is an overriding aim in TYRAD's everyday production practices. However, there are many violations of formal safety rules because workers have to choose between production targets and safety. Even in situations where workers are conscious of imminent danger, there is an increase in informal alternative procedures that are considered to be practical and legitimate shortcuts.

TYRAD's economic and business strategies lead to an abundant use of subcontractors who are not socialized in the organization's culture. Therefore, they can only be controlled by external formal rules. At the same time, the more workers differ as to organizational backgrounds, the less they share the same frame of reference, and the higher the probability of communication failures.

Members of work groups performing dangerous activities constantly emphasize the necessity not to change the composition of their teams. Their greatest fear is the possible introduction of new team members unknown to them and thus "unreliable and unpredictable under conditions of crisis." Whatever formal licenses they might have, new recruits to a team are perceived as being unaware of "how the work is done in practice" and therefore are considered a safety threat. Such statements underline the importance of informal group norms and communication patterns in dangerous work situations: New entrants may be unaware of patterns believed to be essential for the safety of the group.

Concern also arises as a result of a human resource policy that requires experienced foremen to be withdrawn from the shutdowns. Group members feel that they are left with a less experienced leadership [who] is too dependent on formal rules.

At TYRAD, the office is the locus of power, planning, and control. Here, formal rules and procedures are designed and issued, and field workers and their work teams are evaluated according to criteria developed by office management. Field workers see their colleagues in the office as nonpractical bureaucrats who have no insight into the problems of everyday work and only create a lot of unnecessary red tape. Thus many formal rules and procedures are regarded as bureaucratic spinoff or, in the worst case, as tools of power. Contacts between office people and field workers are limited. Both categories follow different career paths. The differences in educational backgrounds and skills also contribute to the gap.

It is easy to see that these differences not only lead to varying frames of reference, but also hinder effective communication. Take, for example, the risk monitoring reports made by team leaders in the field: In many cases office employees consider these badly—or even incomprehensibly—written; in some cases, the office asks for rewriting, which provokes frustration and irritation on the shop floor.

TYRAD's managers believe that an acceptable level of safety can only be reached if people are held responsible for the mistakes and errors they make, so they apply utilitarian sanctions. At the same time, managers see as one of the most significant problems of TYRAD's risk control policy the lack of employee openness and the difficulty in motivating workers to participate in toolbox meetings, where managers and workers come together to discuss work safety.

These negative sanctions provoke a calculative attitude in workers. It often seems as if the main questions guiding safety behavior are: Can I be held responsible, and how can I evade my responsibility? This attitude leads to a strengthening of bureaucratic ritualism and a cover-up of violations of safety rules. The overall effect is a split between those who control safety policies and those who execute them. It also implies a serious distortion in communication patterns: Crucial behavior is hidden from those in charge.

Hidden Rules

Like any other organization TYRAD has hidden rules. From our perspective, three types are relevant. The first relates to the blaming culture mentioned. Colleagues in the field tend to protect each other vis-à-vis those in power. So, in case the drafting of an incident report is inevitable, all subcontractors and field supervisors related to the incident will sign the report. In this way, no single person is to blame. This also makes it almost impossible for management to discover the causes of the incident.

A second type of hidden rule can be associated with a pattern that I call pleasing one's superior. An example is the idea that just before personnel evaluations take place, it is not considered very wise to write an incident report, as it produces a lot of paperwork for the superior involved.

The third type relates to safety itself. Despite the fact that formal rules are in some cases ritualized or evaded, there is a real understanding of the danger of the job. Therefore, workers are very selective: Only those rules considered useless and senseless are violated. In many circumstances, workers have their own informal rules to guarantee each other's safety.

Conclusion

The more managers consider a situation risk prone, the more they try to control that situation by issuing formal rules and procedures that in fact decrease controllability of the situation. Hence, workers tend to add informal rules in order to maintain control.

Our research leads us to two issues of great importance for the improvement of risk control practices. The first is the relationship between the general business strategy of the firm and the shape—and hence effectiveness—of its risk management practices. The TYRAD case study shows that general business strategy may set the boundaries for risk management. In this respect, the company's problem is basically that the general business strategy and risk management policies are formulated in unlinked management layers. And TYRAD is not the exception to the rule. A firmer integration of relevant dimensions of strategic management and risk management will certainly be a worthwhile enrichment of integral risk management.

The second important issue deals with another relationship: Risk management aimed at the social context of primary production processes has everything to do with managing human resources. However, risk management can only gain from human resources management if the latter is not restricted to the supply side of the internal labor market—recruitment, selection, training, and rewarding of workers—but broadened to the demand side, the very design and structuring of work processes.

2

Risk Assessment

The biggest assessment challenge we face actually is educating managers as to their role in identifying risks. A risk manager or risk management department cannot identify all risk within the company. The goal, I guess, is to get my colleagues to recognize that risk assessment is not something a risk manager does to the organization, but rather something the organization does to itself.

Risk Manager
Multinational Medical Device Manufacturer

Our biggest assessment challenge is to get new internal customers from acquisitions or new ventures to understand that we don't want to run their businesses, just understand and help.

Risk Manager
Multinational Financial Services Firm

Perspectives

Cost of Risk Up 8.8 Percent as Survey Base Differs

Michael Bradford
Reprinted with permission from *Business Insurance,* December 20, 1999.
© Crain Communications Inc. All rights reserved.

Risk managers are finding that a competitive insurance marketplace doesn't always add up to a lower cost of risk. The 1999

RIMS Benchmark Survey found that, while many insurers continued to cut rates last year or kept increases slight, any savings were more than offset by respondents' higher retained liability losses.

Those losses helped drive a year-to-year increase in the average cost of risk for U.S. nonbank companies, the first such increase in six years. Their average cost of risk rose to $5.71 per $1,000 of revenue in 1998, an increase from $5.25 per $1,000 in 1997. The increase follows a steady annual decline in the average cost of risk since 1992, when it was $8.30 per $1,000 of revenue. The average cost in 1998 was nearly identical to the 1996 figure of $5.70.

"It's very interesting that the cost of risk actually rose [in 1999], given the soft market," said Sue Anne Mitro, vice chairwoman of the Risk & Insurance Management Society Inc. [RIMS] research committee. "I would not have anticipated those results."

The survey acknowledges that the results appear to have been "skewed upward" by higher costs incurred by a group of new participants in the study. "Some very large companies with very low costs of risk" participated in the previous survey but not in the 1999 survey, the report notes.

James Gamble, senior manager with Ernst & Young L.L.P.'s Business Risk Solutions practice in New York, said that "it's somewhat in the nature of a survey of this type that changes in respondents from year to year can have an impact." Ernst & Young and RIMS conduct the survey jointly.

He pointed out that, in the current survey, a "large portion of this respondent base takes large retentions," and some were hit with big losses. "Retained losses have more volatility than premiums and other types of costs," said Gamble. "With premiums, the changes are usually marginal from year to year; that's not necessarily the case with retained losses."

The survey, which is conducted annually, shows that in 1998, retained liability losses for U.S. respondents rose sharply, to $1.62 per $1,000 of revenue from $1.17 per $1,000 in 1997.

Overall, liability costs per $1,000 of revenue increased to $2.43 in 1998, up from $1.93 in 1997.

While those costs were rising, average liability premium costs moved up only slightly, to 79 cents per $1,000 of revenue in 1998 from 76 cents per $1,000 in 1997. Mitro, who is a member of the RIMS benchmark steering committee, pointed out that retained liability losses make up a "very volatile segment of the cost of risk," and 1998 proved to be a year in which survey respondents—and the overall cost of risk—were particularly affected by those losses.

The survey considers the cost of risk to consist of the following: insurance premiums; retained losses; internal administration; outside services, including consulting, captive management, and other vendor services; financial guarantees; and fees, taxes, and similar expenses.

The results are intended to be used by risk managers to benchmark their risk management functions. The survey can be used to determine, among other things, how a company's cost of risk stacks up against that of others in its industry.

Mitro, who is manager of risk and insurance at The Hillman Co. in Pittsburgh, said she uses the annual survey for several tasks, including sizing up her company's cost of risk against industry averages, preparing risk management reports for management, and performing due diligence on potential acquisitions. In addition, she said Hillman uses the results to evaluate whether the companies with which it is considering doing business are carrying insurance limits that are in line with industry averages.

The 1999 survey contains a new "All Respondents" report, which compares costs for organizations with less than $1 billion in revenue against those for organizations whose revenues exceed $1 billion, allowing users to compare themselves with organizations of a similar size. "I find this extremely useful," Mitro said of the new section, which she uses to determine how costs for Hillman, a diversified holding and investment company, compare with those of other firms.

Survey results were based on questionnaire responses from 737 U.S. respondents and 79 Canadian respondents. Respondents included deputy members of RIMS, members of the American Society for Healthcare Risk Management, certain Ernst & Young clients, and other companies that responded to the previous year's questionnaire.

Figures for U.S. banks were based on deposits and therefore were not included in overall ratio results. The bank figures are included in survey data on items such as limits and retentions where deposits are considered as revenue.

While U.S. risk managers watched their cost of risk rise, the average cost in Canada fell to its lowest level in the last ten years. Declines in property/casualty costs led the reduction in Canada, according to the survey.

The cost of risk in Canada fell to $1.74 Canadian ($1.18) per $1,000 Canadian ($678) of revenue in 1998, down from $2.13 Canadian ($1.44) per $1,000 Canadian in 1997. Liability costs fell to 76 cents Canadian (52 cents) per $1,000 Canadian of revenue in 1998, down from 83 cents Canadian (56 cents) per $1,000 Canadian the year before. Property costs dropped to 72 cents Canadian (49 cents) per $1,000 Canadian last year, down from 94 cents Canadian (64 cents) per $1,000 Canadian in 1997.

Administrative costs in Canada, which include costs for outside services—including broker compensation, consulting fees, and third-party administrator fees—were up to 51 cents Canadian (35 cents) per $1,000 Canadian of revenue, from 46 cents Canadian (31 cents) per $1,000 Canadian in 1997.

U.S. risk managers saw their workers compensation costs move up slightly last year, according to the survey. The increase to $1.96 per $1,000 of revenue from $1.93 per $1,000 in 1997 is mainly attributed to a rise in workers comp insurance premiums. Those premium costs jumped to 48 cents per $1,000 of revenue from 36 cents the year before. Retained workers comp losses fell to $1.52 per $1,000 of revenue in 1998, from $1.57 per $1,000 in 1997.

The survey also showed a growing concern among risk managers regarding employment practices liability risks. Of the 737 U.S. respondents, 212 reported purchasing separate EPL coverage, at a total cost of $39.5 million in premiums. [In 1998],

172 respondents from a pool of 876 surveyed reported buying the coverage in 1997, for a total of $19.1 million in premiums.

Property risk financing costs moved up in 1998 to $1.07 per $1,000 of revenue from 93 cents per $1,000 in 1997. Retained losses showed a significant jump to 53 cents per $1,000 of revenue, from 34 cents per $1,000 in 1997.

The survey said that, while the increase in self-assumed losses can be attributed to changes in the composition of the respondent pool, "the volatility of the results cannot be ignored."

But while some property costs were up, property premiums costs fell slightly in a continued soft market, the survey notes. Those costs were down to 56 cents per $1,000 of revenue, from 59 cents per $1,000 in 1997.

U.S. companies saw administrative expenses rise to 51 cents per $1,000 of revenue in 1998, from 46 cents per $1,000 in 1997. Those expenses include costs for outside services, which partly consist of consulting and TPA fees; broker compensation; captive management; and costs related to risk management information systems.

The average risk management department budget rose by just one cent, to 25 cents per $1,000 of revenue in 1998. That scant increase came even though the average department added 1.2 employees to its staff last year.

The survey also found that risk managers are more frequently exploring the idea of integrated risk programs, although the number of respondents who have actually put together such programs did not increase.

Copies of the 1999 RIMS Benchmark Survey are available from Insurance Publishing Plus Corp., Suite 500, 11690 Technology Dr., Carmel, Indiana 46032-9952. Telephone orders can be placed at 800-211-3257 or 317-843-2523, and fax orders at 317-816-1001. Ordering information also is available online at www.ey.com/riskmanagement/survey. The cost is $395 for RIMS members, $445 for RIMS associates, and $495 for others.

Introduction

Risk assessment is the fundamental activity of risk management. Risk management tools, techniques, and strategies cannot be applied until an entity identifies and understands its risks.

Assessment involves three distinct but closely related elements: risk identification, risk analysis, and risk measurement. The purpose of this chapter is to enable readers to develop an appreciation for the governing concepts and practices of systematic, organization-wide assessment. To that end, the chapter begins with the development of an assessment framework that is based on the Organization Risk Management (ORM) concept. That is followed by a discussion of identification methodologies. The balance of Chapter 2 is devoted to a discussion of risk analysis basics and applications, and to a presentation of risk measurement principles. Both qualitative and quantitative dimensions of measurement are presented and analyzed.

The Risk Assessment Framework

The Organization Risk Management concept, coupled with the notion of the COCA organization, imposes a rather stiff challenge for the practicing risk manager. In principle, the ORM view asserts that risk management is the management of all organization risks, whereas the COCA organization establishes that risks arise from all the contracts, obligations, commitments, and agreements that jointly form the basis for an organization's existence.

A moment's reflection on the implications of these two concepts will reveal the daunting challenge of identifying, analyzing, and measuring every single risk in an organization's risk portfolio (and doing so in a systematic, timely, and ongoing basis at that). We reasonably may wonder how even to begin such an undertaking. In this section we will set forth the framework for comprehensive risk assessment, but with an important caveat: It will be impossible to assess all risks because organizations are highly complex and exist in a dynamic environment. Thus, though the ambition of risk assessment is lofty, the effort to assess must be leavened with a healthy dose of humility and skepticism.

Risk Assessment Begins with Contracts, Obligations, Commitments, and Agreements

The concept of the COCA organization is a basic assumption of risk assessment, and consequently its premises must be restated briefly here.

An organization like a business is the result of many years of conscious and rational, spontaneous and opportunistic, and required or unavoidable arrangements entered into between the business's owners/managers and resource holders. These arrangements mainly serve the declared purposes of the business, but sometimes impose purposes on that business (e.g., a mandate from the Environmental Protection Agency). These arrangements can be described as either contracts, obligations, commitments, or agreements (COCAs). Each is defined as followed:

■ *Contracts* are legally enforceable arrangements that meet the ordinary tests of offer and acceptance, consideration, legality of purpose, and legal capacity. The employment contract is a well-known example. Another would be an arrangement to deliver goods at a fixed price and time.

■ *Obligations* are also legally binding arrangements that are required of an organization—though, typically, they are not the fruit of party/counterparty offer and acceptance. In other words, obligations are legally enforceable, but often are imposed on an organization. A good example would be an OSHA mandate to modify a worksite to improve safety.

■ *Commitments* also may appear to fulfill the test of an agreement (defined below), but the concept of a commitment is intended to convey self-imposed duties. The duty of present generations to future generations is cited in current debates about social security and is a good illustration of a commitment. Certainly, moral and ethical values represent pervasive commitments. The principal governing characteristic of commitments is that only one party need by involved in the formation and implementation of a commitment. As an example, many corporations are committed to the communities in which they reside. While not legally binding, such commitments may strongly influence corporate behavior.

■ *Agreements* often may enjoy legal enforceability—like contracts and obligations—but the term is intended to connote less formal arrangements between parties that may fall somewhat outside a legal sphere. Participation in voluntary associations (e.g., Chambers of Commerce and professional associations) are good illustrations of such arrangements.

Taken as a whole, the COCAs that constitute a business are referred to as that business's *risk field* (see Exhibit 2-1), such that an organization becomes exposed to risk through the COCAs. The risks that arise from the risk field collectively are defined as the business's *risk profile*. This chapter includes an extended discussion of both of these terms and what they mean in the risk assessment process; first, however, a few final words are necessary regarding COCAs.

COCAs either create risks for the organization or they serve as a portal for risk. For example, an employment contract will specify certain contractual matters that are unique to that contract pertaining to salary, job duties, measures of performance, and so on. In that sense, the contract is creating expectations, duties, and rights that have enforceability. Absent the contract, the business would not encounter the risks. However, that employment contract might also allow external risks to pass through to the business. For example, the Americans with Disabilities Act (ADA) exists independently of individual employment contracts, but by entering into an employment contract the organization becomes exposed to risks associated with providing reasonable accommodation for employees.

COCAs can further be characterized by the possible risk-distributing characteristics of the arrangement. A commitment to

Exhibit 2-1. The risk field

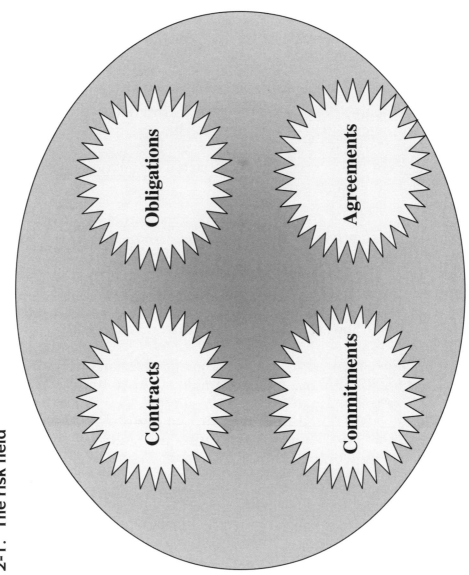

some moral value does not permit risk distribution to occur, as it is a single-party, self-imposed duty. However, a multiparty contract with vendors may create numerous opportunities for distribution. In general, distribution and transfer of risk would seem to be a function of some—if not all—of the following factors:

- The number of parties to the arrangement
- The relative negotiating strength or leverage of the parties
- The legal or moral enforceability of the arrangement
- The risk-bearing capacity of the parties
- The relationship of a particular arrangement with other COCAs
- The influence of external interests (i.e., external to the specific arrangement)

Finally, COCAs have a history, and while the process of risk assessment tends to focus its efforts on describing what exists and how it might be managed, there always is value in understanding why the arrangement exists in the first place. One of the challenging complications of the ORM view of risk management is that it forces the matter of interdependencies (and history) to the forefront of analysis. In later chapters the book discusses some decision-making methods, but almost invariably these methods assume "independence" of exposure—that is, it is assumed that a collection of risks (e.g., motor vehicles) are independently exposed to risk. If the relationships or interdependencies between these exposures are too strong, statistical analysis diminishes in its power to predict and measure.

The irony of this limitation of statistical analysis is that it tends to force risk managers to view interdependency as a nuisance to be assumed or controlled in analysis, whereas the ORM view plainly states that interdependencies are the point (or at least a key point) in understanding organization-wide risk management. COCAs are entered into, more or less, intentionally, and they are expected to serve a common mission or set of purposes for which the business exists. It would, in this light, be absurd not to wonder about the interrelatedness of risks and COCAs, so when analysis of the risks within COCAs occurs, it must be plainly understood that each contract, obligation, commitment, and agreement is expected to have an impact on other COCAs.

Environmental Sources of Risk

COCAs are the risk field, but additional concepts must be introduced to help in the assessment process. For example, while the risk field is the point of contact between a business and a risky world, it would be useful to develop a basis for categorizing the various sources of risk. This book relies on a model that incorporates seven environmental sources of risk as described here and shown in Exhibit 2-2:

1. *Physical environment.* Geological and climatic risks arise from the physical environment.
2. *Social environment.* Consumers' changing tastes and preferences, morals/values, as well as demographic factors, can all give rise to risks.
3. *Political environment.* Political institutions and decisions create responsibilities, interests, and expectations that produce risks.
4. *Legal environment.* The formalized legal system establishes rights and duties that create risk for organizations.
5. *Economic environment.* While often influenced by the political, social, and legal environments, the global economic system has a degree of independence that warrants separate analysis.
6. *Operational environment.* The manner in which an organization goes about its work gives rise to a wide range of risks, most of which are influenced by the other environments.
7. *Cognitive environment.* The environment of the mind; a manager's knowledge may be influenced by absence of information, attitude toward risk, misinformation, or even mental limitations, which can rise to both risk and uncertainty.

Exhibit 2-2. Environmental sources of risk

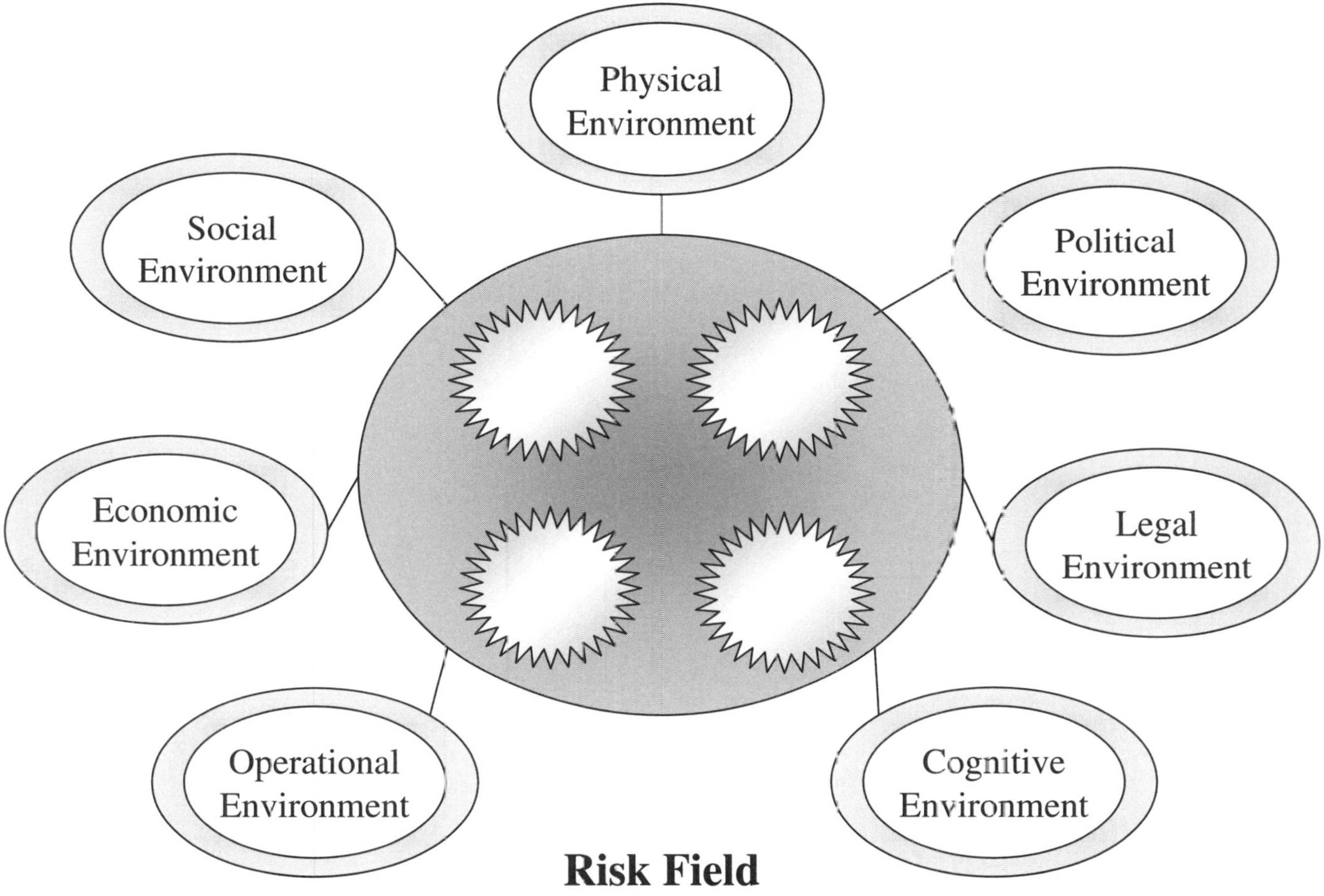

Political Environment

Legal Environment

Cognitive Environment

Physical Environment

Social Environment

Economic Environment

Operational Environment

Risk Field

There are a number of different ways of categorizing environmental sources of risk, but a commonly adopted approach is to identify the physical, economic, political, legal, and social environments as external environments, while the operational and cognitive environments are internal (i.e., internal to the organization). And, of course, within each environment are subcategories.

There certainly is overlap among these environments, but each is sufficiently distinct and the separation enhances analysis. In general terms, risk assessment involves a scan of each environment for the dual purpose of being able to describe the environment and to identify risks that arise from each of these environments.

Hazards and Risk Factors/Perils and Opportunities

The specific purpose of environmental scanning is to identify characteristics that give rise to risk. In the nomenclature of risk management, this means that assessment is concerned principally with discovering hazards (which produce perils) and risk factors (which produce opportunities).

Hazards are conditions of an environment that elevate either the likelihood of loss or the potential severity of losses. Ice on a roadway elevates the likelihood of an accident, and at least indirectly can influence the extent of the damage should an accident occur. Sometimes, an entire environment is deemed hazardous—such would be the case of the social/political environments in Kosovo—but more commonly hazards are nodes within an environment that can be detected through careful investigation.

Perils are actual causes of loss, so assessment ultimately is concerned with understanding how hazardous conditions produce losses. After all, most cars driving on icy roads do not crash. Thus, recognizing that hazards exist only partly explains the nature of a risk.

Risk factors are a speculative risk analog to hazards. Certain features of, say, the economic environment are favorable to gain (as well as loss); exchange rate differentials can be profited from with timely investing. These risk factors produce opportunities that

Insights

Insurers Stymied in Managing Enterprise Risk

Rodd Zolkos

A new study shows that insurance company executives believe enterprise risk management will help them improve their own companies' performance, but they are widely dissatisfied with their progress toward addressing risk on an enterprisewide basis.

Respondents to the Tillinghast-Towers Perrin survey of insurers were particularly displeased with their companies' progress toward managing operational risks. Many also indicated that their companies were not doing a good job of prioritizing risks or optimizing business and risk management strategies based on risk/return requirements. And, though they stressed the value of establishing a framework to guide their companies' risk and capital management activities, many indicated the lack of such a framework at their companies.

"These companies are less disappointed in their ability to get their arms around operational risks than they are dissatisfied in the current tools and techniques to do it," said Jerry Miccolis, the Parsippany, New Jersey–based Tillinghast-Towers Perrin principal who conducted the survey.

"I think that dissatisfaction comes from the fact that they're so well equipped on the financial side," Miccolis said. Given the extent of the tools and techniques available to their companies to address financial risks, the executives surveyed won't be satisfied until they can address their operational risks "with the same level of rigor," he said.

The survey findings are based on responses from sixty-six chief financial officers, chief actuaries, or chief risk officers whose companies are in major markets worldwide. Respondents ranked in order of importance the top-five issues their companies face today as: earnings growth, revenue growth, return on capital, expense control/reduction, and competitive risks. Eighty percent of those responding indicated they believe enterprise risk management will help them address the top issue before their companies—earnings growth.

"Clearly it's a clear line of sight for them between risk management and earnings growth," Miccolis said.

Nearly half—47.4 percent—said an enterprise risk management approach would help them address revenue growth; 97.1 percent said it would help them deal with return on capital concerns; 57.1 percent said it would help with expense control/reduction; and 62.2 percent indicated enterprise risk management would help them address competitive risks.

And 100 percent of those responding said enterprise risk management would help them address the next two concerns on their list—earnings consistency and capital management/allocation.

Only 20 percent of the executives surveyed reported that their companies have chief risk officers [CROs], and those that did were primarily non–North American companies. While only 8 percent of the North American companies responding said they had chief risk officers, 40 percent of non–North American companies indicated they have CROs. Of those companies that reported having chief risk officers, 46 percent have had the position for less than one year, 46 percent for two to four years, and 8 percent for five years or more.

"I don't think a chief risk officer is a necessary condition for enterprise risk management, but the movement to CROs is part of the same phenomenon," Miccolis said. "They are intimately connected concepts."

Although nearly all the executives surveyed said they believe it is important that their companies integrate risk into their strategic, operational, and financial planning, only 83 percent reported that their companies actually do so.

The chief barriers to integrating risk into a company's planning included: tools, cited by 50 percent of those surveyed; organizational turf, mentioned by 47 percent; processes, cited by 40.9 percent; and time, identified by 39.4 percent of respondents. The executives surveyed cited technology, interest rates, distribution channels, reputation/rating, and expenses as the most important sources of risk their companies face.

Such risks also were among those most often identified as being actively managed by the respondents' companies; in each case, at least 80 percent of respondents said they were being managed. In the case of expenses, 92.1 percent said that risk is being actively managed by their companies.

Although people/intellectual capital was ranked as the seventh most important risk source by all respondents, only 59.7 percent [of respondents] said it was a risk their companies actively manage. Not surprisingly, perhaps, people/intellectual capital also ranked at the bottom in terms of respondents' satisfaction with the tools and techniques used to assess, mitigate, and transfer those risks. Only 34.5 percent expressed satisfaction with their companies' assessment and measurement of people/intellectual capital risks; only 33.3 percent were satisfied with the tools and techniques they are using to mitigate those risks; and only 28.3 percent were satisfied with the tools and techniques they are employing to retain or transfer people/intellectual capital risks.

Although it was ranked as the top source of risk faced by the companies of the surveyed executives, technology fared poorly in terms of respondents' satisfaction with their companies' mitigation and risk retention/transfer tools, techniques or processes. While 62.7 percent of those surveyed said they were satisfied with their companies' assessment of technology risks, fully half said they were not satisfied with their technology risk mitigation efforts, and only 48.2 percent were satisfied with the tools, techniques, and processes their companies use to retain or transfer those risks.

The level of satisfaction among surveyed executives with the tools, techniques, and processes their companies use to address another highly ranked exposure—distribution channel risk—fell within a similar range. Only 61 percent indicated they were satisfied with their companies' approach to the assessment of distribution channel risks; just 52.6 percent were satisfied with the tools, techniques, and processes their companies use to mitigate those risks; and less than half—49.1 percent—

said they were satisfied with the risk retention/transfer methods their companies employed in that area.

Copies of the report, *Enterprise Risk Management in the Insurance Industry Benchmarking Survey,* are available inside the United States by calling Tillinghast-Towers Perrin at 800-525-6741; outside the United States, a copy can be ordered by contacting the nearest Towers Perrin office.

offer upside outcome potential. For example, a finance officer may use an arbitrage situation (e.g., misalignment in exchange rates) to speculate on rate movements, an opportunity that may produce returns greater than otherwise would be available.

The identification of hazards and risk factors involves a process known as *environmental mapping* (see Exhibit 2-3).

The operational environment is particularly complex, and the challenge of mapping is considerable. For example, at a minimum, we would expect to recognize hazards/risk factors in each of the following categories:

- Financial
- Professional
- Legal
- Physical
- Contractual
- Technological
- Process
- Human resources
- Products or services

Naturally, some overlap occurs when we consider such things as physical hazards—is this a physical hazard of the operational environment, or is it a hazard arising from the broader physical environment? While this is the type of question professors love, it probably is of modest concern to the practicing manager. If fire is a hazard arising from, say, natural causes and also arises as a hazard of a product assembly process, it is probably sufficient to note that

Exhibit 2-3. Environmental mapping

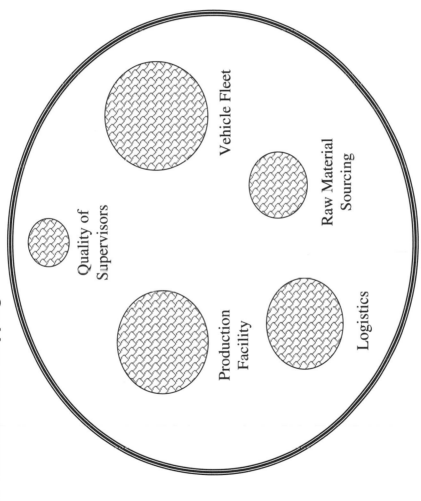

Operational Environment

fire is a reasonably important risk for a business. Categorization assists in organizing our thinking about risks—it is not intended to restrict our ability to do so.

Exposures to Risk

We already have explained that contracts, obligations, commitments, and agreements are the risk field where the risk portfolio arises. These risks may be characterized as the product of the environmental sources of risk; but as a practical matter, the COCAs are directly responsible for the production of the risk or serve as a conduit.

Looked at from another direction, the COCAs bring the exposure to the risks (see Exhibit 2-4). In other words, a business has elements that become exposed to risk through the creation of COCAs. It is not fruitful to spend too much time on making terminological distinctions, however, because commonly the creation of a contract in many senses spontaneously generates exposure. For example, a business's financial assets become exposed to a number of risks the instant an agreement is signed with a key customer.

While COCAs create exposure in a general sense (i.e., the business is exposed to loss), there is an analytical value in categorizing types of exposures. There are five exposure types. They are the substance of Chapters 4 and 5, but are outlined briefly here:

1. *Physical asset exposures* (e.g., motor vehicles, buildings, computers, inventories, brand equity, revenue, and expense flows)
2. *Financial asset exposures* (e.g., money, investment instruments, debt obligations, derivatives, and insurance)
3. *Human asset exposures* (e.g., employees, managers, board members, and key stakeholders)
4. *Legal liability exposures* (e.g., directors and officers liability, employment discrimination, product liability, and environmental impairment liability)

Exhibit 2-4. Exposures in the risk field

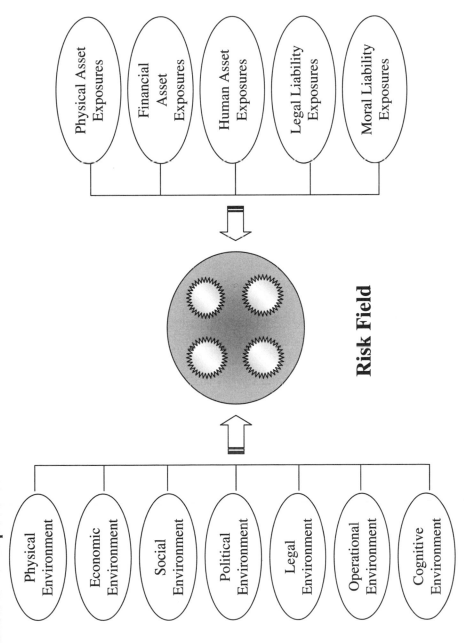

Physical Asset Exposures

Financial Asset Exposures

Human Asset Exposures

Legal Liability Exposures

Moral Liability Exposures

Risk Field

Physical Environment

Economic Environment

Social Environment

Political Environment

Legal Environment

Operational Environment

Cognitive Environment

5. *Moral liability exposures* (e.g., ethical and value-based commitments and obligations)

It is practically true that risks mean nothing without exposure. An icy highway in central South Dakota certainly is a hazardous condition, but if no one drives on the road there is no exposure. In the context of Organization Risk Management, exposure is the trigger and while managers may naturally be concerned about certain hazards where no exposure exists, a discussion of such circumstances does little to advance the purposes of this book.

Risk Identification Tools and Techniques

Ideally, a risk manager would like to develop a process for identifying risks that aided in comprehensiveness and allowed for some degree of confidence that identification was systematically and consistently undertaken. This section describes one such approach, although readers should note that a wide variety of methods might be adopted and, in fact, the unique attributes of an organization will be most influential in the approach that ultimately is created.

A Comment on Risk Checklists

A rather straightforward way to initiate an identification effort would be to acquire a risk checklist and use it as a road map for evaluating an entity's risks. Certainly, risk checklists abound; virtually all insurance agencies, brokerages, insurance companies, accounting firms, and management consultancy firms have them, as do many professional associations.

The benefits of having a checklist are fairly self-evident. However, there are problems with using them. To begin, virtually all available checklists are derived from insurance industry sources and thus tend to limit assessment to insurable risks. Second, by design such checklists are standardized methods, so they may not be suited to any particular organization. Third, the presence of an existing checklist permits an organization to miss an important opportunity, which is the chance to think broadly and critically about its own exposure to risk.

The balance of this discussion assumes that some type of organizing idea is present—whether a customized or standardized checklist—to govern the identification process.

Sources of Information

Conventionally, risk assessment processes rely upon the following sources of information:

- *Environmental scans*. Critical to the risk assessment process is the initial effort to characterize and understand the environmental sources of risk. The sources of information for evaluating the physical, social, economic, political, legal, operational, and cognitive environments will be varied. However, the environmental scanning process should at least produce answers to such questions as:
    —What is the general nature of the environment?
    —In broad terms, what is our business's exposure to this environment?
    —What are the specific hazards or risk factors in the environment?
    —How does our business see itself being exposed to hazards and risk factors?

Ordinarily, a risk assessment document will include a short narrative discussion of each environment. The purpose of the scan is descriptive rather than analytical; the information sources discussed in the following sections will aid in analysis.

- *Financial documentation*. As a starting point, budget forecasts, financial statements, 10K reports, and other financial documents provide a very good starting point for analysis. In principle, financial analysis can yield at least:
    —The overall financial position of the business
    —General representations of resource flows

—Broad identification of physical and financial assets (i.e., exposures to risk)

—Material events and activities that may impact future budgets and planning

—The overall organizational structure of the business

—Some reflection of goals and objectives of the departments and units within the business, as well as the overall business objectives of the firm

—General descriptive information on the firm's industry and general competitive issues

■ *Legal documentation.* Relevant legal documentation is difficult to summarize because it differs significantly from business to business. However, certainly a review of existing contracts would be central to such analysis. In addition, review of relevant statutes, regulatory rules, and laws pertinent to the business is critical. Commonly a risk manager relies heavily on the firm's legal counsel to conduct a significant portion of the analysis.

■ *On-site inspections.* There is no substitute for actually seeing a firm's exposures to risk. A formal risk assessment process would include comprehensive site visits, and such inspections probably should be a regular feature of the ongoing risk management process.

■ *Interviews.* Plainly, employees and managers are the best source of information on risks pertinent to their scope of authority and activity. Talking to all levels of employees is further considered important because relying on managers only can result in an "official version" of facts and circumstances that may not be accurate. The benefit of interviews also is strategic. By involving employees in the identification process, risk managers signal the importance they place on employee input, and this participatory approach facilitates institutional buy-in when the risk management program is rolled out, as well as offering a chance to introduce the principle that risk management is part of everyone's job.

■ *Statistical analysis.* Certain important areas of risk management are amenable to statistical analysis—for example, worker injuries, motor vehicle risks, general liability, and employee benefits utilization, to name the most obvious. Furthermore, process or operations analysis can be important in analyzing work processes, material flows, and other operational sources of risk. Such data may be internally available, but often the firm's insurance companies can furnish data that can provide important understanding of particular risks.

■ *Benchmarking/best practices.* Several efforts have been made in recent years to develop risk management benchmarking standards, and the work of the Risk and Insurance Management Society, Inc. (RIMS) has been particularly significant in this regard. Benchmarking involves the development of standards or measures of practice for a wide-ranging set of risk management practices. Third-party claims administration and other vendor costs, loss control cost/benefit performance, risk manager compensation—each represents a practice that has been subjected to analysis.

Best practices differ from benchmarking measurement. Whereas benchmarking is concerned with showing "average" or customary practices, best practices is an effort to find standards of excellence and to emulate them. Less work has been done in this area, but for many businesses, a best practices approach may be more meaningful. For the practicing risk manager, it could mean investigating businesses similar to one's own and selecting the top-performing firms within that grouping for intensive analysis.

Benchmarking and best practices are identification techniques, to be sure, but they also are risk measurement tools and can aid in the selection of risk control measures.

■ *Consultancy services.* There are numerous sources of professional advice and service that can be useful in risk assessment. Notably, insurance agencies and brokerages have highly competent consultants who can provide valuable assistance, and often their service is considered part of the overall servicing of the insurance that is purchased through their brokerages.

Several risk management consultancies specialize in certain industries and can provide a wide range of highly specialized services. More technically specialized consultancies also exist—actuaries, claims management, safety and security, engineering, legal, and so on—and they may have a particular value with challenging risk assessment projects.

Risk Analysis

Previously, the discussion of risk assessment introduced the role of hazard and risk factor analysis in the overall risk assessment undertaking. However, till this point, little was said specifically about analysis processes.

The roots of risk analysis can be found in operations management and safety engineering principles and practices. Furthermore, specializations have evolved over time bringing particular technical processes to bear on environmental risks, construction risks, workplace safety risks, and roadway safety, among others. For the purposes of this book, it is sufficient for readers to know that these specialized areas of expertise exist. The remainder of this section is devoted to a conceptualization of risk analysis that can be flexibly employed in a variety of settings.

The Risk Chain

Losses (or gains, for that matter) may be reduced to a set of interlocking elements, thereby allowing for close analysis and examination. These elements collectively are known as the Risk Chain (see Exhibit 2-5), the "links" of which are as follows:

- *Environment link*. Refers to the general conditions in which loss or gain events occur.
- *Hazard/risk factor link*. Within environments, certain conditions elevate the chance of loss or gain, or the potential magnitude of loss or gain.
- *Exposure link*. Refers to the nature and condition of the organization's exposure, whether asset or liability.
- *Peril/opportunity link*. Refers to the process through which the

Exhibit 2-5. The Risk Chain

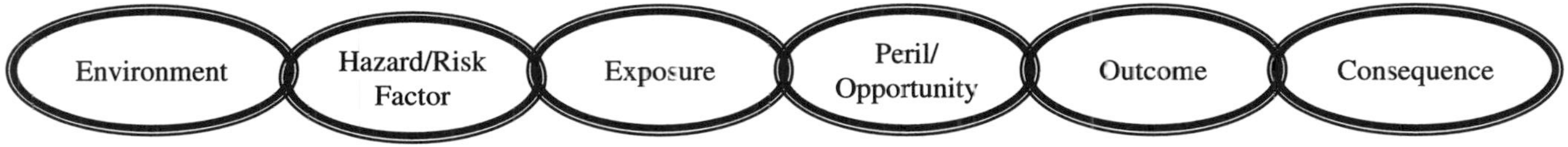

Environment — Hazard/Risk Factor — Exposure — Peril/Opportunity — Outcome — Consequence

interaction of hazard/risk factor and exposure produces loss or gain.

- *Outcome link.* Refers to the direct and measurable impact of the hazard/risk factor on the exposure.
- *Consequence link.* Refers to the longer-term effect of the loss or gain on the organization.

There are numerous schools of thought regarding the appropriate perspective or organizing idea in conducting a risk analysis. Some view analysis as a mainly scientific process, whereby events are mapped and modeled with the hope of developing a highly detailed picture of risks. Often, this view is accompanied by a somewhat "engineering-based" perspective that focuses on the mechanics of accidents.

Others view analysis as largely a matter of behavioral psychology. In other words, accidents and events are characterized by the "human dimension" (e.g., fault, carelessness, malicious motives, and improper training).

In general, either or both views may be appropriate at any given time. The main point would be for a risk manager to be open to a range of possible interpretations.

As a practical matter, the following comments can be made regarding use of the Risk Chain concept in risk analysis:

1. *The environment link is best understood in the context of the broader environmental scan mentioned previously.* The evaluation of specific risks or events should be placed in a wider-ranging view of the overall convergence of environments on an organization. Thus, if one is examining the environmental link of a problematic series of accidents in a production facility, the physical environment may explain a great deal of the problem—but one may find that the operational, social, and legal environments (e.g., a history of insufficient spending on safety) provide a deeper appreciation of the ultimate sources of the problem.

2. *The hazard/risk factor link relates to the conditions that exist within a given environment that elevate probabilities or potential magni-*

tudes. Carrying forward the example of accidents in a production facility, the environmental link would compel us to consider all such facilities as an environment, whereas the hazard/risk factor link would force us to identify potential and real accident sites (e.g., slippery floors, negligently maintained machinery, and improperly lighted areas).

3. *The exposure link isolates the actual loss exposures.* Obviously, in the case of industrial accidents, workers and managers would be the principal exposure units—though one easily might imagine that visitors, physical and financial assets, even public goodwill and regulatory relationships, and moral and ethical values also could be exposures. Beyond simply identifying the exposures, consideration of this link would entail describing the nature and scope of the exposure. In the case of a production facility accident, were new or veteran workers involved? Many workers or a few? Were they on the night or daytime shifts? These are but a few examples of the kinds of questions that may arise.

4. *The peril/opportunity link ordinarily is the focus of much attention and analysis because it is the link that moves a risk from "potential" to "actuality."* For example, not everyone who works at the production facility is injured. What are the elements of a hazardous situation that actually produce the losses that occur? Analysis often reveals that perils are not singular elements but are the product of a convergence of elements (e.g., improper equipment design and carelessness). Quantitative assessment of frequency and magnitude (e.g., how often do accidents occur, and what is their impact when they do occur?) logically will be associated with this link.

5. *The outcome link is associated with the immediate and, mainly, direct effects of an event or accident.* An on-the-job injury raises a number of questions for the risk manager; specifically, what is the nature of the injury—bruises, broken limbs, concussions? In addition, the outcome link forces an examination of immediate or initial accident response efforts. Were supervisors adequately trained to respond quickly? Did response efforts worsen the situation?

6. *The consequence link may not be relevant in some circumstances, but it exists as a reminder that the effects of an accident may be long term*

Insights

Risks Cause for Indigestion

Sarah Veysey
Reprinted with permission from *Business Insurance,* March 27, 2000.
© Crain Communications Inc. All rights reserved.

One in four risk managers in the food and drink industry is anxious about the adequacy of available insurance coverage for potential damage to his or her company's image or reputation.

A new survey, "Corporate Image in the Food and Drink Industry," reveals that the fifty-one U.S. and U.K. risk managers for food and beverage companies questioned saw accidental and deliberate contamination as the biggest threats to their companies' reputation. Conducted on behalf of Lloyd's of London by Insurance Research & Publishing, the survey also found that one in four risk managers is concerned about the adequacy of insurance coverage for damage to their company's reputation.

Respondents were provided with a list of thirteen risks and asked to rank each risk, on a scale of one to five, according to its potential damage to corporate image. Among the top-five risks cited were accidental product contamination, rated at 4.46 out of 5; extortion or sabotage to products, rated at 3.98; specific product-related health and safety issues, 3.86; environmental issues, 3.74; and loss of intellectual property, rated at 3.51.

The respondents were next asked if they had any concerns about the availability of insurance coverage for each of the thirteen risks. The risk managers in the survey responded that they were most concerned about the adequacy of coverage for the same top-five risks that they perceived to be potentially most damaging to corporate image, though they ranked the risks in a different order.

This time, the biggest area of concern was coverage for the loss of intellectual property. More than one-quarter of the respondents to the survey expressed concern about the availability of insurance coverage for the loss of intellectual property.

In a similar study carried out [in 1999] by the Association of Risk Managers, 21 percent of respondents said they were concerned about a lack of coverage for intellectual property. "The fact that intellectual property is difficult to quantify means that it is equally difficult to place a value on reduction of its worth as a result of an insurable event," said Mark Butterworth, chairman of AIRMIC [the U.K.'s professional association of risk managers].

"Factors such as competitor behavior, consumer reaction, and poor management can affect the value of an organization's intellectual property," said Butterworth, who is risk manager for Prudential P.L.C. "However, these are not necessarily covered by traditional insurance products and require innovative solutions from the insurance industry."

Ian Harrison, an underwriter at the Lloyd's agency of Beazley Furlonge Ltd., said that companies are beginning to realize that they must offer solutions to the problem of loss of intellectual property. "There has been a sudden realization that there is a gap between liability and property coverage. Neither can adequately cover the damage to intangible assets or reputation," Harrison said. "Filling that gap is classic Lloyd's territory. Risk managers in the food and drink industry are turning to us for innovation."

Along with environmental issues and specific product-related health and safety issues, a lack of coverage for accidental or deliberate product contamination was the second-largest area of concern, with 18 percent of respondents expressing worries about the adequacy of insurance coverage. In addition to the damage this can cause to a company's reputation, recall costs can be huge. But until recently, many companies did not purchase insurance to cover their product recall costs. "Despite the damage associated with a recall, many companies either do not purchase cover or are not aware that such cover is available," according to the survey.

Harrison said that this situation is changing, however. "There is a growing demand for this kind of coverage. Organizations are beginning to recognize the value of their brands, be it on a balance sheet or not," he said. "This is particularly true of the food and drink industry, where damage to a corporate reputation or brand is most physically represented in recall." The majority of respondents to the survey, 65 percent, said that the brand name was the most valuable asset contributing to a corporate image.

"The research findings of the food and drink survey concur with the views of risk managers in other sectors. This sector makes up a large proportion of fast-moving consumer goods, where the success of many products is heavily reliant upon the strength of the brand," said Robert Chase, special risks underwriter at Lloyd's agency Kiln.

The top-five assets forming corporate image, according to respondents, were: brand name, 65 percent; quality, 47 percent; product/product innovation, 35 percent; company image/reputation, 33 percent; and staff, 33 percent. According to the report's authors, the prominence of brand, together with innovation and image/reputation, highlights the importance of intangible assets to these companies.

"This, together with the finding that risk managers are concerned about obtaining adequate cover for these risks, shows how knowledge and knowledge protection are at the forefront of risk management thinking in the industry," the report stated.

But the survey revealed that, despite the perceived worth of intellectual property and brands to food and drink companies, most companies in the industry do not attribute balance-sheet values to these assets unless they are involved in the purchase or sale of brands. Only 39 percent of respondents said that their organizations gave values to intangible assets, and among those, only 30 percent said that their companies had done so for more than five years.

Even some of the biggest names in the food and drink industry do not actively attribute balance-sheet values to these assets, according to the survey. For example, at the end of 1998, Coca-Cola's net assets were valued at $19.1 billion—less than one-quarter of the $83.8 billion estimate of the company's brand value by branding consultant Interbrand.

Despite the fact that the majority of respondents to the survey saw the brand name as the most important factor contributing to corporate image, only 29 percent of respondents to the survey said that their companies would make attempts to place balance-sheet values on their intangible assets in the future, while 46 percent stated that they would not.

The report also revealed that concern about the safety of genetically modified foods is on the increase. Recent media attention on genetically modified food scares in general has highlighted the potential influence of media coverage on consumer awareness, the report said.

A poll carried out by the research agency Mintel and cited in the Lloyd's survey revealed that the percentage of consumers concerned about genetically modified foods rose to 47 percent in April 1999, from 36 percent in August 1998. Several retailers in both the United States and the United Kingdom have removed genetically modified ingredients from their own brands in recent months. "Such was the concern generated by the media that many companies removed GM foodstuffs from their products/shelves in an effort to reduce the damage to their image," the report said.

Copies of the report can be ordered from Andrew McKenzie, 44-207-327-5832; or andrew.mckenzie@lloyds.com.

and indirect. For example, a spate of accidents may lower employee morale for an extended period of time, or the situation may have broad labor relations consequences. There may also be ramifications with the future costs of workers compensation insurance.

One is tempted to frame risk analysis as a highly statistical process, which it may be. However, the preceding discussion suggests that intuitive and qualitative approaches may be wholly appropriate for certain situations.

Readers should make note of one critical caveat regarding risk analysis. There is a strong and obvious motivation to focus on an analysis of past losses. Losses tend to be known and remembered, and naturally data exists to explain what happened, how much it cost, and even who was to blame. However, from a risk management standpoint, a mapping of past accidents only can be quite misleading. There may be dozens and dozens of incidents that occur in the production plant that do not result in losses, but may be important to know about. For example, a dangerously slippery stairwell may have numerous near-misses but no actual accidents. Focusing on accidents alone and ignoring near-misses in a risk analysis may have undesirable consequences. It may give risk managers a comfort level they don't deserve, distract the risk manager from looming or real problem areas, and negatively influence the distribution of risk management resources.

Risk Measurement

Ultimately, the purpose of risk assessment is not just to identify and understand risks but also to rank them in some way. The ranking of risks is important because it will influence the allocation of risk management resources. Specifically, risk measurement requires the risk manager to develop yardsticks for measuring the importance of risks to the firm, and to apply these yardsticks to identified risks.

The distinction between direct and indirect costs is important to the discussion of risk measurement. Direct costs are a direct consequence of a peril acting on an asset. If a fire damages the roof of a business, for example, the direct loss is the cost to repair and replace the damage to the roof. An indirect cost is related to the damage caused directly by the peril, although the financial consequences are not a direct consequence of the action of the peril on the asset. For example, the inability of a business to operate out of its facility during roof repairs may force it to incur expenses in renting a temporary facility. Indirect costs often are hidden, although their consequences may be greater than those of direct losses.

Hidden Costs/Benefits of Losses and Gains

Considerable research has been undertaken to evaluate the relationship of indirect costs to direct costs in loss-producing situations. Much less evident is work examining the direct/indirect *gain* relationship. This section briefly addresses the latter before turning to a fuller discussion of the losses.

The ORM idea forces risk managers to think more completely about the overall impact of risk, which means that attention must be paid to upside potential. Naturally, positive outcomes would have direct and indirect characteristics. For instance, investment in a new production process may produce direct benefits in that new revenues may occur. However, new jobs, advantageous competitive positioning (for other products), possibilities for strategic alliances, and greater public/customer support and loyalty all may be the result of that investment.

With respect to direct and indirect costs, a number of studies have been undertaken to better understand the impact of losses on organizations. A rather well known set of industrial accident studies, for instance, seemed to suggest that the ratio of 4:1 (i.e., $4 of indirect losses for every $1 of direct losses) was a common phenomenon. While this ratio is widely disputed as anything other than an abstract rule of thumb, it does suggest an important risk measurement point—namely, the "total cost of risk" is greater than the "direct cost of loss."

The phrase *cost of risk* has special meaning in risk management, historically serving as one particular way of measuring the impact of risk on an organization. Indeed, the Risk and Insurance Management Society (RIMS), the leading professional association of business sector risk managers, has undertaken a "Cost of Risk Survey" that should become the risk cost benchmark. However, the likely credibility and widespread use of the survey's results should not mask the fact that the fundamental definition of the cost of risk is not fully agreed upon by practitioners. Most working measures of the cost of risk include the costs of losses (e.g., insurance premiums, uninsured losses, and administrative costs such as claims management services), and certainly these are obvious candidates for inclusion. However, the costs of uncertainty are not so obvious or easy to measure. The salary of a risk manager certainly is a knowable cost of uncertainty, but the misallocation and inefficiencies of resource deployment due to uncertainty are not so easily seen. Fear and worry among managers, employees, and other stakeholders also take a toll, but measurement of those costs is problematic.

The point is that risk exacts direct and indirect, quantifiable and unquantifiable costs on the firm; therefore, risk managers must be alert to the fact that the overall impact of risk extends far beyond the visible effects. Striving to incorporate a more comprehensive measurement is critical to managerial success, because the case for investment in risk management (made to upper managers) becomes more persuasive when the full effect of risk is known and appreciated.

Dimensions of Exposure to Risk

Information is needed concerning at least two dimensions of each exposure. If there are pure risks and speculative risks, then the dimensions of exposure in each case are defined as follows:

Pure Risks

- The frequency of the number of losses likely to occur
- The potential severity of those losses that do occur

Speculative Risks

- The frequency of both positive and negative outcomes
- The range of magnitude of possible outcomes

For each of these two dimensions, it would be desirable to know at least the value in an average budget period and the possible variation in the values from one budget period to the next.

Such data can be directly useful in determining the best methods for handling an exposure to risk. For example, multiplying expected loss frequency and average loss severity provides an estimate of the expected value of losses. This estimate can be compared with the amount an insurer charges for insurance protection, and estimates of possible variation allow the risk manager to estimate the likelihood that losses will exceed the cost of insurance.

An advanced treatment of risk measurement exceeds the scope of this book. Therefore, the purpose of the remaining discussion within this chapter is to help readers gain an intuitive understanding of the concepts that support more sophisticated measurement approaches. Furthermore, the ideas we offer serve a useful function when statistical data are limited or nonexistent—a fairly common circumstance in real risk management situations.

Measurable dimensions of risk are shown in Exhibit 2-6. This risk matrix provides a conceptual structure to the risk measurement challenge. For example, cell I represents risks that are low frequency/low severity; these risks only infrequently result in loss, and when loss occurs, it is relatively unimportant. Cell III represents risks that are low frequency/high severity; losses occur infrequently but each loss is costly. Cell VII represents risks that are high frequency/low severity; losses occur with great frequency but each loss is relatively inexpensive. Cell IX represents risks that are high frequency/high severity; losses occur with great frequency and are costly each time they occur.

From a practical utility standpoint, this matrix is limited for two reasons. First, *high, medium,* and *low* are relative terms. Second, the model is a single period model—that is, it doesn't easily capture the fact that losses may recur over an extended time period. However, as an introductory idea, the matrix helps readers through a basic distribution of risks into four broad measurement classifications.

The measurement matrix helps frame a rather intuitive overall measurement of an entity's risk profile. A risk manager is able to group risks into broad categories that can serve as a "first round" effort to separate the important from the unimportant, the problematic from the manageable. For example, the risks falling into the upper left hand quadrant of the matrix (roughly, cells I, II, and IV) appear to be rather harmless in the sense that they produce events occasionally and those events are of minor consequence. This is the realm of "risk toleration," which signifies that little or nothing may

Exhibit 2-6. Measurement matrix

Magnitude

	Low	Medium	High
Low	I	II	III
Medium	IV	V	VI
High	VII	VIII	IX

Frequency

need to be done other than to monitor those risks that could change frequency and magnitude characteristics over time.

Contrast the previous cells with those found in the lower right hand quadrant (roughly, cells VI, VIII, and IX), where the likelihood of events is high and the impact of events is dramatic. One rarely encounters such risks in the assessment process, largely because the frequency and magnitude characteristics could not have escaped the attention of even the most distracted of managers. Organizations that encounter these risks don't last long—or conversely, if it is a huge upside risk, the windfall benefit will only last for a limited period of time. Still, firms look for such fertile opportunity-producing circumstances, and sometimes they succeed (e.g., possibly by exploiting a favorable geographic resource, such as an excellent climate or beautiful scenery).

The remaining cells represent the "messy middle"—those risks that produce events frequently, but at low magnitudes (the lower left hand quadrant), and those that rarely produce events, but when those events occur, they are dramatic (the upper right hand quadrant). Anticipating the discussion in Chapter 3, one might argue that the former risks are risks to be controlled while the latter, echoing the discussion in Chapters 6 and 7, are risks to be financed and transferred.

A Brief Comment on Frequency and Magnitude Measurement Terminology

One method for estimating event frequency is to consider the probability that a given method of exposure to a single risk will result in an event during a year. For example, a risk manager may estimate the probability that a single storage facility will be damaged by fire or the probability that a franchise will be sued for failing to ensure sanitary preparation of food. One traditional, non-numerical approach to estimating probabilities uses four measurement values, which are

1. *Almost nil* (i.e., in the opinion of the risk manager, the event will not happen)

2. *Slight* (i.e., though possible, the event has not happened at the present time and is unlikely to occur in the future)
3. *Moderate* (i.e., an event has happened once in a while and can be expected to occur some time in the future)
4. *Definite* (i.e., an event has happened regularly and can be expected to occur regularly in the future)

Most exposures to risk are more complex than single-peril/opportunity or single-exposure estimates would imply. For example, a given building can be damaged from windstorm, earthquake, or flood as well as from fire. The value of financial assets can be influenced by foreign exchange rates, inflation, monetary policy, and interest rates. In addition, a single peril/opportunity may influence multiple assets. The accuracy of event-frequency estimates can depend on whether the relationships between perils/opportunities and objects exposed to risk are considered. These considerations return us to the issue of the amount of information the risk manager has on the nature of the risk. Most risk management decisions are made on the basis of what the risk manager considers a reasonable subset of full information. Almost any decision can be improved by additional information allowing more precise estimates of possible outcomes and their likelihood. The risk manager's judgment is needed to integrate all available information and use it to develop estimates.

Two measures commonly used in reference to event magnitude are the maximum possible outcome and the maximum probable outcome. For the moment, consider occurrences causing only one type of loss or gain, in which case the:

■ *Maximum possible outcome* is the largest outcome that possibly could occur.
■ *Maximum probable outcome* is the largest outcome that the risk manager believes is likely to occur.

The maximum probable outcome, which is the most commonly used magnitude measure, depends on the nature of the peril/opportunity causing the outcome as well as the person or object exposed to that outcome; usually the maximum possible outcome is not affected by the peril/opportunity being considered. For example, a small business leasing office space from a commercial property manager faces the possibility of fire and theft losses to its office equipment. The maximum probable outcome (loss) to the tenant may be the full value of this equipment in the event of a fire, but it may be limited to the value of the items that have high value relative to weight and size in the case of theft. In contrast, the maximum possible outcome (loss) is the full value of all the equipment, regardless of which peril is considered.

Finally, the concept of *maximum probable yearly aggregate outcome* is used to apply to a single peril/opportunity (or exposure) or multiple perils/opportunities (exposures). This concept reflects the largest total amount that an exposure unit or group of exposure units is likely to suffer or enjoy during, say, a budget period. Like the maximum probable outcome, this amount depends on the probability level selected by the risk manager, but unlike the maximum probable outcome, this measure does not refer just to magnitude of a single occurrence. Instead, it depends on the number of occurrences as well as their magnitude.

A Comment on ORM and Traditional Risk Assessment

The overall picture developed in Chapter 2 supports the organization-wide approach fostered in the ORM idea (see Exhibit 2-7). Yet readers reasonably may ask whether this scheme relates to more traditional or narrower views of risk management.

It is our view that the ORM assessment scheme is broadly applicable regardless of an organization's philosophy of risk management. For example, even if the risk management function in a particular firm is confined to the management of insurable risks, it remains important for the risk manager to see the firm's practices in the context of the broader risk environment. Indeed, differences between ORM and traditional/narrower practices are most easily reconciled in the area of assessment since it seems that regardless

Exhibit 2-7. A representation of the complete ORM risk assessment process

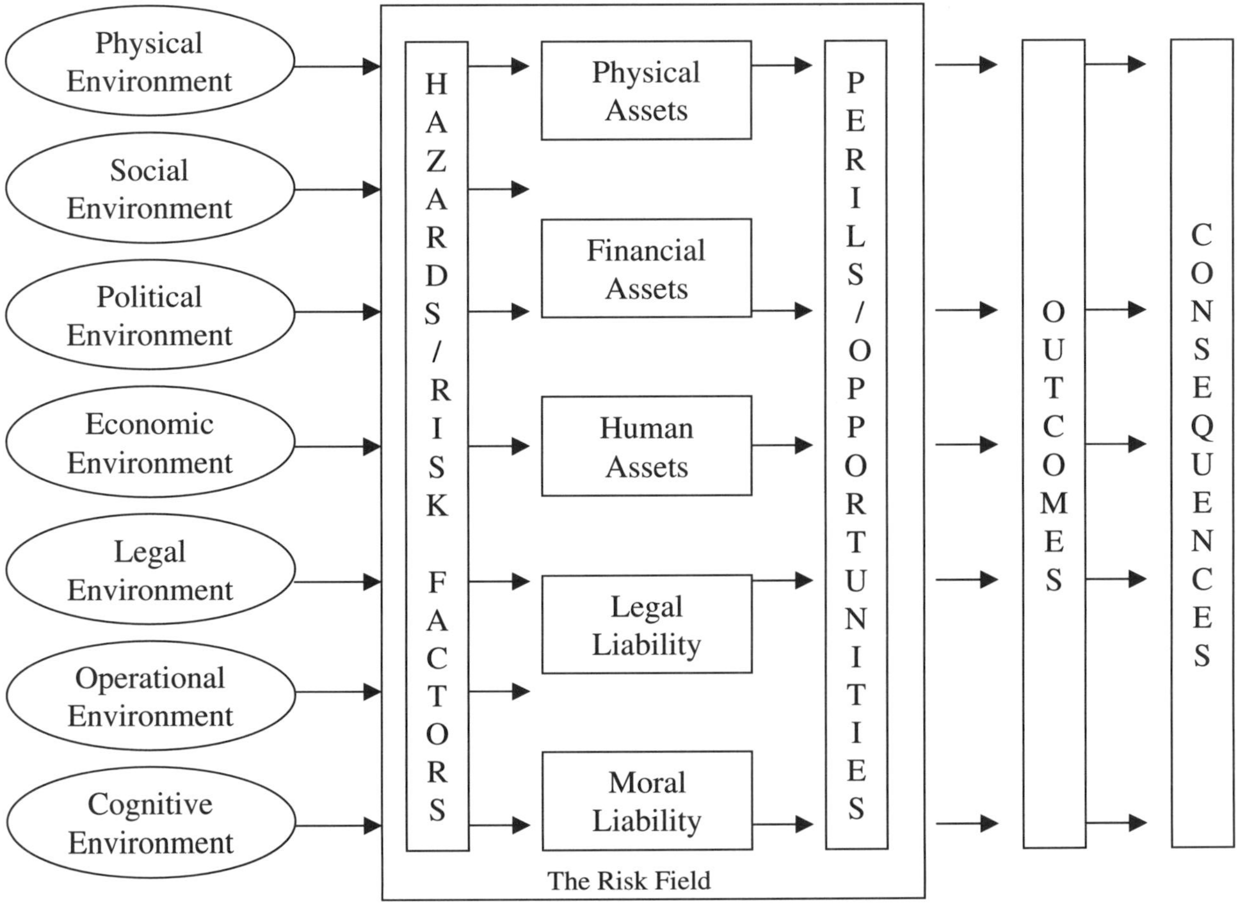

of the risk management philosophy in place, the organization would seek to develop the most comprehensive possible understanding of its organization's risks.

We can apply this argument in a second way when we consider industry differences in risk management practices. A momentary reflection on the assessment model reveals that while all these risks have some impact on each and every organization, it seems obvious that a firm's particular business will greatly influence the relative importance of these risks and, additionally, the individual firm's particular circumstances (e.g., its size, location, history) will lead to further differentiation. Still, at the end of the day, a comprehensive model facilitates perspective and permits organizations to better understand their unique risk attributes.

Read More About It

When in Doubt, Simulate

Mark Jablonowski
Reprinted with permission from *Risk Management* magazine, November 1998. Copyright 1998 by Risk Management Society Publishing. All rights reserved. For more information call 212.286.9364. www.rims.org/rmmag

Risk management decisions are governed by the element of chance. All accidents have some likelihood, or probability, of occurring. We do not know exactly where or when the next mishap will occur, or what effect it will have.

In order to assess how well a plan achieves the hierarchy of risk management goals—survival, stability, and cost minimization—we need to see the complete effects of the entire distribution—the pattern of variation of an event—on plan performance. To get a better feel for the effects of risk management decisions in this probabilistic environment, we can turn to simulation.

Simulation is a powerful tool. When conducted by a computer, it can offer wonderful opportunities for understanding what risk management is all about, and how we can do it better. To realize the full potential of this tool, however, we must use it carefully and understand its limitations as well as its strengths.

Encompassing a variety of techniques that attempt to model the underlying chance processes of risk, all simulations attempt to re-create reality in a setting where the major variables are controlled by the analyst. Using simulations in risk management, we can observe the effects of the entire distribution of accidental losses arising from an exposure, and their probabilities, rather than focusing on a few summary measures (e.g., average and variance).

Various options for the handling of risk can also be introduced into the simulation. By testing risk management mechanisms in a realistic yet controlled setting we can arrive at an accurate assessment of what various alternatives can and cannot do for us. We can also use simulation results to iteratively adjust risk management programs for optimum performance.

Overall, simulation lets us achieve a level of confidence in our decisions that would not otherwise be attainable.

Simulation Fundamentals

To understand simulation, and how it can be useful to risk managers, we need to understand the concept of probability—the long-run relative frequency of some random event. While it is usually expressed as a number, probability is not an abstract mathematical construct. It is a physical property: the pattern of outcomes that emerges from multiple repetitions of an event. Simulation is the modeling of such real-world qualities.

The mechanism of simulation is very simple. Say we want to examine the likelihood of automobile collision losses, considering now only the annual frequency of a collision, not its severity. Through statistical analysis and expert judgment, we find that the probability of an auto collision loss in any year is one in ten, or .1.

Our simulator is a fishbowl filled with colored ping-pong balls. To represent the probability at hand, we use ten balls. Nine are white and one is black. We mix the balls well and draw from the bowl without looking, to introduce randomness. The draw of a black ball represents "accident" and a white ball, "no accident." By making ten draws from the bowl (each time replacing the drawn ball), we can observe the loss frequency for a simulation of ten years.

Assume that each accident results in a fixed loss amount of $1,000. While this loss amount does not represent a financial danger, we may be willing to introduce some stability at a reasonable cost. The cheapest insurance policy we can find costs $175. Simple actuarial mathematics tells us that this premium is $75 above the average loss of $100 per year. This is expected since the insurer must recoup long-run costs plus the expense of doing business, including a reasonable profit. Our question, however, remains: Should we purchase insurance for collision losses?

We are in a much better position to assess the value of the charged premium by simulating a large number of accident years. We might forgo insurance on the reasoning that we can make up the losses in a relatively short period of time. Nonetheless, the variability observed during the simulation might alert us to the $75 per year we pay above expected cost as a true value.

A bit of logical reasoning based on averages and variance might bring us to the same conclusion. The circumstances, however, can get much more complex. Consider a fleet of 1,000 autos, each subject to distinct frequency and severity probability distributions. Our choice in that case may be among various insurance, retention, and loss financing plans.

To deal with more complex situations we abandon our bowl of colored balls in favor of the computer. Simulation capabilities have been around since the dawn of the computer age. Only relatively recently, however, have the speed and storage capabilities enabled desktop simulations of complex phenomena.

All computers can be made to generate random number patterns. These numbers are the computer analogs of our colored balls. With some mathematical manipulation, we can get random numbers that suit a variety of theoretical probability distributions. We can also quickly and simply manipulate the distributions themselves, using a variety of "what if" scenarios.

Spreadsheet programs offer easy-to-use and accessible

technology. Most have a variety of random number and probability distribution routines built in. They also allow for graphic examination of simulation results. This permits an often-neglected aspect of simulation—visualization. Visualization, the ability to see articulations of random outcomes, can add greatly to our appreciation of alternative risk management techniques. It supplements the processing capabilities of the computer with what remains the world's most powerful information processor—the human mind.

Simulation for Decision

There are many options for treating the financial results of accidental loss. These alternatives are offered by traditional insurers, financial institutions, and a variety of consultants. Each present numbers to prove their superiority. Under conditions of randomness and using the element of chance, a well-crafted simulation offers the most effective method of assessing risk management options.

To illustrate the use of simulations in the practical risk management setting, let us look at a real-life risk financing analysis. The company under study, a large manufacturer, needed to choose between loss financing ("chronological stabilization") for all-risk property exposures using either the traditional method of commercial insurance or a spread-loss captive arrangement using its parent company's captive. A probability distribution was assessed for losses in the layer $1 million (the frequency-based retention) and $10 million (the financial "danger level").

The simulation was carried out using a spreadsheet program. For the purpose of this simulation, the three loss categories under study were represented by their midpoints: $1.5 million, $3.5 million, and $7.5 million. Loss scenarios were simulated by assigning random number outcomes in accordance with the estimated probability distribution. In terms of our simple analog simulation model—the bowl filled with colored balls—imagine that the black balls are now marked with the three possible loss amounts. The bowl is then filled with white balls ("no loss") and the numbered black balls in proportion to the given probabilities.

The combination of spreadsheet resources allowed management in this case study to observe the alternate effects of the two proposed financing mechanisms. By definition, both the commercial insurance and captive spread loss options were equal in long-run average losses. As simulation makes clear, nothing in alternative risk financing mechanisms can magically reduce the expected value of losses.

The captive option, however, had a much lower transactional cost. The counterbalance was increased variability. Management was able to assess the variety of possibilities and probabilities associated with both options using the simulation and thereby understand the potential increase in plan variance. Simple summary statistics could not have conveyed this. The captive spread-loss plan was chosen.

This type of analysis is easily extended to multiple exposures. Using simple assumptions about the theoretical probability distribution of loss and spreadsheet program add-ons, we can simulate the annual aggregate losses for each of the firm's exposures in a single spreadsheet column. The columns can be added together to assess the combined potential of all sources of accidental loss. Risk management program structures (e.g., deductibles, risk transfer, and financing plans) can then be applied. This allows the risk manager to observe the performance of the complex whole in a microcosm.

In addition to plan testing, simulation can be used as an aid to plan development. The outcomes of a risk management plan can be observed via simulation, and adjustments made to the plan to improve efficiency with respect to the risk manager's goals. For example, a rough retention level may be chosen based on considerations of loss frequency. The retention level can then be fine-tuned using a simulation and observing the resultant variability of earnings. The parameters of a computer model (e.g., a retention level) can be easily varied. The computer can also be programmed to vary the parameters of the model in a systematic fashion, thus permitting us to search for those that achieve optimal performance.

Simulations can also be run using deterministic, or fixed, inputs. Fixed-input simulation models are used to focus on the effect of specific data. For example, we may want to test the effects of two large losses occurring within the experience rating period of a loss-sensitive premium allocation plan. Rather than wait to observe such a phenomenon in many random simulations, we can enter the proscribed loss data directly and observe the outcome.

Using the fixed-input method can be useful in testing risk management plans for worst-case or unusual conditions that may be difficult to simulate randomly. They can also be varied more deliberately than random inputs to ascertain the response characteristics of a model. This can be useful at the development phase of a model to assess its completeness prior to testing with random inputs.

Deterministic simulation modeling must be used carefully, however. The results of fixed-input simulations must not be confused with those created with randomly generated data. Consider the practice of simulating the effects of differing retention levels by using data of previous years' loss. It is unlikely that this exact sequence will repeat itself under most real-world conditions. Decisions based on such analyses may be misleading. Since most (and the most useful) simulations involve randomized inputs, these tend to dominate.

Using Simulations Effectively

Relying on computer outputs without understanding the quality of the inputs and underlying model structure is dangerous. It behooves all users of simulations to understand the model's limitations, and specifically and completely note them as an essential part of any simulation study. The promise of simulation can only be realized by those who recognize these limitations and take them into consideration.

Randomness is only one type of uncertainty the risk manager faces. Another significant incertitude results from our imperfect knowledge under complex conditions. We may not know the exact distribution of probabilities that an exposure entails. As a result, our simulation outcomes will be tainted with that same uncertainty. A powerful computer cannot improve on the shortcomings of our assumptions.

Computers can help us deal with knowledge imperfection by allowing us to try a variety of possibilities and observe their outcomes. We may engage in formal or informal analysis of the sensitivity of our risk management option to various model assumptions. Our policy choice can then be adjusted based on this type of uncertainty analysis.

While identifying speculations makes our simulations more credible, will our results still be informative? That depends on the extent of the guesswork underlying our assumptions and data. In most cases, we have sufficient confidence in both to draw conclusions that may be considered at least useful approximations.

Validation is the general process of assessing the accuracy of our simulation models. The first step in validating a simulation model is to lay out all the assumptions that go into model construction, identify their limitations, and determine how these limitations may affect the working of the model. Initial testing of the model, with possible iterative development, is also a good idea. Visualization should be incorporated into all stages of model development. This may allow us to spot subtle defects that may be buried in the simulation's programming.

A high level of knowledge about simulation and its workings is never a substitute for understanding the phenomena to be simulated. This is essential to remember when working with consultants (actuaries) from outside our organization. Actuarial model building is based on fitting theoretical probability distribution to past loss data. As this data is usually very limited, considerable conjecture goes into the model construction, introducing the problem of uncertain assumptions.

A consultant must understand our business or be given proper guidance early on. Most consultants are quick to add qualifications in their reports that limit their liability in the event of model inaccuracies. This places responsibility for the results of the simulation modeling exercise squarely with the risk manager.

Additional accuracy can be obtained by going beyond statistical estimates. One important source of loss probability information for simulations is scenario-based risk analysis. In scenario analysis, logical models of the loss process are developed into flow charts. These event trees trace the logical progression of a loss from an initiating event (e.g., fire, earthquake, product defect) to various scenarios. Probabilities of events along the progression from initial event to final outcome determine the likelihood of the result. Using a scenario-based assessment, we can identify probabilities for events that, due to their rarity, have not yet been statistically observed. The probabilities of various loss outcomes, and their estimated loss potentials, can then be used directly in the simulation model.

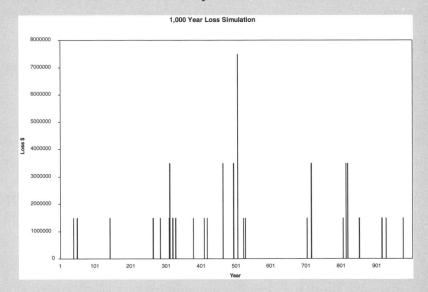

Risk management is an intuitive exercise. It is based on collective experience that is difficult to articulate using precise rules and mathematical formulas. Simulation gives us a tool to expand this intuition. It lets us re-create reality under a variety of scenarios and observe the results. In a very real sense, simulation introduces the art of experimentation to risk management. As an aid to, and not a replacement for, the risk manager's intuition, computer simulation is invaluable.

Read More About It

Cyberchecklist

Emily Q. Freeman
Reprinted with permission from *Risk Management* magazine, May 2000. Copyright 2000 by Risk Management Society Publishing. All rights reserved. For more information call 212.286.9364. www.rims.org/rmmag

Cyberrisk Evaluation

Cyberrisk	Probability Estimate	Financial Impact	Risk Quadrant	Possible Loss Scenario	Potentially Insurable ?
Computer Fraud: Wrongful taking of tangibles (money, securities, and other property) and intangibles (services, intellectual property, and data) carried out by employees or non-employees.	L/M/H	L/M/H	T or R	Part-time accounting department employee used computer system to siphon off inventory and deposits.	Yes
Theft of Electronic Information and Electronic Information Assets: Wrongful taking of software code, supplier information, confidential or proprietary information, including intellectual property, source code, customer data, electronic informa-				Financial institution has a major loss due to theft of proprietary information, including investment, trading, and trust information.	Yes

Cyberrisk	Proba-bility Esti-mate	Finan-cial Im-pact	Risk Quadrant	Possible Loss Scenario	Poten-tially Insur-able ?
tion as a result of un-authorized access or unauthorized use of computer networks.					
Theft of Computer System Resources: Computing or tele-communications re-sources are used for other than official, approved business purposes.				Telecommunications company found that an employee had suc-cessfully tapped long-distance service to run a private illegal enterprise.	Yes
Threats/Extortion: Threat to commit a computer crime or to use information gained from a com-puter crime in ex-change for money or personal gain or to embarrass the com-pany.				An outside, unknown group with a political message threatens [to] put an embar-rassing message and graphics on the web-site home page, un-less the group's manifesto is pub-lished. Site is taken down to examine se-curity issues.	Yes
Malicious Acts (At-tacks): Modification or dam-age to systems or data for the purpose of nuisance, sabo-tage, malicious acts, revenge, political or social motivation, pranks, or entertain-ment.				Part-time program-mer is terminated [and] that evening was able to enter the building and log suc-cessfully onto the sys-tem. An entire critical database was deleted causing significant overtime and data re-construction costs.	Yes
Disclosure of Elec-tronic Information and Electronic In-formation Assets: Unauthorized disclo-sure of proprietary or confidential informa-				A company has a sys-tem penetration, which results in de-tails of their software product/code being published on a hacker website [causing] sig-	Yes

Cyberrisk	*Proba-bility Esti-mate*	*Finan-cial Im-pact*	*Risk Quadrant*	*Possible Loss Scenario*	*Poten-tially Insur-able?*
tion stored in an electronic form, as a result of a computer crime, malicious act (attack), or unintentional mistake made by authorized IT/IS personnel in the normal performance of their jobs.				nificant loss of competitive edge and future revenues.	
Damage to Electronic Information and Programs by Human Error: Damage to computer programs and electronic data caused by an unintentional act or mistake made by authorized IT/IS personnel in the normal performance of their jobs.				Accounting application upgrade insufficiently tested resulted in duplicate records posted to customers' accounts and inaccurate balances. Compensatory payments and extra expense [needed] to correct problems.	Yes
Mechanical Breakdown: Electrical or mechanical breakdown that causes damage to computer equipment, electronic programs or data, and possible network disruption.				Company's only web server suddenly fails due to a malfunctioning internal part, causing loss of data and downtime.	Yes
Physical Loss: Damage to computer equipment, media, and data due to a physical peril such as fire, water damage, vandalism, etc. Catastrophe perils are earthquake, windstorm, and flood.				Data center severely damaged by a hurricane that requires immediate activation of an alternative "hot site." Significant damage to data center, equipment, data, and restoration/extra expenses related to the disaster.	Yes

Cyberrisk	Probability Estimate	Financial Impact	Risk Quadrant	Possible Loss Scenario	Potentially Insurable ?
Harmful Code: Implantation, introduction, and spread of computer viruses, logic bombs, Trojan horses, and other forms of malicious code.				Virus infects hundreds of thousands of computers causing widespread damage and destruction of data, and total losses to the computer's motherboard.	Yes
Denial of Service: Attack causes a degradation of performance or loss of service (outage or interruption) to a website or network application.				Unwanted electronic e-mail (spamming) took so much of a company's web server handling e-mail that it resulted initially in a degradation of service, followed by a system crash.	Yes
Loss of Service: Computer system outage, "crash," degradation of performance caused by an unintentional mistake or error made by authorized IT/IS personnel in the normal performance of their jobs.				Financial services web business grew beyond initial design expectations. Additional capacity was required and an upgrade was installed that malfunctioned and caused several hours of outage of the website. Significant liability, loss of revenues, loss of market cap, and regulator concerns.	Qualified yes— collapse of Internet backbone computers may not be insurable.
Off-Premises Service Interruption: Physical perils (e.g., hurricane and fire), attacks, accidents, and malfunctioning of network communications infrastructure, including satellites, telephone lines, cable, electrical lines, and fiber-optic cable.				Transformer fire—a result of mistakes during a maintenance operation at a substation—causes widespread power outages, affecting computer systems in a large metropolitan area.	Qualified yes

Cyberrisk	Proba-bility Esti-mate	Finan-cial Im-pact	Risk Quadrant	Possible Loss Scenario	Poten-tially Insur-able ?
Dependent Businesses: All perils listed can occur to a critical supplier, vendor, or customer, resulting in contingent business interruption and extra expense.				Security of a router at a web hosting company is disabled by mistake resulting in a successful malicious attack.	Qualified yes
Liability Errors and Omissions: Most of the direct risks listed above may also trigger litigation if third-party electronic information, systems, and revenues are involved. Errors and Omissions exposures are created by the use of, connective nature of, and dependence on Internet technologies that cause financial harm to third parties without bodily injury or tangible property damage. Overall exposure depends on the role and level of involvement, as well as the scope and nature of the contractual relationship. Likely plaintiffs include consumers, business partners, business customers, vendors, e-merchants, and financial institutions.				A financial institution's network security was breached and hackers stole information on the institution's high-net-worth customers. Customers filed lawsuits regarding the unauthorized disclosures. An unknown hacker stole the credit card information of cardholders from a credit card processing center. The issuing bank sued for all its processing and administrative costs to reissue the series of card numbers. A computer virus was spread from the e-mail system of a supplier to its customer, which resulted in the deletion of thousands of files in its purchasing system. The customer sued for its lost revenues and extra expenses.	Yes

Cyberrisk	Proba-bility Esti-mate	Finan-cial Im-pact	Risk Quadrant	Possible Loss Scenario	Poten-tially Insur-able ?
Intellectual Prop-erty Infringement (Direct and Contrib-utory): Patent infringement (especially software and business process patents) Copyright infringe-ment (e.g., plagia-rism and framing) Trademark infringe-ment including trade dress (e.g., use of domain names, "cyber-squatting," metatags) Misappropriation of trade secrets (i.e., re-search and marketing studies, processes, customer lists, undis-closed new products or services offerings, etc.)				A company's use of domain name consti-tuted trademark in-fringement of another company. Defendant website was sued for using the plaintiff's name within HTML codes embedded in its web page so that a search engine will be tricked and call up the defen-dant's site when the plaintiff's name is used in a search string. A business process patent is the source of litigation regarding use of a process that provides ease of use to customers visiting the site.	Yes
Content and Adver-tising-Related Of-fenses: Defamation, espe-cially online com-mentary and discussion, including employee statements made over the In-ternet about third parties. Examples: Trade libel and product dispar-agement; pornogra-phy/obscenity/hate sites; use of testimo-nials/endorsements;				Names and images of famous persons are used without permis-sion in the advertising and content of an In-ternet game site. Statements regarding the competitor's products are deemed to be false and con-stitute trade libel and disparagement.	Yes

Cyberrisk	*Proba-bility Esti-mate*	*Finan-cial Im-pact*	*Risk Quadrant*	*Possible Loss Scenario*	*Poten-tially Insur-able ?*
invasion of privacy, cyber-stalking; mis-appropriation of publicity rights; mis-appropriation of ideas under implied contract; unfair com-petition (i.e., com-parative claims, passing off false or deceptive advertis-ing/trading, Lanham Act 43 (a), trade-mark dilution); edito-rial errors and omissions (i.e., harmful imitation and reckless inducement).					
Privacy: Privacy issues con-cern utilizing infor-mation that identifies a person or an entity for a purpose that was not intended and for which permission was not received. Major differences among privacy regu-lations exist through-out the world; the most significant vari-ation is between the European Data Di-rective and privacy regulations in the United States. In ad-dition, there are spe-cific state privacy protection laws (e.g., Virginia Privacy Pro-tection Act). Also refer to the Child On-				FTC enforcement ac-tion is directed at a website that prom-ised not to share any optional information without the custom-er's permission. The owner of the website is alleged to have marketed and sold to third parties all the information, including that deemed optional and information col-lected from children. These parties, in turn, used this information to target the mem-bers with unsolicited e-mail ads.	Yes

Cyberrisk	Proba-bility Esti-mate	Finan-cial Im-pact	Risk Quadrant	Possible Loss Scenario	Poten-tially Insur-able ?
line Privacy Protection Act of 1998. Inadequate privacy policy on website (failure to disclose information being collected; use made of this information; failure to allow consumers a mechanism to view and modify the information collected), unauthorized release of confidential information (i.e., financial, medical), and failure to allow the consumer to ''opt-out'' of the use of private information relating to such consumer. Violation of a stated privacy policy may result in regulatory action or litigation.					
Other E-commerce Risks: Authentication (validity of a transmission, message, or originator) and non-repudiation (a cryptographic service that legally prevents the originator of a message/purchase from denying authorship or denying the transaction at a later date). A legitimate customer denies responsibility for a transaction.				A valid credit card is used by an unauthorized buyer, who proceeds to have merchandise shipped to an address, other than the address of the credit card holder. Fraudulent investment scam utilizes a website that appears to be legitimate and fools investors to commit funds. The parents of a child who tried to fly off a balcony sue the de-	Yes

Cyberrisk	Proba-bility Esti-mate	Finan-cial Im-pact	Risk Quadrant	Possible Loss Scenario	Poten-tially Insur-able ?
Merchandise misrep-resentation and ful-fillment.				signer of a virtual re-ality software on the Internet.	
Regulatory violations (e.g., Uniform Com-mercial Code).					
Breach or enforce-ability of clip-wrap agreements; en-forceability of dis-claimers.					
Products liability; warranties and con-tractual guarantees.					
Corporate E-mail: Type of information and content con-tained in e-mails is "discoverable" in lit-igation from third parties and employ-ees. Failure of secur-ity (e.g., passwords and encryption) may result in disclosure of proprietary infor-mation (possible in-dustrial espionage) or public embarrass-ment.				Racially derogatory e-mail messages are cited in major civil suit against a com-pany.	Yes
Unauthorized access to stored e-mail; e-mail harassment, pornography, and threats to innocent users of the Internet.					

Read More About It

The Fire Fight

Glenn Anschutz
Reprinted with permission from *Risk Management* magazine, July 1999.
Copyright 1999 by Risk Management Society Publishing. All rights reserved.
For more information call 212.286.9364. www.rims.org/rmmag

Fires in commercial buildings cause billions of dollars in damages and injure thousands of people. Poor maintenance is often the culprit in power plants, factories, and other industrial facilities. But a dangerous lack of awareness compounds the problem in commercial and public settings. Why are fires still a threat in our high-tech world? With today's sophisticated fire detection and suppression systems, it would seem that fire loss could be prevented or at least controlled.

Fire, however, continues to damage, injure and kill.

Much has been done to tackle the problem using new fire protection methods that incorporate better design, training, special equipment, preventive maintenance, inspection, and testing. These techniques have worked well in reducing incidents of fire and controlling those that occur. Even so, sprinklers, fire pumps, and alarms often fail to operate properly—sometimes with costly, even fatal, results.

On Christmas Day in 1992, for example, a lube oil fire resulted in the deaths of three workers at a cogeneration power plant. Automatic sprinkler protection was provided for most of the plant, but the systems had been turned off. Had the system been operational, the fire could have been controlled. This is the kind of problem risk managers should be aware of.

The risk of fire in commercial buildings is often overlooked. While the potential in an electrical plant or chemical factory is obvious, owners of an office or residential or retail complex might not consider their facility to have a significant fire risk. They couldn't be more wrong.

The National Fire Protection Association (NFPA) reports that heating and cooling, electrical, cooking, and other tools and equipment sparked about 35 percent of all commercial fires between 1991 and 1995, exceeding arson. During that period, there were 156,100 commercial fires, which caused $2.8 billion in direct property damage, 190 deaths, and 3,100 injuries.

Approximately 16,000 fires were caused by electrical distribution system problems, more than 10 percent of the total number of fires. Another 20,000, or almost 13 percent, were due to other equipment such as furnaces, kilns, motors, and generators. An additional 10,100 fires, or 6.5 percent, were ignited by heating equipment.

Electrical Fires

Electrical fires can be devastating to property, people, and the bottom line. At a high school in Oklahoma, a short circuit smoldered for more than two hours before it burst into flames, destroying the structure and causing $1.75 million in damage. It took sixty fire fighters from six communities more than six hours to bring the blaze under control. Luckily, it was a Sunday night and no one was in the building—all that was left standing were portions of exterior brick walls.

The NFPA points out that most fires can be prevented with better fire protection programs. A combination of factors, however, including neglect and reduced corporate spending, hinder such projects. Electrical equipment, for example, is often out-of-sight and out-of-mind, hidden behind walls or forgotten in closets and basements. This makes it easier to ignore or put off necessary preventive maintenance.

Corporate downsizings and business restructurings often result in the reduction or elimination of maintenance jobs. As personnel experienced in fire protection leave, tasks often go to inadequately trained personnel or fall by the wayside.

Otherwise skilled technicians and mechanics are not necessarily qualified to perform inspections, testing, or maintenance on fire protection systems. These systems have unique features and are usually subject to specific code requirements. Proper training must be provided to ensure compliance and avoid problems.

Having a maintenance contract for a particular protection system does not guarantee that all necessary tasks will be performed, either. Evaluate your provider and track its efforts. Find a new vendor if your current one is not performing adequately.

Additionally, regular fire department inspections are no substitute for a fire protection equipment inspection and testing program. Often, fire department officials are unfamiliar with automatic fire suppression systems: Their emphasis is on rescue, manual suppression, and hazards to their personnel.

One comment often heard by fire protection consultants is: "We comply with the state's requirements." But simply because a program complies with the standards of a local jurisdiction or fire department does not mean that the protection is adequate. A more stringent and safe set of standards is provided by the NFPA.

A New Approach

A decade of corporate cost-cutting has forced fire safety specialists to find innovative ways to defend against fire and explosion hazards. One methodology—called risk-informed fire protection—has been developed over several years in highly hazardous industries, such as chemical processing and nuclear power generation. It is now, however, attracting wider attention as facility managers everywhere struggle to stretch already-thin maintenance budgets. As the learning curve for this methodology grows, leaders within other industries seem increasingly eager to test its effectiveness.

A risk-informed, performance-based approach to fire protection offers an increasingly acceptable alternative to strict adherence to code requirements alone. Such assessment of a facility's fire protection systems may be more reliable for two reasons. Depending on the facility, process, system, or budget, strict adherence to code could be too costly to implement and maintain. In addition, codes are usually written to apply to a typical situation or configuration. But, exceptional situations often arise, requiring more or less stringent, or even different, fire protection methods.

The approach also presents a more realistic prediction of potential fire and explosion hazards for a given system or process, or for an entire operation. It provides solutions based on performance of established goals, rather than on prescriptive requirements with implied goals. Solutions are supported by data from operators and management about processes, equipment, and components; the buildings or structures housing them; operating and maintenance personnel; and the fire protection systems already in place. An analyst factors in not just the severity of a likely fire or explosion—usually measured in dollars—but also the probability that it will occur.

For example, based on the equipment operator's knowledge and experience, a fire in a given turbine generator has an 80 percent chance of igniting. Based on the knowledge and experience of the fire protection engineer, the sprinkler system protecting that generator is 90 percent likely to be able to contain and suppress a fire. Because the risk-informed, performance-based methodology quantifies the likelihood of a fire hazard—and the likelihood that the fire protection system will contain or extinguish it—it provides a more realistic prediction of the actual risk.

Wider Acceptance

The International Fire Code ([updated] in 2000) is currently incorporating language that will increase the acceptability of performance-based, rather than strictly code-based, fire protection methods. Similarly, the NFPA has begun to develop performance-based fire standards that will be instituted by 2000. Within the next five years, facility designers and managers will witness increasing tolerance within these codes toward performance-based alternatives.

The Future of Fire Protection

With workplace fires accounting for numerous deaths, injuries, and billions of dollars in damage, it's clear that commercial fires remain a significant problem. This is neither acceptable nor necessary. Fires can be avoided with proper loss prevention techniques and contained with loss control measures.

Every business, big and small, must dedicate more attention to this devastating problem. Much can be done to improve safety training and the maintenance of equipment and fire suppression systems, including incorporating new methods, such as risk-informed fire protection. Not all fires can be prevented, but setting that goal can go a long way toward reducing the number of costly and tragic events that threaten the public, employees, and businesses.

3

Risk Control

I have been a risk manager in several different industries, and the thing that has always struck me is how different basic risk management programs can look from business to business. I mean, similar fire prevention activities have a completely different feel and context when one sees them in a large manufacturing plant as compared to a senior citizens' home.

Senior Risk Manager
Specialist Construction Materials Manufacturer

The best thing that we have done in the risk control area is to have frequently occurring risks, such as workers compensation, impact an operating unit's bottom line. It is amazing how effective all other loss control efforts become when losses reflect directly on a unit's P & L.

Risk Manager
International Transportation Firm

Perspectives

Contracts Can Transfer Risk

Rodd Zolkos
Reprinted with permission from *Business Insurance,* March 13, 2000.

Many companies overlook the role that risk management can play in ensuring that contracts meet risk transfer requirements, according to one expert.

"A lot of organizations automatically run any contract by their legal department, but they don't automatically run them by the risk management department," says Ilene Roberts, a vice president with Riggs, Counselman, Michaels & Downs Inc. in Baltimore. "You need both."

Contract situations that need a risk management/insurance review include any contracts with insurance requirements, any contracts with hold-harmless or indemnification agreements, as well as any contracts or situations that should have such provisions, Roberts says. "It's really important to understand that there are lots of situations where there is no contract or it's (only) a one-page work order." Even in those cases, however, it's important for risk management to review the agreement and make sure the company is protected from exposures that might emerge from the contractual arrangement.

[When] entering into a contract with another company, "there are two ways to get you into their insurance," she says. "One is through contractual liability insurance. The second way is as an additional insured." Both approaches have flaws, she says, "so the thing to remember is you want both. You want an indemnity provision in the contract, and you want to be named as an additional insured."

Roberts frequently sees companies making such mistakes as using incorrect or outdated terminology in their contractual risk transfer agreements, failing to include additional insured requirements, or entering into contracts that lack indemnity agreements or whose agreements are inadequate.

Another common mistake is allowing an indemnity agreement with provisions that may be feasible today but won't be a year down the road. "Try to remember to think long-term," Roberts says. "Don't put things in that may not be attainable two or three years from now." Roberts also often sees vague or undefined requirements, and she advises risk managers to "try to be specific."

Moreover, she frequently encounters contracts that mistakenly require an insurer to give notice of modification or non-renewal of the contract counterparty's coverage. "I see that a lot," she says. "And insurance carriers will not provide notice of modification or nonrenewal simply because insurance policies expire." Consequently, the contract must hold the counterparty responsible for providing updated insurance information.

Among the recommendations Roberts makes to risk managers is to conduct insurance reviews of contracts before they're signed. "After it's signed, it's too late." She also recommends that risk managers avoid contradictory clauses in contracts and unattainable requirements, and that they ensure that contract requirements accurately reflect the intent of the parties to the contract.

Roberts draws attention to contractual risk transfer for environmental exposures, for which many policies are written on a claims-made basis. "If they're going to carry claims-made coverage," she says, "make sure there is a requirement that they carry it for a number of years after the project is completed."

She emphasizes that it's critical that a company designate someone in the organization to monitor the contractual insurance requirements and the insurance information provided by the contract counterparties. "Please don't forget that one. That is one of the most overlooked issues. It's amazing how many people will sign contracts and throw them in a drawer and nobody's seen them since, until somebody has a claim," she says.

Introduction

Broadly speaking, risk control can be defined to include any measures taken by a business to prevent, eliminate, or reduce losses; enhance the probabilities of gains; minimize the severity of losses that do occur; or maximize gains. In addition, measures taken to reduce uncertainty arguably would be added to the definition.

The breadth of the definition and the scope of practices that fall under that definition present something of a challenge for the practitioner. In some respects, almost anything a manager does may relate directly or indirectly to this definition of risk control. While this certainly is true enough, such inclusiveness does little to deepen the reader's appreciation of the specific characteristics that constitute a risk control measure. The purpose of this chapter is to work within this broad definition to provide a tight discussion of core risk control measures. The discussion will allow readers to understand the specific contribution of risk control to overall management efforts.

To this end, the structure of Chapter 3 is designed to address the following questions:

- What are the practical working characteristics of risk control?
- Can we generalize risk control measures into categories of action?
- What is the evidence of risk control effectiveness?
- What is "mandated" risk control, and how does it influence an organization's motivation to control risk?

That last question will be particularly important. A high percentage of activities that may reasonably be categorized as risk control are undertaken either due to regulatory requirement or administrative rule. Workers compensation law, the Occupational Safety and Health Act, Environmental Protection Agency (EPA) and federal grant requirements—all illustrate the influence of federal and state governments on the practice of risk control in private sector organizations.

What Is Risk Control?

Risk is pervasive, and its effects are both obvious and subtle. In developing the concept of Organization Risk Management (ORM), this book introduces the idea that firms are "collections of contracts, obligations, commitments, and agreements." A firm's exposure to risk either arises from those relationships or risks "pass through" those relationships. For instance, a firm's contract with a labor union gives rise to commitments and obligations that create specific contractual risks for the business. However, that contract also serves as the means through which the firm's workers compensation obligation manifests itself.

A reminder of the ORM view of firms is useful in this chapter, because any discussion of measures to manage/control risk must begin with an appreciation for how a business becomes exposed to risk. Any effort to build a comprehensive program of risk control must first consider that the portfolio of risks a firm possesses is built over time—sometimes purposefully, sometimes not—and that the risk portfolio in some sense represents an assemblage of risks that connect to larger, interrelated purposes. In other words, all organizational risks have interdependencies. More will be stated on this subject later in the chapter.

These concepts may suggest to some readers that an organization is free to pick and choose the risks to which it is willing to be exposed, and to a certain extent this is true. However, while a business may choose to avoid many risks by simply not allowing exposure to occur, there are instances in which a firm simply has to accept a risk.

What, then, is risk control? Risk control is any strategy, program, tool, or technique that seeks to avoid, prevent, reduce, or eliminate risk and uncertainty. This book's view of risk control would also include those measures undertaken to increase a risk's upside potential, whether through actions to increase the probability of favorable outcomes or the magnitude of those favorable outcomes.

A discussion of the second part of this definition, "upside risk control," could quickly degrade into hairsplitting over the meaning of specific words. For instance, when one says that risk control involves measures to increase the probability of favorable outcomes, the question may arise, Is this accomplished by reducing the downside possibilities, or by fundamentally affecting the upside in such a way that it is more likely to occur? Readers should rest assured that while this question is interesting enough in the abstract, it really is of minor concern in this book. Most often, risk control measures will deal with the management of downside potential, but in doing so the upside potential (where it exists) is directly enhanced. Perhaps an obvious example would be a program to reduce back injuries among maintenance workers, which if successful would have a direct and powerful influence on productivity.

For introductory purposes, we now turn to a discussion of risk control techniques and characteristics. The approach to this objective will be to break down the subject of risk control into the following areas:

1. Risk avoidance
2. Risk transfer and distribution
3. Risk/uncertainty reduction
4. Loss prevention
5. Loss reduction
6. Risk neutralization

Risk Avoidance

It may be possible to construct a hierarchy of risk control strategies, tools, and techniques using a cost-based metric. Almost invariably, the technique of *risk avoidance* would serve as the foundation. Risk avoidance involves those tools and techniques that enable the business to completely avoid exposure to the risk in question. While this technique seems simple enough, it is worth analyzing briefly the specific elements of avoidance, since analysis will prevent confusion when additional risk control techniques are introduced.

To begin, in its most basic form, an avoidance decision means that the risk in question simply does not exist. The risks, for instance, that may be created by entering into a contract with a vendor do not exist if the contract is not signed. This view of avoidance creates some problems, however, because it requires that an avoided risk simply does not exist for anyone (in the previous example, the vendor cannot contract with anyone else). For example,

> **Risk Avoidance**
>
> In the 1970s, a major candy and confectionery manufacturer faced a problem. Red dye number two had just been found to be a carcinogen. While the manufacturer did not use red dye number two in any of its candies, consumers were expressing concerns about all red dyes/additives. Taking a public relations stance, the manufacturer decided to eliminate all red candy colors from its product lines. Interestingly, approximately fifteen years later, after the concern over red dye had passed, the firm reintroduced the red candies with a major marketing campaign. In this example, both the actual and perceived risk were avoided.

destruction of nuclear weapons can help a nation avoid the risk of nuclear explosion *and* the risk does not fall on anyone else.

This is a rather rigorous definition, because a single firm often has little ability to eradicate a risk fully and completely through avoidance. Moving a proposed warehouse from an earthquake-sensitive region is "avoidance" in the conversational sense of the word, but strict application of the definition would require the risk of earthquake to physically disappear.

As Chapter 1 indicates, this book is about management of risks in business organizations, so motivation to act is centered on "exposure to risk." Therefore, practically speaking, risk avoidance is accomplished by ensuring that the firm is unequivocally unexposed to the risk and, whenever possible, that the risk does not exist in any physical sense.

Relaxation of the definition may create some confusion. For instance, when the discussion turns to "risk transfer" later in this chapter, readers may reasonably wonder whether a firm transferring an exposure to risk to a general contractor is avoidance. Perhaps the confusion is moderated a bit by observing that the risk still rests with a stakeholder to the firm who may bear the risk but who can exert some direct influence on the business.

Risk avoidance is the foundation risk control measure, to a large extent because it is close to costless—at least usually. Choosing to not expose an organization does not typically consume many resources (economic, human, or otherwise). However, avoidance is not always costless. Avoiding a risk means avoidance of the benefits (upside), if any. In addition, avoidance of a particular risk may actually make other risks more problematic. This final point is critical enough to warrant a small illustration.

Consider the example of a manufacturer that had two bridges crossing a river running through the center of the property where production facilities and warehouses were built. The business closed one bridge due to structural problems, but the rerouted traffic over the remaining bridge increased the traffic volume to such a level that the second bridge collapsed a few months later. Avoidance of one risk changed the fundamental nature of a related risk.

Lastly, avoidance may not be possible for at least three reasons. First, the law may mandate responsibility for the risk. Indeed, this is such a fundamental issue in risk management that it will be discussed at some length later in the chapter. Second, the risk may be so fundamental to the purposes of the business that avoidance is not conceivable. A mining company could avoid the risk of mine collapse by closing its mines, but such a move would rather defeat the point of being in the mining business. Third, the risk may not be avoidable in any real and physical sense. A firm whose clientele is located exclusively in the San Francisco area may very much wish to avoid the risk of earthquake, but it cannot happen without leaving that area.

Risk Transfer and Distribution

Previously, readers have been introduced to the concept and application of the COCA organization. The idea reemerges here in support of a second risk control tool—risk transfer and distribution.

The principal means by which a firm becomes exposed to risk is through the contracts, obligations, commitments, and agreements (COCAs) into which it enters. In Chapter 2, this insight serves as the basis for the entire risk assessment framework, showing how a risk manager may begin to develop a more comprehensive understanding of the business's exposure to risk. That chapter's discussion also alludes to the fact that entering into these COCAs affords the best opportunity to "manage" the risks that attach to the COCAs. The following discussion elaborates on this notion.

The term *risk transfer* is a little misleading and takes on at least two distinct forms in risk management. It is misleading because while the actual risk itself may be transferred from one party to another, more commonly it is only responsibility (financial or otherwise) for the risk that is subject to transfer. The term is further confusing because of practical usage. Risk transfer is most widely used—almost interchangeably—with the term *insurance,* and it is true that insurance is an important risk transfer (i.e., risk *responsibility* transfer) contract. But there is a plethora of other transfer mechanisms where the term also applies. Although the discussion that follows focuses on noninsurance transfers, readers should note that the distinction is rather arbitrary—contractual transfers of risk differ only in degree rather than in kind.

The burden of risk is both economic and psychological (and sometimes "moral"). Therefore, the purpose of risk distribution is to transfer one or more of these burdens to another party. A firm's ability to do so is influenced by a number of factors—for example, the parties' willingness to accept the risk, their negotiating leverage, and so on (see Chapter 2)—so it must be stated at the outset that many risks may not be transferable or distributable. Discussion here focuses on circumstances where the possibility of transfer exists.

As noted previously, most transfers entail a transfer of responsibility for risk rather than transfer of the risk itself, but certainly *tangible risk transfers* do occur. For example, a sale/leaseback arrangement for storage facilities could be characterized as a tangible transfer because the risk of, say, fire to the facilities transfers from seller

Insights

Modified-Duty Program Helps Home Depot Build on Success

Judy Greenwald

Home Depot Inc. considers its modified-duty program for returning injured employees to work a success.

Eighty-five percent of the injured employees at Atlanta-based Home Depot who participated in the program last year made the transition from injury, to lost time, to modified duty, and then to full duty within a twelve-week period. And the remaining 15 percent of employees in the program were able to move—with no time lost at all—from injury to modified duty, says Stephanie Perilli, Home Depot's occupational claims manager. More than 3,500 injured workers participated in the program.

Perilli and Bart Canon Jr., director of risk management for Home Depot, [say] the modified-duty program [is] part of a revamped risk management program. Canon notes that Home Depot, which currently has 950 stores, is growing rapidly. By 2004, he said, the chain will have more than 1,900 stores and a half million employees, up from 200,000 at year-end 1999.

In 1998, Canon says, the company took steps to enhance its risk management services, "create the safest environment possible," and reduce the total cost of risk to increase shareholder return. The company's culture played a major role in the approach it took in that effort. Home Depot has certain core values, including excellent customer service, shareholder return, entrepreneurial spirit, taking care of its people, [showing] respect for all people, doing the right thing, and strong relationships. "Our redesign had to enhance all of these," he says.

The initiatives included a risk management department redesign; a workers compensation claims redesign, including the modified-duty program; and a liability claims redesign. It also included an information systems redesign, safety program assessment and redesign, and increased store participation.

Discussing the company's return-to-work focus, Perilli says the best practices approach adopted by the company includes promptly reporting all claims through an outsourced claims reporting service. In addition, the claims operation was reorganized into eight dedicated regional claims teams "solely dedicated to Home Depot," says Perilli.

Other elements of the program included implementing a centralized, dedicated telephonic case management unit, which involves a team of nurses responsible for managing the medical aspect of Home Depot's workers comp claims. The company also is using a national medical provider network to support medical management initiatives.

The modified-duty program involves the use of teams to manage claims. Each team has three partners, each of whom has a distinct function in the process.

First, there is the telephonic case manager, who is responsible for the medical aspects of the claim and for obtaining a timely release to return the employee to work. "They are interfacing with the medical community," [Perilli] says. A Home Depot customer service representative assists in modified-duty replacement and acts as an employee and store advocate. In addition, a claims examiner is responsible for compensability issues, benefit payments, and other statutory and legal requirements.

All three team members work with a "very sophisticated electronic feed," says Perilli. After an incident occurs, it is relayed to the claim reporting center. The center, in turn, conveys the data to the team members. Then each [member of the team] gets to work. The claims examiner, for instance, will investigate facts, determine compensability, value the case and set reserves, pay benefits, insure statutory compliance, manage litigation, and see the case through to conclusion.

"We identify very specific tasks" as part of modified duty, says Perilli. And modified-duty assignments are productive, she stresses, and don't involve "counting paper clips." The employee is kept "very, very busy."

Canon stresses, however, that Home Depot does not advocate permanent modified duty. Twelve weeks is the maximum

> duration, with some modifications. In cases where there is a question as to whether an employee can return, "we really deal with it on a case-by-case basis," says Perilli.
>
> Fred Scardellete, vice president, disability management product development for Philadelphia-based Intracorp, provides health care and disability management services and works with Home Depot. Intracorp's best practices are built on providing important communication links with employees, ensuring that doctors set expectations with employees, and facilitating return-to-work options.
>
> Discussing the issue of managing growth, Scardellete says you cannot "just add heads as you go." Improving efficiency comes first, while adding on-site headcount comes second. Other elements of managing growth include automating manual processes to free up staff, using alternative staff for certain functions, and rarely using additional off-site support.

to buyer. Contrast this with the purchase of fire insurance, where the original owner remains exposed directly to the fire risk.

The sale/leaseback strategy suggests the outright difficulty of absolute risk transfers (i.e., both tangible and responsibility risk transfer). If a business sells its storage facilities to a property management firm, but then leases back the facilities, the risk has not been transferred in any conversational sense of the word. The business has simply exchanged one form of exposure for another. This is not necessarily a bad thing, but the illusion of absolute transfer can create dangerous misunderstandings. Equally, risk distribution (i.e., where more than two parties are involved) may actually contribute to the confusion regarding the ultimate responsibility for a risk.

The importance of appreciating the distinction between an absolute transfer of the risk versus a transfer of responsibility versus a transfer of the tangible exposure cannot be underestimated in the current outsourcing climate. Increasing efforts to contract out services and functions elevates the issues that underlay a motivation to transfer or distribute risk. Quite simply put, when a firm contracts out its food services to an outside provider, another party enters into the risk management equation. That vendor may supply the workers, the foodstuffs, the cooking equipment, and the administrative apparatus necessary to perform the task, so in a sense the tangible risks of harm have been transferred. But the responsibility likely has not been transferred. The firm still possesses a general responsibility for the safety of the food served in its cafeterias. If the private service provider declares bankruptcy, many outstanding liabilities and obligations likely will revert to the contracting firm.

A skilled risk manager would correctly note that responsibility for a risk also can be transferred in such a situation by requiring vendors and suppliers to demonstrate financial ability to accept risk. For instance (and this is explained in greater depth in Chapter 8), a firm can insist that its contracting service provider supply certificates of insurance to ensure that risks such as worker injury and motor vehicle accidents are covered and unlikely to revert to the firm.

However, while tangible risk and the responsibility for risk can be transferred, two issues arise that become critical for the firm. One is the cost of monitoring and the other is the cost of a loss of direct control. First, the monitoring cost can be appreciated by realizing that a certificate of insurance states nothing more than that insurance was in force when the certificate was issued. It is possible that the service provider could discontinue insurance coverage immediately after being awarded the contract. Ongoing assurance that financial responsibility will not revert to the firm is labor intensive, and when all such arrangements are considered it could occupy the time of one clerical worker. Second, even if financial responsibility can be transferred and assured, there is the related problem of general or moral responsibility. A firm can be held responsible in more than a financial sense. Inappropriate or even illegal actions by the service provider reflect badly on the firm and can contribute to an erosion of customer goodwill.

This scenario shows the "loss of control" issue that bedevils outsourcing and partnering initiatives. A firm will retain a general responsibility for most of its business risks, no matter how sophisticated the risk transference. That transference typically means a loss of control over the day-to-day activities that influence or give rise to the risks. It may still be in the best interest to both the business and its stockholders that a service is outsourced, but the loss of direct control is not costless. Therefore, just as direct monitoring costs must be factored into the decision to outsource, so must the indirect costs associated with loss of control.

Risk/Uncertainty Reduction

Chapter 2 explained the nature of the relationship between risk and uncertainty. Risk is, in a sense, a state of nature whereas uncertainty is more a state of mind; yet, the two concepts are intertwined. This relationship is important to remember, because it serves as the basis for asserting the centrality of risk/uncertainty reduction as a risk control tool.

Uncertainty can be the result of many factors, and indeed, it may not be possible at any particular time to understand which factors are in play. A person may be genetically predisposed to having a certain outlook on life, and this may affect uncertainty levels.

Risk/Uncertainty Reduction

The Y2K case presents an interesting illustration of uncertainty reduction. By 1998, the looming problem became a topic of concern across the world. The potential crash of computers and the ensuing havoc had begun to promote various types of responses—including survivalist-type strategies. As firms and individuals spent more time exploring the problem and obtaining more information, the problem began to diminish in relative importance. By the time the clock rolled over to January 1, 2000, the Y2K issue was a minor inconvenience. The dissemination of credible information to the public helped reduce uncertainty.

Upbringing, life experiences, culture, and other factors can be influential. One would be hard-pressed to explain how a risk manager might affect these influences on risk and uncertainty—although it certainly is arguable that a risk manager has a responsibility to make a firm's management team more self-aware of the influences of these factors on its decision making.

The more obvious and tangible uncertainty reduction efforts can be directed at *information management,* a term used here in a broad and general sense and not specifically connoting its more specific information technology meaning.

Plausibly, the increase in knowledge of a particular risk results in a reduction of uncertainty. If one knows more about the causes of motor vehicle accidents, for example, it is likely that judgments and decisions regarding driving behavior will be more sound. Notably, the actual underlying risk is not changed; rather, the driver's understanding is changed for the better. The cloud of uncertainty is thinned, allowing the decision maker to act with greater clarity.

This example can be extended broadly to the firm exposed to risks. If an effort is made to systematically understand the environment in which the firm exists, overall uncertainty can be reduced and better—and more consistent—decisions may be made. Thus, a part of the risk manager's role is to ensure that the business has systematic means of gathering and analyzing information that is relevant to the organization's life.

Information management comes with some caveats. First, information gathering is not costless. Second, more information does not automatically reduce uncertainty, as that information may be contradictory, unclear, highly technical, or difficult to analyze. Third, the information may be inaccurate, which may lead to incorrect conclusions. One need only reflect on how many elegant scientific theories rested on the supposition that the earth was flat to appreciate the potential problems arising from a sophisticated analysis based on faulty information. Fourth, additional information does not solve all the contributing factors underlying uncertainty. Case in point: Previously we alluded to the notion of genetic and psychological influences; it is easy to imagine that the interplay of

Insights

Some Employers Seeing Big Payoffs

Meg Fletcher
Reprinted with permission from *Business Insurance,* January 31, 2000.
© Crain Communications Inc. All rights reserved.

A trio of large employers with successful ergonomics programs can offer some reassurance to employers alarmed by recent proposals on musculoskeletal disorders made by the Occupational Safety and Health Administration [OSHA].

Effective ergonomics programs are in the long-term best interest of employers—as well as that of their workers—according to representatives of Intel Corp., the City of San Jose, and 3M. The workers at these leading employers are among the 50 percent of all U.S. workers protected by some type of ergonomics program, though such programs currently are found at only about 28 percent of all worksites, according to OSHA.

Successful ergonomics programs reduce injury rates an average of 70 percent while cutting costs and raising productivity and employee morale, according to more than ninety case studies by the General Accounting Office and others. OSHA calculates that its proposed ergonomics regulations would prevent 300,000 painful and potentially disabling injuries annually and save $22,500 for each MSD [musculoskeletal disorder] prevented, for a total of $9 billion each year.

The proposed regulations would target workers performing manual handling or manufacturing tasks, but also would apply to most general industry worksites where one or more workers report work-related musculoskeletal disorders after the final standard takes effect.

Critics have argued that OSHA's proposed standard unnecessarily interferes with employers' operations and the current state workers compensation systems.

Intel Corp. in Santa Clara, California, launched its ergonomics program in 1992 ''because that was the thing to do,'' says Earnest Ray, occupational ergonomist for the microcomputer component manufacturer. The program already complies with OSHA's proposed regulations.

Intel's ergonomics program won the 1999 national Outstanding Office Ergonomics award from the Center for Office Technology [COT] in Alexandria, Virginia. The program serves Intel's 65,000 workers with the help of a database of worker-specific workstation requirements, such as height of work surfaces and keyboard placement preferences. The data is invaluable because workers frequently change workstations, Ray notes.

In addition, Intel's program emphasizes immediately treating musculoskeletal cases before they become more serious, which "really pays for itself," Ray says. "Musculoskeletal disorders are relatively easy to treat and prevent," if a company establishes a good ergonomics program, he says.

Company statistics demonstrate the effectiveness of Intel's program: Its lost-day severity rate, which reflects restricted duty or lost time per 100 workers, dropped from 37.2 in 1993 to 1.4 in 1999. Over that period, the company also saw a 93 percent drop in its rate of recordable cumulative trauma disorders and a 96 percent drop in its lost-day rate. The program is "a huge morale booster" and has reduced workers comp costs "dramatically," Ray says.

Intel also found that fraudulent claims were not a problem. And compensating workers was not an issue, as the company continued to pay workers their full salary.

Intel is so committed to the concept of ergonomics programs that the company would go one step further than most if OSHA's regulations go into effect, Ray says. He would consider expanding the criteria Intel uses to screen vendors to include a review of their ergonomics programs.

Meanwhile, the City of San Jose is distributing copies of OSHA's ergonomics proposal to members of its 120 voluntary employee ergonomics teams, which help assess and improve worksite conditions for 5,500 full-time equivalent workers, said Marynka Rojas, safety and ergonomics manager. The city won the COT ergonomics award in 1998.

The city's program, established in 1994, includes workstation or worksite evaluation and design, informational lectures and self-assessment classes, and product evaluation. "I'm doing this so people don't panic," she says. Reviewing the proposed federal standards also helps team members learn that the city already is "pretty much in compliance" with the OSHA measures, including those mandating job analyses, workstation evaluations, and training. If the regulations become law, however, the city would have to tighten its record-keeping requirements.

In some ways, Rojas prefers the federal standard, as it contains a clearer and more detailed definition of a "health care professional" who is authorized to provide treatment. California's less comprehensive standard lacks such a definition.

In addition, "one of the neatest things is the 'Quick Fix' option" in the federal standards, which does not necessarily require use of expensive equipment, she says. For example, a video display terminal set too low for ergonomically correct viewing can be raised to the appropriate height by placing it on top of a thick telephone book, rather than by buying a more expensive, box-like support. In addition, "you don't need to spend $1,600 on a chair," she says.

If OSHA's proposal becomes law, many employers undoubtedly will "panic initially," or at least have "an eye-opening experience," she says. It is important for them to remember that "there are cost savings involved, but it takes three to five years before you see any." San Jose, which has about $10 million in annual workers compensation claim costs, has saved about $6 million total in incurred claim costs since fiscal year 1995–1996 as a result of a program that combines ergonomics, safety, wellness, and return to work.

In addition, Rojas does not anticipate a problem with the proposed federal pay mandates for workers with MSDs, because the city's payment policies already exceed state workers comp maximums. But, she adds, "For many industries I can see that being an issue."

The federal mandate calls for an employer to pay a worker on modified duty at least 100 percent of his or her pre-injury, after-tax earnings, while the worker unable to do any job would receive at least 90 percent of such earnings. Critics of OSHA's proposed compensation plan say it exceeds payments called for under many states' workers comp laws and that it would increase costs to employers.

Reducing MSD symptoms also has improved worker morale and their lives at home, Rojas says. It also has improved their job longevity, which is a challenge in Silicon Valley's competitive job market.

In addition, the fifteen-year-old ergonomics program at St. Paul, Minnesota–based 3M is considered an essential "smart business practice" that has improved worker health as well as the productivity and efficiency of its 71,000 workers worldwide, says Nancy Larson, the company's manager of corporate ergonomics. If the federal OSHA standards become law, "we could live with it," she says, though she would like to see the federal compensation mandate be modified. Currently, 3M pays injured workers at the levels required by individual state workers comp laws.

In addition, Larson emphasizes the need for early identification of potential MSD hazards, which helps in efforts to engineer them out of the workplace. She also encourages workers to report symptoms early, so that physical problems can be minimized.

"more information" with subtle psychological factors may produce unexpected results. For instance, certain psychology of risk studies suggest that attitudes toward risk are influenced by the form in which information is obtained, when it is obtained (e.g., recently or long ago), and whether it resonates with private fears and apprehensions. Nevertheless, it probably is a safe proposition to state that more information usually is better than less information.

Loss Prevention

Loss prevention involves all techniques and strategies that reduce or eliminate the likelihood of losses occurring. Readers should note

Loss Prevention

While interventions such as the requirement that stockroom employees wear lumbar support belts often are cited as good examples of loss prevention, there are other more subtle examples. The hiring process is long and complicated within many firms. Part of the complication is the number of federal laws that must be obeyed. Asking inappropriate/illegal questions can expose a firm to lawsuits. Training employees involved in the hiring process as to the scope of allowable questions can head off many possible lawsuits.

that outright elimination of losses—while the preferred outcome—is not commonly the expected outcome in risk management. Rather, loss prevention is seen as a concentrated attack on loss frequency with the intended outcome of reducing losses to some tolerable level.

The discussion of risk analysis in Chapter 2 suggests how the study of risk can give rise to the solutions necessary to manage the risk, and nearly automatically such analysis will point most directly to loss prevention measures. For example, a thorough study of the causes of lower back injuries among maintenance workers may help pinpoint improper lifting activities, physical fitness factors, time-of-day considerations, and inadequate equipment as contributing factors. In turn, each of these factors can be controlled through a variety of interventions—from teaching proper lifting techniques, to lumbar support belts, to training and conditioning programs, to changes in management techniques—resulting in a lowered frequency of injury.

Chapter 2 also introduces the Risk Chain concept, which is helpful in isolating the points of intervention. Loss prevention can either attempt to alter or eliminate the hazard, the peril, or the exposure to a particular risk. As an example, the following loss prevention measures can be undertaken to address each link in the Risk Chain.

Hazard-Based Prevention Actions

Hazard 1:	Untidy, improperly maintained equipment storage facility
Action:	Cleaning and maintenance protocols
Hazard 2:	Flooding
Action:	Water resource management
Hazard 3:	Overweight workers
Action:	Counseling and exercise opportunities
Hazard 4:	Waste water management
Action:	Properly maintained treatment facilities
Hazard 5:	Icy and/or deteriorating parking lots
Action:	Snow removal, salting, regular maintenance, and repair schedules

Peril-Based Prevention Actions

Peril 1:	Fire
Action:	Fire resistant construction materials
Peril 2:	Earthquake
Action:	Retrofitting buildings
Peril 3:	Emergency response practices
Action:	Emergency response policy and training
Peril 4:	Poorly lit parking facility
Action:	Lighting; escort and security services
Peril 5:	Slippery retail store steps
Action:	Installation of nonskid surfaces

Exposure-Based Prevention Actions

Exposure 1:	Maintenance workers
Action:	Proper training, adequate equipment
Exposure 2:	Truck fleet
Action:	Regular maintenance and inspection schedule
Exposure 3:	Computers

Action:	Y2K evaluation and resolution
Exposure 4:	Accounts receivable records
Action:	Backup records with off-site storage
Exposure 5:	A firm's bond rating
Action:	Financial accounting, auditing, and management procedures

In a sense, the allocation of certain loss prevention measures to particular elements of the Risk Chain is arbitrary—often one is hard-pressed to understand whether a particular measure addresses the hazard or peril. However, such fuzziness is of little concern to the practicing risk manager; the examples we provide are intended mainly as an illustration of concepts rather than as a blueprint for action.

One final word is necessary regarding loss prevention. While loss prevention largely focuses readers' attention on measures that prevent bad things from happening, they should not forget that reducing loss frequency improves the prospects of good things happening (in risk situations where upside risk exists). For example, if a firm were able to cut workers compensation losses by 40 percent, funds normally used to finance such claims would be available for more productive investment. Or, taking measures to reduce risks that negatively affect bond rating will mean lower ongoing debt servicing costs. Loss prevention, often, can be seen as "gain enhancement," which may be an important element in persuading top managers to allocate resources to prevention measures.

Loss Reduction

Bad things will happen to a firm even when risk management is practiced. Loss reduction includes those measures taken to limit the impact—direct and indirect—of losses once they have occurred.

Chapter 2 cites an important observation about losses; that is, that the indirect and consequential impact of a loss can outstrip the obvious and direct impact. If interventions can take place after

---

Loss Reduction

Sprinkler systems are a great example of loss reduction. They do not stop fires from starting, but they do limit the damage that a fire can cause. One caution regarding sprinkler systems should be mentioned, however. Firms must be confident that the proper fire suppression system is used. A water-based suppression system may be fine in stairwells, but actually could cause more damage than it prevents in a computing center.

---

a loss to limit or prevent indirect and consequential losses from arising, such losses—even very large ones—become much more manageable. Rapid response measures, fire suppressant systems, seat belts, CPR training, lifeguards at swimming pools, catastrophe management plans, all represent techniques and tools that can contain loss costs. Even when an event has progressed to a courtroom, as in a product liability case, litigation management strategies can be used effectively to intervene and limit losses. Occasionally, subrogation opportunities arise in court settings in which a firm may seek to recover for damages it has paid to a plaintiff by seeking redress from some other responsible party.

Risk managers extend loss reduction to the level of salvage strategy. Since losses rarely are total in actuality, the ultimate cost of loss can be offset by efforts to salvage damaged property.

One aspect of loss reduction has become so important that it demands separate attention: contingency or catastrophe planning and management. Indeed, recent history has done much to enable catastrophe management to be seen as a distinct area of management, which certainly is good because it represents an important aspect in overall management planning. However, readers must recognize that catastrophe planning really only becomes effective if it is done in an organization that has an established commitment to risk management. There are philosophical and practical reasons why this is true, but for purposes of this book it is sufficient to argue that the failure of most catastrophe planning efforts is due to the absence of a champion within the firm who can advocate and advance catastrophe planning efforts—and, of course, oversee the execution of such a plan. Naturally, a risk manager is the appropriate individual to perform this role.

With the preceding qualifier in mind, this section turns briefly to the subject of catastrophe planning.

Catastrophe Planning and Program Implementation

A catastrophe (or sometimes, contingency) plan is a document that establishes an organization-wide, integrated, and coordinated effort to manage emergency or large loss events. What constitutes a catastrophe is determined by the firm; it most certainly is not a fixed concept. In any event, the planning process closely follows strategic planning models as it requires top management/elected official direction and support, but will also require development efforts at all levels of the organization.

In brief, a catastrophe plan requires a business to develop a disaster scenario and then to create a coordinated series of actions, plans, responses, and measures to control the effects of that disaster. In its broadest sense, it is a risk reduction initiative in that it assumes the disaster has already occurred and that the principal objective is containment. However, that simplification is misleading because the individual measures that may be taken to control and minimize the loss may exhibit a wide range of characteristics. In other words, a successful catastrophe management plan will include avoidance, prevention, transfer, reduction, and neutralization elements.

Finally, as was the case with loss prevention, readers should momentarily consider the upside risk aspects of loss reduction. One may argue that measures taken to specifically enlarge positive outcomes might be related in some way to loss reduction measures. For instance, capitalizing on an opportunity to purchase land for a warehouse at a windfall price may be characterized as the mirror image of a situation where a loss is limited through measures to reduce costs of loss. Little time will be further spent on this observation, except to emphasize that risk management also entails (or can entail) efforts to maximize the positive possibilities that risk presents.

Risk Neutralization

The final risk control tool considered is risk neutralization. Neutralization refers to those measures taken to reduce the effects of risk to zero (or near zero) through arrangements to offset one risk with another. While in most technical senses, risk neutralization (often referred to as "hedging") practices fall under the heading of "risk financing," the idea is broad enough to include in a discussion of risk control practices. We mention the concept in this chapter for purposes of introduction and note that, in practice, debates over whether it is a "control" tool or "finance" tool are rather rare. To a practicing risk manager, it only matters that a particular measure works.

Neutralization differs from avoidance in that the risk still exists and is directly borne by the firm. Neutralization differs from prevention in that no efforts necessarily are made to influence the frequency of loss, nor is neutralization like loss reduction because

Risk Neutralization

The idea of neutralization through "separation" has many forms. Having separate warehouses in different locations can reduce the possibility that one event will harm a firm's entire inventory. Automobile dealers are particularly sensitive to this problem. If all of their vehicles are kept on one lot, a tornado, hailstorm, or even a disgruntled former employee could spell disaster. Also, school districts with bus fleets may be strong proponents of separation. Not only does separation prevent catastrophic losses, it also may improve service efficiency—especially for districts covering large geographic areas.

no direct actions are taken to impact the magnitude of loss (or gain).

Hedging arrangements (discussed in Chapter 6) are the obvious illustrations of neutralizing efforts, but one can find numerous examples of techniques where taking the opposite position on a risk does not fit traditional financial hedging practices. Resource pooling often can be construed as a type of hedge position, with mutual aid agreements being good illustrations. Newspaper firms in neighboring communities often enter into commitments with each other to neutralize particular risks. An agreement to share printing equipment does not eliminate the risk of a resource-taxing loss, nor is the risk transferred. Rather, the cooperating firms have packaged together their exposure to a disruptive event in such a way that neither firm will have insufficient resources if and when they are needed.

A scholarly reader may wonder whether we are actually describing "risk pooling." Pooling entails a combining of risks in order to improve predictability of, say, loss experience and to reduce the likelihood that participating members will have insufficient resources in the event of a large loss. The distinction between risk pooling and mutual aid agreements is made in two ways. First, the mutual aid agreement doesn't involve an actual comingling of resources but rather a commitment to participate if events arise. Second, the commitment is not principally financial, but is based on performance of some action.

This discussion may strike some as hairsplitting, and certainly pooling and neutralization have many common properties. The value in making this narrow distinction is to remind readers that while risk pools and hedging strategies mainly are characterized as financing arrangements, there are circumstances in which the neutralization (and even pooling) idea does not follow a distinctly risk financing story line.

Finally, another—somewhat lesser—risk control tool should be mentioned because it is related conceptually to neutralization and pooling. "Separation" is a strategy whereby the resources of one entity are physically separated to minimize the risk of total destruction of assets. Storing equipment in multiple locations is an example, and occasionally firms will strike agreements whereby they separate assets among those firms. This does not "neutralize" the entire risk, but it does tend to reduce or eliminate the chance of catastrophic loss.

An important modern variant on separation is "duplication." Backing up computer records and storing them off-site provides an important type of separation that virtually eliminates or neutralizes the chance of total loss.

Mandated Risk Control

Although management of risk, and particularly the controlling of risk, is a practice that serves the interests of a firm, there are many circumstances in which risk control is not merely a good idea—it is the law. This phenomenon is called mandated risk control.

For practicing risk managers, compliance with mandated risk control is a challenge. Depending on the range of the risk manager's responsibilities, the monitoring of present and new requirements can consume a great amount of time and effort. To begin, the federal government may be generating risk control requirements from a wide range of programs and agencies, including the Environmental Protection Agency, the Occupational Safety and Health Administration, the Americans with Disabilities Act, the Social Security Administration, the Employee Retirement and Income Security Act, even flood insurance programs. Also, general legislation by Congress often has elements that give rise to risk control considerations. The federal courts render decisions that have, or can have, risk control implications.

Of course, the federal government is not alone in imposing requirements on businesses. Occasionally, international governing bodies impose expectations, as is abundantly in evidence in the nations of the European Union. More commonly in the United States, the state and local governments create additional requirements. Workers compensation laws are obvious illustrations of this point, but most states also have occupational safety programs, environmental protection programs, and a range of public safety and health policies that impact directly on risk control activity within firms.

A Final Word About ORM and Traditional Risk Control

As was the case with risk assessment, the discussion here is flexible enough to address risks that fall within the traditional risk management purview or the broader organization-wide perspective. Equally, these techniques will differ in importance, form, and execution when we compare practices across industries. Yet the generic roots of these techniques are immutable. Therefore, for instance, though "avoidance is avoidance is avoidance" in a conceptual sense, the industry and organization context would seem to matter a great deal. As just a simple illustration, the use of risk avoidance is greatly circumscribed in public sector organizations and there are many risks that such organizations cannot avoid. Conversely, a new business may be able to employ the avoidance technique as a very active means of managing and moderating its overall business risk.

Read More About It

Expanding Environmental Risk Management

Dan Anderson
Reprinted with permission from *Risk Management* magazine, July 1999.
Copyright 1999 by Risk Management Society Publishing. All rights reserved.
For more information call 212.286.9364. www.rims.org/rmmag

DuPont has reduced toxic releases 74 percent since 1987, halved its landfill waste, and cut its $1 billion-per-year waste treatment bill by $200 million. 3M's Pollution Prevention Pays program, one of the first corporatewide efforts to avoid waste from the start—rather than clean it up later—has eliminated more than 1.5 billion pounds of air, land, and water pollution, for a total cost savings of $790 million. Are the DuPont and 3M programs [considered] risk management initiatives or more general environmental management strategies? Actually, both.

Environmental risks were virtually ignored by business, government, and society until the 1970s. At that time a regulatory approach to managing environmental risks was set in motion with the passage of various legislation, including the Clean Water and Air Acts, RCRA, and CERCLA (Superfund). While necessary to protect the environment, regulations were often resisted by business and considered unnecessary and excessive.

More recently, an entirely different approach to dealing with environmental conditions has been evolving, namely the development of environmental management as an integral part of overall business strategy. Sustainable development and environment-friendly systems and products are emphasized, in proactive, rather than reactive, ways—with a positive, rather than negative, orientation. Environmental management systems are seen as adding value, creating a competitive advantage, improving community image, reducing costs, and enhancing the bottom line.

And they often have a significant risk management element. While the DuPont and 3M programs are clearly environment-friendly, they also result in reduced risks and potential liabilities for these organizations.

Risk managers can and should be a part of developing and operating environmental management systems. While risk managers are currently involved in environmental issues, substantial opportunities exist to expand this participation. Finally, as will be argued [here], risk management training and techniques are well suited to contribute to developing effective environmental management systems.

Environmental Programs

Environmental management programs and organizations have been developing at a rapid pace. Most are private sector–based and voluntary. Many incorporate the concept of sustainable development. And some of these programs are seen as complementing, and in some cases replacing, environmental regulations.

ISO 14000, issued by the Geneva-based International Organization for Standardization, is a series of management system standards covering such areas as process documentation, training, life-cycle assessment procedures and management reporting, and accountability for environmental performance. Section 14001 creates the specific standards for environmental management systems. ISO 14000/14001 certification is particularly important in Europe and Japan, where it is often a requirement for business transactions.

Coalition for Environmentally Responsible Companies is a nonprofit organization, established in the United States in 1989, that sets forth ten environmental principles for member organizations. Some of these have direct application to risk management, including reduction and disposal of wastes, risk reduction, and safe products and services. [Coalition] members include General Motors, Sun Company, Bethlehem Steel, Polaroid, BankAmerica, Coca-Cola, and The Body Shop.

The Responsible Care Program, established in 1988 by the Chemical Manufacturers Association, is one of the best examples of an industry-specific program setting benchmarks for environmental performance. Willis Corroon set up a program in conjunction with the Responsible Care Program, whereby participating firms can receive up to a 30 percent reduction in EIL [environmental impairment liability] premiums through a premium modification factor process. The American Petroleum Institute set up a similar program in 1990 called Strategies for Today's Environmental Partnership. Given the considerable pollution-related risks of the chemical and petroleum industries, these programs are important steps in environmental management.

The Global Environmental Management Initiative (GEMI) was formed in 1990 in the United States in response to heightened awareness about the changing demands of conscientious consumers. GEMI's core mission is to help businesses achieve environmental, health, and safety excellence. GEMI's twenty-six corporate members include Anheuser-Busch, Bristol-Myers Squibb, Browning-Ferris, Coca-Cola, Colgate-Palmolive, Coors, Dow, DuPont, Eastman Kodak, Georgia-Pacific, Goodyear, Johnson & Johnson, Lockheed Martin, Merck, Motorola, Occidental Petroleum, Olin, Procter & Gamble, Southern Company, and Waste Management.

The International Chamber of Commerce (ICC) created the Business Charter for Sustainable Development in 1991 in Rotterdam, Netherlands. Sixteen principles for environmental management are set forth by the charter, which has been published in over twenty languages, including all official languages of the United Nations. The ICC encourages member companies to express their support and implement the charter and its principles.

The international Factor 10 Club was founded in October 1994 in Carnoules, France. Presently it has sixteen members from ten countries, including India, Canada, the United States, Japan, and most of Western Europe. The Factor 10 Club was formed in response to mounting concerns over the uncharted role of human-induced global material flows and the ecological ramifications of their unchecked growth. Strategies supported by the group include increasing resource productivity through new technological approaches and ecological tax reforms.

The Natural Step is a principle-based program founded in 1989 by Swedish cancer scientist Karl-Henrick Robërt. Its purpose is to encourage and support environmental systems thinking and sustainable development strategies in corporations, cities, governments, unions, and academic institutions.

The United Nations Environmental Programme (UNEP) created the Industry and Environment Centre to work with business and industry, national and local governments, international groups, and nongovernmental organizations. The program acts as a catalyst, providing a platform for dialogue [and] encouraging the move from confrontation to cooperation, from words to concrete actions. The "Statement of Environmental Commitment by the Insurance Industry," which has been signed by seventy-four insurers from twenty-five countries, arose from UNEP.

The World Business Council for Sustainable Development is a coalition of over 120 international companies united by a commitment to the environment and to the principles of economic growth and sustainable development. Its members are drawn from thirty-five countries and more than twenty major industrial sectors. It has a global network of fifteen national business councils, as well as regional business councils and partner organizations in developing countries.

The foregoing is a sampling, not an exhaustive compilation, of some of the more active and important environmental efforts. Besides encouraging sound environmental practices, these programs and organizations provide a wealth of experience and information for corporations planning to expand their environmental efforts. (Visit *Risk Management* online at www.rims.org/rmmag for links to these organizations.)

Application

Risk managers have been and are currently involved in managing numerous environment-related risks, such as oil and chemical spills, harmful products, transportation accidents, waste disposal, workers' health, and natural disaster damages. With a broadened role, risk managers are particularly well suited to contribute to the creation of effective environmental management systems. Traditionally, risk managers have been concerned with internal environmental risks that adversely impact the business. However, by adopting a more expansive approach, the risk management process can also be applied to external environmental risks—those that adversely impact the environment but may not have immediate adverse effects on business.

Through this expanded approach, risk managers can weave various aspects of their programs and strategies into environmental management. This, in turn, benefits the environment, the risk management program, and the organization itself.

Risk assessment is the identification and evaluation of potential losses. Techniques include flowcharts, fault tree analysis, questionnaires, checklists, financial statements, inspections, interviews, and records of past losses. Risk managers systematically assess supplier networks, manufacturing processes, and distribution channels for loss-causing scenarios. They are familiar with all business operations, which is critically important for assessing environmental risks.

Risk identification and assessment techniques could be expanded to examine adverse environmental effects. Supplier networks, manufacturing processes, and distribution channels could be analyzed for situations that produce environmental damage. For instance, organizations committed to environmental management are looking upstream in their various business sectors to eliminate potentially harmful situations. Companies such as International Paper and Westvaco have eliminated elemental chlorine in their paper bleaching mills so that it will not cause environmental harm downstream.

Loss control, including loss elimination, prevention, and reduction, is a key component of environmental management. For instance, the European Union's environmental policy calls for a high level of protection, rectifying environmental damage at the source, and taking preventive action. Loss control is particularly important and cost-effective with the environment, because once a harmful substance gets into the air, waterways, soils, and aquifers, it becomes extremely difficult, costly, and often impossible to remove.

Loss control is a key risk management tool that can be used to control environmentally harmful activities. Linda Bagneschi, an environmental consultant, emphasizes that "from a risk management standpoint, source reduction is preferred to recycling and treatment options, because it is likely to pose the lowest environment risk." Today, industries are developing new technologies to reduce the generation of hazardous waste and toxic discharges. The chemical industry alone has reduced emissions 60 percent in the last six years.

British Petroleum provides another loss control example related to a potentially even greater environmental problem. In a speech by CEO John Browne, British Petroleum became the first oil company to publicly acknowledge that greenhouse gases are contributing to global warming, and that the burning of fossil fuels, like oil, will need to be reduced. At the same time, Browne saw the alternative energy source of solar power as a business opportunity: British Petroleum now has 10 percent of the world solar power market.

Disaster planning is a critical component of an organization's risk management program. Tornadoes, hurricanes, floods, and fires, as well as terrorist activity and criminal acts such as bombings and kidnappings, have been the traditional focus; but recently, environmental disasters have been included within the scope of disaster planning.

For instance, in the United States disaster plans are mandated for facilities producing or transporting hazardous substances under the Emergency Planning and Community Right-to-Know Act. Recently, the European Union expanded the Seveso Directive, originally introduced in 1982 following the 1976 major dioxin accident in Italy. The new directive will require many more companies to institute major accident prevention policies, including a requirement to prepare on- and off-site emergency plans.

Product design and assessment, including quality control, is another crucial aspect of the risk management process. Products liability has been one of the largest loss producers for risk managers. In the environmental area, the Design for Environment (DFE) program facilitates the creation of products that are easier to recover, reuse, or recycle. All the effects that a product could have on the environment are examined during its design phase, which includes a full assessment of all inputs to the product and analyzes how customers use and dispose of it.

It seems reasonable that a products liability control program could be coordinated with a DFE program to produce products that minimize both liability claims and environmental harm. Risk managers would obviously have to rely on DFE experts and consultants, but given their substantial expertise in products liability, they can and should be part of DFE teams.

Monsanto provides a relevant example. Chairman Robert Shapiro is one of the leading proponents of sustainable development. In 1997, he spun off the chemical business, Monsanto's original core business, to focus on its agricultural, food, and pharmaceutical units. In August of 1998, Monsanto was the first to genetically engineer corn resistant to root worm, which causes $1 billion in damages annually to corn crops. Root-worm-proof corn will mean farmers can avoid the expense and potential hazards of using insecticides, thus decreasing Monsanto's products liability exposure from these toxins. (Editor's note: We would be remiss not to mention the fact that there is substantial controversy arising out of recent research revealing that genetically engineered crops may produce a wind-borne pollen that can kill monarch butterflies. Monsanto is one of the major producers of Bt corn, the crop in question.)

When DFE programs are combined with ecolabeling, a strong marketing tool with positive business effects is created. Germany is particularly active in this area. It is estimated that some 80 percent of potential customers recognize the Blue Angel label and one-third are influenced by it in their purchasing behavior.

Risk financing associated with environmental risks is innovative and dynamic. The risk manager's skills are increasingly important in assuring that the business takes appropriate advantage of developing risk financing arrangements.

The environmental insurance markets have expanded beyond EIL and other legal liability products. A wide variety of coverages are now available and growth is particularly evidenced in real estate–related coverages like environmental remediation insurance and stop-loss (cost cap) policies. Competition in environmental insurance markets is now vigorous, with active involvement from four major insurers: AIG, Reliance, Zurich, and Kemper.

The development of more compulsory environmental liability insurance laws will require the attention of risk managers. For instance, for companies operating in Germany, the Environmental Liability Act, which took effect in 1991, requires some 20,000 facilities to carry environmental coverage. This became the impetus for the HUK-Verband (Association of Casualty Insurers) to take the lead in developing a stand-alone environmental liability insurance policy.

Climate change and global warming have the potential to

greatly increase property damages and resulting business interruptions due to natural disasters. Risk managers will need to be alert to changing risk patterns and adjust their risk financing accordingly. To date, such risk financing innovations as catastrophe bonds, catastrophe options on the Chicago Board of Trade, and the California Earthquake Authority have primarily affected insurers and reinsurers, but risk managers may directly employ similar measures in the future.

Finally, one of the more exciting risk financing areas involves the transfer or capping of environmental liabilities via innovative risk financing contracts. Sedgwick has put together two substantial deals involving T&N and Hanson P.L.C. T&N, a former British asbestos manufacturer, now in auto parts, effectively capped its asbestos liabilities through a finite risk reinsurance arrangement. In the event that future asbestos claims exceed a certain amount retained by T&N, Sedgwick placed $825 million of excess coverage with a group of three reinsurers, Munich Re, Swiss Re, and Centre Re. On the day the deal was completed, T&N stock rose 22 percent.

In the second deal, Sedgwick assembled $800 million in environmental remediation coverage for Hanson P.L.C., a British building-materials company. The policy, the largest of its type ever written, will provide coverage to pay for any cost overruns associated with the cleanup of some 200 sites nationwide, including several state and federal Superfund sites. It is reinsured by Centre Solutions, a member of the Zurich Group, and European Re, a member of Swiss Re Group.

Challenges Ahead

In his *Harvard Business Review* article, "Beyond Greening: Strategies for a Sustainable World" (January 1997), Stuart Hart states that "sustainable development will constitute one of the biggest opportunities in the history of commerce." These opportunities will include a place for risk managers. To maintain business growth within environmental constraints is going to require fundamental changes in business processes and living practices. Risk managers can respond to these shifts with innovations to reduce, manage, and monitor environmental risks for both organizations and the environment, including natural resources, and public health and welfare.

As noted, corporate involvement in environmental management is increasing. While some have become involved because "it is the right thing to do," most have discovered that it also makes good business sense. Costs can be reduced, company value enhanced, and profits increased. A positive environmental philosophy and strategy can be a substantial competitive advantage, particularly if a company is the first within an industry to adopt such policies.

It will be important for risk managers and others to be creative and take the initiative to involve themselves in developing environmental management systems. Currently, a large number seem to be out of the environmental loop. As reported in the 1997 Cost of Risk Survey, risk managers have primary responsibility for environmental risk control/engineering (claims management) in only 31 percent (39.7 percent) of those firms surveyed. If not leading, risk managers need to at least be part of the firm's environmental, health, and safety department and environmental team if they expect to be involved in developing corporate environmental management systems.

In the 1990s we witnessed the development of holistic or integrated risk management. The hazard, legal, and operational risks traditionally handled by risk managers are being combined with financial (e.g., currency, interest rate, credit), business, and political risks to construct an overall risk profile of a firm.

Similarly, internal environmental risks are now being combined with external environmental risks to create overall management systems that are an integral part of business and strategic management. As holistic risk management has provided challenges and opportunities, so environmental management provides the possibility for worthwhile contribution.

Read More About It

Breathing Easy

Sandy Moretz
Reprinted with permission from *Risk Management* magazine, February 1999.
Copyright 1999 by Risk Management Society Publishing. All rights reserved.
For more information call 212.286.9364. www.rims.org/rmmag

It is widely recognized that a safe working environment reduces employee accidents and illnesses, minimizes turnover, sustains worker productivity and morale, and helps manage variable costs such as workers compensation. More and more companies are investing in products and services geared toward creating optimal working conditions. This worthwhile trend, however, brings increased job complexity for safety professionals; providing a safe environment can be a daunting task for a risk manager, who often wears several hats. How do you make the right decisions about worker protection, keep up-to-date with Occupational Safety and Health Administration (OSHA) regulations, and handle the mountains of required paperwork?

The Challenge

To ensure proper protection, the risk manager or safety professional must assess each job, determine what is needed, and document all decisions.

Don Garvey, senior construction industrial hygienist at St. Paul Fire & Marine Insurance Company, notes that the construction industry presents unique challenges to the safety professional. "On a typical construction job, today you have a vacant lot, tomorrow you have a hole in the ground and a couple of weeks later walls are going up. The workplace changes by the hour." These jobs frequently involve exposure to airborne contaminants that require workers to wear respiratory protection.

Documentation is a critical part of safety management. As Garvey points out, when faced with an inspection by an OSHA compliance officer, nothing counts "until it's on paper." If you can't produce a document that proves you did fit testing, for example, you could be in trouble. OSHA's respirator standard requires the employer to develop a written program that includes sections on respirator selection, medical evaluations, fit testing, use in both routine and emergency situations, maintenance, training, and evaluation of the program's effectiveness. There are extensive record-keeping requirements as well. Fit testing, training, exposure assessment, respirator selection, and program evaluation records must be kept.

Record keeping is an issue for small and large businesses alike. In small businesses the owner is also often the safety director. Paper and pencil might be used for keeping records. When Garvey was a safety professional in a Honeywell facility, he kept a paper list of names and dates tacked on a bulletin board to remind him when employees needed respirator fit testing. "At my facility we had fifty people trained for respirators and our in-house policy called for an annual fit test," Garvey recalls. He'd check the list every week or so to see whose test was coming up soon, but it was hardly a fail-safe measure.

The issues are different but no easier for large businesses. A risk manager for a large contractor can be responsible for hundreds of employees on job sites all over the country—sites that might change daily.

Regulations

As a former OSHA compliance officer in the state of Washington, Garvey is familiar with the difficulties businesses have understanding federal regulations, which tend to be long and confusing. Tracking changes in the regulations is also a challenge. In 1998, when OSHA revised its twenty-seven-year-old respirator standard, the agency pointed out that construction contractors and general contractors/operative builders would be among the groups most affected by the changes because of their high use of respirators.

Solid Software

Garvey was at an American Industrial Hygiene conference a couple of years ago when he first became aware of a software package developed to help companies comply with OSHA respiratory protection regulations. "I thought this could be very helpful to contractors," Garvey says, "because a lot of them need help writing respirator programs and keeping track of employee records, such as who's had fit testing, medical evaluations, and training." The compliance software looked like a good solution. It can walk a risk manager step-by-step through what needs to be done. You don't have to be an expert in the regulations to complete the process.

The initial software program, however, was geared toward general industry. Garvey points out that contractors won't use safety materials or programs developed for general industry because they simply don't apply. In general industry, for the most part, the facility environment doesn't change much from one day to another. But in the typical construction job, the workplace is in constant flux.

Garvey approached a software development specialist about adapting the program for the construction industry. With one of his colleagues, construction services manager Dale Daul, he helped translate the general industry terminology into more specific construction industry terminology.

Benefits of the Program

According to Garvey, the software makes complying with industry standards for contractors easier and quicker. "For example, instead of having to go to a file drawer and flip through files to see if John Smith has been medically evaluated to wear a respirator, the safety director can click, click, click and pull up the whole history of John Smith."

The software is especially helpful in reminding safety professionals when workers need annual training and fit testing, two requirements of OSHA's revised standard. "Each time you boot up the program, it brings up a file that says Sally Doe and Joe Smith are due for fit testing within twenty-five or ten days, et cetera," Garvey says. The audit trail also is a popular feature. You click on an audit prep screen and the program prepares a report for an auditor.

"Well-designed health and safety software helps assure safety program administrators that the process of following good industrial hygiene practice has been adopted," says Dr. Sharon Garber, a software development specialist in 3M's Occupational Health and Environmental Safety Division. "Further, it instills confidence that a good logic trail and documentation are in place, and helps simplify program compliance in the event of an audit by an outside party."

"A well-developed safety and health program at the company level can have a tremendous impact on reducing the overall burden of illness and injury in the workplace," agrees Dr. Donald Bodeau, an occupational medicine physician at Luther Midelfort, a Mayo Health Systems integrated hospital and clinic in Wisconsin. "It can reduce direct costs as well as insurance premium dollars."

Bodeau, who often helps industrial clients choose the proper respirator for a job, notes that respirator safety is a particular concern for contractors because of the many airborne contaminants to which their workers are exposed. Since construction job sites change constantly—and permanent methods to rid the air of contaminants are impractical—respirators are routinely used to help protect workers. "I think of a construction site as an uncontrolled environment, in contrast to an industrial factory, which at least lends itself to engineering controls and air sampling methods," Bodeau says.

Software helps free up time for the risk manager to focus on other tasks. To be effective, respirators must be chosen according to what contaminants a worker will be exposed to, and they must fit well and be worn properly. That means they will vary by job and have to be fitted to each worker individually, inspected periodically, and discarded or have filters and cartridges changed when necessary.

"You can write a very nice respirator program with a computer and audit it very nicely, but you've still got to go out and do things like medical evaluations and fit testing," Garvey notes. "And a computer will not go out on the job site and remind a worker to put on his respirator. It will not get the worker to wear the respirator or enforce its proper use. That's still up to company management. It's important to understand both the benefits and limitations of software as a tool in order to use it wisely,'' he concludes.

It's clear, however, that for companies whose employees wear respirators, software technology offers a time- and effort-saving advantage.

Read More About It

Out of the Dark: Shedding New Light on Risk Management Training

Harvey B. Lermack
Reprinted with permission from *Risk Management* magazine, October 1999. Copyright 1999 by Risk Management Society Publishing. All rights reserved. For more information call 212.286.9364. www.rims.org/rmmag

How much does your organization spend annually, in human and financial terms, on personal injuries, insurance, environmental, property loss and damage, fines, and penalties? How does this affect productivity, morale, and the attainment of your organizational objectives? How much improvement could you enjoy if every member of the workforce were properly trained to identify, prevent, and manage risks in their workplace?

Traditional safety, environmental, and health training programs often do not provide the results your organization requires. You should have an overall strategy to change the culture, with training properly designed and delivered according to that strategy. Otherwise, you are not enjoying the maximum benefit from your investment and are probably wasting a significant amount of time and money.

As risk managers, we are responsible for identifying the most significant threats to our workforce. We must also make sure that people know how to prevent accidents or manage them properly when they do occur. The stakes are high-potential injuries to our employees, damage to our customers' products and businesses, negative impact on our communities, and costs to our company and shareholders.

As a major transportation company, Conrail has implemented an innovative approach to risk management training, covering virtually the entire workforce. As a result, we have substantially reduced our accidents, injuries, and cost of risk.

Conrail is a class 1 freight railroad that employs a large, decentralized workforce. Employees frequently work alone or in very small groups, with little direct supervision and a great deal of self-direction. Everything they do can have a dramatic impact on safety, environmental quality, and our products and services. So, it is vital that they understand the full weight of their decisions.

As with many railroads and other companies, Conrail traditionally had a rules-driven approach to regulatory training. Training materials were developed and delivered by subject matter experts, in response to the rules of the Federal Railway Administration, Environmental Protection Agency, Occupational Safety and Health Administration, and others in the alphabet soup of regulatory agencies. The training did not always address the most significant needs of our employees, and [it] did not leverage available time and resources. In fact, we often followed what I call the three R's method of training:

- Rules-driven
- Regulatory
- Reactive

In 1994, we determined that a significant change in approach was required to improve our safety performance. Facing similar issues in many different areas, the company brought those groups together into a new risk management department, reporting directly to the executive in charge of operations. In this way, we were able to take a holistic approach to risk management and prioritize and address the most significant issues with the optimal allocation of resources. The new department eventually included safety, environmental, health, damage prevention, hazardous materials management, police, industrial hygiene, claims and litigation, and insurance.

We embarked on a wide range of programs and processes to improve our performance and to ensure that all the decisions made by Conrail employees were risk-adjusted. Top management became heavily involved. We developed new incentives for people at every level. We measured our performance and provided continuous feedback and reinforcement for our employees. Most significantly, we improved our communications and training processes.

In revising our approach, we drew on all our skills and resources to develop a training curriculum that would attain our objectives and improve performance. The resulting three-step process is described [here].

Three Training Steps to Improved Safety and Risk Performance

- *Awareness*. Identify, assess, and control on-the-job risk.
- *Occupational*. Target preventive training to specific job groups.
- *Behavioral*. Involve everyone in risk management to change behaviors.

A New Approach

To leverage our limited resources, we enlisted the help of subject matter experts, client departments, and training department specialists. We formed teams to develop and deliver training to each key department in the railroad.

Members of the development teams attended course design training together, regardless of their experience. The teams then shared their various perspectives—the client departments described the key risks their people face; the subject matter experts explained the regulatory requirements that address those risks; and the training experts talked about how to adapt effective adult learning principles. With this foundation, the teams set out to design and develop effective training techniques.

In each department and every division, we identified and

recruited opinion leaders with the aptitude and attitude to serve as volunteer trainers. These included over 250 line workers (such as engineers and conductors), supervisors, safety committee members, and managers. Every trainer received extensive content and platform skills training that emphasized on-the-job awareness, occupational training, and behavioral safety.

Awareness

Each member of the workforce learned how to identify, assess, and manage risks at their workplace in one- or two-day training programs. Using adult learning techniques, we created scenarios directly related to their daily work, videos, overheads, and case studies. The small training teams then worked together to draw upon their experience to identify and assess the key risks they could face on the job. The remainder of each session was spent discussing how to prevent and manage these risks.

This accelerated learning helps employees create a framework that builds on their previous experiences and training. The training need not be expensive—just relevant to the work. It has certainly helped our employees to better understand their work environment and the impact they can have on safety.

Occupational Training

The training development teams also worked together to pinpoint the required regulatory and preventive training. They analyzed the key risk issues, the relevant regulatory training requirements, and our prevention priorities. They reviewed our current training, looking for overlaps, gaps, and redundancies. They then developed a matrix of training needs that focused on the key risks of the client departments. Finally, they came up with delivery plans to provide maximum coverage, leverage available resources, and minimize the time required of the trainees.

Behavior Management

Once the training is complete, it is important to ensure that the new skills are actually transferred back to the job. At Conrail, we use behavioral safety. In a nutshell, we have everyone in the company involved in identifying key behaviors, observing the employees practicing them, and providing feedback and positive reinforcement. In that way, we are able to measure the effectiveness of our training efforts at the workplace.

What You Can Do

You can quickly assess whether you can improve your organization's performance with a similar approach. Here are some basic questions to get you started.

1. Do all your employees understand the basic concepts of risk management (e.g., how to identify, prevent, and manage risks)? Do they feel empowered to assess their own worksite and to address the appropriate issues to prevent accidents from occurring?
2. Does your regulatory training target the people who actually need it? Is someone responsible for ensuring that there are no gaps or overlaps? Do you leverage the resources and training time to their best use?
3. Who conducts the training? Is it done in-house or is it outsourced? Are complete records and course evaluations maintained, and are materials revised as necessary?
4. Is your training appropriate for adults? Is it a data dump, or do people really participate and achieve long-term learning? Are your instructors qualified, and does the training result in actual behavior change on the job?

By implementing an integrated risk management training program, you can reduce injuries, incidents, and expenses. (The training approach described in this article won the 1997 Award for Outstanding Performer in Training from Lakewood Publications.)

4

Asset Exposures to Risk

Certainly we worry about tangible property—planes, equipment, hangars, and so on–but our real concern is continuity planning; that is, what happens after a loss. We really can't afford to be down for long, but ironically, new management practices like just-in-time have actually cut our margin for risk and error. As a result, the continuity issue has only gotten more serious for us over time.

Risk Manager
Major American Airline

As a manager of real estate, preservation of property is important, business interruption to our company and customers is yet more important, but loss of life or limb is our paramount concern.

Risk Manager
Property Management Firm

Perspectives

Top Priority on Bottom Line

Sally Roberts
Reprinted with permission from *Business Insurance,* March 20, 2000.
© Crain Communications Inc. All rights reserved.

As the concept of enterprise risk management continues to evolve, risk managers are beginning to focus on the exposures most likely to affect their company's bottom line—namely, business risks.

Although exposures such as decreases in customer demand, increases in costs of raw materials, and problems in distribution have been traditionally absorbed by corporations as the costs of doing business, there is little doubt that these risks can severely affect earnings.

In fact, New York–based Mercer Management Consulting recently found that, of the 100 Fortune 1000 companies that suffered losses of more than 25 percent of shareholder value from 1993 to 1998, 95 percent of the losses were primarily caused by strategic, operational, or financial risks. The most frequent primary cause of the stock drops—occurring at twenty-four of the 100 corporations studied—was a shortfall in customer demand, Mercer found. Competitive pressure and the cost of overruns were the primary causes for stock drops at twelve and eleven companies, respectively.

Experts say that, as more corporations focus on their business risks and as technology continues to evolve to better identify and analyze these risks, more corporations are exploring various risk transfer options. In addition to several stand-alone policies that offer insurance protection when such business risks trigger earnings shortfalls, several companies, including Winnipeg, Manitoba–based United Grain Growers Ltd. and Boston-based FMR Corp., have recently transferred operational risks to the insurance market as part of overall customized enterprise risk programs.

Experts say that these types of deals remain more the exception than the rule in the market right now, but the trend is gathering momentum.

"We see the theoretical becoming more of the practical every day," said John Gantz, a principal in charge of global corporate marketing for Swiss Re New Markets in New York, which helped craft the programs for UGG [United Grain Growers] and FMR [Fidelity Investments].

Carl Groth, senior vice president and alternative risk transfer director for Willis Risk Solutions in New York, which worked with Swiss Re on UGG's program, noted that "most companies out there are taking a look, at various levels of interest. It is new, and any given company has a number of priorities," Groth said. "Some companies have a casual interest, and some have a serious interest."

"I see operational risks and operational risk transfer to the insurance industry as a big deal, and it will be a bigger deal in the future," predicted Bernard Friemann, president of the financial risk management division of Reliance National Insurance Co. in New York. "There is no doubt in my mind that the snowball is starting to gather speed as more of these types of solutions are done," Friemann said.

Marty Scherzer, managing director of Marsh Risk Finance, a unit of Marsh Inc. in New York, said that "firms are recognizing that there are more opportunities to address risks that they previously thought were unaddressable." As a result, "firms have devoted more senior management time, more money, and a higher level of interest in trying to figure out ways . . . to address those risks."

At the same time, "the market is developing specialty products to address business risk problems and is working with clients in a consultative mode to customize solutions with insurance, capital markets, and risk mitigation techniques," Scherzer said.

Experts stress, however, that the focus on business risks is a by-product of the larger enterprise risk management movement, which many employers have recently embraced. Regardless of whether a company transfers its business risks, it is important that it analyze its entire risk landscape and truly understand the risk drivers in the company.

When the concept of enterprise risk management first emerged, the focus was whether a corporation was purchasing risk transfer products in the most-efficient way, explained Randy Nornes, managing director and enterprise risk practice leader for Aon Group Inc. in Chicago. Within the last year, however, "the focus has shifted dramatically," he said. Senior management is now viewing risk as a critical element of the business and "as a baseline decision-making tool," he said.

This is a cultural change within corporations to take a team approach to viewing risks, he said. Whether those risks are eventually transferred into an integrated policy or a stand-alone insurance policy doesn't matter, Nornes said. "It's a huge breakthrough for firms to want to look at all the risks of the corporation."

This presents opportunities for risk managers, according to Susan R. Meltzer, president of the Risk & Insurance Management Society Inc. [RIMS]. "The need for risk management has been underlined at the senior management and the board of directors level," she said. "The key that has come out of this is that the board needs to understand the full array of risks that face the organization. Risk managers need to adapt their understanding of risk and their ability to report on risk in a way that is meaningful to senior management," said Meltzer, who is assistant vice president, insurance and risk management for Sun Life Assurance Co. of Canada in Toronto.

United Grain Growers took a team approach when it formed an executive committee to reassess its total risk portfolio about three years ago, explained Michael J. McAndless, risk manager. "This is not a one-person initiative," he said. "It's really a cross-functional, multirisk, multifaceted job that requires skills brought to the table by the treasurer, the CFO, the risk manager, the operational managers, and analytical types."

After identifying forty-seven areas of risk, UGG's committee narrowed the list to the top six. Of those six, only one—environmental risk—was traditionally insurable. After determining that it could manage four of the other operating risks internally, UGG decided that in addition to environmental risk, it needed to try to transfer its weather exposure off its balance sheet.

In the end, UGG developed a three-year integrated program that covers most of its property/casualty exposures, as well as coverage for downturns in its grain-handling business. Since variables other than weather existed that affected UGG's grain-handling revenue, the policy is triggered when its grain-handling volume falls below a volume index set by a Canadian national commission.

FMR Corp., better known as Fidelity Investments, also recently secured a catastrophe program that includes coverage for such operational risks as system failures, counterparty risk, and rogue trading within the company.

While operational risk coverage for UGG and FMR is part of larger enterprise programs, at least one industry is taking advantage of stand-alone earnings protection insurance policies. A number of ski resorts have bought policies to hedge one of their biggest business risks—drops in the number of paid skier-days, said Joseph M. McNasby, president of MDM Group Associates Inc., a Steamboat, Colorado–based managing general agency.

Three years ago, MDM developed an all-risk earnings protection policy that covers a ski resort's loss of income due to a significant reduction in paid skier-days resulting from any cause or combination of causes not specifically excluded. These causes may include a lack of snow, ice storms, road closures, a poor economy, airline strikes, and problems with airports. The policy excludes property damage, fraud, pollution, and other losses that are within the resort's control.

"This takes the crystal ball away from the business owner," McNasby said of the policy. "If you can protect yourself from all these unknowns, then you can eliminate a substantial amount of financial risk that can severely affect the value of the company's earnings."

MDM's policy is triggered when the number of paid skier-days—minus the number of season tickets and complimentary tickets issued—falls below a number agreed upon at the beginning of the ski season. The policy, which is subject to deductibles and coinsurance, has limits up to $50 million and is underwritten through Lloyd's of London syndicates and other London offices of various insurers, McNasby said. It is distributed through other brokers, such as Aon Group Inc., Willis Group Ltd., and Acordia Inc.

Vail Resorts Inc., which bought the earnings protection policy for the first time this season, announced in January that the policy will help the resort offset lower-than-expected financial results for its 1999/2000 ski season. Crested Butte Mountain

Resort in Crested Butte, Colorado, also bought the policy for the first time this season.

[MDM's] McNasby said that eighteen major ski resorts have bought the policy, and "we're getting calls like it's no tomorrow from the rest of them." In addition to ski resorts, MDM also is targeting airlines, cruise ships, state fairs, and expositions. Like the paid skier-day policy, policy triggers are based on the number of passengers and attendees.

In addition to MDM, at least two other insurers offer stand-alone earnings protection policies that cover business risks. Tamarack American, New York–based Great American Insurance Co.'s specialty unit, recently unveiled a policy called Revenue-Guard, which offers up to $50 million in coverage against revenue hits from any of nine defined enterprise loss events. These events include losses caused by new market competitors, currency fluctuations, and changes in consumer buying habits.

Sherif M. Zakhary, senior vice president and head of Tamarack's executive protection/financial products division, said that although Tamarack has yet to bind a policy, he is "more than optimistic" that it will this year. "We are well in the process of getting the applications filled out and educating companies and brokers that are interested," Zakhary said.

Meanwhile, Reliance National last year introduced an "Enterprise Earnings Protection Insurance" policy that responds to an earnings shortfall due to operational business risks, financial exposures, and/or natural and manmade hazards beyond management's control. The all-risk policy has limits of up to $50 million. While the insurer has yet to bind a full EEPI policy, Reliance National is confident that it will do so in 2000.

"During the last year, we spent most of our time educating brokers and clients about the concept of our product," Friemann said. "We found that lots of brokers and clients already had initiatives going to identify operational risks and were doing things to try to understand, mitigate, and decide whether risk transfer was the right answer," he said. "It's a big thing to bite off and chew, and it takes a while to get your mind around the concept . . . and get comfortable with the issue."

Introduction

Chapters 2 and 3 present and discuss the subjects of risk assessment and risk control. Various methods of identifying, analyzing, measuring, and treating risks are considered and explained—but the nature and character of the risk exposures themselves are never explained. A more thorough discussion of the risk exposure begins in this chapter and extends through Chapter 5.

The discussion of assessment in Chapter 2 introduces the idea of exposure to risk, and it is noted there that exposure is a key ingredient in the concept of Organization Risk Management (ORM). Absent exposure, an organization risk manager mainly is unconcerned about risks and uncertainties.

Understanding the nature of exposure is important. In a broad sense, an entire firm is an exposure, but this notion provides little technical insight into the nature of particular exposures to risk. A much more meaningful approach, suggested in Chapter 2, relies upon a categorization of exposures into asset and liability groupings. The five categories are

Asset Exposures	*Liability Exposures*
Physical Asset Exposures	Legal Liability Exposures
Financial Asset Exposures	Moral Liability Exposures
Human Asset Exposures	

This chapter introduces the asset exposures, while Chapter 5 deals with liability exposures. Readers should note that some imprecision will arise in the use of these classification systems. For instance, is workplace safety a human asset issue or a legal liability issue? The practical answer, of course, is that it is both. While this may be a fact of some concern to scholars, it will be of little consequence in this book since it only really matters that an assessment methodology identify workplace safety as a risk management issue. The fact that a situation can arise both in the context of human asset exposure analysis and in legal liability exposure analysis only reinforces the notion that workplace safety is an important issue.

The intent of this chapter and the next is not to achieve comprehensiveness in the treatment of the exposure classifications. Rather, the purpose is to provide a broad frame of reference with respect to organizational exposures to risk and to have readers develop an appreciation for two key aspects of risk exposure:

- The fundamental nature of each exposure to risk
- The matter of exposure valuation

Physical Asset Exposures

Conventionally, traditional risk management has concerned itself with the protection of physical assets, particularly regarding risks leading to direct physical harm of those assets. Not surprisingly, traditional risk management practices in this area have been shaped by the notion of "insurable risks." Indeed, probably nowhere else in all of risk management is insurance more influential in forming the concepts, terminology, and parameters of discussion than in the area of physical asset management.

Terms such as "direct, indirect, and time element losses" will be important to the readers' understanding of physical asset exposures, as will be the variety of valuation methods that have arisen from insurance practice. However, the insurance-based frame of analysis has limitations, especially regarding the nature and character of speculative risks. There is not a widely accepted language in the risk management field to discuss physical assets in the context of their contribution to productivity or profitability. This is not to say that such language does not exist elsewhere—it does—but it is accurate to say that concerns about upside potential have not been part of the traditional risk management world.

Of course, consistent with all other changes occurring in business, the barriers that exist between pure and speculative risks also are falling. For instance, when a professional sports franchise considers its participation in the development of a new sports facility, it is rather limiting to look at the facility only with respect to its ability to attract hazard-driven risks (e.g., fires, vandalism, windstorm, or earthquakes). Risk factor–driven risks also attach to the facility, and the distinctions seemingly fail to warrant separate examination. For example, seating capacity—which has a direct impact on profitability—cannot be separated from physical safety and premises security considerations. They all are part of a singular decision.

Because risk managers are concerned about all risks, the discussion that follows seeks to reorient traditional language in a way that opens full consideration of the wide range of effects of risk on physical assets.

How Are Physical Asset Exposures Classified?

There are numerous ways that one may categorize the wide range of physical assets a firm could possess or for which it would have responsibility. The more salient of these approaches are:

1. Property asset type
2. Cause-of-loss (gain) type
3. Loss (gain) type
4. Interest

Property Asset Type

The simplest form of categorization is by property classification type. Physical assets are classified broadly as either *real assets* or *personal assets*. Real property refers to land, fixed structures on that land, and—more or less—attached appurtenances of those structures. Personal property basically is everything else.

A slightly different wording would characterize property as either fixed or movable, and this slight change in the language more plainly reveals a core risk management concern. That is, although exposure to risk is changeable, a fixed asset's exposure to risk is more constant and knowable than is an asset whose physical location changes. Portability introduces a new dimension to the nature and character of risk.

The fixed and movable property concepts do belie a strong insurance influence. Historically, underwriters were uncomfortable with assets that moved from one place to another. Simply put, it was more difficult to ascertain the likelihood of harm. Because the insuring of movable property required specialized knowledge, the development of the insurance industry followed two parallel tracks—one dealing with fixed property (e.g., fire insurance) and one dealing with movable property (e.g., marine insurance). Although the separation between the two tracks is nearly imperceptible to the outsider today, the problematic distinctions are still manifested in policy language, exclusions, pricing, and even claims management procedures.

Cause-of-Loss (Gain) Type

This typology is based upon the nature of the peril or opportunity that affects or may affect a physical asset. There are a number of ways that perils can be broadly classified. Somewhat consistent with the language Chapter 2 introduces relative to risk assessment, one can describe peril categories as *natural hazard–based* or *behavioral hazard–based*. Perils arising from natural hazards are generally obvious to most readers and include forest fires, earthquakes, freezing weather conditions, and hurricanes. Behavioral hazard–based perils actually have intuitively obvious illustrations (e.g., vandalism, riots, assassination, or theft), but also include a range of broad social, political, and economic phenomenon that arise from collective behavioral influences. Changes in consumer preferences for, say, a particular product certainly are the result of individual changes in preference, but it is the accumulation of changes in behavior and preference that create the risk for a firm. Likewise, investment behavior of an individual may be linked to the overall behavior of the investment marketplace, but the aggregated behavior is distinct from individual behavior. Thus, behavior hazard–based perils include phenomena that are not directly traceable to an individual's behavior, but are nevertheless the result of it.

One could make the exact same argument about *risk factor–based opportunities*. A business located on a beautiful lake with recreational potential may find that natural risk factor opportunities may be exploited to make the firm more attractive to potential employees. Behavioral risk factor–based opportunities might be seen in changes in brand loyalty among customers.

Type of Loss (or Gain)

Physical assets can be typed by the nature of the impact of peril/opportunity on the asset. These impacts would be direct, indirect, and consequential. *Direct impacts* would be an actual physical result—a delivery van is damaged in an accident, or heavy snowfall improves the quality of the skiing season for a resort in Colorado. *Indirect impacts* would be those that influence the value of an asset without directly or physically affecting that asset—the destruction of one part of a building may lead to the tearing down of the undamaged portion, or the rerouting of traffic because of highway construction might benefit a resort by bringing more travelers its way. *Consequential impacts* (often called net income, or time element impacts) refer to effects that occur as a result of a direct or indirect impact—a fire at corporate headquarters means that the business must rent a temporary facility while the new building is constructed, or the heavy snowfall season generates higher revenues for the ski resort over an extended period of time.

Interest

It certainly is in keeping with the COCA (contracts, obligations, commitments, and arrangements) view of organizations to observe that the best perspective of physical assets is not obtained by considering their tangible characteristics alone, but by understanding the enforceable interests that attach to physical assets. This is especially important when considering the matter of exposure, because in a practical sense, a firm's exposure to risk is dictated by the enforceability of its interests. Put plainly, the loss of

Insights

Managing Operating Risks a Control Issue

Rodd Zolkos

Reprinted with permission from *Business Insurance,* February 28, 2000.

Beyond lessening the direct impact of operating losses, managing operating risks can address another major concern—shareholder reaction to news of the losses.

"There have been small losses that have led to very big reactions in share prices," says Lisa K. Polsky, managing director at Morgan Stanley Dean Witter in New York. "Because when the market thinks you don't have control, they tend to react very dramatically. It's not necessarily the size of the loss, it's how does the market react to the loss of control," Polsky says. "If you get it wrong, it can cost you your business."

Polsky notes that banks have devoted considerable time and effort to managing such exposures as market risk, credit risk, and liquidity risk.

"The new up-and-coming kid on the block is operating risk," she says. Examples of operating risk include error risk; transaction processing risk; technology risk; regulatory risk; fraud risk, such as unauthorized trading; legal risk, such as whether a customer has the authority to trade derivatives; sales practice risk; and accounting risk.

In the banking area, addressing operating risk is "also important because the regulators are telling us it is," Polsky says. "We'd like to solve it before they solve it for us."

In fact, Stefan Walter, assistant vice president at the Federal Reserve Bank of New York, notes that on the international level, as part of an effort to amend the Basle Capital Accord, "A lot of thinking has been going into how to deal with operational risk." The accord is a set of standards set by the central bankers of the G-10 countries addressing capital adequacy and the behavior of international banks.

Walter thinks awareness of operational risk management

"has increased dramatically" within financial institutions. "Clearly, senior management is giving it a lot of attention," Walter says.

Jennifer McElroy, executive vice president at Aon Financial Services Group in New York, suggests that in attempting to define operating risk, "what's important is that the definition be in line with your firm's operating activities." She also suggests that risk managers and their companies view the effort to address operational risk concerns "as just another step" in the move from traditional stand-alone insurance programs to broader enterprise risk/holistic programs.

Polsky notes the importance of finding a way to measure operational risks. "You can't manage it if you can't measure it. But it's impossible, if not impractical, to quantify every type of risk," she says. "The answer, the way we approach it . . . step number one: You have to understand the key drivers of risk in your firm.

"The second thing is that you've got to develop policies around those risks," Polsky says. "And your policies should read like motherhood and apple pie. Once you have your policies, you have to develop procedures around them," she says, noting that it's important to assess whether those procedures are "adequate to control the risk" as well as "are they practical?"

There will always be some exceptions to the procedures within a firm, she says. In some cases, they might not be practical with regard to certain operations; in others, implementing the procedures might be more expensive than the cost of the risk itself.

But any exceptions must be written down and must be approved by senior management, she advises. And, Polsky says, "No one wants to be on the exception list. This isn't the hit parade." Consequently, many of those business areas initially included on the exception list find a way to implement the procedures for their operations before the list makes its way to senior management.

Once the operating risks have been identified and procedures are in place to address them, it's essential to track risks,

Polsky says. In doing so, "You've got to translate that data into information . . . and you must report that information to senior management in a way that they understand it. The next thing is follow-up."

McElroy notes that insurance solutions are being developed to address operational risks, though she cautions, "Obviously, any insurance solution isn't going to represent a perfect, 100 percent hedge."

But Lars Schmidt-Ott, head of the global banking practice at Swiss Re New Markets in New York, says, "The question here is: Can insurance replace your equity and to what extent?" He asks risk managers to imagine that their companies had faced major losses and found themselves needing additional equity. "Do you think that's a good time to go to the market to increase equity?" he asks.

"If you look at insurance as a tool, it has all the benefits that will solve the problem," Schmidt-Ott suggests. With insurance addressing the operating loss, the company's overall profit and loss statement can remain intact.

Schmidt-Ott notes, though, that insurance is not meant to replace the entrepreneurial risk taken by a company's shareholders. "It is also not our intention to guarantee top management bonuses," he says.

In the long run, the development of portfolios of diversified liability classes should allow insurers to take on operating risk at competitive prices, Schmidt-Ott says. "So basically, the insurance industry is in a position to take those risks, price it, and hold it more effectively than the bank."

an expensive piece of construction equipment is defined as much by whether a firm owned, rented, or was borrowing it as by the physical nature of that asset or the manner in which it was lost.

Ownership interest obviously is a key interest in property, and the law clearly delineates the rights and obligations owners have with respect to physical property. However, lenders, tenants, vendors, lessors, contractors, franchise holders, and licensees also may have enforceable interests in some property. The important insight to take away is that the contract-, obligation- commitment-, or agreement-based nature of risk can inform one's thinking about physical asset exposures to risk and (as Chapter 2 mentions) provide the means to managing exposure to physical asset–related risks.

How Are Physical Asset Exposures Valued?

At first blush, one may presume that the matter of valuing physical assets is rather straightforward. The value of a particular asset is a function of its purchase price—or so it may seem.

However, with only a moment's reflection, readers should realize that the purchase price of some asset has very little to do with its value to the organization. It would seem that the value of replacing that asset is more likely to reflect the economic impact of a loss or gain on a firm. Naturally, replacement value is the coin of the realm for insurance companies, and this is no accident. The insurance promise is to "restore loss," and so the valuation challenge is to determine the cost of restoring, replacing, or rebuilding a physical asset. To put it in a slightly different context, the generally accepted method for valuing physical assets is to set a value on that asset at the moment after it has been damaged, destroyed, or lost. As Chapter 7 discusses, there are several approaches to determining a value for replacement, but the idea of replacement cost is important to introduce here.

There is an important extension of the valuation question that must be considered. The valuation challenge really has to be addressed on two levels. The basic level, as mentioned already, is the replacement value—the *intrinsic value* of the asset. The cost of replacing a delivery van is, say, $30,000. The secondary valuation level is the economic value—or *contributory value*—of an asset.

The contributory value of an asset is the value it adds to the organization. For example, the intrinsic value of the aforementioned van is $30,000, whereas the contributory value would be judged by the value that vehicle adds to the customer service performance of the firm (naturally, this valuation has a quantitative and qualitative component). Perhaps a slightly more obvious illustration of this point would be assets that generate a revenue stream. For instance, the value of commercial rental property can be measured on the basis of its cost of replacement, but equally, that facility could be measured by the present value of rental income streams. Which is the right value?

Both are right, but they serve different purposes. The contributory value, though represented as a secondary value previously, probably is the first consideration in determining an asset's value. If that asset does not have a contributory value to the organization, arguably the determination of the intrinsic value is mooted. For example, a firm's vehicle repair shop may contain old or damaged auto parts that would or could not be used in any way. Do those assets contribute to the value of the firm and the services it provides? No, and because that is the case the intrinsic value of those assets is immaterial, unless salvage opportunities exist.

Savvy readers will recognize the discussion of contributory value as a conversational application of the financial concept of "firm value." The value of a publicly traded firm is defined as the present value of future earnings less expenses. Likewise, within a firm the value of each asset is judged by its contribution to firm value. A complete discussion of the firm concept would require an extensive foray into modern finance theory, so it probably is adequate for readers to understand that the notion of contributory value has widely agreed-on theoretical foundations.

Financial Asset Exposures

In a very general sense, financial assets are a subset of physical assets, inasmuch as a stock certificate or a dollar bill are exposed to many of the same perils as are automobiles, computers, and warehouses. Indeed, conventional insurance coverages can be purchased to protect against physical losses (e.g., fires, thefts) of financial assets. However, financial assets are further exposed to a set of risks being characterized as financial risks (e.g., price, credit, interest rate, currency exchange, counterparty, and so on).

With only a bit of reflection, it is easy to realize that the management of financial risks can be extremely important to an organization. After all, a diminishment of value to some asset as the result of a windstorm is not any more (or less) real than a diminishment of value due to a downturn in the economy. Indeed, further reflection may yield the observation that financial risks and traditionally insurable risks probably share common features (more on this later); from a firm's perspective, the principal risk management concern is that an asset may be diminished in value and not so much how that diminishment would occur. Risk managers want to undertake measures to ensure that value is retained within a firm, regardless of the potential causes of loss.

The observation that the management of financial risks is important and shares some common features with insurable risks is interesting, but until recently it was an observation of abstract rather than real concern. That is because financial tools were not widely available to manage many of these financial risks. Of course, the risks themselves existed for hundreds of years, and methods existed within the banking and investment community to limit risk. However, it has been the advancing sophistication of derivative contracts (e.g., forwards, futures, options, and their various permutations) that has allowed greater access to the tools of financial risk management and the formation of markets for pooling and distributing financial risks. This has led to the steady erosion of boundaries between capital markets and the insurance industry. The result has been the emergence of "alternative risk financing," a phenomenon that is meant to suggest tools and products that combine features of financial instruments with insurance (or insurance-like) contracts.

Although in a sense "assets are assets," financial assets possess an important feature distinguishing them from physical assets— their value is derived from some other asset (and that other asset may or may not be possessed by the holder of the financial asset). Certainly this is obvious if we think about, say, a fuel oil futures contract. The contract offers a right to buy or sell oil at some future date and a set price. The price of that contract is based on the price of an underlying asset, the fuel oil itself.

The notion of financial assets as "derivative" creates a further important distinction when we compare physical and financial assets. In a traditional insurable risk, the notion of insurable interest is critical. It means the policyholder has a legal interest in the exposed asset (i.e., if a loss occurs, the insured suffers an economic loss). Insurable interest is crucial in controlling for moral hazard. Policyholders are somewhat less likely to intentionally cause losses to assets where they possess an insurable interest. In the case of financial assets, the moral hazard question is not quite as clearly addressed. Certainly an investor/owner in a company has little interest in that company suffering from negative performance. However, two things can happen that introduce potential moral hazard: First, if investors hold a well-diversified portfolio of investments, they may be much less concerned about the fortunes of any one particular stock. Second, in some instances, certain financial instruments enable an investor to take an opposite position on a particular asset (indeed, this is the particular genius behind most derivative products). In extreme instances, investors even may be hoping for an underlying asset loss to occur.

Another interesting distinction between physical and financial assets is that the latter are both sources of risk and—possibly—risk management tools. Therefore, the purchase of an options contract presents financial risks to the buyer, but (in conjunction with other assets) it also might be an effective risk management tool.

We can conclude that physical asset risks and financial asset risks have important distinctions, but they also have common features that may be amenable to risk management treatment. However, with the bewildering array of financial instruments available, is it possible to generalize about the nature of the exposure?

Yes. Exposure to financial risk arises either from holding financial assets or issuing them. The holding of financial assets is the result of investment policy and practice, while issuing (e.g., bonds) is more commonly the result of capital budgeting policy and practice. This is an important insight in the context of the COCA concept as it suggests risks arising from arrangements entered into to serve the broader purposes of government.

How Are Financial Assets Valued?

The physical and human asset sections of this chapter present discussions on asset valuation. Unfortunately, a similar discussion here will take the book far afield from its central purposes. Indeed, pricing financial assets is a theory-driven business that would require a high degree of technical knowledge among readers before even beginning such a discussion. Let it suffice, then, to give this formal definition of financial assets and their value:

> Financial assets have a value determined at issuance that 1) may nevertheless vary widely during the asset's life due to the market's assessment of its value at any given point in time and that 2) will be influenced by a range of outside factors, such as the state of the economy and governmental monetary policy, which produce risks that 3) may be managed within the market through the use of sound investment management or risk management strategies.

Human Asset Exposures

Humans—whether stakeholders, managers, or employees—constitute the third asset exposure area. Risk produces outcomes that can either diminish or enhance this particular asset in ways that are not dissimilar to physical and financial asset exposures. However, the particulars of this exposure are unique and deserve special attention.

There are numerous perspectives that one can adopt in organizing thinking about human asset exposures. The approach employed in this book is to characterize key human asset risks as:

Insights

Protecting Property in Risk Manager's Plan

Mark A. Hofmann

Keeping not only people but also the company protected from harm is a key part of the risk manager's job. For Theodore G. Jeske, risk manager of Historic Tours of America Inc. [HTA], this means looking at the unique exposures of each city in which HTA does business. In addition to Key West, Florida, where HTA is based, the company also has operations in Boston; San Diego; Savannah, Georgia; and Washington.

In Key West, HTA's biggest exposure is the hurricane risk; in San Diego, a key concern might be earthquakes. Plans currently call for the company's Washington operations to act as the headquarters should a natural disaster strike Key West.

Each operation in a windstorm-exposed area has a list of actions that need to be taken before a storm hits, as well as procedures for what should be done during and after a storm, says Jeske. "Once the storm is past, we get ourselves up as quickly as we can," he says, noting that "we're really at the mercy of the federal emergency management folks," who decide when tourists can reenter an area hit by a storm.

HTA also has earthquake disaster response plans, should a temblor strike its San Diego operation, he says.

The Key West plan was tested during 1998's Hurricane Georges and passed with flying colors, he says. "We were up within a day after Hurricane Georges."

Jeske currently is working with his broker, Willis North America Inc., to ensure that his plans are up to date. And he is working with one of HTA's insurers to update a business continuation plan. "I'm in the process with Royal of developing a new business continuation plan for HTA headquarters, and then we're going to take that same plan and go to each city and work with the general managers on how do we customize it for their city," Jeske says. Royal & SunAlliance Insurance Co. writes HTA's auto, workers compensation, and liability insurance. "I used Royal because they've been so helpful. It was a natural thing to go to their loss control experts," he says.

"I don't want a big thick book that nobody's going to read," he says of a disaster response plan. It would be preferable, he says, to have a thin guide that would provide answers to such questions as: "We had a serious accident, I've got the press calling me. What do I do?"

[He adds,] "Probably one of the biggest challenges is to make sure that I treat each city individually. They're all part of a big corporation, but I want to treat each city individually, because they all have unique exposures."

1. Premature death
2. Disability and poor health
3. Old age and retirement
4. Unemployment
5. Poverty
6. Productivity

Poverty and productivity are unique among these risks in that they may be the result of the other four risks, but also may be viewed as risks in their own right. A brief descriptive discussion of each human asset risk follows:

1. *Premature death.* One may argue that one's own death will always be premature, but the concept of premature death has a rather widely accepted interpretation. It is a death "where outstanding obligations remain." Some books further refine this definition and focus on outstanding economic obligations (e.g., debts, dependent children and spouse, other financial commitments), but this book adopts a broader view to recognize that these obligations may be emotional or psychological, or in other ways noneconomic. Certainly, the death of a popular figure within an organization can affect the morale of surviving members, even when economic impacts are not visible.

2. *Disability and poor health*. The rise in importance of the risks of disability and poor health is partly due, perhaps surprisingly, to society's improved ability to prevent premature death. In the past, accidents resulting in injury to individuals quite often resulted in death to those individuals, mainly because of the unsophisticated nature of medical care. Advancements in public health and sanitation indirectly and directly influenced mortality as well. Illnesses and injuries were caused by poor public sanitation, and this squalor and filth also contributed to heightened mortality rates.

In contrast to premature death, disability and poor health reveals a number of dimensions that contribute to the complexity in managing the risk. One is either alive or dead, but disability and health exist along a spectrum. Furthermore, there are parallel subjective and objective elements to health (or its absence). A person objectively could be in very poor health but "feel" that he or she is doing well. The converse equally can be true.

3. *Old age and retirement*. Old age brings with it the heightened possibility of death, disability, and poor heath, but it also presents the economic challenge of retirement—or, to put it more broadly, economic security. The nature of the challenge presently is confounded by the fact that people generally are living longer and preferring to retire earlier. Supporting retirees once was the exclusive responsibility of younger family members, but of course the mobility of modern society has limited the practical ability of families to meet this challenge, which in turn has given rise to various social insurance and security programs that are intended to (mainly) supplement private saving and support efforts.

Current demographic trends conspire to create an enormous "aging challenge" for societies and organizations. The post–World War II populations within developed nations all have variations of the baby boomers, and so the major economic powers all must struggle with the challenge of managing an increasingly numerous and long-living elderly population. Uncertainty limits society's ability to fully comprehend the impact of this phenomenon since it has never really been seen before in the modern age.

4. *Unemployment*. People may suffer unemployment or under-employment as the result of poor health and disability. Unemployment may also be the result of broad economic and social factors, as well as individual attributes such as ambition, education, and ability.

Like disability and poor health, unemployment differs from premature death because it is a rather complex risk. Duration is an issue of importance in understanding unemployment, as is cause of loss, the nature of the economic environment in which the unemployment is occurring, and contributing social and political factors.

From a business perspective, one may reasonably wonder why a risk manager would choose to be concerned about the risk of unemployment to other employees. The simple answer is that state and federal governments mandate interest through the unemployment insurance program. The less simple answer is that while laying off employees reduces costs and can permit an organization to manage its way through economic difficulties, the dismissal or laying-off of employees can have significant effects on organization performance and effectiveness. Certainly, morale can suffer significantly.

5. *Poverty*. Poverty may happen because of premature death, disability and poor health, old age, or unemployment, but importantly, it also is the result of human capital factors. A person's lack of or level of education can contribute to poverty, and the inability or unwillingness of individuals to "invest" in their own development can lead to inadequate resources.

One must plainly state that sloth and indolence are contributing factors—and indeed, social critics today seem to characterize poverty as being largely the result of laxity of morals, laziness, moral hazard, and a failure to take responsibility for one's own life. While this criticism is partly fair, students of risk management must also recognize that random events, uncontrollable factors, and misfortune often play a part. A challenge for risk managers is to sort through the poverty issue and understand or appreciate the complexity of causes behind poverty.

As a final note, organizations may not believe themselves concerned with poverty, since most of their employees will not be poor. However, many people in poverty are "working poor"; inadequate resources is a day-to-day issue for many employees. In addition, like unemployment, state and federal governments mandate interest in poverty inasmuch as taxes support numerous public assistance programs—including recent innovations in welfare-to-work programs.

6. *Productivity*. Productivity may be broadly construed as the "investment risk" associated with human assets. Training and personal/professional development are investments made in employees with the expectation that they will become more effective, efficient, and useful.

In a sense, reducing the other human asset risks may dramatically influence productivity. This observation reveals a rather traditional risk management orientation, in that it suggests that human asset risk management is best practiced in controlling bad things in the hope of indirectly enhancing good things. However, the Organization Risk Management idea gives voice to the notion that risk management should include efforts that directly contribute to the likelihood of "gains" or even contribute to the magnitude of gains. Certainly training and education are tools that may be properly construed as upside-risk management techniques.

How Are Human Asset Exposures Valued?

Development of a singular method for valuing human life simply is not possible—at least not in any generally accepted sense. Clearly, life does have an economic value, and most risk management measurements of the human asset exposure to risk incorporate fundamental economic considerations. For instance, a widely adopted valuation approach is to estimate the lost earnings of an injured or deceased individual and to produce a "present value" by discounting those future lost earnings.

Readers readily will recognize the flimsiness of the assertion that human life is fully measurable in economic terms. Unfortunately, most management books rather weakly make this point and then wave off the trickier discussion of what the noneconomic value of human life might be. But not here!

Business firms have legally enforceable duties and, of course, the possibility of civil or criminal penalties may be factored into the human life value equation. However, the real concern for risk managers is judging the moral values associated with human well-being. Western societies have universally embraced the idea of the sanctity of life, and though contrary behavior abounds in day-to-day life, one would assume that this is a general valuation assumption that mainly is uncontested. Therefore, risk managers should be cognizant of the fact that:

- Total life value may not be quantified, yet that indeterminate value is nevertheless extremely high.
- The moral value is extremely high, although it is noncomparable in the sense that people will reasonably disagree with the value at the margin.
- Although the moral value is high and noncomparable, efforts to come to terms with these characteristics are important.

An absolutely key point in understanding moral valuation is the recognition that individuals have a fundamental right to contribute to moral valuation of their own life. As a practical matter, this means that individuals should have a role in the evaluation of and subsequent management of risks to which they are exposed. Certainly, individuals should be made aware of risks to which they are exposed, and ideally they should have some say in decisions that affect those risks.

A Final Word About Asset Exposures

Physical, financial, and human assets represent a rich diversity of exposures to risk, and the challenge of managing them in an integrated fashion is not an easy one. However, this chapter has produced a few central themes that must be carried forward.

First, these assets all are "speculative" (readers may want to refer to the Risk Management Terminology section in Chapter 1 for our definition of the term). These assets are susceptible to loss or diminishment, but also may prove to be productive. The goal in managing asset exposures would seem to require a focus on maximizing the productivity of assets through a concerted effort to both minimize possibilities of loss and enhance the likelihood of gain. This proposition, while seemingly simple, shows that the purpose of risk management is not simply (or only) to prevent losses from occurring, but rather to find a philosophical balance between reasonably controlling the downside of risk while not unnecessarily muting the chance of gain. This point is fully discussed in Chapter 8.

Second, "interest" in assets matters. Whether it is an enforceable ownership interest in some building, a legally assertable right that is protected by the Securities and Exchange Commission, or the interests we necessarily have in our own persons, an appreciation of risk and the management of risk needs to incorporate recognition of the relevant interests in play.

Third, morality matters. While certainly true with respect to human assets, morality also matters with the physical and financial assets of a business. These assets are held in trust, and firms have a moral as well as legal responsibility for the responsible use of those assets.

Fourth, measurement of asset values is problematic. In a very narrow sense, the benchmark valuation of any asset is its apparent value after a loss has occurred. However, this statement fails to incorporate a number of salient issues. For one thing, it fails to reflect a value of upside risk, and for another, it does not clearly suggest the effect of indirect and consequential losses on the total cost of loss. In addition, the "post-loss" measure does not address the contributory value issue. To wit, an asset may have a determinable replacement value yet not really contribute anything to the overall value of the firm. Thus, it seems that an asset's value to an organization is—firstly—a function of its contributory value. Only secondarily, then, is its replacement value relevant.

Finally, one can begin to see the point of risk interdependency, which is first raised in Chapter 1 and further developed in Chapter 2. The holding of assets is a strict violation of the concept of independence of exposure to risk if for no other reason than there is a single "holder" (i.e., the firm) of those assets. But more practically, a business easily could be characterized as "clusters of assets"—a warehouse filled with merchandise; a vehicle fleet garage filled with trucks, vans, and all the necessary equipment to support fleet activities. The brief tour of asset exposures provided in this chapter reminds readers that risk's possible impact on assets is complicated and challenging to comprehend—and these possible effects must be considered in any plan to manage the asset exposure to risk.

Read More About It

Reputation at Risk? Software Solutions for Reputation Risk Management

Jim Kartalia
Reprinted with permission from *Risk Management* magazine, May 2000. Copyright 2000 by Risk Management Society Publishing, Inc. All rights reserved. For more information call 212.286.9364. www.rims.org/rmmag

Although the majority of corporate risk managers would not have been directly affected by the riots against the World Trade Organization in Seattle or the protests in Washington, D.C., these events represent ominous red flags. Growing anti-business virulence poses new strategic risks for all corporations.

The introduction of new social responsibility initiatives for businesses, by well-meaning nongovernmental organizations (NGOs), needs to be scrutinized and assessed for the strategic business risks it implies. [See the "New Rules."] Corporations will be held more accountable in their own countries and abroad. And the reactions of aggressive media, regulators, judicial groups, politicians, and juries heighten the chance that business culprits will be punished, as evidenced by the enforcement of tough corporate sentencing, including higher fines and imprisonment for corporate executives.

In response to these evolving concerns, a new business

management concept has developed—reputation management. Because reputation is the most strategic of assets, and thus at the greatest risk, reputation management has generated a great deal of interest. And for risk managers facing these new strategic challenges, the information technology that is coming on stream will be critical for success.

Reputation and Risk Management

Reputation is a broad and far-reaching asset incorporating concepts such as corporate image, goodwill, and brand equity. It is a compilation of views held by all of the firm's stakeholders—investors, clients, customers, employees, suppliers, partners, vendors, media, financial analysts, special interest groups, politicians, labor unions, shareholder activists, and regulators. The growth of the global marketplace, as well as the consequences of instant information exchange, intensifies the critical importance of a firm's reputation.

A recent survey by Lloyd's of London revealed that 62 percent of risk and insurance professionals say e-commerce crime and loss of reputation, or brand, are two of the most significant risks businesses face today. Corporations are now operating in a business climate influenced by major societal themes, including increased scrutiny by investigative reporters, threat of litigation, pressure to adhere to global responsibility standards, and accountability to political and special interest groups.

The positive characteristics of a robust and healthy reputation are undeniable. The flip side is that board members and executives now realize that reputation is a long-term, fragile strategic asset that can be easily tarnished or damaged if not carefully protected. For example, Nike, [Coca-Cola], Waste Management, Commonwealth Edison, Bank of New York, and Sara Lee have spent, collectively, hundreds of millions of dollars building and enhancing their reputations, yet all [have] experienced negative events, resulting in unfavorable stakeholder perceptions, reduced shareholder value, and large and unnecessary expenditures of executive time and resources. The reputation-damaging situations these firms experienced were not acts of God or Mother Nature, they were manmade and entirely preventable had the reputation risks that caused them been identified early enough.

Sara Lee, the well-known food and apparel company, has experienced less than spectacular share performance since 1998, and according to *Forbes* (April 3, 2000), "the troubles [for Sara Lee] started with a few bad hot dogs—the wiener-borne Listeria that killed twenty-one people last year came from Sara Lee plants in Michigan."

Like most corporate crises, the problems for Sara Lee started well before the tragic news—deaths caused by its products broke in the media. According to the *Chicago Tribune* (April 17, 1999), prior inspection reports from the U.S. Department of Agriculture (USDA) document serious problems at the Michigan food plant, including: live and dead cockroaches near ovens; caulking in poor condition, leading to problems with insects; old meat and debris strewn across the floor; unclean areas left for days on end; liquid dripping from refrigeration units directly onto hot dogs; and plastic strips and slivers of metal in meats.

For an executive at a food concern, these problems should be clear warning signals, telltale signs that something is seriously amiss and that a potential reputation disaster is waiting to happen. But what if the executive is unaware of these reputation defects or risks and does not even have the chance to take aggressive, remedial action? What if a USDA inspection report remains "stuck" in the plant manager's inbox? How then does the executive protect consumer health, employee safety, shareholder value, and corporate reputation? How does the risk manager mitigate risk and protect all corporate assets if he or she is completely unaware of existing risks to a major corporate asset—its reputation?

More than likely, the executives at Sara Lee's Chicago headquarters found themselves with this exact problem. They had no early warning of the serious food safety and facility cleanliness problems at their Michigan plant.

It is not only Sara Lee executives who would have benefited from an early warning of reputation risk problems. Would not

Nike executives have benefited from an early warning of worker abuse and safety allegations at their overseas plants? Would not Coca-Cola's upper management have benefited from information regarding problems at their European bottling concerns, or information about domestic racial discrimination allegations? Would not Bank of New York officers have benefited from earlier knowledge of the supervisory lapses that allowed for the embarrassing international money-laundering scheme? And would not have Columbia/HCA Healthcare benefited to learn much earlier than it did about incidents of Medicare fraud that resulted in a $745 million civil settlement and multiple criminal investigations?

All of the corporate executives at these companies could have benefited from an early-warning system—an enterprise reputation risk system, that helps identify, categorize, and measure the potentially damaging reputation defects across the entire enterprise, from top-to-bottom, on a daily basis. Executives armed with this timely and crucial reputation risk knowledge can properly assess any given situation and apply the appropriate solution, before the reputation pimple turns into a festering reputation boil.

The fact is, most corporate reputation disasters are entirely avoidable or preventable if executives and board members are informed early enough about existing reputation risks. Early identification, correct recognition, negative impact measurement, and early involvement of executive management are key to preventing negative incidents from being transformed into public relations nightmares and career-ending disasters. If these executives had utilized an enterprise reputation risk system, then all corporate stakeholders would have been much better protected and the plaintiffs' lawyers would have had a lot less work.

Enterprise Reputation Risk Technology

Historically, risk management professionals have been aggressive adopters of information technology, the objective being better identification, mitigation, and prevention of risk events.

The application of computer power has been especially signifi-cant in financial and operational fields. For the management of strategic risks, however, risk managers have typically found a dearth of IT solutions. That is beginning to change.

Reputation risk management requires a knowledge solution that is enterprisewide in scope and scale. To fit this need, the technology solutions used must embrace the entire enterprise and be leading edge, knowledge-based, and easy to learn and use.

Enterprise-enabled software, or EES, which can be utilized across the entire organization, facilitates accurate and rapid identification of reputation risk incidents and the subsequent proper management response. For a solution to be used enter-prisewide, it needs to be both flexible and customizable so that multiple departments can effectively input information and data and retrieve the reputation risk knowledge of others. EES fos-ters the sharing of interdepartmental expertise, achieving the diverse knowledge base necessary for quick and successful solu-tions. EES allows information to be shared among departments, and, as a by-product, produces a low total cost of ownership per user since the installation, administration, support, and training costs are spread.

With state-of-the-art technology, newer software applica-tions are straightforward and intuitive, and ideally should:

- Include an attractive and elegant functional interface that makes them easy to learn and comfortable to operate.

- Include a Multiple Document Interface (MDI), which allows the end user to open multiple risk incident forms and various application features (queries, reports, etc.) at once without having to close down other forms or activated features. MDI capabilities make it easy to view, edit, enter, cut, copy, and paste information among multiple open records.

- Be based on relational element management (REM) database architecture. An REM database structure allows indi-vidual information elements to exist independently or to be relationally tied to risk issues or incidents. REM database architecture provides a solution that allows independent pieces of information to be treated and tracked without unnecessarily creating new risk issues or incidents.

■ Be based on an open database standard that allows for easy exchange of data among various types of applications (word processing, spreadsheets, project management, other databases).

■ Provide for a total enterprise reputation risk measurement capability that allows risk managers to benchmark past and present reputation risk performance and identify trends.

A sophisticated enterprise reputation technology solution should also provide simple and efficient document storage and retrieval capabilities. Reputation-damaging incidents and their subsequent investigations can generate an overabundance of miscellaneous documentation. This might include a scanned newspaper or magazine article, a fax document from a regulatory agency, a word processing letter, a spreadsheet of data, an e-mail from a colleague, a legal notification from a state or federal court, a newsgroup's web page, or a digital photo. Using advanced software technology, today's enterprise reputation risk application can easily handle the "paperwork."

Total Reputation Management

Once an enterprise reputation knowledge solution with advanced information technology characteristics has been identified, the potential application needs to be assessed for requisite features. These will work in concert to focus the attentions of risk managers and executives on the firm's most strategic asset—its reputation, the risks associated with this asset, and the management of the reputation, which includes preventing reputation defects that cause irreparable damage. The technology can perform only as well as the processes of the Total Reputation Management (TRM) plan.

It is important to understand that reputation management is, essentially, quality management. Executives across all spectrums of industry are familiar with the success of Total Quality Management (TQM) programs implemented in tens of thousands of businesses nationwide, with the sole purpose of eliminating defects. The TQM techniques that have been so widely successful in improving products and services can also be applied to eliminating defects that could destroy the corporate reputation. With today's information technology, there is no rationale for not having a reputation risk system that embodies the TQM techniques.

The TQM techniques used to eliminate defects are quite simple.

1. The defect (an incident or issue) is identified.
2. The defect is categorized and ranked.
3. The defect is analyzed for causal factors.
4. The defect is measured and benchmarked.
5. A defect prevention program is built and implemented, based on the knowledge gained from the previous four steps.

Utilizing this same structure, an effective TRM program encourages and promotes an atmosphere of corporate and interdepartmental cooperation and shared reputation solutions. If based on a true information knowledge solution, it protects the organization's reputation for each and every stakeholder, as well as the substantial corporate investment made in advertising and public relations campaigns. It embodies and promotes identification, prevention, communications, and crisis management. Each of these steps can be partially or entirely fulfilled most efficiently through proper use of reputation management technology.

Identification of the vulnerabilities, issues, problems, and perceptions that affect an organization's reputation is crucial. Is the firm a good employer? A trustworthy partner? A positive community neighbor? A quality provider of goods and services? A responsible global citizen? A financially successful concern? A protector of the environment?

Multiple methods of identification are available: opinion

polls, interviews, Internet feedback, surveys, focus groups, toll-free hotlines, community and other stakeholder relation programs, and formal and informal dialogue meetings with special advocacy groups. Identification must be combined with measurement and benchmarking. A complete inventory of identification methods allows the corporation to quantify and compare the results of the identification process. If a firm can identify, measure, and benchmark the factors that determine a reputation, it will have the information to conduct a thorough analysis of causal factors, maximizing solutions for building, sustaining, and protecting its reputation.

Prevention is the least costly and most efficient means to protect a treasured reputation. Preventing defects that can tarnish or destroy a reputation saves an extraordinary amount of anguish, time, effort, and money.

It starts with the published policies and procedures that all organization employees are expected to follow and implement. These should be a reflection of the reputation that the firm wants to achieve. If a company wants to be known as a safe and friendly place to work, its policies should assure the employees they will not suffer from discrimination, harassment, or safety issues. If a firm wants to be a good community neighbor, its programs should allow employees to contribute and participate in community programs and services, as well as promote a clean local environment.

With these policies in place, a firm lays the groundwork for the implementation of an enterprisewide defect reporting system. In any given department, whether human resources, communications, ethics, compliance, safety/security, hazard/pollution, investor and public relations, legal/governmental, sales, customer service, finance, or MIS, defects will and do occur. Large or small, all defects should be reported immediately to the senior level. Almost without exception, crisis postmortems show that the primary reason trivial incidents mushroom into devastating scandals is that the so-called ''trivial'' events were not reported soon enough or at a high enough level.

An enterprisewide defect reporting system integrated into the reputation management program is critical because:

■ Protecting the reputation necessitates the full coverage that an enterprise reporting system provides.

■ Executives and board members need an early-warning system. The sooner they are made aware and involved, the likelihood that a crisis or scandal will erupt is diminished dramatically.

■ Corporations need to build a reputation risk knowledge base of issues, incidents, and problems, as well as the outcomes, results, and solutions. Historical information about incidents, combined with the information gained from the identification process, provides management with a powerful and complete knowledge database to help build better training and more successful prevention programs.

■ A complete and accurate database is fundamental for both internal and external auditing processes. Executives and board members need verifiable and audited data to confirm if reputation risk objectives are being met and whether the prevention programs are working successfully.

Communication strategies have long been used to create product demand, establish brand recognition, and build corporate identity. Effective communications can build up a substantial reservoir of goodwill that provides a buffer when unforeseen events do occur. Communications can manage and enhance the impressions the public receives, creating the desired loyal relationships. An effective program is not only the province of a firm's investor and public relations professionals, though. Corporate risk management, ethics, compliance, human resources, and marketing also provide valuable input and are essential to formulating a sound and well-rounded communications program.

Crisis management, disaster planning, and emergency preparedness are tactics to have in place before ''bad things happen to good companies.'' Inevitably, a negative incident or a damaging event will occur at even the best managed corporations. During a crisis, a firm that has already used identification, prevention, and communications to build up a large reputation reservoir of goodwill will survive the crisis in much better shape than those that have ignored TRM principles. Advocates of TRM also have the luxury of knowing how to react to a crisis. Professionally and expertly handling a crisis situation can make the difference for a successful outcome. Compare the outcomes of the Tylenol poison scare handled by Johnson & Johnson versus the Alaskan oil spill handled by Exxon.

The advent of new information technology will be of significant aid to those risk managers planning to address and manage the risk confronting their firms' reputations. Risk managers, executives, and board members need all the technological wherewithal they can muster in this day and age of reputation risk. Corporations coexist in the age of liability, where lawsuits and legal piranhas are a fact of life; the age of transparency, where the slightest transgressions are magnified thousandfold by aggressive journalism and transmitted worldwide in nanoseconds; the age of responsibility, where NGOs and stakeholders are demanding the best corporate citizenship and protest until they receive it; and the age of accountability, where punishment can be expected. Firms that professionally manage and protect their reputations with fervor and technology will be the competitive winners in this very risky age.

New Rules

Several initiatives have been established in order to promote greater responsibility among corporations. The following are some of the most influential:

- The Global Sullivan Principles serve as a guide for responsible corporate behavior and provide important external perspective. The objectives of the principles are to support economic, social, and political justice by companies where they do business; to support human rights and to encourage equal opportunity at all levels of employment; to train and advance disadvantaged workers for technical, supervisory, and management opportunities; and to assist with greater tolerance and understanding among peoples.

■ SA8000, derived through consensus and based on internationally accepted conventions, provides a uniform standard for social accountability. Whether SA8000 principles are applied internally or used as a tool to manage suppliers, they can make a positive contribution to the well-being of any business. Benefits of implementing and registering to SA8000 may include: improving or maintaining company's image; increasing employee morale and productivity; improved community relations; meeting customers' requirements or expectations; [uncovering] new market opportunities; and gaining competitive edge.

■ The Global Reporting Initiative (GRI) promotes international harmonization in the reporting of relevant and credible corporate environmental, social, and economic performance information to enhance responsible decision making. The GRI pursues this mission through a multistakeholder process of open dialogue and collaboration in the design and implementation of widely applicable sustainability reporting guidelines.

■ The OECD (Organization for Economic Cooperation and Development) Guidelines for Multinational Enterprises are recommendations to help ensure that multinational enterprises operate in harmony with the countries in which they operate. They set nonlegally binding standards covering a broad range of operations: employment and industrial relations, environment, information disclosure, competition, financing, taxation, and science and technology.

A Good Rep

Academic research, market surveys, consultant studies, and major business publications conclude that a strong reputation is a strong competitive edge. Significant advantages of a solid reputation are:

- Superior share valuation
- Improved access to capital markets
- Reduced marketing costs
- Premium pricing capability
- [Ability to attract] the best employees and [ensure] their continued retention
- Increased productivity and employee morale
- Loyal (repeat) customers
- Higher level of respect and deference from the press, politicians, and even the plaintiff's bar
- Preferred relations with advocacy and special interest groups
- Easier crisis management response

Read More About It

The Stamp of Success?

Walter Luker
Reprinted with permission from *Risk Management* magazine, May 1999.
Copyright 1999 by Risk Management Society Publishing. All rights reserved.
For more information call 212.286.9364. www.rims.org/rmmag

The term *highly protected risk* (HPR) is primarily associated with fire sprinkler systems, but much more is required in order to minimize industrial property losses. HPR involves complete facility protection, and its value goes beyond just the security of physical property.

One significant loss potential for an organization is the loss of a market for a product. This uninsurable danger can have devastating effects. If a company's product is destroyed by a fire, its customers simply find another supplier. When this happens, that market is sometimes never regained and the business is forced to close.

The investment in HPR status reaps benefits for all concerned—including a defense against damaging incidents that could shut a company down for good. Risk managers protect the assets and market share of their organization and expect favorable insurance rates and, in some cases, leverage in seeking to insure less attractive properties. And, for the underwriter, HPR means good business with favorable loss experience.

But does having an HPR facility ensure risk management success? Landmark large losses have demonstrated that "highly protected" can create a false sense of security. But there are also success stories. By using the COPE-Plus approach (an improved version of the traditional Construction, Occupancy, Protection, and Exposure considerations), you can create or renovate your facility to make it an effective HPR.

Construction

Analyzing the risk aspects of construction involves an examination of materials and the design of both the exterior shell and the interior components.

Materials should be classified as either fire-resistive, noncombustible, approved, or a combination of these, depending on the use of the building. Fire-resistive construction is composed of heavy masonry material (with no exposed steel) and will withstand fire exposure for a period of time. Noncombustible elements include steel and other metallic materials that will not burn, but will fail within a relatively short time when exposed to intense fire (1,000°F or greater). Approved construction materials will burn under certain conditions, but present a minimal hazard relative to the spread of fire and smoke. Components such as roofing materials and insulation come with an approval or listing from Factory Mutual, Underwriter's Laboratories, or other building codes or authorities.

The presence of nonapproved construction materials can offset other favorable HPR features and increase the magnitude of a loss. This is especially true if the presence of such elements is not acknowledged and dealt with.

The layout of your facility's interior is also an important part of HPR qualification. Depending on the use of the facility and the insurable values involved, there may be a need to segregate hazards. This is accomplished using firewalls, fire partition walls, explosion-resistant walls and venting, and detachment (a separate building at a safe distance).

But fire is not the only peril that is mitigated through construction. Consideration must be extended to concerns such as horizontal wind loading on building walls, the resistance of roof covering to wind uplift and heavy hail storms, and roof load design (along with roof slope and drains) as affected by potential excessive water accumulation, snow load, and drifts.

Of course, these items are best handled during the planning and design stage prior to construction. However, the proper measures can help minimize risk in a less than perfect situation.

For example, re-roofing projects present an opportunity to replace combustible Class II Metal Deck (MD) roofs with Class I MD noncombustible materials. The landmark fire in Livonia, Michigan, in the early 1950s is testament to the combustibility of Class II MD roofs, due to the adhesive used, its application, and the insulating materials. A fire beneath such a roof can heat the underside of the steel deck and cause combustible vapors to escape along the seams of the decking, allowing a fire to spread above the sprinkler system and far beyond the initial fire site.

(If the roof is wood-constructed—heavy plank or plywood—the exposure can be minimized only by controlling ignition sources and providing automatic sprinkler protection. If the values are very high, you can expect an underwriting impact.)

Here is an example of how an HPR improvement might materialize: A loss control engineer notes that the MD roof covering a large, high-value warehouse is in poor condition (leaking and subject to wind loss). She recommends re-roofing with approved Class I materials. The risk manager stresses the importance of these materials with plant management and corporate or project engineering. After appropriate specifications are included in the roofing contract, plans are submitted to the loss control consultants and the needed approvals and follow-up inspections occur.

Now, if a high-challenge fire occurs in this warehouse, the roof would not be a negative factor. Knowing this, insurance companies should grant lower-cost coverage. Without this HPR process, the replacement roof might have ended up with unprotected polystyrene insulation, which is great for energy conservation, but even more combustible than the original roof.

Keep in mind that local building codes represent minimum standards, based on experience and practicality with various types of structures. Large collapse losses normally involve conditions that exceed those anticipated by the standard or code committee. These major incidents are triggered by a combination of abnormal and undesirable factors such as heavy snow followed by a heavy rain, a deep freeze, and then more snow, along with high wind conditions. Considering this, don't be surprised if your loss control consultants offer recommendations that are more stringent than building code. Their advice may relate to industry loss experience and merits consideration.

Occupancy

Occupancy relates to the operations, processes, and storage within a facility. These issues impact other aspects of the COPE-Plus approach, the most common being combustible loading within buildings and the sprinkler protection required. Of equal importance is the facility layout relative to the separation of hazardous processes and storage. The remaining occupancy considerations concern the production process.

The manufacture of most products requires hazardous operations, both routine and specific to the product. These are referred to as common and special hazards, respectively.

Common industrial hazards include boilers and heating equipment that run on natural gas, propane, fuel oil, etc. These hazards can be controlled using the appropriate equipment design, including combustion safeguards and interlocks. Basically, a unit should be designed to automatically shut down as a result of an unsafe condition. Using such safety control measures and properly maintaining and testing equipment significantly reduces the danger these processes present.

Other common occupancy hazards include electrical equipment and power distribution systems, air compressors, and combustible cooling towers. For these, there are specific standards and maintenance procedures, such as using infrared scans to identify potential malfunctions in electrical systems.

Special hazards involve processes and equipment that present a greater potential for loss unique to a specific industry.

For example, the heat treating of metal components occurs within a furnace at around 1700°F. Once the metal is white hot, it is moved to the next compartment of the furnace and plunged into a quench bath of combustible oil or water. Automatic doors and flame curtains are required to prevent an explosion. Some heat-treat operations also involve many furnaces in a large area, adding to the loss threat.

Other special hazards include the chemical recovery boilers used in the pulp and paper industry, and chemical reactors. Adherence to property loss control standards and guidelines can incorporate these volatile aspects of industry into an HPR system.

Protection

Protection, or more specifically, automatic sprinkler protection, is a requirement for HPR status, unless the risk involved is what underwriters refer to as "pig iron under water"—it absolutely cannot burn. Additionally, there are other special protection systems required for special hazards, including deluge water spray, dry chemical, and carbon dioxide.

It is important to remember that all sprinkler systems do not provide equal protection. The size of piping within the sprinkler system network can vary up to 300 percent, the opening of the sprinkler head upward of 200 percent. The system design is based on the discharge density over an area. This is measured in gallons per minute per square foot of floor space and ranges from 0.10 gpm per sq. ft. to 0.60 gpm per sq. ft.

System design must match combustible loading and any changes to that. Take, for example, a design of 0.45 gpm per sq. ft. over a 3,000 sq. ft. area for a finished goods warehouse. If the commodity is changed (e.g., more plastics), the additional heat released from a fire could open heads in a 6000 sq. ft. area. As heads beyond the design area of 3,000 sq. ft. open, the already inadequate density of 0.45 gpm starts to decline. The domino effect, as the fire area keeps increasing and the density keeps decreasing, results in feed mains being pulled apart as the steel load-bearing structure fails within ten to fifteen minutes.

An adequate sprinkler system also depends upon an adequate water supply. Connections to public mains are common and often sufficient to maintain HPR status. But as combustible loading and values increase, there is a need for multiple, stronger water supplies, such as booster fire pumps (arranged to increase the pressure where water supply volume is adequate) or fire pumps with suction reservoirs. Fire pump installations should be in strict accordance with recognized standards. Inspection, maintenance, and weekly testing are also critical. A landmark fire occurred in an HPR facility where the power supply for the electric motor-driven pump happened to be routed through the initial fire area, and failed. Conditions became worse when the diesel engine shut down because of a lack of combustion air (due to an attempt to conserve energy) and another classic domino effect was sparked.

Because the layout and storage arrangements for many facilities are often revised, team effort between risk management and loss control is critical. If management has advance notice that protection will be affected because of a potential change, they can consider the added adjustment costs in their evaluations and budgets. If the problem is identified after the change is made, it is likely that the needed protection upgrade will be delayed. During this period, a major loss could strike, such as the landmark roll paper fire in 1969 that occurred when upgraded sprinkler protection was being planned.

Finally, consider alarm systems, guard service, and combinations of the two. Quality alarm systems are invaluable in alerting facility personnel to an emergency and transmitting the signal to an off-site center.

Exposure

Exposure is normally out of the risk manager's control except during initial site selection and construction. Exposures arising from neighboring properties, aircraft landing strips, railways, and flood zones, which can develop after a site has been selected and developed, provide tricky circumstances for risk managers. For such unavoidable exposures, some mitigation can help to maintain HPR status.

For example, it is possible to build on a site not originally considered a flood zone, but due to continual construction, paving, and grading, storm drains and waterways may not be able to handle extended, heavy rainfall. Address this issue by developing emergency action plans for flooding.

Or, if your organization decides to build in an earthquake zone, consult with local earthquake design specialists in addition to your loss control consultants. Proper design can make a drastic difference in the event of a serious earthquake. Pay attention to items such as sway bracing for sprinkler systems and earthquake actuated shutoff valves for natural gas lines.

Plus

The closer you can come to meeting the preferred COPE features, the safer your facility will be, and the more likely it will rate the status of HPR. But in order to gain the full benefit from your investments, more is required.

There are programs related to the human aspect of property loss control, including procedures for maintaining and testing protection equipment, handling unusual occurrences and emergencies, and dealing with the hazards that humans sometimes create. Critical Plus programs include:

■ *Facility Protection System Inspection and Testing Procedures*. An effective program will insure to the greatest extent possible that protection systems remain in service.

■ *Handling Impaired Protection*. Many landmark fires in HPR facilities happen when protection is out of service.

■ *Permit System for Cutting and Welding*. Hot work precautions listed on the permit should be followed every time such work is done outside of designated maintenance areas. This applies to both facility personnel and outside contractors.

■ *Plant Emergency Organization (EO or PEO).* The effective use of a fire extinguisher can douse a fire in its initial stage before the operation of a single sprinkler head, but employees should be well trained and backed up by coworkers. During a major incident, someone would notify the fire department, appropriate evacuation would take place, hazardous processes would be shut down, and others would respond in accordance with their assignment and training (sprinkler valve attendant, fire pump attendant, etc.).

In conclusion, no, HPR status cannot ensure success; property losses will always occur. But the odds of successful prevention and mitigation can be improved with engineered protection by considering all the COPE building blocks, supplemented by effective Plus elements.

Reality Check

Given unlimited financial resources, the development of a nearly perfect HPR building would be simple. However, most risk managers typically deal with preexisting, imperfect facilities and budget constraints. Even though you may fall short of perfection, you can maintain HPR status by identifying, controlling, and monitoring deficient circumstances, as well as using the Plus techniques. Of course, in some cases, where modification is not affordable, an underwriting impact (higher rates and deductibles) may be necessary.

Read More About It

Flexible Structure: Managing Financial Risk

Simon Jegher
Reprinted with permission from *Risk Management* magazine, January 1999.
Copyright 1999 by Risk Management Society Publishing. All rights reserved.
For more information call 212.286.9364. www.rims.org/rmmag

In my ten years managing finance/treasury departments, I have spent considerable effort addressing the financial imperatives of two of Canada's largest corporations: cash management, including banking and committed lines of credit; external financings, averaging $1 billion per year, in the global capital markets; early calls of publicly held debt; derivatives; pension funds; debt rating agencies; and all the other associated functions that are the bread and butter of our daily corporate finance lives. Yet I always felt a need for a greater structure that would bring together these functions and the people who implement them—a flexible structure that would encourage the innovation required to create financial benefits and shareholder value.

While on vacation two years ago on a peaceful, somewhat remote island off the west coast of Florida, I spent a few evenings churning out concepts, financial instruments, risks, and functions as they randomly occurred to me. Before I knew it an entire wall was blanketed with yellow notes. The next few evenings were spent rearranging the ideas and concepts into a structure. While none of the parts of the process are innovative on their own, my subsequent discussions with both Canadian and U.S. corporations and investment bankers point to the fact that, other than in financial institutions, a unified and comprehensive financial risk management focus is likely an exception.

The objective of such a process is, first and foremost, to address the key policies relating to financial risk exposures. For example, credit ratings are too often seen as simply the fallout of financial performance, not the result of policies tailored to attaining a specific rating that addresses a firm's long-term capital requirements. A credit rating policy can set up other capital structure strategies and an appropriate fixed/floating composition of the debt portfolio.

Another objective of a unified process is to foster a consolidated perspective of financial risk—not only the risk to the company itself, but its subsidiaries and parent, where applicable. Similarly, for companies with defined benefit pension plans, the plan's assets and liabilities must also be incorporated into this consolidated perspective, recognizing that financial risks affecting off-balance-sheet items can have significant impacts on cash flows and net income. Finally, a comprehensive process brings to light the dynamics between disciplines, thus focusing various operating units on common objectives. For example, liquidity policy will affect the timing of capital market transactions just as foreign exchange policy will affect the nature of derivative strategies.

Policy Development

The first step in creating an active financial management process is the identification of the various risks.

■ *Liquidity Risk*. Even companies with a highly tuned focus on customer and shareholder value can go bankrupt because they lack short-term liquidity. Short- and longer-term cash forecasts, combined with worst-case business and economic scenarios, are vital for the development of a corporate liquidity policy. In turn, this policy will drive ceiling short-term debt levels, the size and term of committed bank lines of credit, and the timing of fixed, long-term financings.

■ *Foreign Exchange Risk*. A question: Unless your company is a financial institution, why are you taking any foreign exchange risk at all? Corporate risks should be taken in areas of the company's core expertise. However, analyzing your corporation's FX exposure will raise some interesting questions. What exposures are built into the supply procurement process? If you have a defined benefit pension fund, what is the potential impact of currency exposures? While currency risk is integral to the pension fund's investment diversification strategy, an FX gain or loss could impact the sponsor corporation's cash contributions to the pension fund. These and other questions particular to your firm's operations will raise policy issues that might otherwise go unaddressed.

■ *Interest Rate Risk*. The key policy issue that determines a firm's interest rate risk is capital structure. Thereafter, the primary measure of a company's debt portfolio interest risk should be duration, which is driven by cash flows, as opposed to simply utilizing the average life of the portfolio. Ideally, the duration of the debt portfolio should be equal to the duration of the firm's assets—an objective that is difficult to apply to most companies unless they are financial institutions. Having established a duration policy, the key implementation decision is determining a fixed/floating mix of debt that satisfies both liquidity and interest rate policies. At Bell Canada, we have assessed a number of theoretical, custom-designed studies, all of which point to an approximate 80 percent to 20 percent mix of fixed/floating debt as being the most effective over the longer term.

■ *Counterparty/Credit Exposure*. A key advantage to derivatives as a risk management tool is that they allow for the modulation of duration without necessarily increasing liquidity risk. The best example is borrowing long/fixed and swapping into floating. Similarly, derivatives can be a cost-effective and flexible vehicle for implementing a foreign exchange policy. Their use, however, comes at a price. Derivatives result in counterparty credit exposure which itself requires a clear policy and operating controls. This policy should address credit criteria and specific credit limits on a consolidated corporate basis, including any exposures that undoubtedly exist in the pension fund's equity and debt portfolios. Given the publicity surrounding their occasional abuse, the use of derivatives might be seen as a hard sell to a board of directors. My experience has shown that boards are receptive to derivative use if there is a clear objective of restricting their use to managing, controlling, and reducing risk combined with appropriate internal controls and reporting.

Quantification

Having identified the firm's financial risks, the next step in the process is to quantify the dollar risk associated with each of them. This requires a dynamic financial model that incorporates the firm's consolidated financials, long-term business plans, and off-balance-sheet items such as pension fund assets and liabilities, leases, derivatives in place, and securitization transactions such as the sale of receivables. Quantification will require a risk assessment based on various business and economic scenarios.

Assessment

The next step in the process involves a thorough assessment of the business and operating environment. For example, how is the firm's business correlated to the economic cycle? A high correlation might imply that the firm is capable of assuming higher interest rate risk, assuming rates increase as the economy heats up. Similarly, a firm whose markets are aggressively under attack and whose base technology is undergoing rapid change should consider taking relatively lower financial risks. (While this sounds obvious, too many firms groping to be competitive attempt to reduce financial costs by making short-term capital market bets.) Another aspect that requires assessment is the firm's prospective view of its long-term debt credit ratings. This total environmental assessment determines the appropriate level of financial risk.

Risk Tolerance

The level of risk tolerances that a corporation is prepared to accept should encompass the aggregate of all the identified financial risks and is dependent on a number of factors. How much variance in budgeted earnings and cash flows is tolerable to management, the board, and the shareholders/capital markets? What will be the reaction of the rating agencies to different levels of earnings and cash flow volatilities? How much room for variance exists in the company's debt trust indenture tests?

These are just a few of the questions that will need to be answered in arriving at the next step: developing the core financial policies that make up the foundation of the process leading toward strategy development and implementation.

(A point of clarification: The process should not be misinterpreted to imply that finance/treasury should be a profit center. On the contrary, the process is focused on hedging versus speculation. Its operating philosophy is to reduce both risk and cost.

It does require management to take certain views on market movements; but doing nothing to develop risk tolerance policies is in fact speculating with the company's current financial exposures.)

Implementation

Having developed a set of financial risk policies approved by the board of directors, the next step is implementation and assuring that policies are adhered to. The intellectual foundation must be one of managing the entire lower right hand side of the balance sheet as a single portfolio that finances the corporation's operations, with the focus on cash flows generated from both sides of the balance sheet.

Strategy implementation is the more familiar of corporate financial operations and calls for a comprehensive array of tools. The key tool is the development, or purchase, of a financial model for the corporation's portfolio of outstanding debt, preferred shares, and equity. This model should be capable of dynamically simulating the impact of various scenarios on the portfolio and the various financial risks, thus ensuring constant adherence to policy. It must be capable of measuring counterparty exposure and assessing the impact of various derivative strategies. My experience has shown that investment banking firms are in the best position to assist in the development of this model.

Other vital tools in managing the capital portfolio include both a commercial paper program and a medium-term note program. The key advantage of these vehicles is the flexibility they provide in managing the duration of the capital portfolio. Commercial paper can be an important tool in attaining a target floating debt level and medium-term notes are perfectly suited to slotting in debt maturities in years where room exists based on liquidity policy. This flexibility is further enhanced when combined with interest or cross currency swaps.

Communication

In policy development, the decision-making and approving body should be the board of directors. This role for the board is appropriate and consistent with recent studies and recommendations on the subject of corporate governance. In a study entitled "Where Were the Directors? Guidelines for Improved Corporate Governance in Canada," the Toronto Stock Exchange identified five stewardship responsibilities for a board of directors. The proposed financial risk management process specifically addresses two of the five:

1. The identification of the principal risks of the corporation's business and ensuring the implementation of appropriate systems to manage these risks
2. Ensuring the integrity of the corporation's control and management information systems

Thus, obtaining approval from the board of directors with respect to adopting the suggested risk management process should be consistent with the board's own view of its managing responsibilities.

Similarly, communication should be integral to the operational risk management control process. The audience for this communication varies in terms of both the information provided and the frequency of the reporting. From a corporate governance perspective, the key audience is the board of directors or its audit committee. The implementation of a comprehensive financial risk management process might also justify the creation of a finance committee of the board.

Finally, I believe that the debt rating agencies should be apprised of these key financial risk policies and the process in place to actively manage and control them. The very fact that senior management and the board are taking ongoing interest in addressing the very risks that are uppermost in the minds of the rating agencies conveys a positive signal respecting the quality of the earnings and cash flows that support the corporation's outstanding debt and interest obligations.

A Continuous Process

Every process that strives for excellence is circular—after implementation, performance must be measured against the objectives originally defined and the entire process evaluated for continuous improvement. A corporation's financial policies and the capital portfolio that was the outcome of those policies must be reevaluated based on changing corporate objectives combined with altered business and economic circumstances.

5

Liability Exposures to Risk

Growing exposure to legal liability—in my opinion—is the fuel that has propelled the growth of risk management over the past forty years. And the funny thing is that the story is a little different depending on the sector. Obviously workers compensation is an issue for most organizations, but directors' and officers' liability is a big problem in some businesses and not in others. In some it's product liability, in some it's premises exposures. All different, but all stemming from the legal environment.

Risk Manager
Large Metropolitan Local Government

Perspectives

Careful Planning Helps Avoid EPL Claims

Michael Bradford
Reprinted with permission from *Business Insurance,* May 8, 2000. © Crain Communications Inc. All rights reserved.

Employers can lower their chances of being hit by an employment practices liability [EPL] lawsuit with some up-front risk management practices, a group of experts contends.

A thorough, careful recruiting and hiring process helps eliminate some of the causes of EPL claims, says George J. Tichy II, an attorney with the San Francisco firm Littler, Mendelson, Fastiff, Tichy & Mathiason. At the "very outset, you have to con-

---

sider recruiting," he advises employers, because in many cases companies have a workforce that looks "all the same" in terms of demographics, leaving them open to the possibility of discrimination claims. . . .

Tichy says it is wise policy for employers to seek "protected-category employees . . . and certainly older workers, disabled workers, and racial minorities." And, he reminds employers, employment agencies cannot be used to "discriminate for you" and leave the employer off the hook for what might be determined later as discriminatory practices. "They are your agents and you are going to be responsible for what they do. If they do testing, screening, or background checks, please make sure that they know what they're doing."

He tells employers, when advertising for workers, to carefully craft truthful ads. "It is very important that you be accurate in your job description. Avoid promises," Tichy says, because they can be used in litigation filed by an employee who feels the promises were not fulfilled.

"And most importantly, avoid discriminatory statements" in ads, he urges, such as: "We're looking for a bright young person."

To further avoid charges of discrimination, Tichy suggests that when interviewing applicants, employers "use a script. Do not simply wing it." Having a script will help interviewers stick to questions that are open-ended and avoid such queries as: "Do you plan to have children?" or "Where were you raised?" Such queries are ones that could raise questions of preferential hiring.

Sometimes interviewees will volunteer information that an employer would rather not know. For example, if a prospective employee talks about a workers compensation claim he or she filed at a previous workplace, "do not ask follow-up questions," he advises, because denying employment based on such a circumstance is unlawful.

Mercedes Colwin, an administrative law judge and attorney with L'Abbate, Balkan, Colavita & Contini L.L.P. in Garden City, New York, tells employers that they must be precise when crafting job descriptions for new hires.

"Make sure you have the essential functions of the job detailed," Colwin says. As an example of how a poorly crafted description can become a liability, Colwin tells of a nurse who brought a claim against her employer after the nurse lost her job because she could no longer lift patients out of their beds. "The hospital said, 'But your honor, we had a job description and that's an essential function of her job.' But lo and behold, the job description did not say that she was required to lift patients out of their beds. And it cost that hospital a quarter of a million dollars."

If pre-employment skills testing is used, Tichy cautions that the testing "should be relevant" and reflect the actual job skills that the person will need if hired. That way, there can be no disagreement later over whether the hiree knew what was required for the job. Tichy says risk managers should be aware that the Equal Employment Opportunity Commission will resort to subterfuge by using testers to determine whether an employer is complying with antidiscrimination practices.

"This concept of testers is very important for risk managers to recognize," Tichy emphasizes. "The EEOC announced a year ago that they intended to use testers. The tester is an individual whose function is to apply for a job but not to have any desire or intent to take the job."

The tester, he explained, is on hand to determine if the employer's hiring processes are appropriate. "Just keep in mind that each individual who applies is an individual that you should consider in a good-faith way for employment."

Of course, an essential risk management tool for protecting a company in the event of a claim is EPL insurance, says Sal G. Concu, claims counsel with Zurich U.S. in New York. Concu offers a few tips for structuring EPL coverage so that an employer is adequately protected. For example, while [EPL coverage] is available under a directors and officers liability policy, that should not be relied on as the sum total of an organization's EPL coverage.

"A lot of organizations feel that a D&O policy is enough to cover them for employment practices," Concu points out. "The main reason why you might want to do it under a separate policy," he says, is because under a D&O policy, the cost of an EPL claim will erode the overall policy limits. "What happens is, if you have one or two substantial EPL claims falling under a D&O policy, you may not have enough coverage for your directors and officers" in the event they face claims, Concu explains.

And, he notes, an EPL policy should be written to cover non-directors and officers who could have an EPL action brought against them. If it is written as an endorsement to a D&O policy, the EPL coverage will not be broad enough to cover other employees.

EPL coverage typically is written on a claims-made basis, according to Concu, but can be structured to pay claims for acts that occurred prior to the policy period.

Introduction

In this chapter, we turn to the liability side of the exposure balance sheet. The term *liability* is rather broadly construed here to encompass moral responsibility as an exposure issue.

The subject of legal liability is extremely wide and complex, and a full treatment of the legal environment for business would dwarf the other chapters of this book. Therefore, the focus in this chapter is to establish a basic understanding of the American legal system with a specific orientation toward the practical risk management implications for business. To that end, the chapter begins with a short overview of the legal system with particular emphasis on civil law. Notable risk management–related characteristics of the legal system are identified and discussed. Key liability problem areas are explained in some detail.

The chapter concludes with an introduction to and exploration of the moral and ethical responsibility dimension of liability exposures to risk. A central topic of this section will be the challenge of framing moral and ethical issues in a broader risk management context.

Legal Liability Exposures

The American legal system can be described in a number of different but equally valid ways. For purposes that will become clearer as the book progresses, the key attributes of this system are that:

1. It is a system of common law.
2. It is a system that parallels the federal system of government.
3. It is a system that serves extralegal functions.

A System of Common Law

Although the statement is something of a simplification, one might say that there are two broad forms of law practiced throughout the world—codified law and common law. The distinctions are obvious and subtle, but probably it is sufficient to state that code law is based on a fairly explicit set of laws and rulings (think of the Ten Commandments as the prototypical example of code law). France and countries with historic ties to France tend to follow a code-based system—as does the State of Louisiana. Common law is based on judges' rulings and is generally seen as more flexible and adaptable in concept and application. The common law idea arises from Anglo-Saxon law and became influential through the worldwide promulgation of English Common Law in the eighteenth, nineteenth, and twentieth centuries. Of course, this system directly influenced American law, and virtually every aspect of the American legal system—from Constitutional Law to criminal law and everything in between—is traceable to the English tradition.

We are not suggesting that the English and American systems are exactly alike, because the law is culture-bound and so there are numerous important differences despite the common heritage. Indeed, the Americanization of current English law is a much-debated phenomenon in the United Kingdom, and many of the American influences are not held to be positive inasmuch as they reflect attributes of American culture that are viewed with some suspicion by the British.

From a risk management perspective, the principal implication is that common law is fluid and dynamic, and thus susceptible to change and uncertainty. Although the American system attempts to impose predictability through the fundamental principle of *stare decisis* (i.e., through its reliance on precedent), the system also permits creativity, innovation, and dynamic change to occur. This, many believe, is a strength of the system, although one must recognize that it introduces a level of uncertainty that would not, perhaps, exist at quite the same level in a codified system.

A Federal System of Law

For the same reasons that the American political system is a federal system, the legal system is separated into state systems and a national system of justice. The implications for this feature are profound, affecting matters philosophical and practical. For the risk manager, the key issues tend to revolve around the problems in managing exposure to liability arising from at least two largely separate systems of law. Put plainly, a business may find itself liable for damages that result from violations of federal law and have other liability burdens imposed by the state system. A particularly troubling aspect of the dual system is that many legally questionable situations may run afoul of federal and/or state law, and in such situations the plaintiff may have the option of choosing in which legal system an action should be pursued.

One also should be cognizant of the influence of other state laws on a particular business. A rather simple illustration of this is workers compensation law, which is state-specific. In a number of states, a worker injured on the job may elect to pursue a claim either in that worker's home state or in the state of injury. For instance, a North Dakota–based salesperson who is conducting business in Minnesota and is injured there may choose to file for benefits under Minnesota's system, which is relatively more generous in its benefit structure.

Furthermore, the rapid globalization of business gives rise to possible international law impacts on firms. Businesses in the European Union countries experience this on a daily basis, but the use of foreign contractors on businesses' capital projects is seen increasingly in the United States, and this can create vexing jurisdictional issues when disputes arise.

The Extralegal System

This feature is not as prominent as the previous two discussion points, but it is sufficiently influential that it should be mentioned in a risk management book. The American legal system—while clearly serving explicit judicial purposes—also has cultural functions that are not so evident in, say, the United Kingdom. The United States relies on its legal system(s) to mediate many social and cultural issues that are more informally managed in countries with older and more homogeneous societies.

Demonstrating this point is a bit more difficult than is asserting it. However, it may be a contributing factor to the apparent litigiousness of Americans. Culture mediates many aspects of interpersonal relationships, and the fact that American culture grew up intertwined with a common law–based system suggests that the legal system has less obvious functions. For the risk manager, recognition of this fact may help develop some appreciation for the reasons behind many firms' unhappy role as a "deep-pocket target" for litigation. Such recognition may strengthen a risk manager's efforts to broaden litigation management strategies to include information management and public relations efforts.

Legal Liability Problems and Issues

Business organizations are diverse, and in many respects their differences vastly exceed their commonalities. Certainly, one is hard-pressed to find many similarities between IBM Corp. and Bob's Bicycle Repair Shop. Yet there are some common concerns, and

both businesses share many management-related problems and issues—though clearly of differing scope.

For purposes of introduction—and despite the diversity within
the business world—there are a set of legal liability problems and
issues that are rather widely observed, and it is to these matters
that the chapter now turns. They are:

1. The nature and purpose of tort law
2. Contract law as a foundation problem
3. Premises liability
4. Products and services liability
5. Environmental impairment/public nuisance liability
6. Professional liability
7. Directors and officers and fiduciary liability
8. Bailment liability
9. Employment liability
10. Workers compensation
11. Agency liability
12. Motor vehicle liability

The Nature and Purpose of Tort Law

One can categorize the American legal system in several ways: public versus private law, civil versus criminal law, and so on. Depending on the type of business, one or the other of these approaches
may be suitable. However, since the focus of this book is on the
management of risks in business organizations generally, the main
concern for readers will be to appreciate the basic problems common to most private organizations. Thus, treatment of criminal law
is not essential (though, it certainly could be of concern with respect to employee actions), nor is an extended discussion of distinctions between public and private law (again, from time to time the
issues could be important, but not on an ongoing basis). Indeed,
the best use of time and ink here is to focus on civil law and the
key categories within it.

Civil law is that part of the common law system that pertains to the relationships between individuals (and organizations). A civil action is brought by one party against another for alleged wrongs. These actions are taken at the litigant's own expense, and the awards that are granted under the civil system are determined by a jury and/or a judge, depending on the situation. Those awards may include indemnity for loss, punitive damages, restitution, or injunctive relief.

In a civil action, the burden of proof differs from criminal law. Civil liability is based on the "preponderance of evidence" (as opposed to "beyond all reasonable doubt" in criminal law). This standard is a comparative standard, which means that a party must have more evidence supportive of its position than the opposing party presents on its behalf.

Civil law is classifiable into several categories: contract law, torts, equitable actions, and certain actions that fall outside the other categories. A plaintiff (i.e., the party alleging that harm was done) need not necessarily name the type of civil action being pursued, and thus an action may proceed until a determination of its status is established. Of course, the plaintiff must satisfy a judge that a theory of recovery exists before a case proceeds very far.

The parties of a civil action must comply with the rules and requirements that are set forward by each jurisdiction. These requirements relate to the form and procedure for initiating an action, the methods by which evidence is gathered, the nature of communications between parties, and so on. Ordinarily, the plaintiff carries the burden of proving the case, although from time to time the evidence of wrongdoing is sufficiently obvious that the doctrine of *res ipsa loquitur* ("the thing speaks for itself") is applied; in such cases the defendant must carry the burden of proving it is not liable.

Part of the difficulty of facing the legal liability exposure rests in the complexity of the process. Almost inevitably the pursuit of legal redress requires expert legal counsel and additional expertise in the technical matters relevant to the case. This is expensive, but more important, it puts the risk manager in a situation where there

Insights

Carefully Handling Layoffs Could Head Off Lawsuits

Gavin Souter

Large-scale layoffs can create sizable risk management problems that have to be handled with care, risk managers warn.

When people lose their jobs, they also lose their incomes and, consequently, are more likely to file workers compensation claims and make employment liability-related complaints, risk managers say. To minimize any increase in insurance claims and costs after large-scale terminations, risk managers should be involved in the whole process of downsizing, they say.

By making senior managers aware of potential insurance and risk management issues, risk managers can help ensure that terminated employees are cared for as well as possible and that employers are not exposed to large, unnecessary increases in insurance claims.

For example, PepsiCo Inc. went through a major round of layoffs shortly before Christopher E. Mandel, director of global risk management at Tricon Global Restaurants Inc. in Louisville, Kentucky, joined the company in 1993. A year after the layoffs, employees who stayed with the company were still scared about losing their own jobs. "There was a perspective of fear that permeated the place . . . and that was all due to the way it was handled. It was down, dirty, and quick," Mandel says.

PepsiCo had called in consultants to analyze the employment levels at the company. After the consultants filed their recommendations, a "Black Friday" took place. Employees showed up at work and the ones to be fired were immediately escorted to their offices, told to pick up their belongings, and then escorted out of the building, Mandel says. As a result, the company immediately saw a rise in wrongful termination lawsuits from former employees, as well as an increase in workers compensation claims from existing employees who were unsure of their own positions.

In 1997, when PepsiCo's restaurant business was spun off into Tricon, another round of layoffs took place, but this time it was handled with greater sensitivity and fewer problems arose. The first difference was that management explained to the workers that, as the company was no longer owned by a larger holding company, it had to reduce costs to levels more in line with the restaurant industry and that such cost cutting would mean layoffs, he says.

"They told people early that it was a problem that we had to deal with," Mandel says. Employees better understood the reasons and that the firings were not random. As result of taking a more measured and less abrupt approach to terminations, neither workers comp claims nor employment-related lawsuits have increased, Mandel says.

Service Merchandise Co. Inc. in Nashville, Tennessee, also managed to avoid large increases in insurance-related claims when it made large layoffs after filing for Chapter 11 bankruptcy protection in March 1999, [according to] Michelle Scott, risk manager at the retail company. As a result of the bankruptcy, Service Merchandise reduced its workforce by more than 10,000 and closed about 150 stores.

Once management had decided which stores to close, Service Merchandise communicated with the store managers about three to five days before a public announcement was made, Scott says. "That gave them time to get used to it." The employees were also told how long the stores would remain open and were offered financial incentives to stay until the closures. Service Merchandise then supplied placement packages that gave names and numbers of other retail companies that might be looking for new employees and lists of other job opportunities in the area.

At corporate headquarters, workers who were to be laid off were informed of the decision and then were off the property within four hours. But the next day, they were invited to an off-site location to discuss their situation with human resources personnel, Scott says.

The delay gave the employees time to get over some of the immediate emotional impact of losing their jobs and to think of some questions they would want to ask in their meetings the following day, she says. In addition to informing the fired employees about their rights to benefits, human resources personnel offered advice on interviewing techniques and how to write a resume.

Communicating with employees is crucial when wide scale layoffs take place, agrees Billie Fae Fuschi, director of workers compensation at Methodist Healthcare in Memphis, Tennessee. Otherwise, workers comp and other insurance-related claims can surge, she says.

For example, if a company requires that remaining workers take on added work for which they are not properly trained, they are more likely to be injured, Fuschi says. And fraudulent workers compensation claims are likely to increase as workers who know or suspect that they will be laid off look for another source of income, she says.

To help deter fraud, risk managers should ensure their companies have a corporate policy addressing workers comp fraud, post that policy, and make employees aware that the company will prosecute employees who submit fraudulent claims. Also, exit interviews should always be conducted and employees should be asked to sign a statement regarding any injuries they have suffered, Fuschi says. Employees will be less likely to file fraudulent claims if they have already signed a document saying they had not been injured.

is a reliance on outside advisors. Furthermore, conflicts of interest can arise between counsel and client.

Most civil actions are settled between litigants well before the case comes to trial. Other actions are discontinued or thrown out for lack of sufficient support—but they all cost the defendant money and time. This supports the general view that the real risk within the realm of legal liability is not losing a suit but simply being named in a suit, since this alone sets in motion a commitment of resources regardless of the merits of the case.

Those few cases that go to trial and end in a court decision will likely have gone through the process of filing pleadings, pretrial discovery and case preparation, the trial itself, a possible appeal to a higher court, and the final enforcement of the verdict. The awards that are granted fall broadly into the categories of special damages, general damages, and punitive damages. *Special damages* are compensation for direct and tangible losses suffered by the prevailing party—medical expenses, lost wages, and lost or damaged property. *General damages* refer to less tangible losses, such as pain and suffering. *Punitive damages* may be awarded in situations where the defendant's actions are deemed to be grossly negligent or sufficiently outside the bounds of acceptable behavior as to warrant an economic punishment.

Tort Law

The word *tort* means a civil wrong other than a breach of contract. Broadly speaking, torts are either intentional or unintentional (i.e., negligence) actions. Intentional cases—which are not discussed in any detail here—include such things as trespassing, conversion of property, assault and battery, false imprisonment, and defamation of character.

Negligence cases typically involve alleged personal injury or property damage. A plaintiff will be expected to demonstrate (with a preponderance of the evidence) that:

- The defendant had a legal duty to act or not act in a particular way.
- The defendant breached that legal duty.
- The breach of duty was the proximate cause of the loss sustained.
- There were damages sustained by the plaintiff.

Defendants have numerous possible defenses available. Obviously, they may be able to demonstrate that any of the four conditions listed previously is not true. But if circumstances permit, defendents may also invoke a contributory or comparative negligence, an assumption of risk, or an immunity defense.

Contributory or comparative negligence may be invoked when it is permitted and when it can be shown that the plaintiff contributed in some way to the damages sustained. In some circumstances, even one percent "contribution" on the part of the plaintiff is sufficient to allow the defendant to prevail. More commonly, a degree of contribution limits but does not eliminate a defendant's liability.

The assumption of risk defense asserts that the plaintiff was aware of the risks and assumed responsibility for the consequences. Prior to the adoption of workers compensation laws at the beginning of the century, this defense was a virtually airtight defense available to employers who were sued by injured workers.

The third available defense is immunity. In certain circumstances, charitable or religious institutions enjoy a certain degree of exemption from legal liability.

Contract Law: A Foundation Problem

As the title of this section indicates, contract law is a fundamental concern for risk managers. This is because organizations are collections of contracts, obligations, commitments, and agreements (COCAs). Since COCAs are the principal means by which organizations become exposed to risk, the legal issues surrounding these arrangements would seem to be central to managing risks.

Contracts become legally enforceable when four elements are present.

1. There is offer and acceptance by the parties involved.
2. There is consideration offered by the parties involved.
3. The parties are legally competent to enter into the contract.
4. The contract serves a legal purpose.

From an exposure standpoint, any one of these elements may prove to be problematic for a business. Furthermore, parties may be unable to perform, the intent of the contract may be disputed, inherent risks may not be identified in advance (and thus not planned for), and a contract may come to cross-purposes with other arrangements.

Businesses have always had to address contract-related risk issues, meaning that apart from the risks that pass through the contract, the management of the contract itself may generate problems and issues. What has changed in the past ten to fifteen years is the level of contracting for services. Broad pressures to outsource, to seek greater performance efficiencies, and to trim management structures has led to new and extended uses of third-party service providers. The management of these arrangements has expanded the scope of risk management activity so much that many risk managers complain that "contract risk management" has generated a paperwork blizzard in the form of certificates of insurance (verifying that vendors have purchased appropriate coverages), performance bonds, warranties, and credit assurances. One need only imagine the scope and scale of such documentation in a major construction project to gain a small insight on the day-to-day challenge of overseeing vendor and service provider risk management efforts.

Premises Liability

In a practical sense, premises liability is the most commonplace liability exposure any organization will face. The law imposes certain expectations on property owners (or those controlling property) with respect to the duties they owe visitors to those premises. Although the duty varies depending on whether the visitor is lawfully or unlawfully on the premises, it is generally true that visitors have a right to a degree of safety and to reasonable warning about hazards that may exist.

For a business, the practical challenge of managing this exposure is daunting because it could extend from the office steps to parking lots and private roadways, to parklands or corporate campuses, to corporate fitness centers or day care facilities. In addition to being the most commonplace exposure, premises liability certainly is the broadest liability exposure a business will face.

One could easily imagine disaster scenarios in premises liability situations—collapse of a hotel walkway, children trapped in a fire at a private school, and so on. However, well over 90 percent of legal claims arising from premises liability are classic "slip and fall" claims; each troubling enough but not individually catastrophic from the firm's perspective. This observation offers hope to risk managers inasmuch as it suggests that reasonable steps may be taken to prevent or avoid such accidents from occurring.

Products and Services Liability

Product or service liability is an exposure area that arises from the legal obligation businesses have to safeguard customers from the harm that may occur from use of a product or a service.

There are two key aspects of product or service liability that warrant highlighting. First, liability for defective products or services may be the result of a range of legal approaches. For example, plaintiffs may pursue a legal remedy under a breach of warranty doctrine, of which there are several possible types—breach of an express warranty, breach of an implied warranty of fitness, breach of an implied warranty of merchantability, and breach of an implied warranty of title. Breaches of warranty are problematic, at least relative to a claim of negligence, because the plaintiff has only one challenge and that is to prove that a warranty was breached (whereas a negligence case requires the plaintiff to prove duty, breach of duty, proximate cause, and damages sustained). Warranties hold a special status in the eyes of the law, and they are valuable if held and worrisome if issued.

Second, product liability claims that are pursued as negligence actions are largely subject to strict or absolute liability standards. Although the two words, *strict* or *absolute*, have slightly different technical connotations, the general meaning is that the standard of care or duty is so high that it is assumed the defendant is unlikely to meet that duty. On occasion there may be a case where a defendant is able to demonstrate attainment of the standard, but the history of absolute liability shows an evolution toward the notion of an unattainable standard. To explain this in a different way, readers may recall that a conventional tort action requires the plaintiff to establish duty, breach of duty, proximate cause, and damages sustained. In an absolute liability action, the duty is so high that breach is assumed; thus the plaintiff really is left to show only that the assumed breached duty directly led to the plaintiff's loss.

Environmental Impairment/Public Nuisance Liability

Maintenance of a public nuisance conventionally is seen as an area of exposure when the actions of a wrongdoer affect the public in general (though there is such a thing as a private nuisance as well). Historically, legal actions falling in this area included complaints about sirens or whistles disturbing the peace, disturbances due to blasting during construction, and unsafe construction of roadways, to cite but a few examples. Over the past fifteen years, however, this area of civil law has become transformed by the specific public nuisance of "environmental impairment."

One could cite numerous factors behind the growth of the environmental impairment exposure. The "green" movement, governmental activism, the complicated nature of many polluted sites—all have contributed to heightened activity in this area.

Whereas the courts have played an influential role in the evolution of environmental impairment law, state and federal legislation has been particularly important. Numerous enactments regulate the manner in which hazardous wastes are handled and disposed, including the Water Pollution Control Act; the Water Quality Improvement Act; the Clean Air Act; and the Comprehensive Environmental Response, Compensation, and Liability Act.

Risk managers commonly cite environmental impairment as one of the most significant problems they face. In part this is due to the increasing complexity of the law (and, indeed, the environmental impairment problem itself), the fact that strict and absolute liability standards are widely applied in such cases, and because current law makes it unlikely that a potentially responsible firm can evade or avoid responsibility for environmental problems.

Insights

Prepare for Litigation Before It Strikes

James F. Dorion is an attorney and senior consultant with Richard Oliver International—a unit of Willis Risk Solutions—in Naperville, Illinois. Reprinted with permission from *Business Insurance,* March 27, 2000. © Crain Communications Inc. All rights reserved.

Now, more than ever, the expenses associated with litigation are considered a cost of doing business. Even when you win, litigation is a drain on time, energy, and money. As many business leaders realize, it can adversely affect both stock price and merger activity. Fortunately, the risks associated with litigation can be aggressively managed to minimize their effect on your bottom line.

Those who wish to favorably influence the outcome of litigation should be prepared before it begins. An initial step in this preparation is the assessment of claims facing your company and the identification of potential litigation. This will help to properly focus available resources. Your company's potential liability and the claimant's alleged damages should be investigated promptly. Favorable witnesses and/or evidence may not be available indefinitely. A preliminary evaluation of each claim needs to be conducted by someone qualified to spot legal issues and estimate exposures. In addition, the potential to obtain contribution from any other parties also must be assessed.

There may be occasions when the facts that emerge during your investigation implicate your company alone. In such instances, when your liability is clear and the opposition's assessment of damages is reasonable, it is usually best to take advantage of any settlement opportunities. The cost to resolve such cases rarely diminishes with the passage of time.

It is crucial to establish an efficient response system for referring cases to counsel and providing notice to insurers. Such a system will help prevent having a default judgment entered against your company and will obviate battles with your insurer over the payment of ''pre-tender'' defense costs, which it may characterize as noncovered "voluntary" payments. Most insurance policies that provide for a defense require that notice of any suit be given immediately, "as soon as possible" or "as soon as practicable." In some states, prompt notice is a prerequisite for obtaining coverage. Most states, however, require an insurer to prove that it has been prejudiced—that is, suffered irreparable harm—due to the policyholder's failure to give timely notice before it can deny coverage on this basis.

Your response system should include a process for evaluating suits tendered to your company for defense by its business partners and customers. As a business decision, you may choose to defend a lawsuit filed against your best customer if that suit involves your product, even if your company's liability appears questionable in the claim. Leaving this type of decision to the discretion of your insurer could result in damage to your multimillion-dollar customer relationship over a few $10,000 to $15,000 cases.

Special consideration should be given to lawsuits alleging any cumulative injury that may affect multiple policy periods. This type of lawsuit has the potential to trigger coverage under occurrence-based liability insurance policies having effective periods that have already expired. For example, if a plaintiff alleges that your company negligently polluted a site it occupied from 1979 to 1987, you could, in many states, look to the insurance policies that were in effect from 1979 onward to provide a defense to the suit if the terms and conditions of those policies so provide.

Some insurance programs give the policyholder the right to select its own attorney. Selecting defense counsel is an important decision that should not be made in haste or under pressure; these, however, are the prevailing circumstances when most lawyers are selected. For this reason, it is helpful to preselect counsel in jurisdictions where your company does business. An attempt should be made to develop a long-term relationship with particular lawyers, not necessarily firms.

Selection should be based on the lawyer who will actually be handling the case; watch out for the "bait-and-switch" maneuver. For example, you may have been attracted to a firm by a certain well-respected partner, only to discover that an extremely inexperienced associate will be handling your case under the partner's supervision. You don't want to be in the position of paying for on-the-job training. It should be noted that a passive client is not likely to get the best a firm has to offer.

A lawyer's or firm's familiarity with your business should be taken into consideration, but should not be the sole deciding factor. Selection is often best made on the basis of prior experience or referrals. If neither is available, you may wish to consult a reliable directory, such as "Best's Directory of Recommended Insurance Attorneys and Adjusters." Venue should also be taken into consideration. For example, if your company has been sued in a small town, a well-respected local sole practitioner or small firm will often serve your interests better than would an out-of-town big firm. There is a lot to be said for "hometown" advantage in dealing with a given judge or potential jury pool.

Remember that firms with the lowest rates are not necessarily the least expensive in the long run. Although you may reduce the amount you spend on defense costs, you risk ultimately increasing the amount you pay to settle or otherwise resolve a lawsuit. Always choosing the least expensive firm may also give your company a reputation as an easy mark, increasing the number of nuisance suits filed against it. It has been said that the best lawyers are expensive, but the second-best lawyers are very expensive.

Once you have narrowed your list of potential candidates to two or three firms, you can ask each of them to run a conflicts check, and you should contact their references before making your final selection. You should communicate your litigation guidelines and reporting expectations at the outset of a suit, when your leverage as a client is greatest.

Firms should not claim competence in all things. The firm that did a sensational job defending against a severe auto claim may be totally ill-equipped to handle a wrongful-termination suit. Also, be wary of firms that have received negative press concerning malpractice suits or staff defections. Your case will not receive the attention it deserves if the firm is facing such distractions. While seeking optimum performance from your local counsel, it is important to keep an eye on costs. This can be accomplished with the help of an outside litigation manager, through internal procedures and/or through legal bill auditors. Many people fear that lawyers will resist management, so they never try to manage costs.

Traditional hourly billing provides an incentive for inefficiency and delay. Overbilling isn't always the result of fraud; more often, it arises when a firm has been given free rein to bill as it pleases. There is an ever-increasing pressure, especially at large firms, to bill more and more hours per year.

There are alternatives to traditional hourly billing to help combat this trend. It may be useful to work with the firm to set up a short-term budget—60 to 90 days—and then share any cost overruns and/or savings with the firm. This technique is only as good as the budget, though. Some firms have a tendency to inflate their budget estimate for fear of exceeding it. You can counteract this to some degree by making submission of a budget part of the selection process. Competition should keep estimates realistic.

Still other firms attempt to entice potential clients with low-ball estimates, which are often accompanied by unrealistic or excessive caveats. If you have concerns about a low estimate, you should ensure that it is in writing and is binding.

Some firms offer a "blended" rate that offers the legal services of the firm, whether provided by a senior partner or a junior associate, at a rate lower than that of the highest rate charged by that firm, but higher than that charged by junior staff. These arrangements are not always as good as you might think. A blended rate provides an incentive to have junior staff members perform tasks that merit a partner's attention.

A flat-fee arrangement will provide predictability. Also, under a flat-fee scenario, the firm will pay the cost of inefficiency. You may pay more for some services than you would on an hourly basis, but the expectation is that costs will balance out in the long run. An analysis of historical data from your company's litigation files should provide a basis for the determination of appropriate flat fees.

Controlling litigation costs through the use of flat fees requires proactive litigation management. A lawyer who agrees to a flat fee has a financial incentive to do as little as possible on a case. Further, when using a flat-fee per-task structure, the decision of what tasks need to be done should not be left to the firm alone, as it may be tempted to churn cases assigned by clients with deep pockets.

Some services traditionally provided only by law firms may be unbundled and outsourced. There are many high-quality independent vendors of document management and discovery management services that charge rates significantly lower than those charged by law firms.

A common cause of runaway legal fees is over-lawyering. For instance, a partner may be doing work that could be done by an associate or paralegal. The task should be appropriate for the experience level of the individual performing it. Also, there may be excessive interoffice conferences or multiple attorneys attending meetings where one would suffice. If you suspect over-lawyering, an audit of legal bills you have already paid may reveal cause for a refund by identifying improper or questionable charges.

The following general rules should help minimize costs:

■ *Standardize status reports.* Standardized reports are easy to digest and they can be efficiently updated. Reports should concisely highlight developments and contain counsel's recommendations, letting you know whether your case, at a given point, is better or worse. Also, you can condition the payment of invoices upon receipt of these reports.

■ *Limit paper flow.* Eliminate unnecessary duplication of attachments and the drafting of separate letters when copies will do.

■ *Monitor discovery.* It is often not necessary to depose all witnesses designated by the plaintiff. Also, as a side note, when responding to discovery, never yield to the temptation to destroy documents. Apart from the obvious ethical issues, such actions can destroy you in court and in the press.

■ *Keep deposition summaries brief.* Your local counsel should be able to highlight the sections that have the potential to influence your case.

■ *Do not allow block billing.* Each task should be listed separately so you can see its true cost.

■ *Check to see whether disbursements are being billed at greater than actual cost.* Backup documentation should be available upon request.

■ *Do not pay for overtime of clerical staff.* The firm should have enough staff to handle the matter during regular business hours.

■ *Insist on interim bills.* Monthly invoices will allow you to quickly resolve any billing problems by comparing actual fees to your budget soon after the fees are incurred.

There are internal cost-control measures as well. The maintenance of work-product and discovery databases will avoid duplication of effort. In addition, alternative dispute resolution techniques can be used to avoid some of the costs and delay associated with litigation. Plaintiffs may be willing to agree to arbitration or mediation in the hope of achieving a swift and reasonable resolution.

Decision makers need to track cases closely and monitor reserves. If you have posted internal reserves of $250,000 for a particular case, you do not want a call from your defense counsel on the courthouse steps telling you that your best bet is to settle now for $750,000. It is dangerous to rely on intuition alone, as verdict potential can vary greatly depending on geographic location and the reputation of the opposing counsel.

Your local counsel should provide you with a verdict estimate and indicate the probability of each potential outcome. It can be helpful to have input from a neutral litigation manager, who can make an unbiased assessment. You can estimate case values based on either prior experience or sophisticated statistical models. While there is no exact science, experience and legal knowledge can be a useful guide.

A cost/benefit analysis should be done with each case development, and you should question at each point whether it is more advantageous to settle or press on. Understanding each side's arguments will enable you to better evaluate the relative strengths and weaknesses of your case. Reading all briefs prepared by both sides will help you to fully understand the disputed issues.

In summary, if you establish an efficient response system for the handling of lawsuits, carefully select your defense counsel, work to control costs, and make informed decisions, the odds of bringing a litigated matter to a cost-effective, favorable resolution will be greatly increased. The failure to follow one or more of these steps could result in an unexpected and extremely large adverse verdict, or in a defense verdict at a cost several times greater than the amount it would have taken to settle.

Professional Liability

Professionals, however they are defined, possess a legal status that is different from the ordinary person on the street. Simply put, professionals are held to a higher standard of care—more is expected of a professional in terms of knowledge, competence, and judgment in the scope of professional expertise.

Reasonably, one may wonder what constitutes a professional in the eyes of the law. Unfortunately, the concept is somewhat open-ended and there is something of a trend in expanding the concept to include more individuals. Certainly, physicians, lawyers, architects, and others for whom advanced training is essential would fit into the general category of professionals. Somewhat less clear would be managers within an organization, such as financial managers, operations managers, and others with fairly specialized expertises. In addition, a survey of professional liability claims would reveal individual cases where a wide range of occupations (e.g., truck and taxi drivers to pool hall operators) are deemed to be professionals in the context of a particular case.

Professional liability cases are frequently referred to as malpractice cases, and though such cases extend beyond the bounds of what the general public would consider *malpractice,* the word conveys one important element of professional liability cases: Personal/professional reputation is quite closely bound up in a malpractice case, and this upsets the equilibrium that may otherwise prevail. For example, a hospital may be quite willing to settle a case against an emergency room physician because the economic uncertainty of the case outweighs the benefits of litigation—whereas the physician is likely to include loss of reputation in the cost-benefit calculation and therefore is more motivated to litigate the case.

Readers should note that insurance companies offering professional liability coverage deem the risk to be sufficiently different from others that they tend to either specialize in it or exclude it from broader coverages. The nature of the coverage offered also tends to differ in important ways from other liability coverages (e.g., professionals are permitted greater participation in their defense under professional liability coverages).

Directors and Officers and Fiduciary Liability

Although directors and officers liability and fiduciary liability have distinctly different technical implications in the world of insurance, they have some conceptual connections that make a common discussion appropriate.

Directors and officers of a firm may be held legally liable for any number of things. A CEO may drive a company car in a negligent fashion and be subject to the laws that pertain to that situation. A board member may also fall under the scope of professional liability if, for instance, actions or decisions taken are influenced by that official's professional training (say, engineering). However, the term *directors and officers liability* refers specifically to an exposure arising from errors and omissions—as opposed to negligent acts—that an officer commits in the scope of duties. A classic example would be a suit related to a merger and acquisition that alleges the acquiring board failed to exercise the due care in investigating the acquired firm.

One may be tempted to think that the errors and omissions of an director or officer might be an issue of general negligence law (and, as will be seen later, of general liability insurance), but this is incorrect for at least two reasons. First, general negligence matters tend to focus on events that lead to physical damage to assets or physical harm to individuals (e.g., reckless driving damages the car of another as well as that individual). The world of directors and officers liability contemplates economic damages that are— generally—distinct from direct physical harm (e.g., a zoning decision deprives a business of sales to customers) and are not the result of deliberate or negligent acts but of oversights, errors, mistakes, and misinterpretations. Second, directors and officers liability refers to an area of law where executives might be held individually responsible for the errors and omissions they commit. Ordinarily, an employee will be named in an action, but it is the firm that is the principal party to an action due to the concept of agency (discussed later on in this chapter). Depending on the state, however, an employee can be sued as an individual, in certain circumstances, for decisions made, and the firm may have no official standing in the proceeding.

This second point about individual accountability suggests that directors and officers liability is similar to errors and omissions liability in the public sector, where elected officials can be sued as individuals for mismanagement, among other things. In both the public and private instance, there is a particular problem that arises because many legal actions pursued under this area of law will come from stockholders or citizens. If the organization promises to insure or indemnify the board member or elected official, it means that the organization is expending resources to protect that individual against suits filed by the owners of that organization— clearly a troubling conceptual and practical problem. Some laws simply bar an organization from taking such action and the officer must buy insurance to secure financial protection against such suits. Other laws recognize that allowing the organization to buy insurance or indemnify such individuals is a cost of attracting qualified people into such decision-making positions.

The matter of fiduciary liability is related to directors and officers liability in the sense that a fiduciary responsibility refers to the legal duty one party has in managing or controlling the assets of another. In that sense, boards have a broad fiduciary duty to those parties that provide the resources necessary to run the organization.

However, it is true that fiduciary liability tends to refer to managers who have specific responsibilities for the management of distinct assets—say, an employee-funded pension scheme. Generally, the finance or treasury function of a firm will have pockets of fiduciary responsibility for certain funds or pools of assets (e.g., bond proceeds), and that responsibility is to parties outside the organization. It is enough to say that the general legal expectation is that managers behave as if the assets within their trust and care are their own.

Bailment Liability

Bailment liability is somewhat related to fiduciary liability in that it refers to assets that are temporarily in the care, custody, or control of another. An example where such a situation could arise is a privately owned parking ramp. In the broadest sense, the firm has a certain duty to safeguard the automobiles while in its control. A dry cleaning service would have—again, broadly speaking—a similar duty with respect to the customers' clothing.

These two examples are obvious, but they also are equivocal, because laws frequently modify the exposure a firm may have in bailment situations. In the case of a parking ramp, the law may simply allow the owner to issue a waiver (commonly on the back of the ticket) that preempts liability from attaching to the firm. In the case of the dry cleaning service, a similar waiver may be employed.

Employment Liability

It probably is not an understatement to identify employment liability as the most rapidly growing concern for businesses in the

United States. One may be tempted to cite the growing litigiousness of society or even the advent of the "victim" culture, and there probably is some truth to this. However, the expansion of employment liability is due to many complex factors: the aging workforce, the diversification of the workforce, the advancement of women in the workforce, the role of labor unions in business, the wide variety of types of employment found in the business world today, and the various national and state initiatives that are intended to provide equal treatment of individuals under the law. One of the dimensions of employment liability, workers compensation, is so profoundly important in its own right that it is discussed separately in the next section.

When a firm enters into an employment agreement with an individual, the terms and conditions of that contract raise fundamental risks that would exist in any contract: the ability of the parties to perform, the strength of guarantees, and the risk-bearing capacity of the parties. These risks, while important, are not the key risks of the contract. The key risks are not necessarily expressed in the contract but include the array of common and statutory laws that pertain to employment relationships. These laws include the Fair Labor Relations Act; the Americans with Disabilities Act; the Occupational Health and Safety Act; the right-to-know legislation; the Employee Retirement and Income Security Act; the Unemployment Insurance program; the Old Age, Survivors, and Disability Insurance program; and many others. In addition, a range of antidiscrimination measures have been introduced to protect minorities, women, and other groups (e.g., veterans). Complicating matters, some of the pertinent laws come from the federal government and courts, while some others comes from state and local governments and courts.

Workers' Compensation

The subject of workers' compensation is worthy of an entire chapter, if not more. Indeed, the brief treatment provided here may be dangerous in that it may suggest to readers that it is a peripheral or narrow and technical legal matter for risk managers. It is not. In fact, workers' compensation and the general issue of workplace safety are consistently rated as one of the biggest challenges risk managers face.

Workers' compensation is a no-fault system that has been adopted in each state (the federal government and a handful of other nonlocal entities also have similar systems in place) to provide health care, lost income, and rehabilitation benefits to workers injured on the job. Although each state approaches the matter differently, almost any employee who is injured while working is entitled to complete medical care, which is likely to include the appropriate rehabilitative services. While that person is unable to work, lost income benefits approximating two-thirds of that worker's pre-injury gross wage are paid until that individual returns to work. Death benefits are payable to eligible dependents should that be an issue.

Workers' compensation is viewed by scholars as a grand social compromise. Employers guarantee that certain benefits will be paid to eligible workers, regardless of fault. In turn, workers relinquish their right to sue employers for work-related injuries (which is why workers compensation is commonly referred to as the "exclusive remedy"). There have been some inroads into the exclusivity of the workers' compensation system, and occasions do arise when a worker may sue an employer, but such situations remain a minor exception to the general rule.

Although the subject of risk financing arises more fully in Chapter 6, readers should note that workers' compensation statutes compel employers to finance their workers' compensation costs and to demonstrate that they have done so. In six states, employers are required to buy insurance from the state. In all other states, insurance is purchased in a competitive commercial insurance marketplace. Self-insurance is allowed in most states today.

Agency Liability

In light of the increasing reliance on outside vendors and service providers, we need to mention, even if only briefly, the area of law pertaining to agency relationships.

Principal-agent relationships abound in the private sector. Certainly, managers act as agents of the firm that employs them, and the general rule is that—while in the performance of their duties—employees and the firm are the same. Knowledge of the employee is knowledge of the firm; an employee's acts are the firm's acts; and so on.

The principal-agent relationship is problematic within the firm, but there is a degree of control present due to the nature of reporting relationships and natural oversight that occurs. However, a degree of control separation occurs when activities are outsourced and when the day-to-day supervision of agents is not possible. An agent providing outsourced services is still an agent, and the principal is under the same legal expectations.

In truth, the concept of agency liability offers one of the key conundrums faced by risk managers today. Outsourcing of services may make considerable sense in a broad economic context, but for the risk manager it means that the firm retains ultimate responsibility for the activity even while it has loosened its ability to control the activity itself. In principal, outsourcing is likely to make the management of risk even more difficult than it already is (this subject is discussed more thoroughly in Chapter 8).

Motor Vehicle Liability

In general, the rules of ordinary negligence apply in cases involving motor vehicles. If an employee negligently causes harm to another person, that person may sue the firm and will prevail if the tests of negligence are met.

For a variety of reasons, many states have sought to modify the ordinary rules of negligence. To a large degree, these modifications are due to the enormous number of motor vehicle accidents that occur each year and the concern that court dockets would be overwhelmed if all accidents were adjudicated in civil court.

Approximately half of all states have adopted a no-fault scheme that limits an injured party's rights of legal redress. None of the no-fault states is an absolute no-fault state, because tort suits are still possible. The evidence of the efficacy of no-fault laws is equivocal and subject to debate. Many states stop short of a no-fault system but require that insurance be purchased in order for a vehicle to be licensed.

Moral Responsibility

One often hears business leaders justify a rather unsavory action or decision by noting that "no laws were broken." While it always is a good idea to avoid breaking the law, this statement carries with it a whiff of impropriety. One would hope that human behavior is not governed solely by the standards of the courts. Other standards of conduct can and should prevail, and it is important for risk managers to recognize that the ethical domain is an exposure area for business organizations.

The moral responsibility exposure should be defined (i.e., identified and assessed) and measured. The difficulty for risk managers is that standards of ethical behavior are not fully agreed upon in a democratic society. This is not to say that people don't believe in absolute or nearly absolute standards of behavior—it is only to say that America has chosen to tread quite carefully in imposing a single standard of morality on society. How would Americans come to consensus on that standard? Who would enforce it? What would the consequences be?

This does not mean, however, that risk managers cannot think about the exposure area and cannot incorporate analysis into overall risk assessment efforts. At the very least, one should expect a risk manager to consider the moral dimensions of particular considerations and at least articulate the implications of being deemed "wrong" in some action. For instance, a business decision to build a waste water treatment facility should incorporate recognition of the ethical dimension of exposing the community to possible pollution, as well as recognition of the legal consequences of that decision.

This example, however, suggests the difficulty in "measuring" the exposure to moral risk. Unless one is privileged to gaze upon the Heavenly Ledger, it is impossible to gauge the impact. On a more temporal plane, surrogate values may occasionally be appropriate. For instance, loss of public/customer support can sometimes be measured fairly precisely and sometimes can be linked to "ethical performance." While this line of reasoning can be every bit as troubling as the "we didn't break any laws" defense (to wit, 'if the public doesn't mind, why should we?'), it does show that there are ways to think about the impact of ethical risks on individuals and organizations.

In many respects, risk management is all about consequences. If a firm does something, intended or unintended outcomes may occur. Some of the consequences naturally will be moral and ethical, and they may weigh as heavily on the firm as does damage to property or a threatened liability suit. This means that risk managers have to be very conscious of their role in assessing moral risks and taking measures to manage them. Perhaps another way of putting it is to say that risk managers serve the role of the chorus in a Greek tragedy, reminding fellow managers of the consequences of their actions, the fickleness of fortune, and human fallibility.

Read More About It

Hidden Dangers: Taking the Uncertainty Out of Mergers and Acquisitions

John Conley
Reprinted with permission from *Risk Management* magazine, April 2000. Copyright 2000 by Risk Management Society Publishing. All rights reserved. For more information call 212.286.9364. www.rims.org/rmmag

Columbia Energy Group, a large Herndon, Virginia–based power company, had its heart set last year on acquiring Carlos Leffler Inc., a Pennsylvania heating oil company. There was a problem, however.

Leffler's 75,000 customers receive home heating fuel from eight corporate storage facilities, some of which had experienced significant spills, the oil migrating onto others' properties. Columbia Energy's potential pollution liability, were it to acquire Leffler, made its chief legal officer blanch, nearly squelching the acquisition. "My boss is adverse to all risk, but especially environmental risk," explains Nick Parillo, Columbia Energy's vice president of risk management. "He doesn't like it when things come out of the woodwork and crater a deal."

So Parillo was given his marching orders—quantify how much the spills and resultant damage cost to clean up and, in case this expense turns out to be higher than estimated, transfer that risk to a third party. Parillo did just that, buying an environmental impairment liability insurance policy from ECS Underwriting, an Exton, Pennsylvania–based insurance agency.

Like other companies seeking vertical expansion in these heady days of mergers and acquisitions, Columbia liked the assets it saw, but not the uncertain pollution liabilities. Since most mergers today are stock purchases using cash, buyers acquire both the assets and liabilities of the target company. When the liabilities are in doubt or are difficult to fully quantify, as they often are with respect to environmental risks, they can scotch the deal. To remove them in full or in part, companies are turning to insurers in the still youthful environmental impairment liability (EIL) market.

Five years ago, the EIL market would not have been a suitable resource to marriage-bent corporations. Insurance capacity was relatively limited, given the uncertainty over future environmental claim costs. Public sentiment regarding pollution weighed heavily on underwriters who, fearful of a backlash, priced coverage at the high end in narrowly written policies. Since then, as insurers gleaned underwriting experience, they have liberalized their posture, creating what many agree is a bona fide buyer's market.

For companies plying an M & A course, pollution insurance can be an important transaction tool, in some cases the difference between a deal-breaker and a deal-maker. "Were it not for environmental insurance," says Parillo, "there's no question the acquisition would not have worked."

Polluting the Deal

EIL insurance made its debut as a standalone market in 1979, when American International Group, Inc., and its underwriting manager at the time, ECS Inc., introduced the novel coverage. News stories documenting the spectacular devastation wrought by pollution (remember Love Canal?) captured the public's attention, fomenting multimillion-dollar lawsuits against corporations and a flurry of federal and state legislation, including the Resource and Conservation Recovery Act, the Comprehensive Environmental Response, Compensation and Liability Act, and the 1980 Superfund law.

New regulations inspired by such legislation required polluters to provide financial proof they could clean up their past messes. ECS and New York–based AIG created an insurance product that did just that, covering property damage and bodily injury emanating from environmental causes. Few companies, other than those required to show financial responsibility, bought the insurance.

At the time, many believed they already were covered for pollution damage and injury claims under their comprehensive general liability (CGL) policies. Sued for past pollution practices, they filed claims against their CGL insurers to defend them and pay losses. The insurers demurred, and the insureds took their claims to court. Most of these cases have now been settled, allegedly determined to the benefit of insureds.

All this legal turmoil compelled the drafting of a specific exclusion for pollution liability in post-1985 CGL policies. Companies now had two options to relieve their concerns over environmental liability—do nothing and keep their fingers crossed or buy insurance from AIG/ECS. Because the insurance was so costly and restrictive, most did the former.

Who could blame them? The due diligence required of policy applicants was so onerous they had to complete hundreds of forms, not to mention pay for environmental risk audits before AIG would even pick up the phone. Such surveys cost as much as $10,000 per site. "It was a very cumbersome and costly process for potential insureds," concedes David Bennink, vice president of ECS, now part of XL Insurance Ltd. in Bermuda.

As ECS and AIG started to make money from the line, other insurers jumped on the bandwagon. The first was Reliance National, which utilized ECS as its underwriting manager after it parted ways with AIG in 1987. In the 1990s, Zurich Insurance Group, Kemper Insurance Co., Lloyd's of London, Chubb Group, and XL Insurance also took a flyer on EIL. The heightened competition increased capacity, drove down costs, and loosened coverage terms and conditions. For example, buyers no longer have to conduct or pay for environmental site surveys, processes, and costs now absorbed by insurers. And the extensive paperwork is now a four-page application.

"The biggest change in the EIL market is the willingness of insurance carriers to take substantial risk in environmental liabilities," says William McElroy, vice president of New York–based Zurich U.S. Specialties. "The post-Superfund success in underwriting environmental liabilities has clearly emboldened carriers in their willingness to take some speculative risk on environmental exposures. That has manifested itself in all the issues, including policy limits, price, terms, and conditions."

Coverages now absorb first-party cleanup and bodily injury costs and third-party coverages (insurers previously insured only third-party property damage and bodily injury exposures). Related coverages, including business interruption costs, can also be obtained. Limits have skyrocketed, from $5 million in 1990 to pretty much whatever the insured needs. Kemper, for instance, offers $200 million in coverage. If more is necessary, a risk manager can simply stack one insurer's product on another's and toss in a few more million from excess reinsurers.

The best news is price—down 30 percent in just the last three to four years, according to ECS. At present, buyers can expect roughly a 10 percent premium to coverage limit cost, with a minimum premium of $10,000 for $1 million in coverage considered the norm for a one-year policy covering one site. As more sites and policy years are added (underwriters offer maximum ten-year policies), premium expenses drop. A standard ten-year policy can cost as little as 5 percent of the coverage limit, brokers say.

Premiums would fall further were underwriters able to increase their market penetration. Despite the current buyer's market, a supply-demand imbalance persists. In short, many companies with potential pollution liabilities pass on the opportunity to transfer them. "There is still a bit of education needed for companies to understand what this insurance offers," acknowledges Rod Taylor, a managing director in the environmental practice at insurance broker Willis in New York.

"Many risk managers looked at this four years ago and figured it wasn't worth buying. But things have changed so much for the better, they need to take another look."

An Emerging Market

To increase market penetration, the EIL market is trying to entice nontraditional pollution insurance buyers into the fold. Those traditional buyers—companies involved in hazardous materials treatment, disposal, storage, and transport—are required by law to have financial responsibility and, thus, represent a stagnant market. New buyers are sought among automobile dealerships, hospitals, universities, restaurants, dry cleaning establishments, retail stores, and light manufacturing.

Another way to grow the EIL market is transactional business (e.g., real estate lending business and M & A deals). In the corporate lending area, a borrower usually puts up real estate as collateral to the financial institution providing the loan. The bank wants to make sure that if the borrower defaults on the loan, they are not left holding real estate with potential environmental liabilities. Typically, they require a so-called Phase One survey of real estate holdings to determine the extent of such liability. An alternative is EIL insurance, covering the borrower's future first-party and third-party cleanup costs in the event of an environmental issue emanating on the collateralized property.

In the M & A area, EIL insurance is becoming virtually de

rigueur when companies acquire or divest industrial facilities. "It is extremely difficult to quantify in a due diligence process the target company's environmental liabilities, and yet, if it is a stock purchase, you are responsible under joint and several liability rules for these liabilities," says ECS's Bennink. "Instead of worrying about this, we'll worry for you."

Environmental liability can significantly alter the value of a potential merger or acquisition. Even if a company can discern what it believes is the extent of risk, that estimate can fall far short of actual or realized liability. Transferring the liabilities removes any uncertainty. "In the event $10 million turns out to be $100 million, you're covered," Bennink says.

Indeed, the deal-breaker in many M & A transactions often is environmental uncertainty. "You get a dispute between the parties as to what the actual value of the environmental problems are, and who will inherit them," Taylor says. "Will these costs be retained by the buyer or the seller, funded, shared, or result in a discounted deal price? These issues need to be resolved, or the deal breaks down."

Columbia Energy faced just that possibility. "We had hired outside environmental consultants (Chicago-based Dames & Moore), who did both Phase One and Two studies of the target sites, and they made a conservative estimate of what it would cost to clean them up—$7 million," Parillo recalls. "The question was, who would pay for this?"

Parillo sat down with ECS, which decided to use the consultant's estimate as the deductible in a $100 million policy to cover site remediation expenses, as well as third-party exposures, personal injury, and property damage costs. Thus, if pollution-related expenses exceed $7 million in aggregate, the policy picks up the remaining costs.

The policy's premium was about 3 percent of coverage limits, a discount given the number of sites covered and the ten-year term of the policy. Parillo also negotiated a premium return component, so if losses fall below a certain threshold, Columbia Energy is given back a percentage of the premium it had paid. "This feature serves both us and ECS, in that it gives us incentive to keep costs down by cleaning up the sites on our own," Parillo says.

While buyers in an acquisition scenario typically purchase the insurance, sellers also buy it to clean up their balance sheets. "An old-line manufacturing company may want to divorce itself from old liabilities as it redirects itself into becoming a services company," Bennink says. "We're here to help them remove the sins of the past."

"We've done deals for both buyers and sellers, although we prefer buyer-side transactions," says McElroy from Zurich U.S. Specialties. "When you deal with a company buying another, you know they're there going forward. You don't have any problems getting access to properties or records after the closing."

ECS has even sold EIL policies for conglomerates both buying and shedding companies. The United Co., a Bristol, Virginia–based diversified concern with businesses in the oil and gas, financial services, and construction fields, is one such insured. The company recently bought a roofing supply enterprise and sold off a mining supply division, in each case using EIL insurance as a risk transfer tool to effect the transactions. "We use the insurance all the time in our M & A activity," says Thomas Griffin, the company's vice president of risk management.

Not every company can expect cheap insurance and ample coverage. Insurers will raise eyebrows at industrial concerns that have been in business for decades, if not centuries. "When you're looking backwards at historical disposal practices, these are very hard to quantify in terms of future liability," explains Taylor from Willis. "Underwriters are resistant to these risks, although they are becoming less so as the market matures."

Willis recently brokered an EIL product to a 100-year-old shoe manufacturing company that, over the years, had operated multiple tanneries, shoemaking shops, and via a diversification into textiles, a horde of dye shops, sewing shops, and the like. "They had touched a lot of properties over the decades," Taylor notes.

At first, the company (a confidentiality agreement bars Taylor from divulging its name) indicated it had operated at 160 locations in all, thirty-four of which were still active. "As we re-searched their history, interviewing old-time employees and reading archival material, we learned the actual number of loca-tions was closer to 400," Taylor says.

Willis worked with AIG to craft a policy covering all the sites for EIL risks over the next ten years. Says Taylor, "Were some-one interested in acquiring this company today, they'd see it has a very clean balance sheet—at least for the next decade."

Any takers?

Read More About It

Setting the Right Course: Business Ethics

Mary C. Gentile
Reprinted with permission from *Risk Management* magazine, September 1998. Copyright 1998 by Risk Management Society Publishing. All rights reserved. For more information call 212.286.9364. www.rims.org/rmmag

A sophisticated arsenal of tools enables risk managers to pre-dict, model, and protect against such hazards as natural disas-ters, currency fluctuations, interest rate shifts, plant accidents, products liability litigation, and others. But increasingly, the more daunting threats are harder to predict and protect against because they are tied to human behavior. Few precedents exist for building probability models concerning the way people act, but company ethics initiatives can help identify and prevent po-tential problems.

Within a number of organizations, desired ethical stan-dards straddle an often-blurry line between theory and prac-tice. For instance, a Louis Harris & Associates survey reported in *The New York Times* suggests that if you "ask 100 chief exec-utives of America's largest companies whether their employees intentionally circumvent corporate policies when they consider them to be in the way . . . more than 75 percent will say no." But if you ask employees, "half will assert that such control breakdowns occur often."

In fact, the same study reported that "middle managers are three times as likely as CEOs to give their companies low marks for 'monitoring internal controls,' " and twice as likely "to give their companies low marks for both 'developing and implementing procedures to deal with risk' as well as 'communicating risks and related controls to employees.' "

Thus, the challenge for risk managers is not only to develop sources and systems for capturing accurate, complete, and timely intelligence, but also to cultivate receptive and nonretaliatory listeners among corporate leadership. And of course, all the openness in the world counts for nothing if employees remain unconvinced that such receptivity exists.

Where can concerned risk managers turn for support and insight in this ambiguous terrain of corporate values, cultural norms, shifting standards, and organizational honesty? A valuable resource can be found in a corporate ethics initiative. The most forward-looking programs provide a "way of thinking," a mindset for approaching information related to corporate values, employee behavior, and shifting external constituencies.

For example, a multinational telecommunications giant simultaneously embarking on a strategy of managerial decentralization and international expansion is painfully aware that these twin objectives create optimal conditions for inconsistency as well as the potential for real lapses in efficiency, effectiveness, and ethics. They wonder how, and by whom, information about corporate standards and practices will be communicated and interpreted in different cultural and organizational contexts.

Similarly, a Fortune 500 manufacturing firm, immersed in rapid growth through acquisition, runs the risk of encountering regulatory and legal liabilities and damage to its reputation should its pre-acquisition due diligence prove inaccurate or insufficient.

And the closer a mining enterprise looks at a remote Asian-Pacific subsidiary, the more it recognizes potential impediments to implementing the parent firm's health and safety standards and upholding the Foreign Corrupt Practices Act—impediments that are not regularly reported to management because no system exists for sharing such data.

Managerial restructurings, mergers and acquisitions, globalization, heightened media scrutiny and Internet access, and increased shareholder activism—all of these swelling trends share certain features. They all create opportunities for information-based disasters. Corporations may fail to communicate about conflicting values, standards, or cultural norms, or they may do so poorly. Employees who are convinced there is no audience for their concerns internally may take accounts of unethical or unsafe practices to the press or to cyberspace. And increasingly empowered and vocal shareholders can access and use such data easily.

It is precisely these information based concerns that risk managers raise when they are asked to recite potential limitations in addressing ethics-related exposures within an organization:

- How can I obtain information about conditions that are changing where there is no baseline for comparison, no history from which to extrapolate likely scenarios, and no clear sources of unbiased data?

- How can I obtain information about prohibited practices (legal violations, regulatory infractions, or ethical lapses) when individual employees are reluctant to report their colleagues, fearful of retaliation, or suspect that management may tacitly accept or even expect such practices?

- How can I promote the integration of risk-related questions into the development of overall corporate strategy and the daily management of core business processes when these questions are often more difficult to quantify than other risk management issues?

- And perhaps most important, how can I promote a corporate culture where candor and openness to information flourishes, where denial and the preservation of deniability are replaced by receptivity and a nonretaliatory posture toward listening among corporate leadership? And how can I promote this candor while balancing it against a respect for appropriate individual privacy and confidentiality?

A Look Inside

An effective ethics program is concerned with the identification, development, and sharing of information regarding these thorny questions of human behavior and shifting values. Such a program confronts difficult dilemmas with candid discourse and takes the approach that "what you do know, you can respond to and deal with effectively." As Michael J. Critelli, chairman and CEO of Pitney Bowes Inc., phrased it, "You can tell the story or someone else can tell it for you." Seen in this light, a responsible business practice function is a natural partner of the risk manager.

At a time when risk management is evolving, an ethics program can be a catalyst for that transformation. Risk managers are endeavoring to adopt—and to encourage their senior management to accept—a broader, more strategic perspective toward their function in the firm; to take a cross-functional approach in reviewing business processes; to develop a language for addressing risk that is relevant, compelling, and accessible to a wider organizational audience. Most fundamentally, they have been moving for quite some time now from risk protection (insurance) to risk prevention (information and control systems).

The underlying principles of a business ethics practice support each of these shifts. An effective initiative begins with a corporate conversation concerning the organization's primary values and driving principles, requiring a thoughtful and public commitment to those premises by the firm's leadership and making those premises explicitly clear to all employees. Similarly, the program provides a language of shared values and commitments for raising concerns and inconsistencies while representatives from across the organization review the messages given and the practices supported, explicitly and implicitly, across all functions.

The key components of a corporate ethics program are designed to optimize a corporation's information culture. Such components include: organizational assessments; cross-functional and multilevel compliance and responsible practices teams; broad communication programs (including print materials, websites, and training); ongoing assessment and monitoring of business practices (through focus groups, surveys, hotlines, and e-mail); and integration of programs into performance measurements.

Let's look at a few actual examples of potential dangers that an ethics initiative can uncover and address:

1. A multinational financial services company decided it was time to take a closer look at ethical business practices as regulatory scrutiny increased within the industry and, in particular, within the firm's halls. Consumer, investor, and media attention had been captured by some very public loan failures, as well as changing regulations requiring greater transparency in the firm's reporting of commercial dealings.

As the organization embarked on a comprehensive review of employee understanding and compliance with corporate policies and standards, it became apparent that the firm was infused with a "culture of secrecy." Internal policies were not written down, or they were written in many different locations with which only the firm's legal and compliance officers were thoroughly familiar. Some practices were not consistent with changing external and regulatory requirements, and managers within different business functions were not training their staff regarding the changed standards. And employees, understandably, interpreted this lack of attention to consistent and thorough communication of standards and values as a signal of low priority, or worse, active discouragement.

It was through the effort to design and develop a business ethics initiative that these information hazards were made apparent to senior management and a proactive mechanism for addressing them surfaced. Working in tandem with the firm's risk management function, new opportunities emerged for preventing future violations.

2. At another global financial services firm, disaster seemed to have already struck. Found to be in violation of proper practices, regulators demanded that an employee edu-

cation program be developed for all supervising officers. But in the process of satisfying the regulators' demands, the company and its officers uncovered widespread gaps in their procedural manuals and training efforts and, perhaps more important, an active "disinformation campaign" being waged through the informal transfer of supposed wisdom from experienced employees to newer ones. While the corporate values stated one thing, employees believed that what really counted were the numbers, regardless of the official standards. And had they not welcomed a team of ethics experts into their fold to research and develop the required training, senior management would have remained woefully ignorant of regulatory violations waiting to happen, with much greater cost to the company.

Promoting Candor

Ethics and responsible business practice initiatives often uncover other common hazards. A tendency in some firms is to "kill the messenger" when employees or managers try to alert their organizational seniors to potential ethical risks. The frequently heard accounts of whistle-blowers who—after years of unsuccessfully trying to "capture the ear" of their managers—finally take their stories of unsafe or unethical business practices outside the company are unfortunate cautionary tales.

When evaluating potential mergers and acquisitions, for another example, decision makers who do an admirable job assessing future product, asset, and financial synergies often overlook questions regarding the compatibility of business practices and corporate values, or different levels of familiarity with regulated operating environments in the new company partners. A business practices assessment is an invaluable tool for completing the kind of M & A due diligence that uncovers such risks. Today, for example, after hiring 2,000 brokers from the fifty recently acquired branch offices of Yamaichi Securities in Japan, Merrill Lynch must retrain them to understand the differences in American expectations and standard practices. This means that the common habit of lending clients company money to cover losses must be broken.

Perhaps most important of all, managers and experts in business ethics initiatives are familiar with and comfortable asking often-overlooked questions, such as:

- Who are the stakeholders in this decision? Or, put another way, whom are we protecting? An ethics approach answers this question broadly, often uncovering potential victims of inadvertent decisions, or potential perpetrators of unplanned business malpractice.

- Whom can we involve in this decision, or ask for cooperation in addressing this issue? Pressures of time, control, and secrecy often push managers to narrow this list. But, as has been suggested above, a cross-functional and organizationally collaborative response to this question can help managers anticipate and prevent risks.

- What sources of information are we overlooking, and do all employees have access to the necessary information and procedural guidance to make responsible and ethical decisions?

Defining and educating employees about information sources, organizational procedures, and decision-making skills are among the several core responsible business practice functions.

This last function—developing decision-making skills—is particularly significant; the dilemmas that arise in the domain of business ethics are precisely those thorny judgment calls that can bedevil risk managers. They are the moments when an organization must rely on responsible employees to be equipped for dealing with changing norms, mixed messages, ambiguity, and competing pressures (corporate, personal, and societal).

These challenges occur in the best of times as well as the worst. They may result from unexpectedly rapid growth in sales and employee headcounts that places stress on a firm's ability to carefully select staff and ensure they are adequately trained in procedures and standards. Or they may arise from the pressures of increasing competition and price-sensitivity in a mature industry, pushing managers and employees to walk very close to the line when making quality and safety decisions.

These are the types of dilemmas that keep managers awake at night. In the light of day, resolutions are only as effective as the company's communication of values and information. The risk manager who welcomes, supports, and collaborates with the company ethics function gains invaluable help in understanding and resolving the information risks that threaten today's corporations.

Read More About It

D&O Fault Lines

Ty R. Sagalow
Reprinted with permission from *Risk Management* magazine, January 1999. Copyright 1999 by Risk Management Society Publishing. All rights reserved. For more information call 212.286.9364. www.rims.org/rmmag

[Y]ears after securities litigation reform, the D&O [directors and officers] risk landscape is again shifting and risk managers need to be aware of the new exposures. Initially, the 1995 Federal Securities Litigation Reform Act helped reduce frivolous litigation, but today the number of securities lawsuits filed in federal courts is up to pre–Reform Act levels. And plaintiffs' lawsuits that survive motions to dismiss are often stronger than ever and more costly to defend.

There are several trends and forces converging to pose new threats to directors and officers: Plaintiffs' strategy of filing parallel state court actions has created new D&O liabilities such as punitive damages; securities plaintiff attorneys seeking to expand their revenue bases have honed in on employment practices litigation; [and] bankruptcy and pollution liability are emerging concerns.

Certainty?

In this shifting liability landscape, individual directors and officers—and their personal assets—are at greater risk than ever before. Risk managers need to take a closer look at their

D&O policy to make certain that it covers the increasing range of situations under which directors and officers can meet with new and heightened liabilities.

Working out the terms of directors' and officers' insurance can be tricky. Each policy is more like a negotiated commercial contract than an off-the-shelf insurance product. The process is made even more difficult by the ever-changing panorama of liability. Failure to painstakingly explore and evaluate the environment and compare today's risks to current policy language could lead to unpleasant and dangerous surprises when claims arise.

The essence of any contract is certainty of purpose and effect. Coverage certainty should be the central issue when reviewing the nascent and growing list of exposures. This is particularly true for special risks that carriers avoid by writing in exclusions, narrowing definitions, instituting restrictions, or remaining silent on specific issues.

To begin with, risk managers should make sure that directors and officers are covered for various types of litigation, investigations, and damages. They should ensure that their D&O policy provides individual coverage for civil, criminal, administrative, and regulatory investigations, including SEC [Securities and Exchange Commission] and grand jury proceedings. In particular, coverage for any SEC investigations at the early subpoena stage is absolutely critical. Additionally, to protect as fully as possible the personal assets of directors and officers, coverage is necessary for punitive and exemplary damages in securities claims. . . .

Custom vs. Standard Coverage

For example, in a standard D&O policy, the corporate entity is not insured for nonsecurities claims. Contract claims naming both the corporation and directors and officers require loss allocation between the covered directors and officers and the uncovered corporation. This raises a number of questions:

- Should policyholders leave this allocation issue to the time of the claim, perhaps hoping for a more favorable result?

- Should they choose to fight on two fronts, against both the claimant and the insurance company?
- Should they choose to spend the substantial legal fees necessary to negotiate a higher level of coverage, or should they obtain the coverage they need, clearly and expressly?
- Additionally, is it in the best interest of the insurance industry to avoid today's claims until they are reported or to resolve them immediately?

The answer to these questions is a pre-agreed allocation formula negotiated between the insured and the underwriter.

Additionally, standard D&O policies do not provide coverage for government investigations, even those against individual directors and officers.

Bankruptcy

Standard D&O policies contain an "insured vs. insured" exclusion. This excludes coverage of claims against directors and officers brought by or on behalf of the company. In many states, this exclusion has been interpreted as applying to claims brought by a bankruptcy trustee, thus robbing directors and officers of coverage when they need it most—at the time their company is financially unable to protect them.

This uncertainty can be resolved by negotiating policies that expressly cover claims brought against directors and officers by the bankruptcy trustee or examiner in the event the insured company files for bankruptcy. Additionally, in the event of bankruptcy, coverage is necessary for the directors and officers of the Debtor-in-Possession.

Pollution Liability

Current securities laws and accounting rules require companies to report projected expenditures on environmental problems such as pollution site cleanup. These disclosure requirements, and the growing public scrutiny of companies' records, have put a greater focus on pollution control.

Like many other liability policies, D&O coverage features exclusions for pollution-related claims. However, this approach can expose the personal assets of the directors and officers when the insured company does not indemnify claims. Risk managers should request that their D&O policy include coverage for nonindemnifiable pollution claims.

Employment Practices

The frequency and severity of employment practices claims are skyrocketing. Addressing these risks is especially critical given the trend of plaintiffs' attorneys branching out into areas of D&O litigation other than securities. For example, most standard D&O policies contain exclusions for libel, slander, and emotional distress and may not cover claims against nonofficer supervisors.

D&O coverage should expressly address employment practices liability, cover directors and officers for claims brought by employees of the entity, as well as by third parties, and eliminate related employment practices exclusions. This approach helps eliminate uncertainty.

New Challenges

Litigation and legislative trends will continue to shift and affect corporations and their directors and officers in different ways. [For example,] Congress [has] passed federal securities preexemption legislation, as well as year 2000 disclosure legislation. New exposures will also continue to appear as challenges to risk managers and underwriters. In the end, the certainty of D&O policy language will ultimately be the critical factor in providing directors and officers the broadest and most complete personal asset coverage possible. And risk managers will need to be in the driver's seat when negotiating with their brokers to provide their companies with maximum protection.

6

Risk Financing Principles

I don't know if anyone has a clear idea of what is going on in risk financing. The capital markets have entered the scene in a big way. Reinsurance companies are trying to go direct to the end users, and even insurance companies are experimenting with different kinds of financial products. Still, even though I can say "this thing is happening and this other thing is happening in risk financing," I have yet to hear a decent explanation as to what the big picture trends are.

Risk Officer
Automobile Leasing Firm

Perspectives

Risk Financing Alternatives Increasing as Market Grows

Rodd Zolkos
Reprinted with permission from *Business Insurance,* March 20, 2000.
© Crain Communications Inc. All rights reserved.

Although the market for alternative risk financing techniques is growing more slowly than many of its proponents would like, evidence that these approaches are a permanent fixture continues to build.

From catastrophe bonds to weather derivatives, credit wraps to integrated risk programs, the market is broad and diverse; and it is these characteristics that provide the market's principal appeal—the flexibility to address complex risk transfer issues with the most efficient tools.

At the same time more insurers, reinsurers, brokers, and bankers are showing interest in the alternative risk financing arena, a growing number of businesses also are beginning to systematically study their risks, the first step toward taking advantage of the new risk transfer opportunities becoming available.

"The compartmentalization between banking, insurance, and even investment banking is blurring very quickly," says Ed Guzik, head of product development at Swiss Re New Markets Corp. in New York. "For example, treasury people realize that purchasing insurance—purchasing risk transfer in the form of insurance—is almost identical to purchasing a derivative product," Guzik says. "As such, they've come to the conclusion that the product with the highest efficiency . . . is the product that should serve them in the long run."

"Things seem to be getting more flexible," says Carl Groth, senior vice president and director of alternative risk transfer at Willis Risk Solutions in New York. "[W]e're at a point where I believe the industry is going to start changing much more rapidly."

The development of the new risk financing options is driven by both the supply and the demand sides of the equation. On the one hand, risk financing providers are eager to find new business opportunities. From Swiss Re's perspective, "As an entity, we are trying to offer a broad spectrum of products," notes Guzik.

"From a big, macro picture, I think there's a general agreement that the (traditional) market is overcapitalized," says Mr. Groth of Willis. "But insurance has started thinking about investor returns . . . so they're thinking about new ways to underwrite risk."

From the demand side, "there is the growing awareness that a risk needs capital," Guzik says. "People are trying to optimize not only the cost of capital, but the allocation of capital to different operations within the company."

And, on both sides, there is the impact of improved information technology, allowing exposures to be analyzed in ways that weren't previously possible.

"Information today costs next to nothing," Guzik says. "And that puts emphasis not on collecting information and processing information, but on using information in the most effective fashion."

Groth says he's seeing businesses showing interest in using the new risk financing approaches to address a host of risks. One area of growing interest, volumetric risk, is addressed by an element of an integrated program United Grain Growers Ltd. [UGG] put in place this year to protect the company against a downturn in its grain-handling business. The grain-handling trigger in the Winnipeg, Manitoba–based firm's integrated program is a volume index set by a Canadian national commission.

The UGG deal has "created a little bit of momentum," Groth says, adding that he's working on other deals involving volumetric risk. "We're pursuing this with not only other grain companies, but also some of the companies that grow the actual crop. . . . It comes down to whether there's good published data . . . and whether or not there is a good understanding of what causes those numbers to materialize," he says.

Weather risk is another area where businesses are finding new risk solutions. Estimates of the volume of weather derivative transactions thus far range from $3 billion to $5 billion. "We've done a significant number of deals in that area," Groth says. Most have been with energy companies, but businesses such as retailers—whose sales could be affected by weather—could benefit as well.

Credit enhancement is another area of growing interest, and one in which solutions can be readily found from either insurers or bankers. "When we get a request for something like (credit enhancement), we might go to an investment bank before we go to an insurance company," Groth says. The client company could ultimately use either a credit derivative or credit insurance, whichever is the better fit for the risk.

One situation where credit enhancement could come into play is that of a spinoff company whose credit had been guaranteed by its parent. By getting credit enhancement coverage for the spinoff, the parent company can free itself from that credit obligation going forward. "There's an expense involved, but it could be an efficient way of relieving the parent of that obligation," Groth says.

In the environmental liability arena, there is a growing market for coverage of cleanup costs and for related third-party liabilities. "In not all cases can the client achieve a total write-down," [Groth] says. "It depends on the nature of the liabilities, and it depends on the nature of the transaction. But it falls under the category of balance sheet management."

Groth cites the example of a company Willis has worked with that has about $1 billion in potential environmental liabilities on its books. By using a risk financing mechanism, the company obtained $1 billion in potential insurance receivables to offset the liability.

[According to] Swiss Re New Markets' Guzik, for insurers looking to take on other classes of risk, weather derivatives and certain commodity risks that are illiquid or involve limited markets are the most likely candidates for this approach. "Where we can make a contribution is where there are skewed distributions—the potential for a wide swing of volatility, but on a limited-frequency basis," he says. "These are the areas where insurance can do better than capital markets."

In contrast, areas such as foreign exchange or interest rate risk, by themselves, make less sense for insurers, Guzik says. "The capital markets are so efficient in those areas," he says, "which doesn't mean we can't use those classes in connection with other classes of risk, like traditional property and casualty. . . . I don't know that we would do this most efficiently, but these would be done as an accommodation for someone who might want to package risk in an integrated program to advance a holistic approach to risk," he says.

In the area of integrated programs, Groth says, "I know that we have several of those in the market right now, and I think we'll see a couple more of them come to fruition in 2000."

"At the moment, what we're seeing is continuing interest in looking at risk more broadly and more systematically," says

Scott M. Sanderson, senior vice president at Marsh Inc. in Minneapolis. "We are seeing clients who are certainly at the level of doing very in-depth studies."

Such examination of a company's exposure is integral to using the new risk financing approaches successfully, Sanderson says. "We've been pushing this for a couple of years. You can't understand how risks work as a basket unless you do a study of how it hits your organization and how it potentially affects your stock price."

That education is key, Guzik says, in terms of an organization understanding its own risks as well as how some of the new products can address them. "When you look at the actual number of deals that have been done . . . there are a few, but not as many as you might expect, given the amount of effort that has been put into this area over the past three to five years," he says. "What we need, as a market, is time to educate the buyers."

In addition, the industry must achieve greater transparency in the alternative products' pricing before they will become more widely used. "Most of these products are custom made, custom designed," Guzik says, and the amount of time and effort that goes into crafting them "is actually quite substantial. And therefore, the cost of these products is not only reflecting the cost of capital, but also the cost of the time and effort of the underwriters," Guzik says. "Greater transparency—I don't know that it would open the floodgates, but it would broaden the pipeline for these products."

The perception that the alternative approaches are too expensive compared to buying conventional insurance in the current soft market has been the biggest obstacle to their gaining favor, Groth suggests. "The hindrances and the barriers for integrated programs have been, well, [that] the insurance market is soft and risk managers are pleased with the cost reductions in their programs," he says. "So there hasn't been a lot of incentive to fix something that isn't broken."

But Marsh's Sanderson is heartened by the number of companies that are at least studying their exposures and the potential solutions. "I know the marketplace is frustrated because they haven't seen a lot of them," he says. "But a good chunk of this [concern] is 'I want to see it, I want to understand it before I go about fixing it.' And the market doesn't see these until they get to fixing it."

Although the pace may be slower than some might prefer, the alternative risk financing market appears bound to continue growing.

Jayan U. Dhru, head of the insurance capital markets group at Standard & Poor's Corp. in New York, says that bankers and insurance companies constantly approach Standard & Poor's with new risk financing products. "We have not seen all the new products, but we are willing to see any new product that comes on board," he says. "Some of these are very exotic, but what was exotic two years ago isn't exotic anymore."

"There is no way back. We have to move in that direction," Swiss Re's Guzik says. "Buyers will press for some additional values. There's no doubt in my mind." Meanwhile, "We also need to streamline some of the delivery processes we have in place and also admit to the market that some of these products that we've been working on will not fly, and others will not fly at this time," Guzik says.

"I think what we all need to do, all of us people playing in this alternative risk market, is go through some post-mortems and go over those deals on which we spent a lot of money and a lot of time and, for whatever reason, didn't (complete) and ask ourselves 'Why?' " he says. "And in identifying the reasons why those deals didn't come to fruition, we might find answers to crafting risk financing approaches that better meet market needs."

Introduction

Risk imposes costs (and benefits) on organizations. Those costs come in two broad forms—loss costs and the costs of uncertainty. The concept of risk financing refers to those measures and methods taken to finance the costs of risk.

This chapter and Chapter 7 that follows provide an extended introduction to risk financing. This chapter focuses on the development of an overall framework for understanding the bewildering array of financing mechanisms now available. Key terms and concepts such as *insurance, self-insurance,* and *pooling* are defined and compared, as are emerging methods for handling financial risks. General goals and objectives of risk financing also are discussed.

Chapter 7 provides a more in-depth presentation of insurance. Insurance is a financing tool that has technical, legal, and institutional aspects that must be explained and developed separately.

Risk Financing Defined

The introduction to this chapter asserts that risk financing is defined as "measures and methods taken to finance the cost of risk." This is the definition adopted by the book, but it is worth noting that this view is not without controversy.

Historically, the concept of risk financing has been influenced by insurance, which in turn is viewed as being a mechanism associated with financing losses. Therefore, most traditional definitions of risk financing have focused on measures that directly relate to paying losses.

Paying losses is an important risk financing purpose, but financing arrangements also exist to address the costs of uncertainty. Ironically, insurance serves as an example here too, inasmuch as insurance premiums are paid whether or not there are losses. Absent uncertainty about the future, these financing arrangements would not be necessary. However, extending the definition of risk financing to include "costs of uncertainty" forces one to consider that risk financing includes expenditures for safety programs and equipment, risk management information systems, research, consulting services—and indeed—the risk manager's salary.

In a way, this insight is interesting but of limited practical value because while an arrangement to pay the salary of a risk manager is a cost of risk, it does not require any extraordinary measures (unless one can imagine budgeting for the risk manager through the loss savings that position would generate). Likewise, the purchase of lumbar support belts for maintenance workers is a cost of risk but does not require any special financing structure. Nevertheless, the insight has significance to the overall practice of risk management in business organizations.

The importance of the extended view of risk financing is that the financing of cost-of-uncertainty measures is intertwined with the loss financing measures. In a straightforward example, the hiring of a risk manager may be seen as ultimately related to the cost of loss financing because an effective risk manager will drive down loss costs. In a strategic sense, these two expenditures cannot be evaluated independently of one another. Interestingly, some insurance companies are recognizing this fact and are "rebating' "(used in only the general sense of the word) part of the premium to insureds specifically to finance broader risk management costs (e.g., the development of safety manuals, purchase of safety equipment, or purchase of training programs).

Furthermore, the method of financing risk influences the signals sent to those who may control the risk. Incentive programs, for example, can influence safety behavior. By realizing the relationships between the risks and all costs associated with those risks, an organization can begin to approach risk financing in a coordinated fashion, the result being greater financing efficiency, greater risk communication and signaling, and stronger linkages between risk control and financing.

Since there are core technical aspects of risk financing, readers should be clear that the following discussion focuses mainly on measures that are both loss financing and uncertainty reducing. Thus, scant attention is paid to the financing of risk assessment, control, and administration efforts—they are risk financing concerns, to be sure, but require little special attention.

The Risk Financing Grid

Traditionally, risk financing has been subdivided into two categories, insurance and "not insurance." Despite the revolutionary changes that have occurred in the past twenty years, that distinction still influences the thinking of many managers and regulators.

The mismatch between historical categories and current practices creates confusion and limits the chance of grasping admittedly complex topics. In addition, the mismatch creates very practical problems in matters such as regulation of financing products and financial analysis of alternatives. It seems that a reoriented approach to discussing risk financing is necessary.

For purposes of this book, readers can begin to organize thinking about risk financing by first imagining how a firm might "pay for" risks. It seems that the answers would fall out on two dimensions: how financing occurs, and when financing occurs.

How Financing Occurs

Intuitively, one may observe that this dimension is rather straightforward; either a firm finances risks directly or it gets some other party to finance risk. In fact, those two methods represent the core financing strategies of risk retention and risk transfer, which are defined as follows:

- *Risk retention* refers to methods of self-financing. The risk is borne by the firm and, if risk-related costs arise, the firm directly bears those costs. The various ways in which this happens are discussed shortly.
- *Risk transfer* refers to methods of transferring the cost of risk (or more properly, the direct responsibility for bearing the risk) from one party to a non-related party. Insurance serves the purpose of illustrating risk transfer. Through the purchase of insurance, a business has transferred the cost of the risk of, say, fires to an insurance company.

For newcomers to the subject of risk management, the distinction between transfers and retention can create confusion. In an important sense, risk is *not* being transferred in an insurance contract. Certainly the actual risk of a fire still resides with the business; only the economic impact is being transferred. As Chapter 7 shows, the pricing of insurance is undertaken in such a way that over time, an insured is paying for all its losses (because the premium is based on a calculation of average expected losses). What, therefore, actually is being transferred is the timing risk associated with the fire. In other words, most conventional risk transfer vehicles are structured to facilitate a smoothing process whereby the insured is protected from the risk of not having sufficient resources at the time a loss occurs, but in facilitating that arrangement the insurance company is requiring the insured to make payments over time that will—on average—ultimately equal and exceed the cost of benefits paid out.

This example indirectly suggests an important feature of the retention/transfer concepts—they are not discrete methods, nor are they absolutes. Rather, measures to finance risk involve varying degrees of retention and transfer. No single approach to financing is either completely one or the other.

Later in this chapter when the subject of financial risk management is presented, the concept of neutralization will be raised as a third financing method. Neutralization involves the hedging of risk, which is effected by offsetting one risk with another. In a sense, insurance is a type of hedge in that an insured possesses a risk of loss (say, a fire to a building) and a possible gain (the proceeds from a fire insurance policy) that offset one another. While knowledgeable readers will recognize that this observation is only roughly true, the notion of insurance as a type of hedge provides a useful insight, which is that neutralization is a financing strategy that is both retention and transfer.

The advent of sophisticated tools for hedging financial risks (e.g., derivatives) has heightened attention to the hedging phenomenon, and it is very true that the technical complexity of such products has spawned an area of financial risk management all its own. From an organization management perspective, this is all to the good, because the control of such things as interest rate, currency exchange, credit, and price risks is critical to effective management. However, it also should be noted that financial risk management is not a separate (or even superior) matter to Organization Risk Management (ORM). It is a part of an overall approach to managing an organization's risk and, despite technical complexity, involves fairly conventional notions regarding risk and its management.

When Financing Occurs

The second dimension relates to the timing of the financing approach. Conversationally, one can imagine that the financing of risks could occur before, during, or after resources are needed. More formally, certain financing tools are prospective and involve arrangements to accumulate resources in advance of a particular need. Other tools are contemporaneous, so the financing of a risk occurs as the resources are needed. Yet other tools are retrospective in the sense that they are structured to provide financing after events have occurred giving rise to a need for resources.

The risk financing grid presented in Exhibit 6-1 provides a useful method for beginning to organize one's thinking about risk financing tools and techniques. Risk financing tools can be categorized as to who is paying directly for the risk (and how) and when the financing occurs. Later, this chapter covers various tools that may fit into the various cells of the grid, but an important caveat should be offered as well: The cells within the grid are inserted for instructive purposes, but actually the axes of the grid are continuous and not discrete. This means that various tools and techniques may fall anywhere along either axis and are not confined by the boundaries of the grid cells.

The Retention/Transfer Demarcation Line

While it is true that no tool or technique is solely transfer or retention—at least not conceptually—readers reasonably should wonder what distinguishes retention from transfer measures. In other words, what are the characteristic differences by which one tech-

Exhibit 6-1. Risk financing grid

How Financed?

	Retention	Neutralization	Transfer
Prospective			
Contemporaneous			
Retrospective			

When Financed?

Insights

Interest in Alternatives Grows as P/C Rate Increases Loom

Michael Bradford
Reprinted with permission from *Business Insurance,* February 21, 2000.
© Crain Communications Inc. All rights reserved.

The threat of a hardening commercial market is reviving interest in nontraditional ways of funding property/casualty risks.

Insurers and reinsurers are boosting prices for many coverages after years of bargain-basement rates in a competitive marketplace. In turn, companies that are accustomed to low costs and confident of their ability to control losses are looking, in many cases, to retain more risk.

"We are definitely seeing insurers and reinsurers looking for rate increases," says Mark Charron, Hartford, Connecticut–based partner and national practice leader in Deloitte & Touche L.L.P.'s risk management practice. "It's clearly in their renewal strategy this year." As a result, Charron says, "More organizations are focusing on what the alternatives are."

"We are really beginning to see a ticking up in prices," agrees Barbara H. Monaco, vice president with Atlantic Risk Services Inc., a Madison, New Jersey–based subsidiary of Atlantic Mutual Cos. "Companies that in the past were not considering the alternative market because (traditional) prices were low are now giving it a second look."

"We're not seeing anything that looks like a mad rush into alternative funding arrangements, but any time the market becomes less competitive, people start looking for alternatives," says Ralph Korn, a senior consultant with SRG Strategy & Risk Group, a Glendale, Arizona–based subsidiary of Northshore International Insurance Services Group of Salem, Massachusetts.

There still are deals to be found in the traditional market, according to Stephen Beene, branch manager with third-party administrator Ward North America Inc. in Lafayette, Louisiana. "They're there if you can find them and keep plugging away." But the cyclical nature of the insurance business means self-insurance remains a "solid option," if traditional market prices get too high, Beene notes. Self-insuring is "always in the mix" of companies' choices, he remarks. And some companies are getting ready to self-insure.

The Louisiana Association of Self Insured Employers, which has seen its membership grow in recent years, expects more employers to begin self-insuring their workers compensation risks, says Gary Patureau, LASIE's president. "We've had people qualified to self-insure that have not" as workers compensation prices remained reasonable, he says, "but now they are looking to gear up" as those costs rise.

Employers are taking a look at the full range of options, experts say, with captives, rent-a-captives, large deductibles, self-insured retentions, and other alternatives all being considered. Jack Gohsler, senior vice president with Conning & Co. in Hartford, Connecticut, says it doesn't appear that any one type of alternative risk-funding method is getting the nod over others. As the nontraditional market has matured, a range of solid choices has developed.

"A number of the alternative market forms have become more established," Gohsler notes, and, over the years, they have become readily accepted methods for funding risk.

Charron doesn't see employers leaning toward one particular approach, either. "Pure self-insurance represents for many organizations the most cost-effective manner," he notes. "The risks can be predicted, projected, and you can build a program around it."

As interest among employers has picked up, Charron says, Deloitte is "doing a lot more studies around looking at appropriate retention levels. How high can they go? What is the optimum retention level?"

Crown Vantage Co.'s paper mill in St. Francisville, Louisiana, illustrates how some employers are content to manage large portions of their risks. The mill holds a $500,000 retention on its workers comp exposure and buys catastrophe coverage above that amount from American International Group Inc.

Because of its high retention, Crown Vantage, which was spun off from James River Corp. in 1995, operates essentially as if the risk were totally self-insured, says Gary Devall, safety and health supervisor. Claims never have exceeded the retention, he notes. The company's aggressive effort to keep workers safe and quickly return to work those who have been injured keeps workers comp costs low, Devall says. "We stay on the cutting edge" in offering safety training, with an ongoing focus on risks at the facility and participation by employees in loss-prevention programs that can keep down the number of injuries, he says.

Patureau of LASIE believes that "when you administer a tight, well-run self-insurance program, you are going to save dollars in many different areas. Getting the employee back to work quicker" is one of them.

Conoco Inc. carries large deductibles on its property/casualty risks for several reasons, according to Linda Luis, casualty insurance adviser at the Houston-based oil company. "One principal reason we are confident that this is the right choice for our company is our outstanding safety program," she says.

Gaining control over the claims process, especially for workers compensation and general liability claims, is another reason Conoco chooses to self-insure, Luis says. Conoco can say to its third-party administrator, "Hey, that's our money," when deciding how or whether to settle claims, she points out. An insurer, though, might not be as concerned about costs or as appreciative of the company's reasons that a claim should or should not be quickly settled, she says.

As employers assume more risk, they need to emphasize loss control, experts agree.

"Effective loss control is a necessity if you want to have a successful self-insurance program," says Korn of SRG. "If people abandon the marketplace and go into self-insurance, they have got to have good loss control. If losses are out of control, they have no business being in self-insurance."

Charron points out that when companies self-insure, they often allocate risk-funding costs to various units. Because some of those costs are loss-sensitive, those units become more aware of controlling losses.

"It's the carrot-and-stick theory," he says. "The cost-allocation method can promote the kind of behavior you're looking for in the loss control effort."

Employers continue to use captives as a favorite self-insurance vehicle, though the number of new formations is slowing. Korn says that while he believes "there's going to be a resurgence in interest as the market moves into a harder, less competitive market," there is no evidence that there will be "mass (insurance) cancellations and people forming captives like they did in the mid-1980s."

Geoffrey H. Horsfield, assistant vice president in charge of Atlantic Mutual's Commercial Affinity Program business, says: "What we're seeing, from a program perspective, is a heightened increase in any kind of rent-a-captive or captive. What we're able to do is provide accounts that typically were too small to enter the alternative market the ability to combine and access these facilities." For example, Atlantic Mutual provides alternative risk financing solutions for companies with similar exposures.

Industry sources point out that interest in using captives to cover workers compensation exposures is on the upswing. Monaco says California employers are showing a lot of interest as workers comp costs rise in that state.

Korn agrees, saying the tide is beginning to turn in California, where workers compensation insurers are posting loss ratios of as much as 150 percent and asking for rate increases of 30 percent to 100 percent. Many employers had abandoned self-insurance schemes to buy inexpensive workers compensation coverage from California insurers, he says. Now, however, it appears there will be "a movement back to self-insurance, particularly on the part of public entities who are more susceptible to criticism on pricing issues than private companies," Korn explains.

Industry observers point out that much of the increasing interest in captives during the hardening market will be in the form of new business to existing insurers and not necessarily in new formations. "We talk to risk managers who own captives, and they alter their retentions according to what they can buy in the marketplace," explains Kathleen Waslov, editor of *Captive*

Insurance Company Reports (CICR), a Tillinghast-Towers Perrin–produced publication of the International Risk Management Institute in Dallas.

And, Waslov points out, while captive owners are preparing to increase the amount of business they send to the insurers during the hardening market, the number of new companies appears be tapering off.

[D]uring the year [1999], CICR counted 171 new captives licensed worldwide. That figure is expected to rise somewhat when it is rechecked with domiciles and formations that were missed are added to the total. Even so, the final count is expected to fall short of 1998's 305 new formations globally. The captive count had risen steadily since 1995, when 278 new licenses were granted.

The number of new formations among risk retention groups also declined in the past year amid the lingering soft insurance market. "In the last year, three risk retention groups were formed, all in the automobile extended warranty business," says Karen Cutts, publisher of *The Risk Retention Reporter* in Pasadena, California.

That's the fewest number of new formations in a single year since three were formed in 1991. Altogether, there are 67 groups operating, one fewer than a year ago, according to *The Risk Retention Reporter.*

Cutts says: "The risk retention groups that sat their roots down in the early 1990s and late 1980s are continuing to do well. The ones that came along later had a hard time because the market was so soft." Competitive market conditions hampered the groups' ability to attract and retain members.

Cutts expects new formations to pick up soon. "Do I think the hard market will stimulate formation? Absolutely. I'm hearing of several risk retention groups in the pipeline."

nique is construed as transferring a risk while another is seen as a retention measure? The question is more practically relevant than one may think because it bears on a host of legal and regulatory concerns that plague risk management today.

Previously in this chapter, transfer was distinguished from retention by noting that an unrelated party assumes responsibility for the timing and economic consequences of a risk. But what makes a transfer a transfer? Insurance law and regulation provide an important insight in this regard. Among other characteristics that define an insurance contract as a risk transfer are these three:

1. The legal validity of the contract
2. The nature of the consideration of the parties
3. The pooling of risks and resources

The first point is fairly self-explanatory. A risk transfer agreement, both practically and conceptually, must meet the test of legality and validity. This means that it must serve a legal purpose, that the parties must be legally competent to enter into the agreement, that there must be identifiable offer and acceptance, and that each party must give some consideration. A key feature of valid risk transfer contracts is the degree of separation between transferor and transferee. Considerable litigation has occurred over the question of what constitutes "parties" to a transfer agreement. For instance, imagine two companies owned by a holding company. Is transfer of risk from one of those companies to the other a legal transfer? In general, the courts have concluded no. A legally valid risk transfer contract must involve non-related parties. If the risk does not escape the corporate family, the risk is not transferred.

The nature of the consideration given by each party is significant in the case of insurance, particularly, and in risk transference generally. The transferor of risk is generally expected to make an economic commitment to pay for the benefits of transference. Some courts have further noted that the commitment (say, a premium payment) must show some relationship to the risk to be transferred, although this is not a consistent requirement. The transferee (i.e., the acceptor of risk) offers consideration in the form of an aleatory and conditional promise—that is, a promise to perform (e.g., pay a claim) that's conditional on some further event such as a loss, an event that is probabilistic.

The third feature, the presence of pooling, is rather important in the history of insurance law and regulation, but it is a criterion that is under some pressure today.

Traditionally, pooling referred to the notion of a risk bearer (i.e., insurer) accepting many similar risks and pooling those risks together to accumulate funds sufficient to cover expected claims as well as to cover fluctuations from expected levels of claims. The mathematical notion behind pooling is the Law of Large Numbers, which essentially establishes that the claims experience of an accumulating pool of risks becomes more stable and predictable as it grows.

Recently, some revision has been occurring regarding what is actually happening as a pool of risks grows. While historically the view has tended to be that it is the actual accumulation of risks that leads to stabilization, a current proposal suggests that it is actually the accumulation of funds—not risks—that is the secret behind pooling. Put plainly, as a pool obtains more and more funds, they accumulate to a level where they are not only adequate to meet expected payments, but also overwhelm the possible variations that may occur.

For the uninitiated reader this may appear to be a purely academic matter, but this changing view has very important implications for the book. Traditionally, risk transference was closely associated with insurance, and this meant that the distinction between retention and transfer could be (and was) based on evidence of a pool of risks—is a risk-accepting party offering a similar arrangement to many other parties, and are those accepted risks being pooled together for financial purposes? The newer way of looking at transference requires only that an adequate sum of resources be available to cover the promises made under the contract. In other words, it is the "ability to financially bear the risk" that matters, more so than the presence of other similarly constituted risks.

As Chapter 7 shows, regulation of insurance companies is based on the notion that insurers have special obligations worthy of separate oversight. This chapter is asserting that transference is transference, whether it is a traditional insurer selling standardized coverages to hundreds of businesses or whether it is a bank offering a one-off risk transference arrangement to a single customer. All risk transference arrangements—under this line of reasoning—should be regulated, if at all, under a common structure.

That consistent regulation presently is not the case is evident to anyone examining the world of risk financing. Many of the products discussed later in this chapter will appear to the naked eye to be indistinguishable from one another, and yet they are treated quite differently from a tax, legal, and regulatory perspective because some fit the traditional test of "insurance" and some do not.

Risk Financing Methods in Overview

In a sense, the risk financing matrix in Exhibit 6-1 is an open field and the combinations of transference/retention and prospective/ contemporaneous/retrospective characteristics are limitless. However, for introductory purposes it may be useful to characterize a set of alternatives that will represent the distinctions that exist between the prototypical approaches to financing. The grid shown in Exhibit 6-2 offers a possible placement of the examples discussed.

Transfers

Perhaps the best starting point for visualizing the nature of risk transfers is traditional insurance arrangements. Conventionally, insurance companies issue contracts that meet the legal tests of risk transfer. Furthermore, these contracts meet the less tangible criteria one may expect to see. In exchange for the premium paid, the

Exhibit 6-2. "Illustrative" Risk Financing Grid (One Possible Placement of Some Financing Tools)

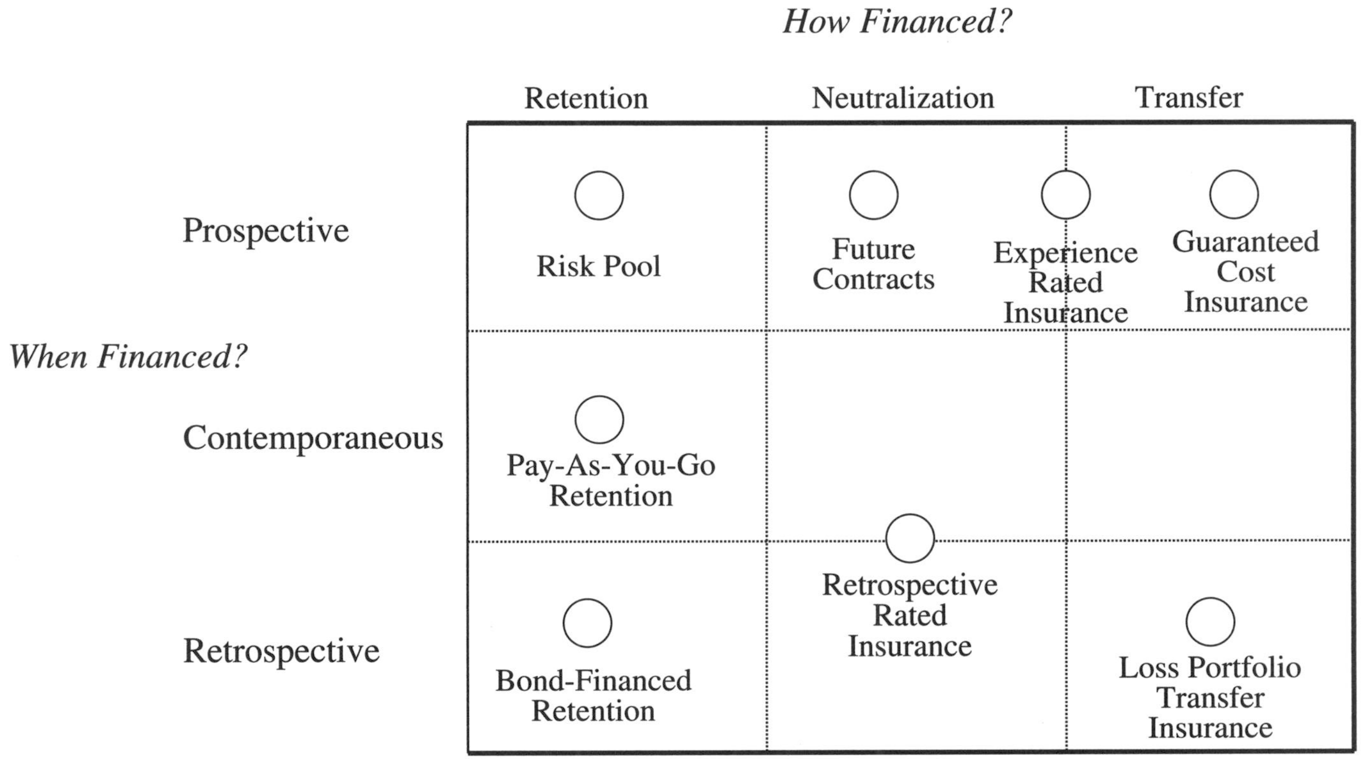

How Financed?

	Retention	Neutralization	Transfer	
Prospective	○ Risk Pool	○ Future Contracts	○ Experience Rated Insurance	○ Guaranteed Cost Insurance
Contemporaneous	○ Pay-As-You-Go Retention			
Retrospective	○ Bond-Financed Retention	○ Retrospective Rated Insurance		○ Loss Portfolio Transfer Insurance

When Financed?

insured is confident that a risk is fully and completely covered. When a claim occurs, the loss is fully restored.

Within conventional insurance coverages, however, the degree of transfer will vary, and this is due to the pricing approach employed and the degree to which the contract represents a reduction in uncertainty as well as risk. Perhaps the best way to illustrate this is to draw the distinctions between guaranteed cost insurance, experience rated insurance, and retrospectively rated insurance.

Guaranteed Cost Insurance

Most insurance that is sold is priced based upon a classification rating scheme, which means that the insurer develops risk groupings and computes the average expected losses for such groupings—which in turn serves as the basis for the premium. In addition, that premium is guaranteed, so it cannot be adjusted to reflect the actual loss experience during the coverage period.

For instance, an individual buying automobile insurance will pay a premium based on the average expected losses of people like that individual (e.g., men age 16–24 who live in rural areas and drive certain kinds of vehicles for business only). The rate does not specifically correspond to the individual and, indeed, it cannot. A single person cannot provide an insurer with sufficient driving history to enable that insurer to develop an individualized rate.

Classification rating, which serves as the principal rating method for personal lines insurance (e.g., auto, homeowners, individual life, and disability insurance) as well as for small businesses and entities, differs fundamentally from the other rating approaches discussed in subsequent sections of this chapter, and it is important to underscore that difference. All other rating methods are based (at least in part) on the actual experience of the insured, whereas classification rating does not. Therefore the earlier discussion that—over time—policyholders pay for their own losses really only directly applies to rating schemes other than classification rating. Certainly, an individual homeowner may discover that claim payments roughly correspond to the premiums paid, but this is a very rare circumstance. Most often, homeowners pay premiums and never suffer losses. Occasionally, a homeowner will receive far more in benefits than has been paid in premiums, but this also is not common.

Thus, when discussing the role of classification rated insurance, it probably is more appropriate to say that the principal benefit being purchased is uncertainty reduction (i.e., no matter how rarely losses occur, the insured is certain that benefits will be paid). Indeed, it is the diminishing role of "uncertainty reduction" in the following rating schemes that signals the movement toward retention.

Experience Rated Insurance

Firms that are large enough to produce a consistent volume of claims typically are subjected to a form of rating known as experience rating. This means that the organization's own loss experience is used—at least in part—to develop the premium that is paid. The degree of statistical credibility that is assigned to the loss experience will vary depending on the amount and quality of that data, but the key feature is that a direct linkage is established between the actual risk and losses and the amount that is paid. This feature, in turn, evokes the concept of "control," meaning that efforts expended to prevent or reduce losses will translate more or less directly into the ultimate cost of risk financing. The degree of correspondence between risk and rate is positively correlated with a move away from transference. Increasingly, the insured is paying its own losses. However, because the experience rating approach still factors in other loss data from similar organizations, it still is a transfer and still provides benefit against "timing risk" and against uncertainty.

Retrospectively Rated Insurance

For very large firms with highly credible loss data, insurers may employ a third form of rating. Retrospective (or retro) rating is based on an insured's own current loss experience. In the sense that it is the insured's loss experience only that sets the price, transference is low. The fact that it is based on current losses means that the timing risk transference also is low. Certain transference protections remain (Chapter 7 discusses them), but while this is legally viewed as an insurance agreement, it does not present much evidence of transference.

Summary

The preceding discussion demonstrates that one factor that moves transference arrangements toward a retention posture is the relationship between the actual risk and the amount that is financed. It also implies that the movement from transference to retention does not precisely correspond with the temporal distinctions between "insurance" and "retention."

Other risk financing characteristics are evident in the preceding discussion. Notably, the timing of the financing mechanism can vary. Guaranteed cost insurances tend to be paid for proactively, as are experience rated coverages. Retrospective coverages, naturally, are retrospectively financed (to a significant degree, anyway). Some types of contemporaneous financing also may be seen in certain products.

The introduction of features such as deductibles, copayments, or other cost-sharing provisions can further shift a classic transference contract toward retention, as can the limits of coverage in the contract. If the exposure to loss is $1 million, but the coverage limit is $100,000, much of the risk is retained.

As a final point, the financial solidity of the insurer would be a dimension of the transference. For instance, a complete coverage of some risk under a guaranteed cost plan may pass the basic test of transference, but if the insurer is of dubious financial quality, the degree of transference must be questioned.

Neutralization

The risk financing grid in Exhibit 6-1 suggests an environment where risk neutralization serves as an intermediate point between

Insights

Industry Axioms Outmoded in New Century: Analyst

Rodd Zolkos
Reprinted with permission from *Business Insurance,* March 20, 2000.
© Crain Communications Inc. All rights reserved.

A number of long-held truths about the property/casualty insurance industry will be found false as the new century progresses, according to industry analyst Sean F. Mooney, a senior vice president at Guy Carpenter & Co. Inc. in New York, who [has] outlined seven twentieth-century property/casualty truths that won't hold true in the twenty-first century.

The first is that branding isn't important, Mooney says.

That might have been true in the twentieth century, when a relationship with an agent provided all the security many consumers needed in making an insurance decision. But the strength of the insurer's brand will take on new significance as more and more insurance purchases are made online in the twenty-first century.

The second truth Mooney expects to fall is the notion that one-stop combinations of banking and insurance into ''financial supermarkets'' won't work.

''When we look to the twenty-first century, I think we're looking at a different reality,'' he remarks. ''In fact, the financial supermarket may be the major place to buy property/casualty insurance.''

The third twentieth-century truth Mooney sees going by the boards is that there will be few strategic alliances in the industry. In fact, he predicts, more such alliances will be crafted, driven particularly by the emergence of new management concepts.

The belief that banking and insurance are fundamentally different businesses also will be overturned in the coming years, the Guy Carpenter economist predicts. ''When you think about the various businesses that banks and insurance are in, there are a lot of similarities,'' Mooney says. As the two industries grow closer, each is likely to employ some of the business techniques of the other, he suggested.

Yet another notion to be dashed is that being "the low-cost price taker is the key to success." In fact, Mooney suggests, "perhaps one of the winning strategies will be to start to think of a premium-price strategy." As an example, he cites Chubb Corp.'s experience with its homeowners coverage, whose customers are willing to pay a higher price in exchange for better service.

The sixth truth soon to disappear in the property/casualty industry is that there is no "first mover" advantage. With more and more technology being employed in the business world, insurers will definitely find it advantageous to be the first to move in a particular direction, Mooney says, particularly in terms of new methods of distribution and new services.

Finally, the notion that property/casualty insurance is about physical risks will not hold true in the twenty-first century. "Information infrastructure has become the central nervous system of the economy," Mooney says. As a result, property/casualty insurers will be developing more and more products to deal with information-related exposures, he says.

retention and transfer. This is not an uncontroversial view. Some observers would argue that neutralization is the "third point" of a financing triangle—that is, neutralization is something distinctly different from the other two financing methods.

In a sense, the model we accept is less important than is an appreciation of the basics that underlie the neutralization concept.

- Neutralization is defined as a financial method for offsetting risks principally through taking opposite positions on a given risk.
- In a perfect neutralization arrangement, the pre- and post-event financial position of the firm exposed to risk is unchanged.
- The risk itself is not treated directly and so the exposure is retained. However, the use of financial instruments allows aspects of the risk to be transferred to a counterparty or distributed into

financial markets. In this sense, neutralization is both transfer and retention.

▪ Instruments that are used to neutralize risks can also be used to speculate on risks.

Risk neutralization serves an intermediate role (i.e., between transfer and retention) in another way as well, which is that it allows risk managers to address a range of risks that are not traditionally insurable but are not risks on which a firm may wish to speculate. Those risks are speculative (in the Chapter 1 sense of the word), but they are not risks that are directly related to the central purposes of an organization. For example, fuel oil prices are a key input cost for businesses, and fluctuations in oil prices present a real speculative risk. However, betting on fuel oil price swings is not (or should not be) a concern for most firms as they are not in the commodity investments business. The firm's main concern should be to neutralize the uncertainty/risk of price changes—that is, to make the input cost more predictable.

The idea of a risk financing continuum makes some sense within the world of risk neutralization, too. Some techniques exhibit higher levels of transfer than do others, and an explanation of that point can be offered by briefly discussing the two most common forms of neutralization—futures and options contracts.

A *futures contract* is an arrangement for securing the future purchase or sale of goods/services and a predetermined price. Forward contracts do much the same thing, but tend to be customized to specific buyers and sellers whereas futures contracts are traded in markets and can be bought and sold anonymously. The purpose of a futures contract is to allow the buyer of that contract to neutralize the risk associated with some particular asset that the buyer will be acquiring or selling at some future point in time.

For example, a firm may be concerned about fixing the price of the heating oil it will purchase in the coming winter. As a basis for discussion, imagine that a supplier is willing to guarantee oil at $20 a barrel for that future delivery date. This arrangement presents a risk to buyer and seller—namely, that the price on the market at that future date will be different. If, say, the market price for oil at that delivery date is $14 per barrel, the buyer is overpaying by $6 per barrel and the seller is earning a windfall $6 per barrel. Obviously, the opposite outcome could occur as well. The seller may choose to speculate on price fluctuations, but the local government may want to neutralize the risk, which it could do by purchasing a heating oil futures contract that would permit it to sell oil at $20 on the delivery date. Thus, at that future date it could buy oil on the market at $14 and—via the futures contract—sell at $20, thereby offsetting the $6 per barrel "loss" it incurred on the underlying purchase. Newcomers to the world of futures should note immediately that the opposite risk is neutralized as well; the firm cannot come out ahead if prices go up.

An *options contract* is one in which the holder has a right to buy or sell some asset at a specified time and amount. (*Put options* allow the owner to sell an asset; *call options* allow the owner to buy.) In this case, however, an options contract may or may not be exercised (futures transactions must occur at the agreed date). So, in the previous heating oil example, the option contract would enable the firm to exercise the option if the price rises—thus assuring that the price will be no higher than $20 per barrel. However, if the price of oil drops, the firm will choose not to exercise the option, meaning it can take advantage of the lower $14 per barrel market price.

From a slightly different perspective, we can say that options contracts and insurance contracts have a great deal in common. If a firm buys an insurance policy, it has purchased an option that it may choose to exercise (by filing a claim when a loss occurs) if it is in the firm's interest to do so. Of course, the policy does not lapse if no claim is filed (which occurs with an options contract), but the similarity is important to observe because it shows how, like an insurance policy, an options contract can transfer risk—to financial markets rather than to an insurance company—while still retaining the more attractive features of the risk.

Discussion of hedging tools and techniques gives rise to a possibly distinct fourth risk financing area (after transfer, neutralization, and retention, the three methods discussed in this chapter)—*risk speculation*. Although we have chosen not to invest much space to discuss this form of risk financing, we believe events are overtaking practices and that financial speculation (or, if readers prefer, "investment") is becoming less distinct as a financial practice. In other words, a dollar spent on a futures contract purchased to hedge a raw materials price exposure is not so different from a dollar spent on the same contract to speculate on price movements.

We reckon that while the world of investment management will continue to retain a distinctly separate identity from risk management, readers should be sensitive to the fact that ORM and nontraditional approaches to risk management all posit that risk taking can be a form of risk management as long as it is rationally considered and corresponds with the overall purposes and philosophy of the organization. Thus, although we would be hard-pressed to point out an organization that fully integrates every aspect of its risk financing in this way, we predict that the time is not far off when retention, transfer, neutralization, and speculation are terms that are used commonly in the discussion of an organization's approach to risk financing.

As a final and separate note, the phenomenon of *risk securitization* should be introduced here because it reveals a different risk financing method that is emerging from the convergence of capital and insurance markets. Securitization, of course, is not a new idea. Mortgage-backed securities are a fairly common example of non-traded contracts being bundled together and sold as securities (the security allows its buyer to earn a revenue stream that is based on the collective cash flows generated by the mortgages). Today, many insurance companies are turning to capital markets to package asset and liability exposures to risk and to sell the risk into the market. For example, insurers can package together insurance contracts and sell securities based on the expected cash flows generated by the policies. For risk managers, the real significance arises from the growing application of insurance securities to alternative risk financing uses. One example would be weather bonds, which pay proceeds based upon a meteorological phenomenon (excess rain or snowfall, for example).

Retention

In a sense, the concept of retention requires little specific discussion. If a firm makes no arrangement to transfer/neutralize a risk, it will continue to possess sole responsibility for the risk and is practicing retention. Inevitably, all organizations practice some degree of retention by virtue of the fact that some risks are not identified and handled in advance.

Allowing for the fact that unconscious retention occurs, the principal concern is with the planned and conscious retention—what widely is referred to as *self-insurance*.

The particular means by which a firm can self-insure are varied. Much self-financing is undertaken on a pay-as-you-go basis, without any special provision for prefunding. This is "contemporaneous" financing in its most basic form. Some organizations extend this approach to a type of prefunding that uses lines or letters of credit that allow an organization to draw on its credit line to finance losses. Other more formal self-financing approaches can be employed as well. They include captive insurance companies (an insurance company that insures only one policyholder; its parent company), risk retention groups and pools, finite risk insurance (a banking arrangement where the risk manager can accumulate funds and obtain certain financial management—even transference—services from the financial institution), among others.

Perhaps more important in our discussion than the means behind self-financing risks is the matter of why risks should be financed in such a manner. Broadly, the decision between transferring and retaining a risk is governed by the following five factors:

1. The degree of control over the risk
2. The cost of financing options
3. The quality/value of services
4. The opportunity cost
5. The tax issue

The Degree of Control over the Risk

In general terms, the more one has the power to control a risk, the less necessary transfer appears. "Control" implies predictability, knowledge of the risk, and the means to manage it. In such circumstances, it commonly is more effective and less costly for an organization to retain the risk and manage it, paying directly for losses when and if they arise.

The Cost of Financing Options

In its most basic sense, an insurance premium is made up of the insurer's estimate of average expected losses to be paid out (plus the costs of adjusting and settling those claims) and the overhead costs of selling that policy (e.g., commissions to agents, taxes, and profit). Depending on the degree of risk predictability, the retention decision is governed by the size and value of the insurer's margin. If, for example, a firm pays $1 million in premium to an insurer and both the insurer and the firm believe average losses are about $700,000 a year, the question becomes whether it is more economically wise to simply set aside $700,000 to pay for losses and forego many (but not all) of the overhead costs.

Interestingly, since about 1993, the commercial insurance market has been so competitive that premiums offered, in some instances, are below the average expected loss costs (naturally, the insurers are hoping to make up the loss through investment returns on those premiums while in their possession). This has made it rather difficult for risk managers to argue for increasing their retention practices, at least on purely economic grounds. Thus, the decision to retain has had to be judged more on matters of control, quality of services, politics, and public relations. Of course, the competitive market may change.

The Quality/Value of Services

This factor also relates to the discussion of cost comparisons. Certainly, the overhead costs of insurance are not deadweight costs to the buyer. They include the technical expertise necessary to manage many risks (e.g., claims management, actuarial, loss control), and this expertise has an economic value.

While in the past the quality and value of these services has weighed strongly against a decision to self-finance, this is no longer the case because most insurers now "unbundle" their services. Thus, a self-financing firm could acquire an insurer's claims services without purchasing the insurance itself. Indeed, the emergence of unbundled services has produced an explosion in the risk management services industry. Today, it is possible to purchase any type of risk management service from insurers, brokers, and other third-party providers. (More is discussed on this point in Chapter 8.)

The Opportunity Cost

Previously it was noted that insurers consider the investment income earned on premiums as an important economic factor in their pricing. One would have to note that this is a lost opportunity for the insured. Thus, for a business, part of the decision to retain is governed by the lost opportunity associated with possessing those funds.

Interestingly, the nature of this "cost" is directly related to whether the risk in question is a "long-tail or short-tail" risk. *Long-tail risks* are those where a significant amount of time elapses between the loss producing event (or notice of that event) and the eventual settlement of that claim. This is a notable feature of liability-related losses where a suit is filed and litigated, appealed, and ultimately closed, perhaps five to seven years after the case has begun.

Short-tail risks, naturally, are those that open and close quickly (e.g., a fire loss or a theft claim). Such risks present little in the way of opportunity costs, whereas the long-tail variety may present a benefit that more than offsets a degree of uncertainty associated with the actual ultimate outcome.

The Tax Issue

For private firms, federal and state tax codes generally recognize insurance as a deductible business expense. Self-financing is treated differently and, for the most part, losses are only deductible when they are paid. This creates a general advantage for insurance over self-insurance.

A secondary dimension to the taxation question is embedded in the matter of insurance pricing. In most instances, insurers are required to pay income taxes and premium taxes, the burden for which falls on the policyholder via the premium paid. In addition (although this is not a tax issue per se), the premium will reflect various charges that may be required by state regulators for high-risk pools, state guaranty funds, and other similar charges. Premium taxes, guaranty fund charges, and the like obviously are not paid by self-financing programs.

General Observations on Risk Financing

Readers wading through this discussion for the first time may still remain a bit unclear on the distinctions between products that are mainly transfer, that neutralize risk (or even speculate), or that retain risk. They should not feel alone! The risk financing market is in a high state of flux and many expert observers have great difficulty in keeping straight the extraordinary range of new methods for financing risk. It probably is sufficient at this point for a reader to feel comfortable by remembering the following main points:

1. Risk transfer, retention, and neutralization arrangements are not mutually exclusive in practice—most risk financing arrangements involve varying combinations of these approaches.

2. The emergence of banks, capital markets, and investment management firms in the risk financing business now presents a number of arrangements for managing financial risks, and these providers are beginning to look at offering products for more tradi-

tional, nonfinancial risks. The entry of these new providers is stirring up the industry.

3. Regulation and the law have not kept pace with these changes, so traditional definitions of transfer and retention now—as often as not—confuse, rather than clarify, the situation.

4. The degree to which retention is attractive to a firm is, more or less, directly related to:

- The control that firm can exert over the risk
- The degree of predictability regarding that risk
- The financial capacity of the firm to bear the risk directly—and notably—to withstand variations from the expected

5. For these reasons, most firms in the United States will continue to seek transfer and mostly transfer financing arrangements (i.e., insurance). In recognition of that fact, Chapter 7 provides an extended discussion of insurance.

Read More About It

The Rent-a-Captive Alternative

Chris Johnson
Reprinted with permission from *Risk Management* magazine, March 2000.
Copyright 2000 by Risk Management Society Publishing. All rights reserved.
For more information call 212.286.9364. www.rims.org/rmmag

One of the sexiest concepts in the alternative risk financing market today is the cell captive or rent-a-captive—a structured insurance facility that enables different portfolios of business to be segregated from each other within one overall insurance company vehicle.

It is not a new concept: Mutual Risk Management in Bermuda has been promoting cell captive or rent-a-captive structures for nearly twenty years, and they have developed variations on the theme. Steve Butterworth, now Guernsey's insurance supervisor, attempted to formalize such structures within legislation as a regulator in the Cayman Islands in the 1980s, and finally achieved his aim in Guernsey in 1997. The protected cell company [PCC] passed into current jargon soon thereafter. Cayman followed Guernsey's lead a year later with their segregated portfolio company legislation.

Gibraltar is currently drafting its own PCC legislation, although its law already allows cell structures to be set up under common law and contract. Indeed, the AIG/Munich Re–owned cell captive, Euroguard Insurance Company, was established in this way in 1996, and has been highly successful for this nascent domicile. Gibraltar is therefore currently the only domicile that allows Europe-wide programs to be written in a cell captive structure without being obliged to use fronting facilities, and the new legislation will strengthen that facility.

Dublin, the other principal domicile in which European business can be written direct, is also considering introducing cell legislation.

A cell or rented captive is not that different from such vehicles as group or association captives, or even agency captives— where entities with a common interest fund losses jointly and reduce overheads by creating a critical mass of premium. Where the cell captive differs is that each entity has a separate experience account and profit (or loss) according to its own insurance results, as if it had its own captive insurer. At the same time, however, overheads are reduced because the costs are shared. It's an ideal halfway house for a company with a relatively small premium income that is attracted by the captive concept.

Rent-a-Captive

According to the 1999 Tillinghast-Tower-Perrin Captive Insurance Directory, there are seventy rent-a-captive operations throughout the world. Seventeen were licensed in 1998.

Various terms are used to describe these vehicles, including cell captive, account solution, shadow captive, and external fund, all of which bear a resemblance to what is defined as a true rent-a-captive or cell captive.

Tillinghast defines a rent-a-captive as a "third-party sponsored insurer or reinsurer organised to handle the risk of multiple insurance programmes.'' As a definition this is adequate, but could use some clarification.

The typical way in which a rent-a-captive or cell captive is set up is that an investor establishes a company with core capital, usually a substantial amount. When Euroguard Insurance was formed in Gibraltar, the core sponsor's capital was £1.5 million. Over time this can be grown: The well-established Mutual Risk Management–owned companies (Insurance Profit Centres) in Bermuda and the Caribbean, which started in the late 1970s, have a core capital of around $186 million.

The entity that is established is an insurance or reinsurance company in its own right, and will issue policies under its own name. However, its clients rent or participate in the underwriting account, and each will normally have a separate experience account allocated to it. Policies will be written for the benefit of this experience account and claims paid out from the experience account—and profit made at the end of the year—may well be distributed back to the client.

Rent or Cell?

The two principal types of sponsored insurance entities are rent-a-captives and cell captives. In a rent-a-captive the client does not participate in the capital of the company, but rather pays an annual fee (rent) to the company for the use of its capital.

Rent-a-captive programs are usually fully funded by the client with liquid assets, although the method of funding can be flexible, including letters of credit and parental guarantees. Close attention is paid to the risk gap—the amount by which the maximum loss possible in the client's program exceeds the premium income in a given year.

In a rent-a-captive, sponsors are usually remunerated by the rental amount, and possibly administration fees or percentages of investment income. Reinsurance commissions may also be retained by the sponsor. Profit from the client's experience account would normally be available for remission back to the client, if desired, in the form of a profit commission.

In a cell captive, it is normal for the client to provide the capital needed to support the business plan. While the core capital is available to meet unexpected years of losses, it is not good practice for it to be exposed as a matter of course to the risks of individual cells. Having a safety net, however, enables solvency rules to be applied in a flexible and simplified way, especially where the regulatory regime enables the rent-a-captive or cell captive to be regulated as a single entity.

In a cell captive, the client will normally participate in the capital of the company by the issue of a separate class or classes of preference shares, which the client purchases for a nominal amount. In order to provide the underwriting capital, a premium is then paid on these shares of the amount appropriate to support the projected business plan.

The cell captive remuneration would normally be achieved by a combination of flat administration fees and percentages of investment income or premiums. The cell captive sponsor would often retain reinsurance commissions, although some may be paid back to the cell. Profits of the individual cells can be distributed back to the client by means of dividend.

Advantages

So why participate in a rent-a-captive rather than set up your own in the traditional manner?

One of the primary advantages is the lower cost of establishing a cell within a rent-a-captive. While pure capital requirements may be similar, there is no need to go through the incorporation process of a company, or license application to local regulators, which reduces the initial setup costs.

Ongoing costs in terms of fees to managers are usually lower in a cell captive than in a traditional captive. However, some argue that when comparing those fees with the elements of remuneration involved in the cell captive, there is not a great deal of difference between the two. There is no doubt, however, that there are savings in costs such as annual license fees and filing fees to local government offices.

Another advantage is the speed with which a cell can be set

up within a rent-a-captive or a cell captive. Again, there is no need to go through a separate incorporation or licensing process; it is merely a matter of concluding arrangements with the sponsors of the cell captive.

Once a cell captive or rent-a-captive is established and the sponsor has gone through the full regulatory process, the regulator will often be willing to take a flexible and more rapid view on the attachment of each program or cell, thereby reducing the amount of time necessary to establish the arrangement.

Further savings in costs can come through the pooling of resources and the sharing of services, for example investment and reinsurance arrangements.

Yet another potential advantage is tax efficiency, although there is some debate as to whether this is effective or not. Traditional captives are usually subject to controlled foreign corporation legislation in the home domicile of the parent, meaning the captive's profits are taxed as part of the parent's profits. This obviates any benefit of establishing the captive in a low tax domicile.

A controlled foreign corporation [CFC] is usually defined as one in which the parent has a minimum percentage interest. If the percentage interest in the cell captive can be shown to be less than the minimum, the insurance operation will not be subject to taxation in the parent's domicile.

In the United States, the normal minimum percentage shareholding for a company to be considered a CFC is 10 percent. The cell captive, however, introduces an interesting possibility. As a company can only be considered to be a CFC, from the U.S. Internal Revenue Service's point of view, if U.S. shareholders constitute 50 percent or more of the shares, it is possible for a U.S. parent to own more than 10 percent of the stock in a cell captive and yet not have it treated as a foreign corporation. (These provisions are in sub part F of the Internal Revenue Code; they are continually under review by and the subject of occasional case law.)

One interesting point in light of the current fashion for cell captives is that the less formal unsegregated rent-a-captive arrangements can be more effective from a tax point of view, avoiding any possibility of revenue authorities holding individual cells to be tantamount to separate companies, and taxing them accordingly.

The tax motive is considered to be questionable in terms of captives generally, as tax authorities throughout the world seek to close the gaps. Ultimately, a captive will either make profits itself and remit dividends to the parent, on which tax will be paid, or reduce costs for the parent, which will enable it to make more profits, on which tax will be paid!

Other than some marginal benefits that can be achieved (for instance, paying a smaller local tax in the captive domicile, which exempts the profit from treatment by the parent domicile tax authority), the tax benefits are purely those of deferral of payment. The focus of captive establishments today is far more to address demand within a company for certain types of cover, or to encourage management of certain exposures and risks in-house.

Disadvantages

Any negative aspects of rent-a-captives relate to the shared nature of the facility. Some companies feel a lack of control or prestige in not having their own captive.

If the decision to join the rent-a-captive facility was influenced by the tax aspect, they may be frustrated by the attitudes of aggressive tax authorities. One major point that should always be highlighted when considering a cell captive or rent-a-captive facility is the segregation of assets. One of the advantages of the cell structure is that under the agreements that are effected when a client enters a structure, each cell should stand alone for its own account in terms of the losses that it pays. Losses in one cell should not affect the capital in any other, but may affect the core capital, depending on how the company is structured.

PCC legislation is being enacted in various territories, as mentioned before, and some Bermuda cell captives are set up under individual private legislation. These provisions seem to give legal effect to the segregation of cells within the structure; however, there are circumstances in which they can be attacked.

There is legal opinion that suggests that although a statute may segregate one cell from another, if the assets of the cells are held outside the domicile where the legislation is effective, the foreign courts may be able to set aside the cell captive legislation and lay claim to the overseas assets. If assets remain in the domicile when the legislation is effective, it is likely that the courts of that domicile will uphold the segregation. It is important when considering the cell captive structure to take account of this aspect.

If a cell captive is set up under common law and contract, the position is clear: Only the parties to the contracts can be bound by its terms, so a court can attack the overall structure if a claim is not met.

In either case, the key is to be selective in the type of business written, and to ensure that highly rated and effective reinsurance programs are written, which cap the cell's (and therefore the company's) aggregate loss to an acceptable level.

Conclusion

The rent-a-captive is not a new concept, but it is actively under development. It widens the appeal of captives to companies whose budget would otherwise make the establishment of a stand-alone a borderline decision. Companies can enter a rent-a-captive cell at a reasonable cost, and then move that portfolio of business into a stand-alone once it becomes significant enough to make such a move viable. In the meantime, protected cell company legislation continues to be drafted in various states, and like the rest of the captives market, is still a buoyant area of business.

Read More About It

Insurance Links to Securities

David Cummins
Reprinted with permission from *Risk Management* magazine, August 1999.
Copyright 1999 by Risk Management Society Publishing. All rights reserved.
For more information call 212.286.9364. www.rims.org/rmmag

Projected catastrophes like a $75 billion Florida hurricane or a $100 billion California earthquake would severely stress the capacity of insurance and reinsurance markets. However, while $100 billion represents approximately one-third of the equity capital of U.S. property-liability insurers, such a loss amounts to only about 0.5 percent of the value of U.S. stocks and bonds. Clearly, if a way could be found to access securities markets directly, it would solve the problem of financing catastrophic (CAT) risk.

In fact, such an entrée into the securities markets already exists—insurance-linked securities that pay off in the event of a CAT loss. These securities are bought by investors, such as hedge funds and pension plans, that receive a premium above usual market yields for bearing the risk of catastrophes. Why would any investor buy a security that creates an exposure to a large loss in the event of a hurricane or earthquake? The answer is that such investments form only a small part of their highly diversified portfolios. CAT securities are valuable to investors because CAT losses are zero-beta events, meaning their correlation with market security returns is close to zero. Zero-beta securities are valuable for diversification purposes because they make it possible for investors to reduce risk for any given level of expected portfolio returns, that is, to improve portfolio efficiency.

Sampling

One version of CAT risk securities are the CAT call spreads currently traded on the Chicago Board of Trade. The payoff structure is identical to excess of loss reinsurance. The contracts pay off when losses exceed a retention level, or lower strike, and continue to pay until losses reach a specified cap, or upper strike.

Unlike reinsurance, however, the contracts do not pay off based on the loss experience of a specific insurer, but rather on industrywide loss indices. The Chicago Board of Trade defines one index point as total industry losses divided by $100 million. Thus, if insurance industry CAT losses are $5 billion, the index value would be 50. The payoff on the option is $200 multiplied by the index minus the lower strike, with a cap determined by the upper strike. Contracts are traded on a national index, five regional indices, and three state indices (California, Florida, and Texas).

To hedge its risk of Florida hurricane losses, an insurer could buy 40–60 September Florida calls. These calls pay off on the Florida loss index for the third quarter of the year (July, August, and September). If $5.5 billion in hurricane losses occur, the index would be 55 and the payoff would be $200 × (55–40), or $3,000 per contract. The contracts are sold or "written" by investors who receive a premium in return for bearing the risk.

Another important type of insurance-linked security is the CAT bond. A CAT bond is similar to an ordinary corporate or government bond in that investors loan money to the issuer (usually an insurer) and receive coupon payments and the eventual return of the principal. Unlike ordinary bonds, however, the return of principal on CAT bonds is contingent on the occurrence of a catastrophe. If a specified triggering event occurs, the repayment of principal to investors is partly or totally forgiven, and the issuing insurer can use the proceeds of the issue to pay claims.

For example, an insurer might issue CAT bonds totaling $500 million. The insurer promises to pay interest on the bond and to repay the principal in a year unless the triggering event occurs. The triggering event might be defined as a hurricane of a specified severity causing the insurer at least $500 million in losses in the southeastern United States. The proceeds of the bond are invested in safe securities, such as U.S. Treasury bonds, that are held in a special trust or by a single-purpose reinsurer. If the triggering event occurs, the insurer is permitted to withdraw some or all of the principal from the trust to pay claims. In return for taking the risk, the investors receive the interest rate on safe securities, such as the one-year Treasury bill rate, plus a premium over and above the Treasury rate. A typical premium for CAT bond investors is about 4 percent (400 basis points).

A third type of CAT-linked security is the catastrophic equity put option. This type of security provides the issuer—again, usually an insurance company—with contingent equity financing. The catastrophic equity put gives the insurer the right to issue a prespecified amount of equity, usually preferred stock, at a prespecified price, contingent on the occurrence of a specified triggering catastrophic event.

The put option may give the insurer the right to issue one million shares of stock at a price of $60, for example. Suppose the triggering event occurs, causing severe losses and driving the insurer's stock price to $40. It then becomes advantageous for the insurer to issue shares at the prespecified price of $60. Again, the option is "written" or sold to the company by investors who are compensated by receiving an option premium from the insurer.

Considerations

There are a number of factors that can affect the success or failure of CAT-linked security offerings, and they are important elements to consider when comparing CAT securities with conventional insurance and reinsurance transactions.

One factor is credit risk—the risk that the counterparty to the transaction will fail to pay when the triggering event occurs. In the case of a CAT bond, the counterparty is the trust that holds the Treasury securities purchased with the proceeds of the bond issue. Because the trust is funded with safe securities and exists only for the purpose of this single transaction, the credit risk of a CAT bond is close to zero.

The counterparties in the case of Chicago Board of Trade

options are the investors who write the options. However, organized exchanges control credit risk through margin requirements, trading limits, and daily settlement, with ultimate guarantees from the exchange's clearing corporation. Hence, the credit risk of exchange traded options is also low.

Credit risk is more important to consider for catastrophic equity put options, because the puts traded thus far are not issued through an organized exchange, much like conventional reinsurance that carries the risk that the reinsurer will fail to pay.

Another important aspect to consider in securitization is moral hazard—the possibility that the insurer will write too much insurance in regions protected by the CAT securities or overreport claims in order to collect more money than is justified. Moral hazard is obviously also a problem in conventional insurance and reinsurance, and provides the economic rationale for underwriting.

Moral hazard is also a potential problem in a CAT security where the contract payoff is based on the losses of the insurer issuing the security. In most of the CAT bonds issued so far, moral hazard is dealt with by including a percentage coinsurance, whereby the insurer collects only 90 percent (for example) of its CAT losses after the triggering event occurs. The purpose of the coinsurance is to reassure bondholders that the insurer will not act against their interests.

One advantage of index-based contracts, such as the Chicago Board of Trade options, is that the payoff is not tied to the experience of any one insurer. The moral hazard of index linked contracts is thus very low. Bonds, or options where the trigger is parametric, eliminate moral hazard. Parametric triggers are based on criteria over which the issuer has no control, such as the strength of a storm (on the Saffir-Simpson scale) or the magnitude (in Richter scale units) of an earthquake. For example, Japanese CAT bonds have been issued where the triggering event is an earthquake of specified Richter scale strength in Tokyo.

One of the most controversial issues in insurance securitization is the importance of basis risk. Basis risk is the risk that the payoff of the CAT security will be less than perfectly correlated with an insurer's losses. For CAT bonds and conventional reinsurance, where the payoff is triggered by the hedging insurer's own loss experience, basis risk is low. On the other hand, where the payoff is based on an index or a parametric criterion, the probability exists that the insurer will collect more or less than it expects.

For instance, an insurer may enter into an index-linked CAT option hedge that pays off for a Florida hurricane causing industrywide losses between $10 and $20 billion. Suppose, for example, that a $15 billion hurricane occurs leading to $4.5 million in losses for the hedging insurer. It is possible that the option contracts will pay only, say $3.5 million, or possibly $5 million, leaving the insurer imperfectly hedged.

Not knowing the degree of basis risk creates problems for insurers because of the uncertainty about the correlation of their losses with the industry loss index. A study currently underway will help to answer that question and give insurers more confidence in using index-linked contracts. The study, conducted jointly by The Wharton School, Applied Insurance Research and the Insurance Services Office, uses simulation analysis to measure the basis risk of insurers operating in Florida, over a wide range of storms. Preliminary analysis reveals that many insurers can hedge effectively using call option spread contracts based on a statewide loss index, and that even small insurers can make effective use of index options.

The Outlook

The securitization of insurance risk has the potential to radically alter the risk management landscape as we know it. The size of potential CAT losses relative to the capital available in the securities markets, as opposed to the insurance industry capacity, is simply too compelling for securitization to fail. Although the CAT bonds issued to date have been private placements, the development of a public market for this type of security is probable within the next few years. The standardization and simplification of CAT bond contracts necessary for the development of a public market will reduce transaction costs to the point where CAT bonds will become feasible for a much wider range of issuers. A wider market will permit investors to better diversify their CAT exposures, thereby reducing the proportionate loss to their portfolios from any given event. Publicly traded CAT bonds could be issued on a wide range of events throughout the world, such as California and Tokyo earthquakes, Australian typhoons, European floods, Florida hurricanes, and so on. Investors can also expect, in the not-too-distant future, the development of CAT risk mutual funds.

Securitization will also be driven by corporations that issue CAT securities directly in capital markets, totally bypassing the insurance and reinsurance markets, and adding to the depth and liquidity of CAT securities markets. In fact, the first issue of a CAT bond by a noninsurer (Oriental Land Company, the owner of Tokyo Disneyland) took place in May [1999].

Securitization will dramatically affect the role of reinsurers. Traditionally, reinsurers have played the role of underwriters and ultimate risk bearers for the industry. In the future, reinsurers will continue to employ their underwriting expertise to select portfolios of reinsurance contracts. However, they will bear less of the risk directly and lay off a higher proportion of risk to the securities markets by buying (and selling) CAT securities. The risk-bearing role of reinsurers will increasingly be replaced by their role as managers of basis risk and designers of innovative hedges for primary insurers.

The future also will bring the widespread securitization of other types of insurance, including automobile property damage, liability insurance, and life and health insurance. Many insurers may find their role shifting away from risk bearing and more toward a role as "originators" of primary insurance contracts. The underlying causal factor is that the uniqueness of insurers and reinsurers lies in their underwriting and risk management capabilities, rather than in their ability to serve as ultimate risk bearers. Capital markets are much better suited to perform the latter function.

Read More About It

Making the Most Out of Capital Markets

John Kollar
Reprinted with permission from *Risk Management* magazine, August 1999.
Copyright 1999 by Risk Management Society Publishing. All rights reserved.
For more information call 212.286.9364. www.rims.org/rmmag

It began with insurance companies looking beyond the limits of traditional risk financing. In the $27 trillion U.S. capital market, they found the only private sector source with the capacity to cover their exposure to catastrophes. The urgency was clear: The past decade has witnessed three of the costliest natural disasters in U.S. history—Hurricane Hugo in 1989, Hurricane Andrew in 1992, and the Northridge, California, earthquake in 1994—with a total $35 billion in insured property/casualty losses.

And the future appears likely to be stormy as well. According to the Insurance Services Office's [ISO] study, *Financing Catastrophe Risk: Capital Market Solutions,* recent advances in catastrophe computer modeling indicate that the United States is exposed to potential hurricane and earthquake damage that could exceed $100 billion in a single year, especially as the populations in particularly susceptible areas—Florida, the Midwest, and California—continue to grow. Yet ISO estimates the p/c industry's total surplus through 1998 at only $333.5 billion. Just one mega-event could wreak havoc, resulting in numerous unpaid claims and unprecedented insurer insolvency.

In securitization, many insurance companies have found an alternative risk transfer mechanism for catastrophe risks that allows them to share risk with investors, reduce the likelihood of insolvency, protect financial ratings, curb premium volatility, and limit economic and market disruptions.

Likewise for risk managers, securitization provides an alternative market for coverage. Although this market has been almost solely the domain of insurers, the financial tools that are evolving from securitization can add value to complicated programs for noninsurers' catastrophe coverage in especially prone areas, such as hotels and resorts in Florida, franchises in the Midwest, local government entities along the Texas Gulf Coast, or large corporate facilities in California.

When the commercial insurance market eventually tightens, the search for new financing methods is likely to intensify. Those risk managers who understand and can use securitization and other alternative means will be better positioned to guide their organizations safely through potential catastrophes.

The Possibilities

ISO estimates that through May 1999, investors had committed almost $3 billion to the capital markets for securitizing insurance risk. There are a variety of products available, fitted to the different needs and limitations of the investor and the risk bearer.

The most common entities are catastrophe, or "Act of God," bonds. These corporate bonds, offering higher yields to investors, are structured such that payment of some or all of the interest or principal is forgiven or deferred when catastrophe losses exceed a specified trigger. This can be based on the catastrophe losses of the risk bearer or of the property/casualty industry as a whole. Particular events—wind speeds for hurricanes or Richter scale magnitudes for earthquakes—can also activate the trigger.

The risk bearers, however, do face higher transaction costs for providing substantial amounts of customized information that allows investors to assess exposure to catastrophe losses and the consequent risk of the CAT bonds they are considering.

Catastrophe options are also growing in popularity. These standardized contracts provide the purchaser (the risk bearer) with a cash payment if a specified index of catastrophe losses reaches a predetermined level or strike price. If catastrophe losses are too low for the index to reach the specified strike price, the option expires.

Option indices are traded on the Chicago Board of Trade and the Bermuda Commodities Exchange. The CBOT index is based on insurers' total catastrophe losses and the BCOE index is keyed to insurers' weather-related losses on homeowners' policies.

The standardized option contract makes it easier for buyers and sellers to liquidate their positions. All a seller needs to do is buy the same number of options with the same strike price as the options he or she sold. Correspondingly, buyers can sell the same number of options with the same strike price as the options they bought.

The key disadvantage of catastrophe options, though, is basis risk—an individual risk bearer's loss experience may not match up with the catastrophe index used in a particular option. For the investor, the incentive to sell catastrophe options is the premium they receive from the purchasers. And unlike catastrophe bonds, investors need not rely on the individual risk bearer's superior knowledge of its exposure and disclosure because the options settle based on the index. Transaction costs are also significantly lower.

Both these and other forms of securitization offer investors a new means of reducing portfolio risk through diversification. Since catastrophes are independent of market or economic conditions, CAT bond performance is unaffected by the trends of other stocks and bonds.

In Play

The right mix of techniques is the key to a successful risk financing recipe. Through the use of computer models and business information, insurers have been able to calculate their potential catastrophe losses. The next step is figuring out how to combine the various methods to create an effective risk financing strategy.

ISO used real exposure data to show how companies can evaluate potential reduction in the cost of CAT risk financing using catastrophe options, along with reinsurance and their own capital.

For example, the cost for a midsize carrier, whose exposure distribution resembles that of the index, is as follows: $53 million with its own capital; $51.6 million (2.6 percent less) with a combination of reinsurance and its own capital; $44.8 million (15.6 percent less) with a combination of catastrophe options and its own capital; and $44.5 million (16.1 percent less) with its own capital, reinsurance, and catastrophe options.

For a large national insurer, whose exposure distribution is less similar to the index, the cost pattern, in the same combinations, is as follows: $144.3 million, $143 million (less than 1 percent less), $132.6 million (8.1 percent less), and $132 million (8.6 percent less), respectively.

Obviously, the benefits of securitization depend on the type and size of the business (and particularly with options, the business's similarity to index patterns), and on what combination of these financing tools is brought into play.

Next in Line

Recently, for the first time, a noninsurance company tapped the capital market to finance a natural hazard risk through catastrophe-linked securities. According to various published reports, the Japan-based Oriental Land Company, owner and operator of Tokyo Disneyland, placed two $100 million catastrophe bonds with two Cayman Island–based special-purpose reinsurers to protect against earthquakes.

The first bond provides Oriental Land with up to $100 million in earthquake coverage. This is provided for a five-year period and the payment depends solely upon the magnitude, location, and depth of an earthquake, regardless of actual property damage. The second transaction provides Oriental Land with a $100 million fully collateralized post-earthquake financing facility. In that case, Oriental Land will issue a $100 million five-year bond to the reinsurer, with no obligation to pay any interest for the first three years.

Clearly, primary insurers—and now self-insureds—can use securitization to supplement traditional reinsurance. Reinsurers can also use securitization to supplement traditional retrocession-reinsurance for reinsurers. And, if and when the insurance market hardens, risk managers will want to explore the use of catastrophe risk securitization as a supplement or alternative to the more common methods of risk transfer.

Securitizing risk with capital market instruments is still relatively new. But is it an emerging trend in risk funding that innovative and alert risk managers will adopt? Or is it an unproven gambit that investors and risk managers want to assess from the sidelines before calling into play? As availability and cost improve, market demand is likely to create a place for securitization in the risk manager's risk transfer arsenal for reducing costs and increasing capacity.

7

Insurance

We still rely on insurance to address many of our risk financing needs, but the quality of services provided by the insurance industry—including brokers—is pretty spotty. Risk managers are often criticized by suppliers as being driven solely by price, but what else is there to base the purchase on when the services are so mediocre?

Risk Manager
International Financial Services Firm

When looking at a broker, we want one that is honest, understands our business, has an appetite for risk, and is creative!

Risk Manager
Health Care Delivery Firm

Perspectives

Financial Reform Brings New Challenges

Rodd Zolkos
Reprinted with permission from *Business Insurance,* March 20, 2000.
© Crain Communications Inc. All rights reserved.

The convergence of financial services industries doesn't pose an immediate threat to commercial insurers, but they should be prepared for some changes. . . . [T]wo S&P analysts outline some of the new challenges that insurers will face, as well as detailing some existing ones.

Vandana Sharma, a director in the insurance ratings area at S&P in New York, notes that commercial lines insurers can offer customers underwriting expertise, loss control expertise, and claims management services, all of which are skills banks don't currently possess. What's more, she says, an alternative insurance market is already developed, with insurance and investment products already being effectively combined to develop financial solutions.

"So, in the near term, it's hard to see where the convergence of financial services is going to change the world of commercial lines insurance," Sharma says.

On the personal lines front, however, banks have the potential of leveraging their existing client bases, reaping benefits from data mining and the ability to cross market a broader portfolio of products.

They also have the potential to benefit from economies of scale realized by combining back office systems and developing customer service synergies. Consequently, Sharma says, personal lines insurance products offer the greatest near-term potential for financial institutions.

With the financial services sector changing, Sharma says the roles of financial institutions are blurring. As those changes occur, the possibility of disintermediation may become a bigger threat to commercial lines carriers as large industrial clients might be able to obtain risk transfer directly through the capital markets.

As the financial services sector evolves, consumer preferences will drive product innovation, Sharma says. "Customer service is going to drive a lot of innovations." Meanwhile, improvements in information technology are driving down the costs of building a multiproduct platform. "Technology makes it possible for us to implement a true multidimensional operating platform," she says.

With industry convergence, the competitive landscape for insurers has changed, and turf wars are only beginning. "Everybody has to develop a strategy and a strategy they can implement," she says. "The ultimate goal is increasing shareholder value."

And companies need both short- and long-term solutions for dealing with the impact of financial services convergence. "It may or may not impact them in the near term," Sharma says, "but they'd better have a solution in the near term for how they're going to deal with it."

Finally, she notes that since companies are venturing into uncharted territory, they need to exercise considerable caution.

Of course, the changes are occurring at a time when the property/casualty insurance industry is already facing tough business conditions, says Matthew T. Coyle, a director in insurance ratings services at S&P in New York. He notes that during the ten years from 1988 to 1998, while the U.S. property/casualty industry's capitalization increased 183 percent, net premiums written increased only 39 percent.

In 1999, though, rates began to firm and several insurers moved to strengthen reserves, primarily insurers in the California workers compensation market, Coyle says. "We think this is only the beginning." He also predicts that a trend toward merger and acquisition activity evidenced in 1999 will continue.

Illustrating the industry's condition, Coyle notes that in 1999, Standard & Poor's downgraded 1.5 times as many insurers' ratings as it upgraded. For 2000, Coyle sees more downgrades of insurers caused by continued compression of margins and capital quality issues. In that scenario expense management becomes crucial for insurers, and consolidation is likely to continue as a result.

"Not surprising, all the outlooks for all the sectors, aside from personal lines, are negative," Coyle says. Benefiting personal lines, he notes, is that those companies "have been more proactive in putting through rate (increases)."

Introduction

The subject of insurance is important for both conceptual and practical reasons. Conceptually, much of our understanding of risk and its management derives from insurance theory and practice, and an appreciation of insurance and insurance institutions provides valuable insights into the management of risks in organizations. Practically, insurance is a financing arrangement of profound importance to most risk management programs.

The "practical" point should be underscored. The expanding definition of risk management has tended to push the role of insurance somewhat to the side—at least this is happening in professional and academic discussions. Unfortunately, for the uninitiated, this can leave the false impression that insurance is of marginal importance to risk managers. Let there be no doubt, insurance remains a critical feature of risk financing programs.

Chapter 7 serves to provide an overview of insurance, which is a tall order. The chapter begins with an introduction of the concept of insurance and its principal characteristics. This discussion is followed by an analysis of the insurance contract—its forms and functions, its content, its pricing, and the contract law that supports it. The chapter concludes with an institutional look at insurance, which will touch briefly on legal forms of organization, functions within the insurance operation, and relevant financial and regulatory issues.

Insurance in Overview

An essay on insurance could address its subject as a matter of mathematical theory, as a legal contract, as a social institution, as a business, and—indeed—in many other contexts. Each context is interesting, but for purposes of this book it may be sufficient to note that insurance has many facets and then move on to a fairly general discussion of insurance in the context of risk management.

Insurance is a mechanism by which the financial responsibility for a risk is legally transferred from one party to another. Insurance is distinguished from other types of contractual risk transfers by the following three features:

1. The nature of the consideration given differs from most contracts

2. Performance differs from most contracts
3. The financial basis for insurance differs from most contracts.

The Nature of the Consideration

The consideration given by an insurer and insured have a rather distinct form. For the insured, the consideration is a payment or promise of payment (i.e., the premium). Conceptually, this payment is expected to bear some financial relationship to the underlying risk in question. For the insurer, consideration is a promise to perform; a promise that is conditional on a chance event (e.g., a loss) covered by the contract.

Performance

Insurance is a conditional and aleatory contract, which means that the performance of at least one party is based on a chance event. By implication, insurance contracts are not commutative, which is to say that they are not exchanges of equal value—at least not as one would conventionally understand that concept.

Financial Basis

For reasons that become more apparent when financial and regulatory issues are discussed, insurance further distinguishes itself by virtue of its "pooling" of risk. Legal disputes centering on whether a contract is insurance or something else often pivot around the question of whether risks have been pooled together so that the "funds of the many finance the losses of the few." The mathematical basis of insurance rests on the notion that the gathering together of similar risks allows the insurer to estimate future losses with greater accuracy, and this ability affords funding stability and predictability, as well as certain economies of scale.

Theory demonstrates that the act of pooling produces a social good in the sense that pooling reduces the aggregate cost of risk that otherwise would be paid by society if pooling were not practiced. A minor debate has arisen in recent years regarding the thing being pooled (see Chapter 6). Traditionally, the view has been that it was the aggregating of the risks (e.g., a number of motor vehicles) that served to improve predictability. Recently, the observation has been made that it is the pooling of "resources" that is the key issue. By accumulating premiums, an insurer can overwhelm possible variations in loss experience, thus providing stability and predictability.

Notably, insurance is a mechanism that addresses the two aspects of the cost of risk. Obviously, insurance manages the cost of losses by indemnifying the insured against the economic impact of loss. Less apparent is the impact on the cost of uncertainty. The presence of insurance can reduce the uncertainty an insured feels about the possibility of loss—which in turn lessens worry and stress and frees the insured to concentrate on matters of greater importance.

Insurance can reduce the cost of risk, but insurance can impose costs as well. As will be seen, the insurance premium is based in part on the insurer's estimate of average expected losses; thus, over time an insured is paying for its own losses. This means that the cost of losses ultimately is paid by the insured and that the insurer mainly is providing a means by which risk of sudden, large, and unexpected losses are traded for the certainty of steady, small, and manageable "losses" (i.e., the premiums paid).

The more difficult-to-appreciate cost of insurance is *moral hazard*. Moral hazard is defined as illegal or irresponsible behavior prompted by the presence of insurance (this is not a characteristic exclusive to insurance since other contracts and arrangements may have the same effect). The purchase of insurance, while clearly a risk management action, might also change the behavior of individuals in such a way as to promote the very losses the insurance was intended to address. A common illustration of this is arson, which in many respects is motivated by the prospect of profiting from insurance proceeds.

Insurance underwriters recognize that analysis of an insured risk involves a kind of two-stage evaluation to determine 1) what the existing nature of the risk is and 2) how the issuance of the policy affects that risk. The premium ultimately is based on some judgment of both elements.

The discussion of moral hazard can potentially carry far beyond the subject of insurance. Virtually any risk management measure can produce a moral hazard effect. For example, requiring maintenance workers to wear lumbar support belts (to support lower back muscles while lifting) may encourage the wearers to lift more weight than they otherwise would. Some have argued that the mandating of seatbelt usage, the wearing of hard hats, or the use of other safety equipment may encourage users to act less safely than they should. On a grand scale, it has been noted that river bed reengineering on major waterways has actually worsened flooding problems by transferring the location of flood-prone areas to new regions that have done little in the past to prepare for such problems. Clearly, moral hazard is a general phenomenon of risk management, not just of insurance.

The Insurance Contract

Insurance contracts share many common features with other contracts. By law they must serve a legal purpose, the parties must be competent to enter into the agreement, there must be offer and acceptance, and consideration must be given by the parties to the contract.

Despite core similarities, common law has recognized that insurance contracts have many features that—when taken as a whole—are unique. As a result, the legal system has evolved a rather distinct area of contract law specific to insurance. These distinctions are discussed next, but first, one overarching characteristic of insurance contract law warrants mention. Whereas contract law in the United States rests largely on a philosophy of *caveat emptor* ("let the buyer beware"), the special nature of insurance has influenced the law in such a way that buyers of insurance and sellers of insurance enjoy certain protections and privileges that commonly do not exist in contract law. Although it is true that regulatory changes in recent years are resulting in less protection for corporate/organizational buyers of insurance than for individual consumers, as a general rule, preferential treatments remain.

Legal Characteristics of Insurance

Insurance contracts are characterized as:

1. Contracts of indemnity
2. Conditional contracts
3. Aleatory contracts
4. Contracts negotiated in "utmost good faith"
5. Contracts of adhesion

Contracts of Indemnity

A contract of indemnity restores a loss. In principle, an insured is returned to the tangible and economic position that existed before a loss. As a practical matter, violations or exceptions to the concept of indemnity abound. For instance, the loss may exceed the policy limits; there may be a cost-sharing provision within the contract, the cause of loss may not be covered or only partially covered, or it may simply not be possible to actually restore an object to its preloss value (e.g., as in case of a priceless work of art).

Broadly, insurance contracts handle the restoration of loss in two ways. The most common is to define the obligation on a *replacement cost* basis. That is, the insurer promises to commit resources to replacing the lost object with a new and similar object. Some coverages modify that promise to an *actual cash value* basis so that the proceeds paid to the insured are reduced by some amount to reflect the wear, tear, physical depreciation, and obsolescence of the lost object. The second method is the *valued or agreed amount* basis, which is a value determined in advance by the insured and insurer.

Conditional Contracts

Some contracts, when agreed to, are fulfilled automatically and with certainty. Others, like insurance, perform based on the condition that some additional event occurs. In the case of insurance, of course, that additional event is a covered loss.

Aleatory Contracts

The notion that insurance is a conditional contract is extended by the fact that the conditional event is probabilistic. Some conditional contracts are based on additional events that are certain to occur, but aleatory contracts are arrangements where the conditional event is a chance event—such as a fortuitous loss. Taken in combination, the aleatory and conditional nature of insurance distinguish it from most contracts, which are commutative. Commutative arrangements are characterized by exchanges of equal value, but aleatory and conditional contracts are rarely, if ever, exchanges of equal economic value.

Contracts of Utmost Good Faith

The standard of utmost good faith implies a somewhat higher expectation for forthrightness and honesty in the insurance transaction. The courts have deemed this to be so because there is ample opportunity for fraud to occur in the buying and selling of insurance. Buyers may withhold information known only to them, which would be relevant to the insurer's decision to underwrite (e.g., a health condition). Equally, the insurer's consideration is merely a promise to perform at some future date, conditional on the occurrence of certain events. And, of course, the insured's ability to ascertain the insurer's future ability to perform is limited.

Contracts of Adhesion

This feature has become less and less relevant as risk management has developed and risk managers have become more sophisti-

Insights

Using Insurance as Capital Adds to Company's Value

Rodd Zolkos

Viewing insurance as a form of capital and risk management as capital management can open the door to managing risks previously considered uninsurable and new sources of risk financing. The return on such a perspective can be significant: the enhancement of an enterprise's value.

"Insurance is a form of off–balance sheet capital," said Brian M. Kawamoto, a director at Swiss Re New Markets Corp. in New York, who coordinated a panel on the changing face of risk financing at [the 2000] Risk & Insurance Management Society Inc. [RIMS] conference. "Think about insurance as a form of financing and how you might be able to use that in your organization going forward," Kawamoto said.

"Risk management is capital management," he said, adding, "Ultimately, when you begin to think like this there's a payoff."

That payoff can include the ability to transfer noncore risks that may dilute the firm's equity capital. Or it can take the form of recognition of more efficient sources of financing and consequently lower costs of capital.

The payoff also might involve the reshaping of an enterprise's risk profile in the eyes of other stakeholders, such as investors, lenders, or clients. Or it can be the opportunity to tap a nontraditional source of capital. "Every CFO likes to diversify financing sources," Kawamoto said.

The "modern tool kit" used to achieve this sort of risk management includes:

- Structured finance, "where you're really using insurance in a corporate finance way," Kawamoto said. These are corporate finance transactions where insurance or reinsurance capital typically is employed to alter an enterprise's risk profile, thereby widening investor appetite.

- Capital relief transactions, which is event-triggered financing to provide either debt or equity capital to the client company. Such transactions provide a way for a company to borrow money if certain events occur, allowing the organization to optimize capital resources.
- Derivatives, which an enterprise can use to optimize its risk profile by trading risks between counterparties using swaps, options, or similar instruments.
- Enterprisewide risk transactions, [which are] deals typically driven by strategic concerns to address volatility inherent in an organization's fundamental business. "Often, these types of transactions may result in improving or promoting shareholder value," Kawamoto [explained]. In some cases, the result in terms of market capitalization can be dramatic. "When you can create billions of dollars in shareholder value you're really talking about using insurance in an opportunistic way," the Swiss Re New Markets director said.

Two risk managers whose organizations have recently implemented programs displaying that sort of thinking also participated in the panel.

For Winnipeg, Manitoba–based United Grain Growers Ltd. [UGG], the process of moving to the integrated risk program the company put in place this year was an evolution rather than a revolution, according to Michael J. McAndless, the company's corporate risk manager. UGG already had good policies, defined responsibilities, well-defined position limits, good risk control practices, and formal monitoring and reporting procedures, he noted.

What the company sought was improved accountability, better structure of responsibilities, improved internal communication, a focus on and understanding of the costs of principal risks, and a risk management system for keying in on the highest risks facing the company, "not just the property and casualty and traditional risks," the risk manager said.

The traditional risk management approach is a defensive posture, McAndless noted, addressing only pure risk in which the only chance is for a loss. It can be applied only to specified insurable areas.

Enterprise risk management, on the other hand, enables an organization to take an offensive or defensive posture, addressing speculative risks that hold potential for either gains or losses and can be applied to general business applications. "We wanted to extend the traditional risk management process," McAndless said.

Ultimately the company crafted an insurance program that included a grain volume trigger to integrate coverage of its core business risk with its traditional insurance program. The integration of the grain volume coverage with the traditional insurance risks combined leverage from a favorable loss history with the portfolio effect, McAndless said, reducing the company's average long-term cost of risk and periodic earnings volatility while making it possible to increase financial leverage.

Judith M. Lindenmayer, vice president, Fidelity insurance and risk management at Boston-based FMR Corp., better known as Fidelity Investments, said her company's enterprise risk program stemmed from the company chairman's desire for coverage for "anything bad that could happen, anywhere in the world."

Late last year, the company took the next step in that approach, putting in place a new three-year catastrophe program that includes coverage for operational risks the company faces. The current program represents an evolution of a prior three-year program that combined conventional and finite risk insurance to blend financial risks facing the company with traditional risks.

Among the lessons she learned along the way was the fact that "it takes longer than you think," said Lindenmayer. "It took us eighteen months to put together the first $150 million program. But at the end of that process we had a policy that could cover anything bad that could happen anywhere in the world."

McAndless agreed that the process is an extensive one and

requires the commitment of the very top officials of an organization. "You don't just go and buy one of these things off the shelf and say, 'I want one of those integrated risk financing products,' " he said.

The UGG risk manager noted, however, that in crafting an integrated program it's not necessary to look to transfer or intensely quantify all a company's exposures; some areas of risk are better handled by internal management controls or even avoidance. "Our business is commodities," he said. "We don't want to transfer that risk, we want to take it. So you don't want to give up everything."

Lindenmayer offered a similar view. "If we sat down to do total risk mapping of everything it would probably be my grandchildren who would finish the process," she said.

But, the Fidelity risk manager said, a business should never assume that a solution simply does not exist for addressing a particular exposure. "You're only limited by your imagination and your ability to craft something that an underwriter is willing to underwrite."

cated consumers. A contract of adhesion is one that is offered on a take-it-or-leave-it basis.

Ordinarily, two parties will jointly draft a document and sign it when they are in agreement as to its wording. However, in insurance this historically has not been true because the insurer has had sole control over the drafting of the contract language. As such, the courts have tended to side with the insured when disputes arose over contract language and meaning. While this still is broadly true today, many risk managers (especially in large organizations) are able to exert considerable influence in contract formation. The result of such situations is a unique contract that—in the parlance of the industry—has been "manuscripted."

Contract Structure

A certain degree of standardization of contracts has occurred in the insurance industry, despite trends toward customization. However, it is not easy to summarize the format because insurance contracts address such a wide range of risks. For example, a life insurance policy would have to address a set of underwriting issues quite different from a product liability policy. Furthermore, some policies apply to groups (e.g., employee benefit coverages), while others apply to individuals.

Nevertheless, for introductory purposes it is useful to have some sense of contract structure. One approach to the subject is to note that contracts generally contain four parts:

1. The declarations
2. The insuring agreement
3. The conditions
4. The exclusions

The Declarations

This often is the only unique part of a coverage document. It contains information on the insured, the properties or assets involved, the coverage amount and the premiums, as well as other matters that are specific to that particular contract. In some types of policies the term *jacket* is used inasmuch as the declarations wrap around a collection of coverages (e.g., property and liability coverages) and coordinate the protection provided.

The Insuring Agreement

The insuring agreement is the meat of the contract. It describes the coverage provided, the perils protected against, the definitions of coverage terminology, and—in general terms—the objects covered.

The Conditions

Part of the consideration given by both parties is compliance with conditions that are part of the contract. The conditions will vary, but they include such material as instructions on how and when losses are reported, what the insured and insurer must do after the loss, and so on. Importantly, a loss could be denied—though fully and completely covered in all other respects—if there is a failure to comply with the conditions section of the policy.

The Exclusions

One might assume that if a contract is silent on a matter, that matter cannot be construed as being part of the contract. However, due to years of litigation over contract terminology, most insurance contracts now include a section that affirmatively asserts that certain things are excluded from coverage. As just one example, acts of war commonly are excluded as a covered cause of loss.

The Pricing of Insurance

Insurance premiums are set to achieve two objectives:

1. To assure that there are sufficient funds to cover the cost of losses and costs directly associated with losses
2. To cover the insurer's overhead costs and profits

Commonly, the loss portion is referred to as the *loss ratio* while the overhead/profits portion is the *expense ratio*. The expense ratio consists of fixed and variable cost units and is loaded into each premium after the loss ratio (sometimes called the "pure premium") has been set. (Loss and expense ratios and other measures for evaluating the performance of insurers are covered again later in this chapter.)

The loss ratio is determined in a number of different ways, but all are based in part on an estimate of the average expected losses the insured is likely to incur. For smaller organizations and for individuals, the standard approach is *classification rating*. Under this scheme, risks are pooled together into groupings that have common attributes. The loss ratio is determined by computing the average losses of risks in a particular grouping. While certain credits or premium breaks may be added, readers should note that the individual insured's own actual loss experience does not factor into the initial computation.

Organizations that are larger may be eligible for *experience rating*. Under this approach the insured is rated first on a classification basis, then the premium is adjusted to reflect the insured's own past loss experience. The degree to which the insured's own experience influences the ultimate premium is dictated by the statistical credibility of its loss experience. Experience rating is used extensively in workers compensation and other liability-related coverages. A key attribute is that future premiums can be directly influenced by efforts to control and reduce risks.

For large organizations whose loss experience has a high degree of statistical credibility, *retrospective rating* may be employed. Under this arrangement the ultimate premium is almost completely predicated on that insured's current loss experience. Thus, after making an initial premium payment to cover basic costs, the premium is determined at the end of the coverage period based on the actual losses that occur during that period. Retro plans also provide a loss capping feature, which means that if losses exceed some predetermined level, the insurer will assume responsibility for excess claims.

Interestingly, while retro rating is used mainly for large insureds, it also can be used by an insurer when a prospective client represents unknown risk. Under the retro plan, the insurer is able to moderate its risk by requiring the insured to bear the cost of its losses up to some point.

A fourth method of pricing is *judgment rating*. Though not seen widely, this approach is used when statistical information is limited or poor in quality. In such cases, an underwriter may offer coverage at a price that's based on an educated judgment of the likelihood of loss.

While premiums do represent expected losses and expenses, they may or may not reflect investment income/time value of money. For instance, under many liability coverages, the premiums paid in a particular year may not be paid out in claims for several years, giving rise to an investment income opportunity. For the insurer, this represents a revenue opportunity and a sort of hedge against unexpected results in underwriting performance. For the insured, it represents a significant opportunity cost. Thus, risk managers are interested in either negotiating into the coverage a recognition of the investment return or they may be tempted to retain the risk and capture the investment income directly.

As a summary observation, readers should note that insurance is priced on the assumption that, over time, an insured will pay in sufficient resources to cover (or more than cover) losses. The degree to which this happens is related in part to the size of the risk insured. For an individual buying automobile insurance, the typical result is a lifetime of premiums paid with few or no claims. Less commonly, an insured may have a claim that dwarves the amount of premium paid in. In other words, only rarely do premiums even roughly correspond with claims proceeds. Insurance experts would note that "uncertainty reduction" also is being purchased and has economic value, but this is an argument that wins few supporters among insureds.

As Chapter 6 indicates, when organizations grow larger and larger, the preceding argument takes hold, however, and it becomes more apparent that over time the loss ratio roughly corresponds with the actual loss proceeds that are paid under a policy. This phenomenon suggests a key risk financing insight—if the loss ratio and the claims paid are generally consistent with one another, then the decision to self-finance is influenced by the economics of the expense ratio (i.e., does that portion of the premium corresponding to the insurer's expenses and profits more than exceed the resources necessary to manage the related costs of retaining the risk, such as claims management costs?).

A Word About Reinsurance

Reinsurance is insurance for insurance companies. Commonly, an insurance company will not wish to bear all the risk it has accumulated through the issuance of policies, and it particularly will be keen to protect itself against the possibility of large losses (either from a single event or an accumulation of small events). Reinsurance companies offer the chance to transfer away the catastrophic portion of the risk portfolio and thus stabilize financial performance.

The inclusion of a brief discussion on reinsurance is important for two reasons. First, a risk manager would not necessarily be aware of the reinsurance arrangements that an insurer has made, because the insured legally is not a party to the reinsurance transaction. And yet the identity and financial solidity of the reinsurer would appear to be material to the risk manager's concern about the security of the risk financing arrangement. A risk manager needs to make appropriate inquiries into the insurer's financial management programs.

Second, as the insurance industry has evolved, reinsurers have begun to deal directly with risk managers and other end users of their products. In part this is due to the reinsurer's quest to diversify its products and services, and in part it is due to the opportunities to do so. Regardless of the cause, reinsurance companies now deal directly with captives and other alternative risk financing schemes, and also directly with larger firms. In many respects, they are providing exactly the same service they provide to insurers (i.e., protection against large losses), but the emerging direct relationship with risk managers is spawning many new innovations, such as *loss portfolio transfers*—which are arrangements where a business can transfer a collection of past losses (yet to be settled or paid out) to the reinsurer as a means of removing loss reserves from financial statements.

Institutional Aspects of Insurance

The insurance industry is widely varied and rapidly changing, and any effort at description runs some risk of becoming out-of-date in short order. For instance, though it is not addressed here except indirectly, the insurance industry is rapidly being subsumed by an emerging global financial services industry. In this new industry banks, capital markets, insurance companies, and other financial institutions are competing in a single, though differentiated, marketplace. Regulation is evolving rapidly to keep pace, and it seems probable that risk managers will soon be able to access risk financing products from investment banks, commercial banks, and directly from capital markets (as well as from insurance companies).

The principal purposes of this section are to describe briefly the structure of the insurance industry, to identify basic issues related to regulation of the industry, and to comment on financial management issues relevant in evaluating the performance and security of an insurance company.

Industry Structure

In general, the insurance industry today can be divided into two segments: life and nonlife (historically called "property and liability," but now changing to conform with international standards). The life industry segment includes individual life, health, disability, and annuity products. It also includes a subsegment known as group life, which includes life products commonly seen in employee benefit programs. Nonlife includes individual and commercial property and liability coverages, as well as a range of specialized coverages such as automobile, homeowners, boiler and machinery, marine, and aviation coverages.

There are about 5,000 insurance companies in the United States. There are fewer life insurers than nonlife, but life insurers tend to be bigger and in total have assets far in excess of the nonlife industry. Insurance companies are legally organized as either proprietaries (for profit corporations) or cooperatives (sometimes called "mutuals," which are not-for-profit corporations). Proprietary and mutual companies are found in all areas of insurance, and the debate over which form is most advantageous has never been satisfactorily resolved, although the proprietaries' ability to access capital markets has led to something of a trend in recent years known as *demutualization,* where cooperative insurers have converted to a stock-ownership form of organization.

Insights

Revenue Growth Slows as Consolidation at the Top Abates

Dave Lenckus
Reprinted with permission from *Business Insurance,* July 17, 2000. © Crain Communications Inc. All rights reserved.

Although relatively small revenue gains last year show that consolidation among the world's largest property/casualty insurance brokers has subsided, brokers' most sweeping evolutionary changes may still lie ahead.

Against a backdrop of mediocre quality-of-service grades from risk managers and their concerns over diminished choice due to broker consolidation, brokers have to find ways to add value efficiently to the risk financing process as their clients look to both new and traditional means to minimize and transfer risk, industry experts say.

As more risk managers seek to protect their organizations from a gamut of enterprise risks, brokers must gear up to direct their clients to those solutions, experts say. At the same time, brokers have the challenge of retaining their core business of placing insurance. They are seeing some risk managers beginning to deal directly with insurers. Other risk managers, concerned about maintaining a competitive broker market, are inviting a newly fortified tier of regional brokers to work on their accounts.

Brokers are adding services, as well as investing in technology, like never before in an effort to meet risk managers' growing service demands. Some observers warn that failing to meet those challenges could expose brokers to "disintermediation"—the buzzword for the phasing out of brokers from the risk management process.

But many others say that, while some disintermediation is possible and even inevitable, the brokerage industry will be around for the long haul.

Even if brokers continue to prove and improve their worth to risk managers, brokers could look very different in the next couple of years. Whether large brokers are acquired by larger financial services companies or they evolve into organizations that offer far more than insurance placement services, one thing is clear, says Russell R. Miller, chairman of the specialty investment bank Russell Miller Corporate Finance Inc. of San Francisco, "Brokerage is a line of business. It belongs in a greater product mix of risk minimization and insurance services."

Meanwhile, consolidation continues among mid-market and smaller brokers. The end of the big consolidation push by the world's ten largest brokers is reflected by their return to single-digit revenue growth last year. Revenues in 1999 grew 6.0 percent, to $14.83 billion from $13.99 billion the year before, when brokers' top-line gain exceeded 21 percent. Even that hefty gain paled compared with brokers' revenue hikes of nearly 40 percent in 1996 and 1997.

The pace of revenue-per-employee growth slowed commensurately as brokers still added employees, though at a slower clip. Brokers' 4.4 percent increase in employees held revenue per employee to an average of $123,363, a 1.5 percent gain from $121,517 in 1998. That gain essentially matched the 1998 increase of 1.3 percent, but the gains in both years fell far short of the 10.5 percent and 5.6 percent increases that brokers enjoyed in 1997 and 1996, respectively.

The continued consolidation among second- and third-tier brokers was reflected by their stronger revenue gains. The 184 smaller national, regional, and local brokers listed in the *Business Insurance* directory reported a 17.4 percent jump in revenues, to $4.40 billion last year from $3.75 billion in 1998.

In addition to revenue growth, the brokers saw an increase in their revenues per employee, which rose 2.0 percent to $118,563 on average in 1999.

With consolidation largely complete among at least the largest brokers, what business expansion and profit growth opportunities lie ahead for them? Some observers question how significant a role brokers will have in the risk financing process in the future.

The prospect of not using a broker "is a realistic possibility for any large insured capable of developing and sustaining its own relationship with a market," including a capital market, says David Mair, a first vice president with the Risk & Insurance Management Society Inc. [RIMS] of New York.

Disintermediation is not a major goal among risk managers now, because most risk managers currently find advantages—most notably, time savings—in using intermediaries, says Mair, associate director for risk management for the U.S. Olympic Committee in Colorado Springs, Colorado. But in the next several years, disintermediation likely will become a "predominant trend," because technology improvements will allow risk managers to develop efficient direct relationships with markets, he says.

Risk management consultant Michael Vogler, a principal with PricewaterhouseCoopers [PwC] L.L.P. in Atlanta, agrees that, while brokers do not face any immediate risk of disintermediation, risk managers now are beginning to size up how to get along without intermediaries.

Insurance industry stock analyst Alain Karaoglan says the risk of disintermediation is high for those brokers whose work adds little of value to the risk financing process. Brokers— companies or individuals—that know only what market to approach and what price to pay will lose their jobs, predicts Karaoglan, an equities research analyst with Donaldson Lufkin Jenrette Corp. of New York.

But disintermediation is neither a new concern nor a bigger risk for brokers than it was in the past, says Ken Crerar, president of the Council of Insurance Agents & Brokers in Washington. The prospect of disintermediation has been overplayed as a result of the boom in e-commerce, which some observers contend will greatly facilitate direct relationships between insurance buyers and markets, Crerar says.

Risk management consultant Jim Swanke notes that risk managers whose organizations have captive insurers increasingly are dealing with excess and reinsurance markets directly. "That's been set in motion and will not be stopped," says Swanke, a principal in the Minneapolis office of Tillinghast-Towers Perrin.

"This was all going to happen anyway," though the Internet

and broker consolidation may have speeded up the evolutionary process, Swanke says. He observes that, similarly, commercial buyers of benefits coverage began dealing directly with markets during the mid-twentieth century, after decades of having used brokers to place their coverage.

But Swanke and others agree that, while disintermediation is the price that any broker could pay for failing both to bring useful services to risk management and to make risk managers aware of brokers' importance, the brokerage industry is not reeling toward oblivion.

"There will always be a role for an intermediary," says Tim Cunningham, a Chicago-based principal with broker consultant INSIGHT Consulting Group of Kansas City, Missouri. INSIGHT's clients typically are midsize and large brokers, though not the world's largest brokers.

Insurance industry stock analyst Jay Cohen agrees. Those with smaller risks lack the time, inclination, or sophistication to handle the responsibilities they give brokers. Large accounts rely on brokers' advice, says Cohen, a first vice president and senior property/casualty insurance analyst with Merrill Lynch & Co. of New York.

Even if e-commerce does cut out brokers from personal lines and small commercial business, larger risks always will require "the human element," says Robert C. Meder, assistant director of new business for New York–based Kaye Group Inc., a member of the World Broker Network.

Indeed, says Cunningham, by facilitating the exchange of massive amounts of data, technology has broken down the "old boy" barriers that some brokers previously faced in winning business and gaining access to markets and facilities.

The result is a growing universe of brokers that earn at least $5 million in commission income annually, according to Thomas W. Harvey, president and chief executive officer of The Assurex Synergy Group of Columbus, Ohio. The network, composed largely of privately owned mid-market brokers, generated revenues of about $1.2 billion worldwide last year.

Wall Street and acquirers of privately held brokers also recognize the promise that well-positioned brokers hold, says John

Wicher, managing director at Russell Miller Finance. In a market where the value of the average broker has not changed measurably, those brokers that have invested in technology and talent, worked to address their clients' needs, and maintained their commission income structure "are doing very well" in valuation, Wicher says.

Also pulling up values are acquisitions by banks and by Internet-based companies with the so-called "click-and-mortar" strategy of building their operating foundations with established brokers, he says.

In the near term, the hardening property/casualty insurance market is a double-edged sword for brokers, Tillinghast's Swanke observes. While it presents brokers the opportunity to boost revenue that has been lacking over the past decade, it also will strain the servicing capabilities of brokers. This is particularly true of the largest brokers, which still are integrating recent acquisitions. Large brokers that do not show their value will lose business—some to direct writers, but more to regional brokers, Swanke predicts.

Risk managers will be ready to move at least parts of their accounts to smaller national brokers or to large regional brokers for several reasons, according to observers. With the talent that those brokers picked up during the shakeout after consolidation, they are showing they can handle the business that large accounts give them and providing a more personal touch, observers say.

Another factor weighing in favor of the smaller brokers is risk managers' lack of satisfaction with larger brokers' service since the advent of consolidation, several observers say. Tillinghast's Swanke says that large brokers have spread their talent too thinly and that consolidation has not led to the promised increase in the breadth of services brokers offer.

Others, including Merrill Lynch's Cohen, say that, while service remains a problem, at least "brokers are attempting to leverage their size."

RIMS' Mair, the organization's executive council liaison to the group's quality committee, says: "I think, across the board, the entire community is doing, at best, a C or C−. There are still too many problems that exist that need not," he says. Those problems include inaccurate policies, a lack of responsiveness and delays on delivering on promises. But brokers are "trying very hard" to remedy the problems, and service "absolutely" is improving.

Vogler of PwC maintains that brokers' service capabilities are "very good." The problem is that brokers are under such pressure to produce business that often they do not "listen real well" to their clients—a shortcoming common among service providers.

The Council's Crerar maintains that the quality of service never has been bad. And with consolidation and integration among the largest brokers largely complete, with their budget allocations for technology averaging a record 10 percent, and with their and Internet-based companies' many e-commerce initiatives, the industry is poised to deliver an array of improved services as effectively and efficiently as ever.

[Crerar] acknowledges that brokers underestimated the cost and the effort required to integrate systems. But, he says, brokers had no blueprint on which to rely. "Is it done? No. Will it ever be done? I don't think so. It's an evolving process."

Still, Crerar maintains that even though large brokers have not yet fully digested their recent acquisitions, industry consolidation has helped risk managers by making regional brokers much stronger.

Assurex's Harvey and the World Broker Network's Meder also point to the international capabilities of their respective networks through affiliations with network members located overseas. Assurex's 68 North American members have 67 affiliates in 55 countries and plans to increase its international presence to 90 or 100 countries within a couple of years, Mr. Harvey said. The World Broker Network's 8 U.S. members have partners in 30 countries.

"The playing field is really leveling," Harvey says. "The challenge is to convince prospects that we can deliver seamless risk management services through independent brokers rather than through a network of branch offices."

Thomas Motamed, executive vice president and chief operating officer for Chubb Corp. of Warren, New Jersey, agrees that risk managers are giving regionals a closer look to maintain competition. "The early indications are that the clients are very happy," Motamed says.

Even so, "there's a clear dichotomy between the large broker and the local agent . . . of service that can be offered," Miller says. That is important because of risk managers' increasing knowledge and financial strength to address problems in more effective and efficient ways than traditional insurance programs. Miller notes that many risk managers today represent organizations that have net worths greater than those of insurers.

Wicher says that the best brokers understand that they must have access to sophisticated financial tools other than insurance in order to best address their clients' enterprise risks. The largest brokers are in a position to meet those many needs, including securitization needs, Wicher and Miller say.

Chubb's Motamed said the largest three brokers—including Willis Group Ltd., in which Chubb and other insurers have invested—have "a broad and deep global reach," attract capital markets and reinsurers, and provide consulting. "So they have more in their arsenal."

Motamed says that regional brokers "probably don't have as much experience" dealing with those providers. Still, he says, "they can do it."

What should risk managers expect the brokerage industry to look like ultimately? Industry observers say that change could be the one constant that risk managers will see.

Many observers expect that consolidation will continue apace among second- and third-tier brokers. "There's still a lot of revenue and expense pressure on smaller brokers," notes Cohen of Merrill Lynch. The largest brokers likely will limit their acquisitions to relatively small targets that would add or round out a niche service, fill a geographical void, or bring onboard a group of coveted producers, observers say.

The exception, some observers say, could be an eventual bid for Arthur J. Gallagher & Co., which is strong in mid-market and public-entity business. But Gallagher President and Chief

Executive Officer J. Patrick Gallagher has said he is committed to keeping the broker independent unless he is offered a deal that he, as a fiduciary, would have to consider.

Some analysts suggest that the largest brokers themselves, after a decade of bagging prized broker game, may become the hunted. Some analysts, including Hugo J. Warns, a principal in the financial institutions group at Baltimore-based investment bank Legg Mason Wood Walker Inc., expect that financial services companies will begin pursuing brokers to round out their portfolios of integrated financial services.

Wicher believes that "the market for securitization, especially relating to catastrophe risk, will continue to grow." That means brokers must be able to access capital markets, he said. But "there is a scarcity of individuals with those capabilities," he says.

At the same time, Wicher says: "One of the most important trends is the recognition that mid-market clients want human resources answers that reach beyond traditional insurance." Brokers who want to be robust in the marketplace by following the example of a handful of Internet initiatives designed to provide that broad-based human resources solution would need the capital to do so, he says.

"Ultimately, there will be one more transaction for the largest brokers," and that could be a merger with a large securities firm, Wicher says.

A more interesting alliance, though, would be one that combines a broker, a management consultant, and a dot-com company, said William J. Kelly, chairman of the International Federation of Risk & Insurance Management and a managing director with J.P. Morgan & Co. Inc. in New York. "Management consultants have far greater breadth of expertise with respect to overall operating risk and associated issues but lack risk funding ability and transactional leverage. A dot-com partner could keep the enterprise ahead of the curve, in terms of its product delivery infrastructure," Kelly recently told a group of Willis Group Ltd. producers.

However the brokerage industry shakes out, observers agree that risk managers will be seeing some important changes over the next few years. "It's a very exciting marketplace," Wicher says.

Because states regulate insurance, most insurers are licensed to do business in only one or a few states. The general public often is surprised to learn this because the largest insurance companies conduct highly visible nationwide marketing efforts. However, the most common form of nonlife insurer is a "county mutual," which writes farm and commercial business in a single county.

As mentioned previously, the reinsurance industry provides large loss protection for the direct or primary insurance industry. Reinsurance tends to be regulated more lightly, and the financial characteristics of this industry segment have led to significant consolidation and globalization in recent years. The leading reinsurers today are international firms that have grown to be very large.

One reinsurer of particular note is Lloyd's of London, which is influential beyond its actual size. Lloyd's has been in the insurance business for more than 300 years, and its experience and reputation make it an opinion leader in the world of insurance. Much of the industry takes its cues from Lloyd's underwriters. Having noted that, Lloyd's has emerged recently from a period of financial difficulty that nearly destroyed the organization. As Lloyd's is not an insurer per se, but is a marketplace for the buying and selling of reinsurance (and direct insurance, too, such as marine and aviation coverage), its reorganization has included allowing other insurance companies into the Lloyd's market. Historically, Lloyd's only permitted individuals to invest in the insurance business (an investment with unlimited liability), but the arrival of corporate investors and participants is changing the picture at Lloyd's.

Distribution Systems

In general, insurance companies have three ways to sell insurance:

1. Directly
2. Through independent agents
3. Through the brokerage system

Direct writing involves either a paid sales force or direct phone sales or—increasingly—the Internet. Independent agents are business owners who represent one or more insurance companies and are paid a commission by the insurer, but are not construed to be employees of that insurer. Brokers are independent business owners who represent the buyers of insurance and approach the insurers on behalf of the buyer. Confusingly, they also are paid commissions by the insurer, though they are legal representatives of the buyer. Many risk managers, in an effort to control the possible conflict of interest that could arise in such situations, negotiate fee-for-service arrangements with brokers. Chapter 8 discusses this issue in some detail.

Reinsurance companies tend to be direct writers, although brokers are present in the reinsurance industry as well.

Regulation of the Industry

As was mentioned, in the United States, insurance is regulated mainly at the state level. Although the Securities and Exchange Commission (SEC) and other federal bodies have an important influence, history and convention have dictated that state governments take the lead in overseeing insurance practices. There has been some movement to consider whether federal regulation may better suit an industry that finds itself in the throes of global competition, and some observers believe that change will occur, but since this is speculative, the focus of the following comments is on current forms and practices.

Structure

Each state has designated an individual who has responsibility for overseeing regulation—that position most commonly is known as the insurance commissioner. The position may be elected or appointed by the governor. Of course, the commissioner will have a staff of some size to undertake the necessary activities.

Powers and Duties

The regulator's principal duties are to license insurers and agents, to conduct financial audits of insurers, to act on consumer complaints, to regulate some rates, to approve some policy language, and to manage the conservation or liquidation of insurers with financial difficulties.

Although each of these duties is complex, the central objective of regulation is to ensure the financial solidity of insurers and to protect consumers against fraud and abuse. Ordinarily, these assurances and protections come in the form monitoring activities and mechanisms for adjudicating complaints. However, most regulators also oversee mechanisms that act as assurances in their own right. For example, each state has created guaranty funds that serve to protect policyholders against financial loss due to insolvency of an insurance company. In addition, there are circumstances when the state directly intervenes to develop markets for insurance when public policy considerations are present (e.g., high-risk programs for motor vehicles or joint underwriting authorities for low-income housing).

The emphasis of regulation has evolved over the past forty years. Early in that time period, the emphasis was on monitoring for financial solvency. Beginning in the 1960s, the focus shifted to consumer protection, and this ushered in an era that de-emphasized financial oversight. Recently, some states have begun to view financial oversight as the ultimate in consumer protection, so there has been some refocusing of priorities. Interestingly, this refocusing has promoted new efforts to focus more regulatory resources on the protection of individual policyholders while reducing resources used to protect corporate or institutional buyers. The logic of this trend, in part, is due to the belief that organizations have risk managers who are able to judge financial security for themselves and do not require quite the same assistance as do individual consumers.

Financial Assessment of Insurers

In part because greater oversight is being shifted to risk managers, it is useful to examine briefly the key financial aspects of insurance companies that influence performance and solidity.

Although a financial performance ratio, standing in isolation, provides little (if any) insight into any organization, a reasonable starting point for thinking about insurer performance and solidity is consideration of a few key ratios.

The loss ratio is, perhaps, central to a basic understanding of financial performance. It is commonly determined by relating losses incurred (i.e., losses an insurer becomes obligated to pay, plus expenses associated with settling the claims—so in that context it is not surprising to recall that an individual premium contains a loss ratio as well) in some period of time to premiums earned (typically something less than the premiums received, owing to accounting rules) in that same period of time.

While the loss ratio is often expressed as a percentage of the premium that is paid by the insured, it is more useful to understand that the loss ratio represents the insurer's estimate of expenses—or almost literally of the "cost of goods sold"—allowing for some degree of variability. Provided other factors are held constant, a high loss ratio implies that a significant portion of a premium will be returned to the insured as benefits and loss-related service, which may be a positive indication. If, for instance, a $10,000 premium were found to have a 90 percent loss ratio, it could mean that the insurer is very efficient, with only $1,000 being retained to cover overhead, taxes, commissions, profits, and salaries. However, if the insurer had planned for a 60 percent loss ratio, the same result would suggest a serious problem. Because the loss ratio could suggest positive or negative performance, it rarely is worth considering on its own.

The expense ratio is another important ratio. In general, expenses would include claims-related costs (e.g., hiring claims adjusters and sending them into the field to investigate accidents), but custom and practice hold that these expenses typically are included in the loss ratio because they are somewhat variable and related to loss costs. Thus, the expense ratio is related to underwriting and other nonclaims expenses. These "expenses incurred" are related to the "premiums written" (i.e., premiums received during a period of time, which is commonly a larger value than premiums earned) and tend to relate the portion of premium dollars that are consumed in paying for overhead and other expenses. Other factors held constant, a low expense ratio suggests the insurer performs in a low-cost environment. Of course, low cost could mean cheap as well as efficient, so the ratio itself can be misleading. Alternatively, a high expense ratio may suggest inefficiency, but it could also reveal an appropriate level of investment in underwriting and loss control. As a rather extreme example of this point, boiler and machinery insurance (i.e., insurance protecting against explosion of boilers, large manufacturing equipment, refrigeration systems, and the like) has extremely high expense ratios, but these expenses are incurred in providing inspections and loss control services that have the net effect of reducing the likelihood of losses.

The *combined ratio* is the sum of the loss ratio and expense ratio. The combined ratio, when adjusted for dividends, often is reported as an indicator of an insurance company's performance. For example, a loss ratio of .65 when added to an expense ratio of .30 yields a combined ratio of .95, which—while not quite correctly—is interpreted as the percentage of premium dollars paid in losses and expenses. In this instance, the insurer collected $1 in premiums and paid 95 cents in losses and overhead expenses, producing an underwriting profit of 5 cents. Logically, a 100 percent combined ratio represents a break-even underwriting performance, while 100+ percent ratios signal problems in underwriting.

Astute readers will note that the combined ratio omits an important source of revenue for the insurer—investment income. While the insurer holds the premiums, it is able to invest those funds. In certain lines of insurance (e.g., liability insurance, workers compensation), that income can be significant because the holding period can last for years. Consequently, the combined ratio often is adjusted by subtracting the net investment income ratio (i.e., net investment income divided by premiums written). A 12 percent net investment ratio would change the above-discussed combined ratio as follows:

Loss ratio + Expense ratio − Net investment ratio = Operating ratio
  .65   + .30   − .12   = .83

Or, put a different way, when investment income is considered, the insurer paid out 83 cents for every premium dollar taken in.

A second basis for considering financial performance is the *premium-to-surplus ratio*—the ratio of net premiums written related to the policyholders' surplus (which is the difference between an insurer's assets and its liabilities). The policyholders' surplus represents, in a sense, the cushion an insurer has to protect itself against unexpected loss costs. In general, a high premium-to-surplus ratio implies that the insurer is vulnerable to adverse events. Put simply, such an insurer would have relatively fewer resources to draw on should losses end up being higher than expected. Typically, premium-to-surplus ratios range from 100 to 300 percent, and analysts advise that companies offering riskier and uncertain coverages should have lower ratios than companies offering traditional and stable insurance coverages.

Readers are reminded that reinsurance is important in judging insurer financial performance. Reinsurance can protect the primary insurer from adverse shocks, but of course, the presence of the reinsurer raises monitoring issues for the risk manager. The financial solidity of the reinsurer becomes an additional subject of inquiry.

The typical firm manager has limited time to conduct financial security analyses of insurance companies (though, as was suggested previously, regulatory trends are tending to put more of a burden on organizations to evaluate insurer financial solidity). Fortunately, this type of expertise is one of the central reasons brokers are used. Brokerage houses commonly have resources to monitor insurer financial performance, and risk managers rely on brokers to steer them clear of troublesome or suspect insurance companies.

Publicly available ratings of insurance companies can also assist a risk manager. Moody's, Standard & Poor's, and A. M. Best's all provide rating systems for financial security and performance. As perhaps the most widely used rating agency, Best's produces a system that grades insurers (e.g., A+, A, B+, etc.). A general rule of thumb is that risk managers should use insurance companies with an A or higher rating only. Of course, like all rules of thumb, blind adherence to the rule can be as problematic as using no evaluation system at all.

Read More About It

Future Shock? An Industry Forecast

Andrew Berry
Reprinted with permission from *Risk Management* magazine, April 2000.
Copyright 2000 by Risk Management Society Publishing. All rights reserved.
For more information call 212.286.9364. www.rims.org/rmmag

The turn of the millennium—especially one free of apocalyptic disasters—has given rise to much speculation about the future. Nowhere is this conjecture more apt than in the insurance industry, the very survival of which has been called into question. Indeed, a health check on the commercial lines insurance industry does not make pleasant reading. Consider: Our product is inefficient. Thirty-seven cents of every premium dollar goes to expenses. This figure has become accepted in the industry; but consider it against other services: the realtors' fees and closing costs on your house, travel agent commissions, stock brokerage fees, foreign exchange commissions, even the expenses added to a consultant's professional fees. These are mostly in the single digits. Despite their high numbers, the U.S. commercial lines industry still attracts $140 billion in premiums annually—and $52 billion in expenses.

Our customers are not satisfied. According to the QIC/RIMS Quality Scorecard, customer satisfaction is below that of the U.S. Postal Service. How many companies still use the post office for their key mailing needs? How did the insurance industry respond to these findings from our customer association? It withdrew funding for the research group. Our customers seek alternatives to our product. The alternative market has grown over the past thirty years to about half the size of the traditional market. Alternative risk financing is arguably an inferior product to insurance, due to the lack of true risk transfer, but aided by lower expense ratios and more control, customers have been steadily substituting this product for insurance.

Our distribution channel is strangled. Thirty-five percent of the commercial lines market is controlled by two intermediaries. (This figure is considerably higher for larger commercial accounts.) This concentration has created a lack of choice and flexibility for both buyers and sellers of commercial insurance. Carriers are consolidating as well, further reducing buyer choice.

We don't understand our customers. In many cases we don't even know who our customers are. The insurance industry remains one of the few that deliberately distances itself from those it is presuming to serve. It has created complexity and confusion around its product. The result? A lack of communication and products that do not meet the needs of the customer. In the Quality Scorecard, buyers gave the industry its lowest scores on identifying needs and creating solutions. It is estimated that traditional insurance products cover only 15 percent to 20 percent of an organization's risk exposures.

Two trends ensure that the state of affairs described here will not be sustained long into the new century: convergence in the financial services industry and the growth of the Internet. The first acts as a significant threat to the continued survival of the insurance industry as we know it, and the second may be the answer to the industry's problems.

Convergence

While much is being made of the demise of Glass-Steagall, convergence in financial services has been going on for some time, and on three different levels:

■ *Convergence in ownership.* The passage of the Financial Services Modernization Act creates the opportunity for banks and other financial services groups to own insurance operations. This is making insurance companies nervous, as banks, it is argued, are better positioned to compete. They have stronger and more direct relationships, lower expenses, and more opportunity for cross-selling. However, there is some question as to whether banks will find insurance business that attractive. Returns are comparatively low, the industry is overcapitalized and hence very competitive, and underwriting losses have been high.

The key decisions facing banks are whether to be in the underwriting or distribution business, and whether to build or buy. The low returns on underwriting and difficulties in building complex insurance organizations favor distribution and buying. The competitive threat from banks appears more remote for commercial lines business than life and personal lines. However, if a bank were to enter the commercial lines underwriting business, it is unlikely to choose the industry's existing distribution and operating structure. E-commerce could provide the low-cost and flexible platform banks need to quickly and profitably enter this market.

■ *Convergence in products*. The 1990s have seen a convergence between insurance and capital markets products. Each has designed products to address the risks traditionally covered by the other. The insurance industry has developed integrated risk products to address both hazard and financial risk. While there has been much talk about integrated risk products, few have moved outside of hazard risk to be truly integrated with financial risk. Instead, we have seen a growth in multi-line policies across traditional insurable risk. Most recently, the industry has launched earnings protection policies to address a broad range of enterprise risks, products that could remove the need for (or duplicate) risk spreading in an investor's portfolio.

The securitizing of risk has allowed companies to finance their hazard risk with capital market solutions. Most securitization deals have been limited to reinsurance type transactions, although there have been two Japanese earthquake bonds placed by corporations.

Increasingly sophisticated risk assessment tools, particularly in the area of covariance between risk factors, will allow flexibility in packaging risk for transfer to external parties. The identity of those external parties will depend on the relative efficiency of their markets. Until the insurance industry reduces its expense base, it will be at a considerable disadvantage in competing for this integrated/securitized risk business.

■ *Convergence in risk management disciplines.* In the late 1990s, we also witnessed the emergence of enterprise risk management, the process by which an organization uniformly assesses and manages all risks to the achievement of its business objectives. There have been three drivers to this aspect of convergence.

To begin with, there were a number of well-publicized corporate collapses, including Perrier, Barings Bank, Kidder Peabody, and Long Term Capital Management. The end of the century also saw an enormous amount of activity in the implementation of new corporate governance guidelines. Most focused on providing greater disclosure to shareholders in an effort to boost equity markets. Many also incorporated guidelines advocating or requiring a system for managing, reviewing, and reporting on all material risks affecting the enterprise.

Finally, there is the potential to increase shareholder value. Financial theory shows an inverse relationship between a company's share price and its risk profile as measured by its historical share price movements against the market. This theory is supported by a Towers Perrin survey, which found that consistency in results (good risk management) accounts for 25 percent of share price.

For the risk manager, enterprise risk management is both an opportunity and a threat. It has gained senior management attention, providing an opportunity for the risk manager to become involved in more strategic activities. However, traditional risk managers are not the only ones eyeing this turf. Treasurers, legal counsel, HR, strategic planners, and internal auditors all have ambitions. Unfortunately, the structure of the insurance industry does not help the risk manager in this competition. Bogged down in administration, many risk managers have little time left to actually manage risk and become involved in these strategic activities. This is a serious problem. Not making chief risk officer may condemn the risk manager to the role of insurance administrator. And even that role may be greatly diminished if the insurer is no longer the preferred risk financing partner.

The Web Advantage

At the end of 1999, there were over 200 million Internet users, of which half were in the United States. Some predict that by 2003 there will be 500 million users, with the greatest growth internationally. In the area of e-commerce, we have only seen the tip of the iceberg. A December 1999 Boston Consulting Group report estimated that business-to-business e-commerce would reach $2.8 trillion in transaction value by 2003. This represents an annual growth rate of 33 percent from the current level of $671 million.

With e-commerce becoming a standard method of operation for all companies, risk managers will increasingly face Internet-related exposures in the areas of intellectual property and legal liability.

In addition, the Internet will have a significant impact on the way risk managers perform their jobs. Two major web forces are the disintermediation of markets and the streamlining of work processes. Both are suited to the commercial lines insurance industry. Allowing buyers to transact online with insurance carriers could reduce the industry's expense ratio by as much as half. Savings would come not only from reduced distribution costs but also from efficiencies in marketing, underwriting, and infrastructure costs. By removing unnecessary touch points in the distribution chain, the time required to transfer risk information would be greatly reduced. With a more efficient product and greater ease of purchase, the industry may attract back some of the customers lost to the alternative market. With more direct communication, new products may be designed to better address the needs of customers.

Disintermediation is only half the story. E-commerce can greatly reduce the administrative burden currently placed on risk managers. Electronic certificate issuance, claims notification, policy issuance and management, reporting, and benchmarking are all possible. Taking people out of unnecessary activities will allow and challenge them to add value in risk assessment and risk control activities.

With all this promise, you would think that the industry is

readily embracing e-commerce. Not so. A June 1999 Booz Allen survey found that insurers are well behind other financial services firms in their online offerings. Fifty-eight percent could not respond to customer e-mail.

A December 1999 Tillinghast-Towers Perrin survey found that three-fourths of insurance executives (both life and property/casualty) see the Internet continuing to emerge as a means of educating and serving customers rather than as a major vehicle for product sales. By contrast, nearly the same percentage of banking and investment management CEOs believe the Internet will become a major sales channel.

If e-commerce is the cure for the insurance industry's ills, why isn't the patient taking the medicine? The main reason is the significant investment insurance companies have made in agent/broker distribution and in existing legacy systems. XML [extensible markup language] standards in the industry may solve legacy integration problems. Channel conflict is a more difficult issue. While most insurers recognize that change is on the horizon, managing that change and potential agent/broker displacement is a significant issue.

Absent any external force, it is unlikely that the insurance industry will adopt e-commerce any time soon. The good news for customers is that convergence and the emergence of competition from entities unencumbered by existing infrastructure investments could force insurers to act sooner rather than later. The buyers themselves can collectively exert pressure on the industry to change. By demanding more direct, efficient, and streamlined solutions, they will speed the adoption of e-commerce. And that just might get us to a situation where risk managers manage risk and insurance companies underwrite it. An old concept for a new millennium.

Read More About It

Convergence

Todd Williams
Reprinted with permission from *Risk Management* magazine, August 1999.
Copyright 1999 by Risk Management Society Publishing. All rights reserved.
For more information call 212.286.9364. www.rims.org/rmmag

In the year 2000, will insurance buyers purchase protection through investment banks using catastrophe bonds, derivative contracts, or other financial vehicles? Will treasurers look to insurance companies to protect against fluctuations in foreign currencies and other financial risks? With insurance and capital markets headed full speed toward a so-called convergence, the answer to both questions appears to be yes, but to what extent, only time will tell.

This article is an introduction [to] the convergence of the insurance and capital markets. The intent of the series is to demystify many of the aspects surrounding this convergence, to explain some current insurance-risk capital market transactions, to identify some of the players, and to examine the potential impact on insurers, brokers and insureds.

Convergence Defined

The Merriam Webster Dictionary defines convergence as ''the act of converging and especially moving toward union or uniformity.'' This accurately describes the insurance and capital markets as each begins to enter certain sectors of the other's business.

For example, insurance companies now issue insurance contracts for certain risks, such as financial risks, that were previously managed or hedged using capital market instruments. On the other hand, investment banks transfer to the capital market certain risks that previously were insured or managed by insurance or reinsurance companies. This mutual turf encroachment is evident in the number of transactions that have been completed by both competing markets over the last twenty-four months.

Insurance Markets

Insurance companies are invading the realm of financial risk managers. One example of the insurance market nipping at the capital market can be found in the much-touted Honeywell integrated insurance program. The deal entailed a multi-line insurance program that provided coverage for certain property and casualty risks, as well as a basket of foreign currencies. Under the integrated risk scenario, the insurer issued a contract that covered decreases in the value of the basket of foreign currencies and certain p/c [property/casualty] losses above a predetermined retention level. Ideally, the program will result in savings over the existing insurance costs for the p/c risks and the hedging costs for the foreign exchange risk.

Clearly, insurance companies have begun to challenge investment banks by "insuring" foreign exchange and other financial risks. But continued movement onto the financial risk side is contingent on the acceptance of integrated risk programs by buyers, the state of the insurance market, the clearing of accounting hurdles (e.g., Financial Accounting Standard Number 133), and the resolution of turf battles between insurance risk and financial risk managers.

Capital Markets

Investment banks and other financial institutions are likewise hungry for new insurance-related business. For example, over the past two years, a number of catastrophic insurance risks have been transferred to the capital markets through insurance-linked securities. One vehicle used by insurance and reinsurance companies to transfer earthquake, windstorm, and other catastrophic risks to the capital markets is the catastrophe (CAT) bond. Under the CAT bond scenario, investors purchase the bond and exchange a principal payment now for future coupon (interest) and principal payments. These payments are contingent on loss experience or the occurrence of a specified catastrophic event. If the bond is not triggered, the investor receives full coupon and principal payments over the life of the bond. If the bond is triggered, the investor may lose the right to future coupon payments, principal payments or both, depending on the type of bond. Organizations employing CAT bonds or similar instruments to transfer insurance risk to investors include USAA, Tokio Marine, Swiss Re, Reliance, and Winterthur.

Other examples of capital market–related transactions include risk swaps, catastrophe equity put options, exchange-traded options, and others.

The Impact

Why are insurers and investment banks entering each other's businesses? From the insurer standpoint, the soft market has forced them to be creative in order to increase profits or maintain market share. They are looking to underwrite financial and business risks that historically have not been insurable. Additionally, insurers are exploring less expensive methods of risk transfer and seeking experience and market share in the new capital market transaction arena. The capital markets are looking for additional investment opportunities and a potential new asset class uncorrelated to the stock or bond market. And convergence is an ideal model for the corporate trend toward enterprise risk management—managing uncorrelated business risk through a systematic, coordinated process.

But the more pertinent question at this point might be: What will convergence mean for the players in the insurance industry?

For insurance and reinsurance companies, convergence will likely mean additional competition from nontraditional players such as investment banks and investors. Several, such as Lehman Brothers and Goldman Sachs, have already started insurance risk groups. Others have formulated similar operations or are in the due diligence stage. In the long run, convergence could result in insurers and reinsurers losing market share to insurance risk capital market transactions.

But there are also opportunities for insurers. Insurance companies such as AIG, X.L., CIGNA Risk Solutions, and Zurich offer integrated insurance products that cover financial risk in direct competition with financial institutions. And many insurers and reinsurers have formed financial risk groups to compete in the insurance-linked securities market, including Swiss Re, Zurich, General Reinsurance, AIG, and others. The ability to quickly adapt to these opportunities will ultimately determine the impact of convergence on a particular insurer.

For brokers, convergence also spells contest and possibility. The foray by investment banks into the insurance business includes using reinsurance brokerage operations to facilitate insurance risk transactions. These brokers could compete directly with insurance brokers on the reinsurance side of the business. Alternatively, Aon, Marsh, and others have established specialty groups to play in the insurance-linked securities sandbox. Could both insurance brokers and investment banks foresee a new asset class in this risk? Insurance brokers will likely play a role in facilitating or originating insurance risk capital market transactions by packaging risks with specific characteristics to sell to interested buyers. This risk originator's role, similar to the role of mortgage bankers, could also be played by insurers. In the long term, insurance brokers could package and transfer risk to either market, whichever offers the more cost-effective alternative.

From the insured's perspective, changes include new product offerings from insurers and potential opportunities for the transfer of insurance-related risk using securities or derivatives. Innovative offerings include the aforementioned integrated products for certain financial, business and weather risks, as well as other nontraditional products such as earnings protection.

The day has already passed when an insured packaged p/c risk for transfer to the capital markets; the day when an insured combines p/c risk and other risks to transfer to the capital markets may not be too far away. In fact, Toyota recently initiated one incremental step toward such transactions. It transferred the residual value of certain leased assets to the capital markets. Although the residual value of leased assets is not p/c risk, the near term could bring the same type of thinking to the insurance arena.

For the moment, however, although insureds have shown significant interest in learning about and understanding the new integrated risk and capital market alternatives, very few have opted for these alternatives over traditional insurance in this soft market.

Future

What convergence ultimately means for the insurance industry remains to be seen. At this stage, increased competition, potential new business opportunities, and additional risk transfer alternatives are already direct results of the trend.

Hang on. The only thing certain about the convergence of these sectors is change.

Read More About It

Transformers—New Tools for Risk Transfer

John Conley
Reprinted with permission from *Risk Management* magazine, March 2000. Copyright 2000 by Risk Management Society Publishing. All rights reserved. For more information call 212.286.9364. www.rims.org/rmmag

There are some new players on the competitive battlefield, vying for the risk manager's attention. Investment banks are creating vehicles that can transform insurance risk into an investment offering, thus opening up another avenue to the capital markets. How do transformers work, and how will the traditional insurers and major brokers react?

Now that the last bricks have been torn from the wall separating insurance from investment and commercial banking, the parties are looking each other in the face and wondering, "What next?" While investment and commercial banks have made tentative assaults in the past against insurers and reinsurers, the onus is on them now to mount a full-scale attack. Meanwhile, as the banks ponder their newfound regulatory freedoms, several reinsurers and insurers are preparing countermeasures.

Here's how the competitive battlefield is shaping up for the third millennium. On one flank are well-armed insurance companies like American International Group, ACE, and XL—insurers with the clout to offer traditional property/casualty insurance, insurance-linked securities, and other alternative risk transfer strategies. On another flank are hugely capitalized reinsurers like Swiss Re and Munich Re—companies with units that specialize in offering traditional insurance, capital market instruments, and alternative risk strategies on a primary basis. And then there are the investment banks, particularly Goldman Sachs and Lehman Bros., each with a reinsurance unit that can transform insurance risks into securities and vice versa. Finally, we have the rest of the property/casualty insurance industry, traditional companies offering traditional product solutions.

They're all battling for the attention of risk managers, many of whom are essentially competing in their own right with captive insurance facilities. Does anyone have a scorecard?

Financial services modernization legislation aside, one wonders why all the strategic repositioning against traditional insurers is occurring in the first place. With property/casualty insurance products at sustainable low prices, why would anyone shop around anyway? "It does seem an odd time for these new strategies and players," says Raymond Dowling, vice president of TP Financial Solutions Ltd., a Stamford-based broker dealer for Towers Perrin Inc. "But companies are always looking for different ways to transform risk, thanks to the historic cyclical volatility in the property/casualty industry. Even though we have gone through this incredibly long soft cycle, there's always a pent-up fear factor that the market will turn. Prudence dictates readiness."

In other words, risk managers should sniff around to sense what's new in risk transfer. If they do, they'll find a changing market, one increasingly focused on customized risk solutions, less so on products. The new customer-focused strategies are marketed by mega-brokers like Marsh, Willis and Aon and several investment banks, underwritten by a few insurers and reinsurers and, in the case of securities, absorbed by institutional and other investors. "It used to be an insurance-driven market in the past, but now we're seeing a more corporate-driven market," says Elizabeth Farrell, assistant vice president at A.M. Best Co. "Risk managers increasingly are being asked to help manage their companies' balance sheets. These nontraditional products cannot be ignored."

Presto Change-o

Among the more innovative strategies are the so-called transformers sprouted by Goldman Sachs and Lehman Bros. Each bank has formed a unit, Arrow Re and Lehman Re, respectively, that underwrites insurance or reinsurance for a corporate client (or ceding insurer), warehouses these risks, and then converts a block of them into a security bought by investors.

These newfangled companies also can transform a derivative into insurance or reinsurance. "The flexibility they provide is enticing," says Carl Groth, senior vice president and director of alternative risk transfer at Willis, in New York. "We're able to bring them a weather derivative that we securitized for a company, and they can take it in and reinsure it. Or we can bring them an insurance policy that they will absorb through the front door and spin out through the back door to investors in a security."

Michael Gelband, president of New York–based Lehman Re, says his company has completed several risk conversions for Fortune 1000 companies, but would not divulge the names of the parties involved. "We're not looking to compete head-on against traditional insurers or reinsurers selling products, seeing ourselves instead as a problem solver," Gelband says. "We have every possible (risk transfer) solution at our disposal, whether it be insurance, reinsurance or something that is capital markets–based. We select the best of these alternatives to solve a client's problems in the most efficient way. As opposed to being on one side or the other—insurance or securitization—we're on both."

Gelband's career up until now has been in investment banking, developing capital market strategies. "Giant insurers and reinsurers are trying to develop sophisticated expertise in the capital markets, but it is not their core competence," he says. "For us, the structuring of options and other creative, analytical solutions to corporate problems is our bread and butter. Lehman Bros. developed the mortgage-backed securities market and the asset-backed securities market. We've spent billions on technology to structure such markets efficiently. Now we're bringing this technology to insurance." To shore up the insurance and reinsurance side of Lehman Re, Gelband has amassed a cadre of what he calls "lifelong insurance people."

As corporations adopt a holistic approach to risk management, essentially obtaining systematic protection for all the risks affecting the balance sheet, transformers will become a valuable resource, says Arrow Re President Kymn Astwood. "Currency exposures and interest rate risks typically are hedged by capital market instruments," Astwood notes. "Arrow Re can be the bridge between the capital markets and the traditional insurance and reinsurance markets to provide comprehensive risk transfer. Traffic can go both ways."

Arrow Re's parent, Goldman Sachs, executed the first insurance securitization for a corporation last year, bought by Oriental Land Co., operator of Tokyo Disneyland in Japan. The $200 million catastrophe-linked securities transaction provides property and business interruption protection against an earthquake in Japan. Goldman Sachs subsequently executed a $566 million insurance-linked transaction providing lease residual value protection to Toyota Motor Credit. Meanwhile, Arrow Re takes credit for several transactions involving credit, currency, and commodity risks, and another that, Astwood says, "helped to facilitate a corporate merger." He would not elaborate on any of these deals.

The reticence of the transformers is not surprising, considering that investors in many of the securities they develop are, in fact, the insurers and reinsurers they also compete against. Why antagonize customers with arrogant boasts of market share? Some observers have noted the irony: While the transformers and other insurance-linked securities are designed to reach beyond insurance capital, in many cases the banks are just carving up and repackaging risks for sale back to insurers and reinsurers.

Expectations are that noninsurer/reinsurer investors in insurance-linked securities will eventually pony up. "Capital market investors are constantly trying to find different asset classes to diversify their portfolios," says Dowling. "The insurance-linked securities generally don't correlate with their other investments and, therefore, provide investment diversification."

Groth says the transformers ultimately will create more price transparency in the risk transfer marketplace. "There's no opportunity for opportunistic pricing, as there can be with traditional insurance," he explains. "Typically, a corporate buyer of insurance goes to an insurance company who writes the risk and then passes it on through a variety of reinsurers. The original insured doesn't learn what the reinsurers are getting for absorbing pieces of the risk, nor do the reinsurers see what price the insured paid to transfer the risk to the primary carrier. The result is high friction costs. With a transformer, however, everything is completely on the table. Such candor will encourage more investors to participate in insurance-linked securities."

Rumors have circulated that Willis is about to launch its own transformer. "I won't confirm or deny," says Groth, "but I will say that there's a strong likelihood we'll see more transformers in the very near future."

Other Way Around

While no one concludes the capital markets, via a transformer or insurance-linked security, will replace the traditional insurance and reinsurance markets, some observers do believe the nature of risk taking in the industry will change. "Ultimately, the insurance industry will become very good at originating business similar to the way banks originate risk," Dowling says. "They will increasingly underwrite the risk—given their expertise in this regard—retain a portion of it, then package the rest and lay it off to pools of investors."

Of course, while the investment banks vaunt their various insurance securitization strategies, insurers and reinsurers are not sitting around waiting for business to fade away. AIG, ACE, and XL offer a range of high-flying financial tools via their own capital market risk laboratories. And reinsurers like Swiss Re and Munich Re have amassed their own singular arsenals, launching units specializing in noninsurance company business. "We're seeing less and less of a distinction between an insurance company and a reinsurance company, and on any given transaction there could be a mixture of both," says Marty Scherzer, managing director of New York broker Marsh.

Swiss Re New Markets, for example, can put together a program for a client covering its hazard risks, financial risks, and business risks, separately or in combination, marketed directly or through a broker. "We use insurance both in the traditional sense and as a corporate finance tool addressing pure balance sheet issues," says Erwin Zimmermann, CEO of Swiss Re New Markets in Zurich. "We try to understand the real volatility issues and then structure a risk transfer to accommodate them. The transfer could be conventional insurance, a capital market instrument or a combination."

As a riposte to Gelband's comment about the transformers' capital markets expertise, Zimmermann counters that investment banks fall short when it comes to insured risk. "They cannot touch a lot of these volatility issues," he says. "They don't have the desire or capability of handling the risk part. An insurer has this appetite because it can take the risk and integrate it into its diversified portfolio of risks."

Al Beer, president of Munich-American RiskPartners in Princeton, New Jersey, says his company is solutions-oriented and not product-driven. "The ART (alternative risk transfer) market is defined by the clientele, not the products," Beer says. "Unlike traditional insurers, we organize ourselves according to the client and not by product divisions. If a religious institution came to us, we would bring in our experts from our dedicated public and nonprofit unit along with experts in property/casualty insurance, sit down, and brainstorm."

Like the transformers, the broad ART purveyors must be careful—the insurance companies they're competing against are also their parents' biggest customers. Farrell from A.M. Best says the emergence of reinsurers as primary competitors causes friction. "If this continues, it could create a market opportunity for non-competing reinsurers," she says. "Managing relationships will be critical."

Evidently, the reinsurers' competition with customers has raised some hackles already. "Needless to say, I have been harangued at many a dinner party, when a long-time traditional client comes up to me and says, 'How could you?' " says Beer with a chuckle. "But, seriously, there have been few problems. Through our approach to managing traditional client relationships we have been able to minimize this as an issue. We don't pretend we're not in this business; our annual report speaks to that. But we're not a traditional insurer; we're an ART player. Our clients must be willing to take on more risk than they would with traditional insurance."

Toward that end, both Swiss Re and Munich Re say they try to partner with primary carriers to provide risk solutions to clients. Groth says such partnerships offer mutual benefits: Insurers gain access to greater capital and sophisticated risk transfer and financing capabilities, while the reinsurers gain access to specialized services. "Traditional insurers have very good claims and engineering services," he explains.

Yet, can these same traditional insurers survive on services alone? Indeed, the craft and ingenuity of the fashionable insurers, reinsurers and investment banks makes traditional property/casualty insurers the wallflowers at the new millennium party. "There are just too many insurance companies out there lacking any distinguishing features," says Dowling. "Everyone agrees there has to be consolidation. Clearly, the carriers that service the Fortune 1000 must think about the need to broaden themselves like an AIG or Swiss Re. These carriers are definitely competing against investment banks and more innovative insurers for business solutions and advice."

Even insurers targeting the middle market must broaden their menus, he argues. "At some point in the not too distant future, mid-market insurers must figure out how to securitize a portion of the risks they're taking on, as a way to release some of the capital they have," Dowling says. "These carriers must operate at a lower level of capital to increase their return on equity. By securitizing a portion of assumed risk, they can offer products at more efficient prices than those companies that are heavily capitalized."

Farrell agrees traditional insurers must follow market leaders and move from a product focus toward a client focus. "They must develop the customized solutions risk managers and CFOs are looking for," she says. "Rather than be just a manufacturer (of insurance products) they must become a service company, sharpening their pencils to develop new alternative risk transfer strategies. Certainly, the recent financial services legislation catapults this need to the forefront, as does the increasing number of competitors that already have these capabilities."

For risk managers, the changes underway among their service providers bode well for the future. "These developments create opportunities to transfer risk more cost-effectively and efficiently," says Groth. "While they may not be efficient for every company, for some they will make extraordinary sense. It all depends on the risk exposures and the combinations thereof."

Groth adds, "If anything, risk managers should be cheered that the stodgy, somewhat hidebound insurance industry of the past is giving way to a more modern, sophisticated business. A new era beckons."

8

Risk Management Program Administration

In this age of broader risk management, one person cannot know and do everything that needs to be done. I am finding in my own situation that I really am doing less and less of the technical things that used to occupy my time, and spending more and more time educating and training managers and employees. I suppose you could say I am an internal risk consultant, but the thing that strikes me is how much of my time I feel like a teacher.

Risk Manager
Regional Power Company

To make the administration of risk management programs work more efficiently, two-way communication between the risk manager and the rest of the firm is the most important ingredient.

Risk Management Panel

Perspectives

Enterprise Risk Policy

Douglas McLeod
Reprinted with permission from *Business Insurance,* January 31, 2000

Until recently, a company complaining about revenue lost to an upstart competitor could expect a terse answer from its insurers: "What do you want from us?"

That may be changing. As the concept of enterprise risk management gains ground, a unit of Great American Insurance Co. has become one of the first to offer a policy covering new competition and other threats to a corporation's bottom line.

Tamarack American, a New York–based Great American specialty underwriting unit, recently unveiled a policy offering up to $50 million in coverage against revenue hits from any of nine defined "enterprise loss events." These events include losses caused by new market competitors, currency fluctuation, and even changes in consumer-buying habits.

In developing the coverage, Tamarack follows Reliance National Insurance Co., which began offering its own "enterprise earnings protection" policy [in 1999]. The two coverages differ in numerous ways, though, including that Tamarack's is a named perils rather than an all-risk policy.

Brokers familiar with the new policy are enthusiastic, though some note there are still wrinkles to be worked out in the policy language, including questions related to claims handling.

"It could be a hell of a marketing tool for the more entrepreneurial brokers," potentially opening doors at new client companies, said Andrew Marks, president and chief executive officer of MLW Services Inc., a New York–based broker. "They're on the cutting edge. Whether it's the right policy or not, only time will tell," said another broker, who requested anonymity.

Tamarack officials spent nearly a year creating the policy, dubbed RevenueGuard, with help from law firm Davis, Polk & Wardwell, said Sherif M. Zakhary, senior vice president and head of Tamarack's executive protection/financial products division. Arthur S. Phillips oversaw the policy's development until his departure as president of Tamarack.

The policy insures against nine enterprise loss events, with policyholders able to choose coverage for some or all of these risks. The risks comprise revenue losses from:

- Business interruption, which—contrary to the standard definition—covers policyholders' inability to make, sell, or distribute products because of weather conditions; work slowdowns; death, kidnapping or voluntary resignation of key executives; or physical product tampering.

- Changes in laws in the U.S. or covered foreign jurisdictions on the safety or possible harmful effects of a policyholder's products, such as warning label requirements; and detrimental tariffs and excise taxes.

- Competition from another company entering the policyholder's market for the first time, as long as the resulting revenue losses exceed 25 percent of revenues for the same product in the prior fiscal year.

The coverage applies if the losses are caused solely by a drop of more than 25 percent in the average, undiscounted price of the policyholder's products or services or if a competitor introduces a product that is similarly named or otherwise resembles the policyholder's product.

- "Cultural risk," which the policy defines as a revenue loss of more than 25 percent from the prior year caused by a change in the public's buying habits, provided the change cannot be explained by any other factor, such as price, quality, or product obsolescence.

- Currency fluctuation adversely affecting the market price of a policyholder's products or the prices paid by the policyholder for imported or exported materials or products.

- Customary financing, defined as the policyholder's inability to get financing for its operations at an interest rate within three percentage points of a defined rate, or the inability of customers to get such financing to buy the policyholder's products.

- Public concern about the safety of a policyholder's products, caused by published studies by a U.S. government agency or a recognized academic or professional body, provided that revenue losses exceed 25 percent.

■ Obsolescence of a product designated in the policy that leaves the policyholder unable to sell the product at a profit in any market, as long as the revenue loss is not attributable to the policyholder's sale of another product.

■ Bankruptcy or other failure of a vendor that the policyholder relies on for services or critical components of a product, as long as it has tried to anticipate the failure and has exhausted efforts to replace the vendor.

The policy also features several exclusions, including losses payable under other property/casualty policies, which this coverage is not intended to replace; accounting changes; taxes; and Y2K-related losses.

Tamarack, backed by co-lead reinsurers General Reinsurance Corp. and Zurich Reinsurance Co., is offering an aggregate limit of up to $50 million, with sublimits of up to 25 percent of the aggregate limit—or a maximum of $12.5 million—for any individual loss event.

The policy requires a minimum self-insured retention equal to 10 percent of the policyholder's prior-year earnings. Each loss event may be subject to additional retentions.

A policyholder must pick a single loss event category for reporting a given claim; a claim cannot overlap two or more loss categories.

Tamarack/Great American will pay a claim using a formula aimed at covering lost earnings to the same extent that a loss event hits revenues. For example, a company may see its total revenues drop from $100 million to $80 million, with $10 million of the $20 million drop—or 50 percent—attributable to a covered event. If the company's earnings before interest, taxes, depreciation, and amortization then fall from $10 million to $5 million, the insurer would pay out 50 percent of that decline as the covered loss, Tamarack officials explain.

The one-year policy is written on a claims-made basis, with a retroactive date to the beginning of a policyholder's fiscal year and a 180-day extended reporting period option.

Claims would be paid only after the end of a policyholder's fiscal year and, thus, would not improve current-year earnings, Zakhary noted.

Tamarack is targeting U.S.-based companies or corporate divisions with annual revenues of $50 million to $1 billion, established operations, and solid earnings histories. Tamarack officials concede the largest corporations are not likely to buy the coverage, because they can absorb the kind of revenue losses the policy covers.

Premiums will vary, based on the buyer, loss events insured against, limits and self-insured retentions, though premiums will range from a minimum $100,000 to a maximum of $3.5 million, Zakhary said.

Brokers familiar with the policy say it fills a void between traditional p/c coverages and financial insurance. But they also express reservations. "It's going to be tough to sell it," said MLW's Marks, noting the underwriting process will require a more time-consuming dissection of a policyholder's business than traditional coverages demand. Another broker said he will be marketing the policy to banks that may, in turn, sell it to loan clients.

One flaw, brokers say, is the pressure the policy could put on companies at renewal time: If a covered event occurs at the end of the policy year but most of the losses don't emerge until the following year, the policyholder may not collect the full loss unless it renews the policy. "It's a very tough sell to say to your client, 'You had your claim at the wrong time of the year, and you're only going to get two-twelfths of the payment,'" a broker said. "You're going to get a lot of angry clients if you do that."

Zakhary, however, said Tamarack is aiming for long-term relationships with policyholders and that the one-year policies are intended to be renewed to provide continuous coverage. The problem may also be mitigated, he added, by the extended reporting period option. "If the (market) sees us slashing and running, it does not bode well for the product."

Introduction

The preceding seven chapters have focused on the "risk" side of risk management. Chapter 8 discusses the management side. The imbalance in emphasis should not mislead readers, however. The main distinguishing difference between effective and ineffective risk managers is an (in)ability to manage. Indeed, in today's environment almost any technical aspect of risk management can be bought, rented, or borrowed—from claims management services to actuarial consultation, legal services, risk audit services, and financing and investment management. It is the management of these technical elements that cannot be outsourced. Only an effective manager understands the organization, its politics and culture, the appropriate means of communications, and how to get things done. Management competence matters—it matters a lot.

The focus of this chapter is on the effective design and implementation of risk management practices within business organizations. The chapter begins with a discussion of risk management mission statements, goals, and objectives. It then turns to program design and implementation. Finally, the chapter deals with several key management challenges: risk communications, contract management, procurement of broker and insurer services, and program audit tactics.

The Risk Management Mission

What is the purpose of risk management in a business organization? The question is more difficult to answer than one may think. Historically, the field of risk management has been dominated by the notion of risk reduction or elimination. Indeed, this book carries a considerable amount of evidence as to the influence of this view. Many of the tools and techniques discussed here address the challenge of preventing, avoiding, controlling, or eliminating risks. One may be tempted to conclude that this book, too, views the perfect world as one that is absent risk.

Setting aside for the moment the impossibility of a risk-free world, there are other reasons to doubt the wisdom of "risk elimination" as the singular mission of risk management. The world simply is too complicated and the typical organization's resources too limited for anything but the most modest of risk reduction to occur. Furthermore, managers—being human—can only know, manage, and do so much. Not only is risk elimination a metaphysical impossibility, it would be far beyond the capability of individuals and organizations to even eliminate a meaningful slice of the risk they encounter.

But, beyond even these constraints, one has to wonder whether the reduction of risk alone (even in a narrow sense) is sensible. For example, as this book argues, the portfolio of risks that constitute a firm's risk profile is interdependent, includes pure and speculative risks, the objective and subjective, and is related to the overall purposes of the organization. Thus, virtually every negative risk is related to or influenced by positive attributes. A simple example is the hiring of an employee. That person's risks of loss are not separable from the productivity and other positive attributes he or she brings to the organization. One can expand that imagery to the organization. It is a complete entity in and of itself, and consideration of hazards and perils cannot really be done absent a recognition of the related risk factors and opportunities.

In addition, singular risks have both upside and downside potential, and the elimination of downside risk may simply eliminate the risk, period. Humans are motivated by the presence of risk, sometimes to run away but often to run toward it. It probably is not putting too fine a point on it to say that the elimination of risk would make for a pretty dull and unproductive existence.

Finally, on the point of risk management mission, one must be reminded that the act of managing risks alters the risks and creates new ones. Recall Chapter 7's discussion of moral hazard, and the notion that the presence of insurance can alter the underlying risk—elevating, for example, the possibility of fire (i.e., arson) losses. Moral hazard is a general problem of risk management; requiring driver's training may encourage more aggressive driving because the trained individuals may have more confidence than they should. Safer roadways can encourage faster and less responsible driving; lumbar support belts encourage workers to lift more weight than is proper; information on a work-related hazard might produce too much caution. In other words, risk management may actually make some situations worse, or at least shift a risk from one exposure to another.

What is the purpose of risk management, then? Earlier, risk management was identified as "serving the overall purposes of the organization," and that definition seems as good a place to start as any.

Businesses exist to make money for owners. Naturally enough, other motivations and aspirations exist in business, but it probably is safe to say that lofty motives mean little if a firm cannot remain a going concern. Thus, readers should assume that the overarching purpose of risk management should be to support that mission.

Depending on the type of business, the overall mission can be further refined. For example, for large publicly traded companies, a rather extensive theory supports the notion that the purpose of such businesses is "firm value maximization." In this rather rigorously defined view, managers should only undertake those things that add to firm value (as measured by share price). Thus, if an investment cannot be shown to translate into growth in share price, it probably should not be undertaken.

It is interesting to note—though the theory cannot be adequately explained in this book—that the value maximization idea poses some interesting problems for risk management. In a broad and general sense, investors can costlessly diversify away many risks through their investment strategy, and thus they can be shown to be relatively disinterested in whether any individual firm manages its risks or not.

The fact that firms practice risk management suggests that managers are not purely pursuing the firm value maximization objective. Indeed, even theorists recognize that other motives may exist for practicing risk management. Those motives may include:

- Managing the risks of stakeholders (other than investors/ owners) whose risks cannot be diversified away
- Complying with requirements of regulators, lenders, and others with enforceable interests in the firm

- Managing or avoiding the extraordinary costs associated with bankruptcy, which often are not factored into investor's valuation of a firm
- Assaying moral and ethical concerns
- Getting managers and employees to moderate the impact of risk and uncertainty on their day-to-day activities

We also should not forget that an emerging trend is the application of risk management principles and practices to the management of upside risks. While this reflects the notion of firm value maximization, it serves as a reminder that the motivation to manage risk does not automatically mean that risks should be avoided, eliminated, or limited. There may be risks where "maximization" is a conscious business decision. Risk taking, in the service of overall firm objectives (whether value maximizing or not) can be risk management, too.

Beyond this, it seems that financial stability and uncertainty reduction likely would be a risk management objective, in the sense that most managers value predictability in their environment. But stability may not be the only thing going on here. Risk management can directly affect the seeking out of new risks, the decisions to take those risks, and the measures that enhance the prospects of success. Therefore, arguing the competence-based risk management goals are driven by stability considerations ignores the important upside potential that risk management provides. Thus, "competence maximization" can be a risk management objective, too.

Risk Management Program Design and Implementation

The traditional venue of risk management is either the finance/accounting or purchasing department within a firm. In an important sense, neither choice is illogical as insurance buying and risk financing clearly could be viewed as purchasing or financial management concerns.

However, the broader view of risk management introduced in this book would suggest that problems can arise from defining risk management as a subfunction of finance or purchasing. Conceptually, the organization-wide stance presented in this book offers many circumstances in which finance/purchasing managers are enormously unqualified to address—political risks, human resources concerns, information technology issues, training matters. Financial issues are critical concerns for risk managers, but risk management is far more than financial management.

Furthermore, as may be apparent at various points in the book, risk management has at least three levels of existence within an organization: political/strategic, tactical/managerial, and operational/functional. The political/strategic level of risk management is concerned with the purview of board members and top managers. It is focused on political risks, by which we mean stockholder and community relations.

The tactical/managerial level of risk management is defined as the provenance of mid-level managers and concerns itself with risk as it affects budgets and interacts with broader goals of the firm.

The operational/functional level of risk management is the ground level and concerns itself with the implementation of specific risk management tools and techniques—safety training courses, accident investigation, enforcement of loss control techniques.

When looked at in this light, one can easily see an explanation for the principal frustration voiced by traditional risk managers, which is the inability to get support from the top officers and the difficulty in persuading department heads and colleagues to take risk management seriously. Conventionally, risk managers sit somewhere between the tactical and operational level—and this is a difficult position from which to effect organization-wide change.

There are two important insights that arise from understanding the levels of risk management. First, one can see that design of a risk management function needs to be cognizant of how organization design influences the management of risk. Second, it strongly suggests that political/strategic support (and, probably, organizational proximity to that level) is essential to effective risk management practice. Let's discuss these points in reverse order.

Political/Strategic Level Support

In both a real and conceptual sense, CEOs are the chief risk officers of their organizations, and it is essential that this dimension of the position be more explicitly known to them.

Commonly, such a revelation will not require, say, the CEO to serve all the functional aspects of risk management, but it does mean that the executive (and, ultimately, the board) must establish a clear position on risk management and delegate responsibility. Equally important, this political level must become more self-conscious of the risk management elements of its executives' actions and decisions. At a minimum, the risk management mission statement must emanate from the political/strategic level of the organization.

Although this need not occur, at least not literally, an individual with organization-wide responsibilities should assume the "chief risk officer" mantle. For example, a senior vice president may assume responsibility for risk management at the strategic level, the added dimension here being that this person could oversee the implementation of risk management within the organization and ensure that risk management is practiced in accordance with overall political and strategic objectives. A notable variation on this idea is the establishment of a risk management team at this organizational level. The key is that risk management policy, however it is implemented, is being set at the executive level of the organization.

The tactical level of responsibility is practiced in this model at the department or division level of the organization. Thus, division-level managers take effective responsibility for risks within their purview—while, as a practical matter, they are likely to delegate the actual practice to their own deputies. Likewise, operational risk management responsibilities are delegated to work unit/individual employee levels.

In summary, this organization-wide approach can be defined as one where there is a top-down approach with respect to strategy, but where the actual practice of risk management—ideally—is rather organic, with every employee being the "risk manager" of risks within his or her area of responsibility. Of course, in such an environment, risk management expectations become part of the job description and performance is evaluated with some recognition of this expectation.

The Impact of Organization Design

The fact that most organizations do not practice risk management in the manner described is a concern, but not a fatal one. Clearly, the model suggested in the previous section is a benchmark—attainable to be sure, but nevertheless at least a way of thinking about actual practices. Deviation is possible, and even desirable in some circumstances, but the model forces one to consider why the deviation exists and whether it is helpful or harmful to the risk management cause. Consideration of deviations may also provide insight into obstacles or barriers to effective risk management.

The scope of organization-wide risk management is sufficiently broad to suggest that—ideally, again—the risk management function within an organization is probably not best suited to a command-and-control structure. Certainly overall direction comes from the executive level, but the diverse range of risks and management needs suggests that more flexible matrix or team-based approaches to risk management are a more suitable functional design.

The matrix/team-based approach to risk management could range from a rather free-form structure where groups and individuals are organized on an as-needed basis to solve risk management problems, to a more organized approach where permanent teams coordinate overall risk management implementation. Temporary teams or assignments would still exist in the more structured form of this approach.

The logic for a team-based approach lies not only with the diverse challenge of managing organizational risks, but also with the organizational design and process issues common with most business organizations. That is, most firms operate with a great deal of functional separation and some degree of autonomy. Exhibit 8-1 illustrates the Organization Risk Management structure.

Insights

Ask a Risk Manager

Reprinted with permission from *Business Insurance*, May 22, 2000. © Crain Communications Inc. All rights reserved.
This column on risk management issues was written by Christopher E. Mandel, director, global risk management at Tricon Global Restaurants Inc. in Louisville, Kentucky, and vice president, member and chapter services, Risk and Insurance Management Society Inc.'s Executive Council.

Some people are predicting substantial increases in workers compensation rates in the near term. How can risk managers best prepare for such a possibility?

Whether substantial market hardening in the workers compensation line will occur remains to be seen. As with most lines of property and casualty insurance, however, such eventualities are hard to predict and harder still to plan for. Nevertheless, there are plenty of strategies available to risk managers to mitigate the potential effects of dramatic rate increases, especially for this line of coverage.

First, while it is more of a long-term strategy, most midsize to large entities can benefit from evolving toward higher and higher retentions. This can be done either through qualified self-insurance—which can be a state-by-state regulatory gauntlet—or through various alternative programs, such as fronted captives.

The first step in properly approaching this shift is to determine the risk-bearing philosophy of your firm. Don't make the mistake of assuming that this is your exclusive purview. Your best "personal" risk management strategy is to present your assessment of what that philosophy ought to be and why and get the appropriate concurrence from the right decision makers.

While many individual managers are risk averse, collective senior teams and boards, recognizing their fiduciary responsibility to stakeholders, will often support different, more risk-assumptive views. In general, an evolution toward greater risk assumption is appropriate and most economically efficient for most entities. There are, of course, special considerations for many firms that would modify this view, such as current yet temporary financial or market stresses, a lack of effective loss prevention and control programs and the like.

Obviously, assuming more risk through increased retentions puts more distance between you and the insurance markets that determine large portions of your cost of risk through their rating decisions. At its purest level, total risk retention insulates you completely from these market forces. After all, the more risk you retain, the less risk you will need to place elsewhere and, thus, the less effect potentially negative market forces will have on your program costs.

There are lots of opinions about what are the most important considerations in risk retention, but here are a few not to be overlooked. And many of these apply to the matter of preparing for a hard market in workers compensation as well. I'll elaborate on some of these later. Meanwhile, ask yourself these questions:

- Do I have at least five years—or, better yet, ten or more years—of accurate loss data that clearly show my trends in this line of risk?
- Do I have a comprehensive understanding of the types of exposures that my workforce represents?
- Are there unusual exposures or past loss trends that could produce unusually large or frequent midsize losses that could result in substantial variability in loss results?
- Do I have a cost of risk and loss allocation program that facilitates management accountability for operational safety?
- Do I have effective management and employee incentives in place to promote a safety-oriented culture?
- Do I have effective loss prevention and control programs in place to minimize expected losses?

- Have I educated management on the relevant exposures and their controllability?
- Can I support a particular level of risk assumption such that management will be reasonably confident that key performance indicators will be unlikely to be negatively affected by increased risk retention?

Getting answers to all of these questions is critical to successfully preparing a program of increased risk assumption or for getting ready for a hardening market for traditional workers comp insurance. I suggest you make use of all available resources, particularly knowledgeable actuaries, to help identify the right answer.

Having briefly covered the question of how much risk to retain, we can now turn to the equally important area of loss prevention and control programs critical to taking on more risk in any area of exposure.

In the workers compensation realm, there are a few key loss prevention and controls that are used widely, though with varying degrees of success. But when constructed correctly and used effectively, they can have a dramatic impact on both the frequency and severity of loss. These include:

- A customized safety program focused on minimizing both the frequency and severity of accidents and injuries
- A mandate for timely loss reporting
- A policy of transitional or modified work
- A comprehensive managed care program to control medical costs
- A comprehensive employee communications program
- A good source of data to measure key performance indicators

A few comments about each will help you understand their potential.

First, a comprehensive safety program, focused both on the areas of loss that are the most frequent and on those that can be the most costly, can be effective only in a culture that makes safety a priority. Thus, this one starts at the top. Get senior management cooperation and regular, visible support for your program and the front line will practice what you've preached. The first priority for getting operations management attention is to ensure some element of financial accountability at the front-line profit and loss level. Make sure it is viewed as fair and easy to understand and administer. Ideally, it will include both incentive and punitive elements, with the emphasis on the former.

Next, it sounds trite, but numerous studies have shown that the earlier and more accurately losses are reported, the less likely injured workers will be to retain attorneys—who run up the cost of claims—and the less each claim will cost, on average, over time. It's a simple fact that quick reporting allows for quick intervention, whether by claim adjusters, medical providers, or supervisors. In fact, each has an important role to play in successful workers comp programs.

Another effort with proven benefits is related to providing light or modified duty jobs for employees during their recuperation. This requires thorough job evaluations and good communications with those treating physicians who make the calls as to whether employees can work at all before full recovery.

The importance of this cannot be overstated. The greater the length of disability, the more likely it will be that the employee will lose the motivation to return as soon as he or she may be able. If it is commonly known that modified jobs are available, most employees will then expect to return earlier rather than later and adopt an attitude that fosters that result.

Since medical costs can often constitute the majority of claim costs, it's critical to get out in front of them. A comprehensive managed care program includes several components, including:

■ A preferred provider arrangement, if not a comprehensive network that either directs or suggests, depending on state law, where employees can be treated most quickly and cost effectively

■ A nurse-based oversight mechanism employable in select cases where special intervention may be warranted

- A solid partnership between your adjustment and managed care providers allowing for joint and cooperative management of the total claim

- A bill review protocol allowing for the appropriate scrutiny of most medical bills for the application of fee schedules

- A field-based nurse/case manager mechanism allowing for one-on-one intervention in the most severe cases

- A second opinion process to ensure accurate diagnoses and to selectively verify the appropriateness of treatment

- Good controls over expenses associated with these services

Communicating with employees both before and after losses occur is another critical part of a successful workers compensation program. The premise is simple—the better the relationship between employee and employer, the less likely the employee will exploit or manipulate the program. Thus, it starts long before losses occur, when you're building and reinforcing a safety culture. At that point, the approach is educational and reveals management's concern.

Once a loss occurs, the attitude should not be just "we want you back soon" but should include a focus on the effect of the absence on the team—on friends and coworkers—as well as on the life of the disabled worker. And the common thread must be a sincere concern for the individual and his or her family.

Finally, good reliable data is as important here as in most lines of risk. Whether it is knowing the average length of disability by injury type or the average cost of medical care by injury code, being able to measure impacts and outcomes affects your ability to prevent and control the frequency and severity of losses. It can also make the difference in a successful proposal to management about a new intervention or program you may want to try.

Good data also allows you to make comparisons among your own divisions as well as with competitors, enabling you to define more accurately what success is for your program. There are plenty of risk management information systems to pick from, but a careful assessment of your needs and the provider's track record is a must. And don't forget to review the portability and cross-functional use of data and the ability of the system to grow as your needs expand.

Employing these strategies will allow you to be more prepared for both a hardening workers compensation market and increasingly complex and more hazardous workplace exposures. And when the Occupational Safety and Health Administration comes knocking, you'll be able to sleep at night as well.

Risk Communications

Risk communications is a phrase that corresponds roughly to the idea of organization behavior—at least as it relates to matters of organization design. In other words, while the previous discussion has focused on the structure of risk management within a firm, this section trains the reader's attention on the matter of the dynamics of risk management programs.

Broadly, the premise behind risk communications is that risk management needs to be effectively communicated inside and outside the organization. Equally important, communications—at least as it is defined here—is central to effective management as well.

The subject of risk communications is a growing field of academic study, though for a number of reasons the work in this area tends to focus on risk and public policy (e.g., inoculations against infectious diseases, earthquake preparedness, roadway safety) rather than on communications within an organization setting. However, some of the key products and insights that arise from the research can be applied—or at least summarized—in our context as follows:

1. Organizational communications should be understood as a system, so any effort to communicate information occurs in an environment where there is a communicator, a communicatee, a

Exhibit 8-1. Illustrative Organization Risk Management Function Chart

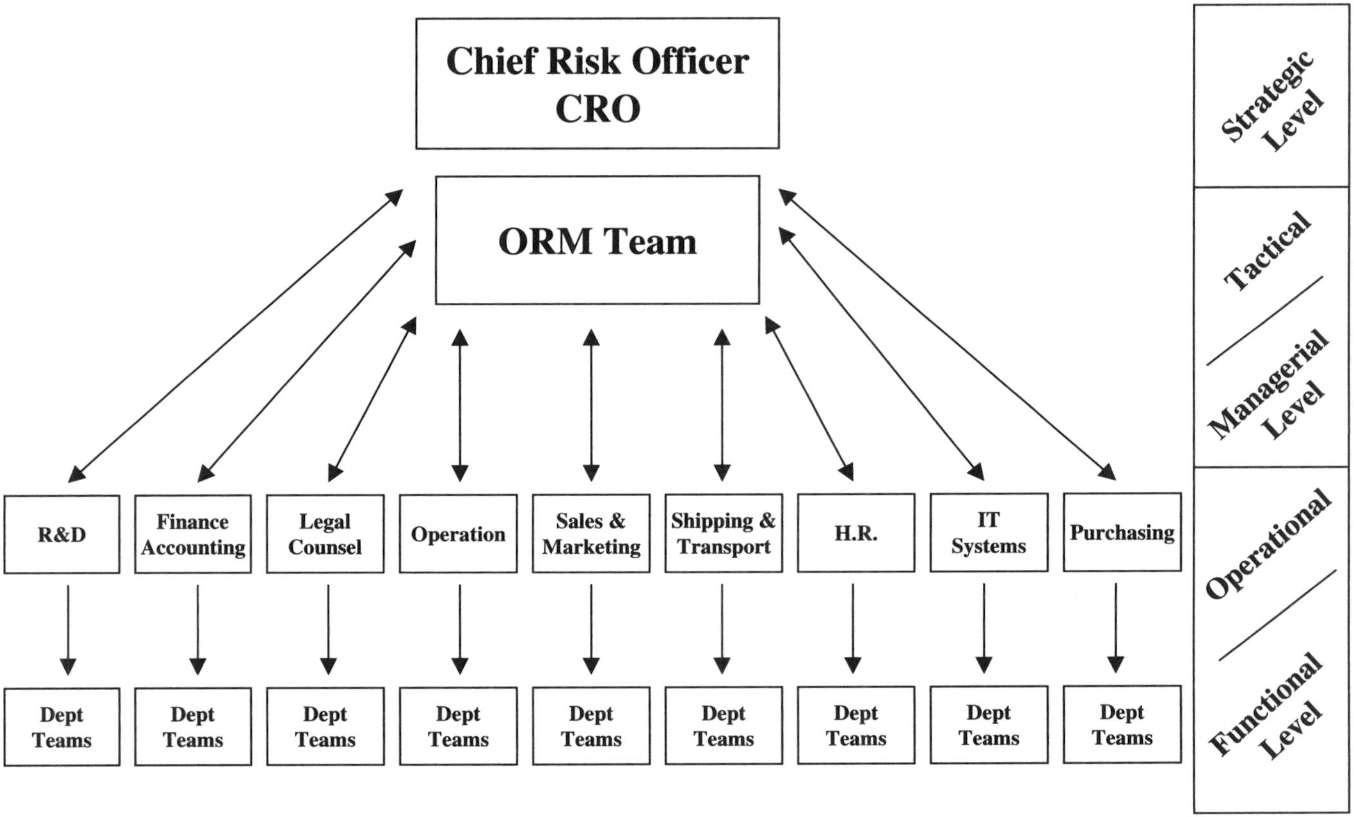

Strategic Level	Tactical / Managerial Level	Operational / Functional Level

Chief Risk Officer CRO

ORM Team

R&D — Dept Teams

Finance Accounting — Dept Teams

Legal Counsel — Dept Teams

Operation — Dept Teams

Sales & Marketing — Dept Teams

Shipping & Transport — Dept Teams

H.R. — Dept Teams

IT Systems — Dept Teams

Purchasing — Dept Teams

message, and a medium of communication. Each element of this system can contribute to the effectiveness/ineffectiveness of the communication effort.

2. Risk presents a number of substantive challenges when communicating information to an audience; for example:

- Audiences typically are not knowledgeable about risk management concepts and principles.
- Technical aspects of risk management are difficult to understand, even when communicated.
- Key risk management issues often require very specific technical knowledge (e.g., engineering, medical, or legal).
- Attitudes toward risk are subjective and difficult to measure and compare.
- Audiences often underestimate the value of risk management.

3. Cultural filters affect people's understanding of risk and can produce unexpected (though not unpredictable) responses.

4. Communication can occur through various media, but in organizations the use of incentive and disincentive tools (implied or explicit) can assist in the effectiveness of the effort.

On the final point, it is worth mentioning that executive-level support is the critical incentive in effective risk communications, but often communication efforts rely on other tools to provide incentives such as rewards, cost allocation systems, penalties, audit evaluations, and the like. The key point is that "motivation" must be understood and incorporated into any effort to communicate.

Information Management

Conventional use of the term *information management* focuses on the use of a Risk Management Information System (RMIS) as a tool toward effective risk management. An RMIS can range from simple spreadsheet-based software to very complicated programs designed to organize, analyze, and manage large amounts of data on risks, insurance programs, claims, certificates of insurance, forecasting, and budgeting.

However, in this book the term is used more inclusively to include all systems and efforts used in an organization to gather and communicate information regarding risks. In this light, information includes decidedly low-tech approaches such as having managers report incidents that may produce claims or establishing organizational expectations that encourage employees to keep risk managers "in the loop" when new or evolving risks appear on the horizon. Equally, information management can include very advanced approaches to automated data management.

Perhaps the simplest way to reinforce the broader concept of risk communication is to say that the approach should enable an organization to answer—at least—the following questions:

- What risk information is necessary for us to have?
- From where may this information/data be retrieved?
- What are the relevant timing issues? When must we have this information?
- How is this relevant information most effectively and efficiently transmitted?
- What will we do with the information?
- Who needs to receive the information captured in this system, when do they need it, and in what form is it best received?
- What are the impediments and filters to the flow of information or data, and how can they be managed?
- What are the cultural and political implications of information management within and outside the organization?

Cost Allocation Systems

Cost allocation systems have an explicit and implicit purpose. Obviously they represent a type of cost accounting mechanism that allows an organization to identify and track costs associated with specific risk-related activities and objects. Less obviously, perhaps, such systems represent an important means of communicating information and providing incentives to managers and employees. To put it simply, managers tend to pay attention when budgets are at stake.

Although there are an infinite variety of approaches that can be taken in designing a cost allocation system, they all seem to have to strike a balance between risk sharing and risk pooling. One might imagine the spectrum of systems to be anchored at one end by a model where all costs are allocated back to the source (i.e., a department generating 45 percent of a firm's overall workers compensation costs is allocated 45 percent of that total cost), while at the other end a system retains all costs at the corporate level.

By considering the two extremes of cost allocation, one can begin to see the potential benefits and problems of such systems. A fully dispersed cost-of-risk model effectively tells managers where losses are being produced, and it provides a powerful motivation to practice risk management. However, many losses are not within the control of unit managers, so there is a question about whether it is fair to assess their budgets when they were simply the victims of dumb luck. Then, from a "good business" perspective, it is hard to argue that a single bad year of losses should wipe out a unit's budget since, after all, it is the customer who obtains services from that unit who suffers ultimately. Thus, there seem to be some problems in a system that fully allocates loss costs back to the source.

A fully pooled environment insulates the various divisions and departments from the vicissitudes of fortune (thus offering a degree of budget stability), but the cost of this approach is that it removes an important incentive for managers to practice risk management.

Consequently, a cost allocation system should strike some balance between distribution and pooling of costs. How that balance is effected will depend on circumstances and preferences, but the following matters should be kept in mind when designing a cost allocation system:

■ Care should be taken to recognize that systems have a tendency to reward good risk management practices in the long run, while penalizing or creating inconvenience in the short run. Good risk management practice has the effect of smoothing out experience over multiple budget periods, while some of the costs of undertaking such efforts are borne immediately. In addition, conventional budgeting creates a strong disincentive to risk management in one important sense—that is, if a unit manager reduces losses and saves money, there is a reasonable chance those funds will not be allocated to the unit in future budget years. Good risk management could result in budget shrinkage over time, which may be good news for executives and investors, but can serve as something of a disincentive for managers within business units. Few managers like to see their budget shrink, regardless of whether it makes economic sense to the firm.

■ Loss experience is likely to be erratic for most divisions or units, so it may take many years before an organization has an accurate sense as to what is going on within that unit and how much of that activity is within the unit's control.

■ Identifying the "cost" to be allocated is difficult. Is it only the direct cost, or the indirect or consequential costs as well?

■ Many programs founder on the difficulty in matching cost allocation precisely with the risk source. For example, risk of worker injury may be influenced by cost allocation, but the impact is likely to be borne by the manager and not the workers themselves. In some circumstances, it is the workers' behavior (and not the manager's inattentiveness) that is the critical loss-producing factor, so cost allocation may be ineffective. Therefore a key question is, Where is the motivational effect of cost allocation being felt?

■ Timing of allocation can become an issue. Budget setting and planning occurs at fixed or regular intervals, whereas the timing of losses largely is random. Are loss costs assessed at the beginning of a budget year or at the end? In and of itself, the timing of assessments can play a major role in the effectiveness of such a system.

■ Simplicity and equity are the guiding stars of cost allocation system design. They should be easy to understand and fair—and they should be perceived to be fair as well.

Contract Management

The phenomenon of outsourcing is of such importance in the business world that it barely warrants comment—except for the fact that 1) outsourcing is a risk-generating activity and 2) a fair amount of the outsourcing may be occurring in the risk management area.

The concept of organizations as collections of contracts, obligations, commitments, and agreements (COCAs) is addressed elsewhere in the book, but it is worth a brief reminder that contract management is a broad and general risk management concern for a firm. Many of the issues that are raised in this section are relevant to all contracts and formal arrangements.

However, the main purpose of this discussion is to focus on the risk management–specific contracts that may be entered into by a risk manager. In principle, these contracts might be numerous. The evolution of the risk management services industry is such that a risk manager today can rent or hire virtually any kind of technical risk management service imaginable. Indeed, except for the risk manager, an entire risk management function could be outsourced, and a current scan of the market would find numerous illustrations of such a practice.

In an effort to give some substance to the notion of the risk manager as a manager of contracted relationships, the following discussion focuses on four illustrative issues:

1. The management of insurance broker/agent relationships
2. Bidding processes for third-party services
3. Certificates of insurance
4. Financially securing risk management arrangements

Although each of these points is specific, it can be generalized to virtually any aspect of contract management a risk manager might encounter.

Managing Brokers/Agents

Agents and brokers each have a different legal status, though the terms often are used interchangeably. A broker is a representative of a buyer in an insurance transaction, whereas an agent is a representative of the seller. This distinction is confused by the fact that historically, both broker and agent services are paid for by the insurance company through a commission.

Agents and brokers are intermediaries in the risk financing marketplace, but it would be misleading to limit one's understanding of them. Due to broad competitive and market forces, most agents and brokers offer a wide range of services, including:

- Underwriting and claims management services
- Actuarial services
- Training, research and education services
- Captive and pool management
- Risk management information services
- Access to capital markets and alternative risk financing solutions
- Risk management audits and consulting
- Loss control services

For businesses that are too small to develop sophisticated risk management programs, a broker/agent can provide much-needed professional assistance in the creation of an effective risk management strategy. Certainly, an agent/broker can provide the knowledge of the insurance market, which will enable the client business to obtain the best insurance arrangements possible. Thus, obtaining the services of a qualified and capable broker/agent becomes key to the creation of effective risk management practices. Even for larger firms with significant in-house capabilities, brokers/agents can bring to bear great expertise in solving complicated risk management issues.

Selection of a broker/agent should be based—at least—on four criteria: marketing competence, consultation expertise, administrative competence, and basis of remuneration.

Marketing competence refers to the broker/agent's knowledge of insurance markets and the relationships with insurers. Consultation expertise means the capacity of that broker/agent to provide a wide range of consultative services *and* the broker/agent's ability to understand the specific needs of clients. Administrative competence refers to the broker/agent's ability to manage the account and the specific services or needs of the client. The remuneration issue relates to the methods of compensation. Previously it was mentioned that brokers/agents are paid a commission by the insurance company, but recent developments in the insurance industry have resulted in the emergence of fee-for-service compensation arrangements. Under the fee-for-service approach, the risk manager negotiates a flat fee for the broker's services, and the broker then finds insurance that is quoted "net of commissions." The cost of either approach may be roughly equivalent, but many risk managers argue that fee-for-service contracts help avoid conflicts of interest and enable them to see clearly what they are paying for the services they receive.

Bidding for Third-Party Services

Most managers are familiar with the bidding process, since firms often require bidding for a wide range of products and services. Thus, little needs be said here, except to offer a few comments on bidding issues particular to the world of insurance and risk management.

It is common for firms to select brokers/agents through rather informal processes because such services often fall outside the rules that govern purchasing. Furthermore, because broker/agent selection often is informal, it tends to be unexamined and—as a result—brokers/agents may retain clients for decades without any kind of oversight or review.

Maintaining a long-term relationship with service providers actually is a pretty good thing in risk management because most risk

Insights

Communication Key to Fighting Workers Comp Fraud

Lee Fletcher
Reprinted with permission from *Business Insurance,* May 8, 2000. © Crain
Communications Inc. All rights reserved.

Fraudulent workers compensation claims are not uncommon, but experts say that by knowing how to respond and what to expect through good communication at all company levels, combating fraud is possible.

"Make the (employee fraud) policy simple and basic. Have the policy and educate the staff. Building in a deterrence system is vital," according to Philadelphia-based John C. Pikiell, director of the Special Investigation Unit for ACE USA Group's Claims Risk Control Services. He emphasizes that if employers send the message that fraudulent claims will be investigated, employees may think twice. For example, a hot line/reward program involves coworkers essentially "telling on" each other, but according to Pikiell, "it works."

Another type of fraud today is from medical providers. Pikiell says that closely monitoring billing practices for product switching, services not rendered, and multiple office visits is an excellent way to prevent consequences of false claims. Also, establishing a bill review program "builds in a detection and prevention system," Pikiell says.

Employers also may commit fraud, he notes. This type of fraud often occurs when companies underreport payroll, improperly designate job classifications, provide false business addresses, and misrepresent their loss history.

Especially when dealing with employee fraud, medical control through selected doctors should be incorporated at a very early state, according to Walter F. Noeske, a Detroit-based defense attorney specializing in workers compensation and insurance defense for Fortune 500 clients. He is a partner with Conklin, Benham, Ducey, Listman & Chuhran.

Noeske says employers should make known to every employee the seriousness of on-the-job injuries. Although corporate policy should be caring and concerned, it needs to be firm. "We want our employees to be happy, but we want them to know that every claim will be investigated. Some employers don't take the extra step," he says. He emphasizes the need to take small, preventative steps in every claim, regardless of its size.

Good documentation is a crucial part of claim prevention and investigation. All gathered information and investigation should be in writing, signed, and dated, according to Noeske.

"Red flags" of potential workers compensation fraud are numerous. Some big indicators, Pikiell says, are unwitnessed accidents, rumors, employees who fail to appear for scheduled medical exams, and injured employees who cannot be reached at a home telephone number.

Pikiell emphasizes the need for rapid response after spotting a potentially fraudulent claim. He suggests immediately obtaining statements from all witnesses and the injured employee, photographing or videotaping the accident site, and securing equipment maintenance or repair records. "Take photos of the (equipment) manufacturer's name and serial number. Down the road, the machine may be obsolete and gone."

Often private investigators are selected to look into the potential fraud. Pikiell recommends using a full-service company that can accommodate surveillance, background checks, and interviews. Be wary of investigators using out-of-date equipment that may make the surveillance easier to spot.

"They can't simply have the tinted windows. They should blend—everybody is looking for that black van with tinted windows," Pikiell says.

It is imperative that all parties work together, according to Noeske. "Effort must be coordinated and controlled. Never presume that anyone is doing anything. Determine and confirm individual responsibilities in writing at onset. Meet or conference to discuss roles and activities. Communicate." Although the steps may seem basic, "don't be scrambling to put these things together a week before a trial," Noeske says.

Although workers compensation claims are often legiti-

mate, it's important to be aware and prepared for any fraudu-
lence that may occur. "Often the good outweighs the bad. If
there are facts that clearly indicate a legitimate workers compensation case, it's okay. That is what workers compensation is
for," Noeske says.

management issues are rather long-term in nature. However, this
approach of relationship building should be based on a rather rigorous process of broker/agent selection (and, of course, this assumes
that the business has choices to select from). And, obviously, periodic rebidding should be built into the relationship management
process to protect against complacency.

The ideal duration for bidding is open to debate. In some instances, bidding may be expected to occur every year. However,
bidding too frequently is as great a problem as bidding infrequently
because annual bidding creates continuity problems, bars economy
of scale possibilities, and entails significant administrative costs.
When yearly bidding is not the norm, most experts suggest a bidding cycle of three to five years.

There is a tendency for bidding decisions to be based on lowest
cost. Unfortunately, buying insurance or risk management services
on a lowest-cost basis is not necessarily a good idea. When purchasing risk financing services, it would seem that financial security of
the risk-bearing entity would be key, as would the quality of services.

Low-cost procurement is, undoubtedly, the principal frustration expressed by insurance companies, brokers/agents, and other
risk financing providers. Understandably, firms must be attentive
to minimizing costs, but the proliferation of risk financing products
means that insurance (and other alternative financing arrangements) is not a commodity—at least it is not for organizational
buyers of such services. Quality and other nonquantitative variables should be considered.

For some organizations, the selection of a broker/agent is handled separately from the selection of the insurance company. That

is, the firm will first select the broker/agent and then work with that organization to obtain insurance. Thus, the firm would issue a request for proposals (RFP) and the responses would serve as the basis for the decision.

This newer approach differs from traditional methods, which asked brokers to find insurance coverage first and then submit their proposal inclusive of insurance coverage. While in general this approach works fine, it tends to promote one practical problem. If three agents are competing to obtain a firm's business, they will shop the market for the best coverage and will invariably contact many of the same insurance companies. This means that the underwriters at these companies will be responding to three different requests for the same customer. While an underwriter's workload should be of little concern to a risk manager, it is not an efficient approach and can result in some problems when time is of the essence.

Certificates of Insurance

When a firm uses third-party contractors, vicarious liability can become an issue. Consequently, that firm would like to assure itself that the third party can finance any losses it creates and that it can cover the firm's exposure to risk as well. This assurance can come in a number of different forms, such as hold-harmless agreements, additional/named insured provisions, and certificates of insurance.

Hold-harmless agreements are contractual transfers of risk that effectively enable one party to escape potential responsibility. Additional/named insured provisions enable a firm to be named as an additional insured on the third party's coverage—a benefit of some import because it allows the third party's insurance coverage to extend fully to the firm.

The certificate of insurance is a document that provides evidence that insurance is in place to provide coverage for a risk in question. Many organizations develop their own certificate form, but there is a widely used standardized form called the ACORD (Agency Company Operations Research and Development) contract. It is generally available from brokers/agents and insurance companies.

Although a certificate of insurance provides pertinent information on the coverage in place, it has some critical limitations. First, it is not an insurance contract, so it does not extend coverage to the holder. Second, the certificate does not necessarily clarify insurance policy language, and it may in fact confuse a risk manager's understanding of the coverage that is in place. Third, it only ensures that coverage is present at the time the certificate was provided, and it does not guarantee that coverage exists at any future point.

Security for Risk Management Programs

State insurance regulators provide certain financial security guarantees for consumers of insurance products, but increasingly businesses are relying on alternative financing arrangements that are not subject to state oversight. Thus, many arrangements require that additional steps be taken by the risk manager to ensure that the program is financially secure.

Commercial banks offer a variety of collection systems and credit-based products to assist the risk manager in meeting the security objective. Collection systems allow a bank to facilitate transactions through document processing (e.g., bills of lading, invoices, certificates of origination). In addition, these services can include enforcement and legal services, foreign exchange management services, and a myriad of related financial risk services.

Credit-based products tend to be related to letters and lines of credit. The letter of credit is a banking mechanism that secures payment of an obligation. It is, effectively, a promise made by a bank to provide financing should it become necessary; and there are many different letter of credit models (e.g., revocable or irrevocable, straight or negotiable, confirmed or unconfirmed). Lines of credit are more narrowly defined and typically act to secure a fairly confined situation, such as a retrospectively rated insurance policy.

Program Audit and Review

Risk management programs should be audited and reviewed periodically, both from an inside and an outside perspective. Conventionally, a risk manager should have in place a process whereby the entire program is subject to an ongoing and thorough audit process (and this includes not just a financial audit and an actuarial audit, when necessary, but also a performance audit). Less frequently, risk management programs would be advised to submit to an external audit. Although outside evaluation comes with some risk, external validation can become a very important tool in promoting the risk management function within the firm.

One review function that warrants a further discussion is the risk manager's role in claims adjudication and resolution. Regardless of whether the firm self-insures or insures its risks, the risk manager has a supervisory role in the claims management process. Because claims management requires technical knowledge, few risk managers retain complete responsibility for the claims process. If the risk is not insured, the risk manager is likely to have one or more third-party administrators involved in the claim management process. However, whether insured or self-insured with third-party administrator services, the risk manager has a general responsibility for setting claims policy, monitoring and advising the administrator, participating in litigation management, and providing decision-making guidance.

A Final Observation: Whither ORM?

The format of this book has relied on the development of the concept of Organization Risk Management as a means of understanding what risk management is today and—maybe—what it should or could be. However we look at ORM, it is a model in the rather textbook sense—that is, it is a tool for organizing our thinking about a complex subject.

Readers reasonably may challenge the applicability of ORM to real-world practices. While the model provides us with a way to think about risk management, the separate issue of whether ORM actually is practiced in organizations is useful to consider.

The importance of this question is elevated by the fact that there is scant evidence of holistic risk management being practiced today. Certainly there are examples of organization-wide efforts, newly minted chief risk officers, and the like; yet the actual adoption of holistic risk management practices is strangely disproportionate with the levels of enthusiasm that exist for the idea of holistic risk management.

Why is this the case? In some respects, the answer can be inferred from practicing risk managers' comments throughout the book, but the picture is not complete. What follows is a structured set of arguments for the limitations of or impediments to organization-wide risk management. Readers should keep in mind that these are arguments rather than statements of fact, for the holistic risk management idea is new and it is rather too soon to say that it will not ultimately prevail.

1. *Who are the ORM advocates?* Beyond the vendors (e.g., consultants, brokers, insurers, and investment bankers), there does not seem to be a natural constituency for the ORM idea, either inside or outside business organizations. A traditional risk manager may attempt to make the case that a broadened brief is important, but selling ideas is difficult if the manager is not appropriately situated within the organization. At several points in the book it has been argued that the traditional risk manager is not well situated to practice organization-wide risk management (let alone, advocate for it).

If this point has any validity, it may be supported somewhat by the evidence within the few organizations where the ORM idea has caught hold. The suggestion here is that the advocate be sufficiently prominent within the organization to make the ORM case. Intriguingly, the chief risk officer (CRO) idea appears to be most fully developed in the financial services world, where—perhaps unsurprisingly—the core business risks are financial and where the chief financial officer is likely to take ownership of the organization-wide risk management idea.

2. *Do organizations do anything on an organization-wide basis?* Certainly, organizations do operate under organization-wide policies and practices, but the notion of holistic risk management (as it generally is argued in the trade press) presumes a rather intensive day-in, day-out set of integrated activities and practices. So defined, we may reasonably wonder whether real organizations are so organized as to accommodate such an approach to risk management. The answer seems to be no. Even the most autocratic organizations exhibit high degrees of loose-jointedness and tolerate a great deal of inconsistency and autonomy. Why should we expect that such organizations suddenly would become highly structured and integrated for risk management?

3. *Do directors and officers really care about risk management?* We think they do, but the book has attempted to show at different points that the executive or board perspective is different from the type of risk management that gets most of the airplay. For boards, risk management largely is a matter of appreciating attitudes toward risk, searching for consensus on risk, and clarifying its political and broader implications.

The important test case on director and officer commitment is in play in the United Kingdom. Under the aegis of the London Stock Exchange, publicly traded firms are now required to—in effect—have a declared position on risk in order to show how corporate goals and objectives (as well as actual performance) align with the organizational attitude toward risk. Curious readers should look for the Turnbull report, issued by the London Stock Exchange, as an explanation of the new U.K. standard.

4. *Is it possible that the idea of ORM is more important than the practice of ORM?* It may be possible that holistic risk management (again, as it is argued in industry circles) may never gain wide favor within the business world, and it may prove not to matter. That is because the holistic risk management concept (no matter how it is

labeled) already has achieved significant success in the following ways:

- Many managers today recognize that risks are pervasive in organizations and assume that addressing those risks is an important managerial matter.
- Various forms of risk management have emerged within organizations (e.g., finance, legal, operations); whether or not they establish links with other practitioners, their presence is a distinct improvement on the past.
- Further developments in board-level risk management may produce philosophical support for risk management, which then may be carried out in numerous autonomous ways within an organization.
- The risk management services industries (e.g., brokers, insurers, accountants, investment banks, and others), in pursuit of the concept of wholly integrated risk services, have unearthed and/ or developed numerous new products (e.g., capital markets financing products, statistical modeling tools, effective risk communications tools) that have a net benefit to businesses.

Perhaps the bottom line for the holistic risk management idea is not that an organization-wide system be imposed on the organization. Rather, it is the recognition among directors and officers that their organization has a policy or position on risk that can provide guidance for all managers and employees. High levels of autonomy probably are necessary for most forms of risk management, and coordination really only becomes necessary when corporate-wide issues are at stake or economies of scale or scope become important.

And perhaps this is the distinction we would make between our ORM idea and the general view of holistic risk management today. The ORM idea does not require a CRO, a risk team, or even a staff level risk manager. It requires, however, that organization leaders explicitly articulate the business's philosophy of risk and then empower managers and give them incentives to address the risks within their spheres of responsibility. ORM is not something that is done to an organization; it is something an organization does to itself.

Read More About It

Three Winning Ways

John Conley
Reprinted with permission from *Risk Management* magazine, December 1999. Copyright 1999 by Risk Management Society Publishing. All rights reserved. For more information call 212.286.9364. www.rims.org/rmmag

Every corporation has a unique array of risks testing the mettle and imagination of corporate risk managers. The following are profiles of three risk managers who took the road less traveled when it came to managing their companies' exposures. One created a singular return-to-work program that is the benchmark today for other companies; another assembled a unique marketing strategy using a novel weather insurance program; and the last opted for a double trigger insurance policy providing smoother earnings projections. Each broke the mold when it came to managing risk. Here are their stories.

Jeanne Brown

Jeanne Brown's organizational skills are legendary among her coworkers and friends. At home, Brown has a collection of some 3,000 salt-and-pepper shakers, all of them catalogued, photographed, appraised, and displayed. At work, she oversees 6,998 employees (Brown is not the type to round off numbers) in twenty-three states for CSR America, a West Palm Beach, Florida–based manufacturer of concrete blocks and pipes and other construction materials. "I'm a perfectionist; I cannot tolerate anything out of order," says Brown, the company's national risk manager and a member of the Palm Beach chapter of RIMS.

CSR America is the U.S. arm of CSR Ltd., an Australian company that entered the market here through acquisition. The first company it bought, in 1988, was Rinker Materials Corporation, then Brown's employer. Within a year, CSR purchased five more U.S.-based concrete manufacturers, ranging in size from about $1 billion in annual revenues to Rinker's $8 billion. Each of these companies was composed of several subsidiaries in a slew of businesses, from sewerage to quarries to drywall. All of them had their own way of handling claims and safeguarding their workers, and only one of them had any claims automation.

Brown, a risk manager with twenty-six years' experience, was appointed CSR America's national risk manager upon the Rinker acquisition. The challenges loomed large. "The various companies comprising CSR America were dealing with dozens of insurers and multiple third-party claims administrators," Brown recalls. "Altogether I counted 16,212 open claims at the acquired companies, some of them going back decades. Meanwhile, CSR kept acquiring additional companies, small mom-and-pop type shops. The data overload was tremendous. I decided simplification was the key."

Brown opted for a single insurance company (St. Paul), a single TPA (Crawford & Co.) and a single claims administration system (STARS from insurance broker Marsh). She also worked with Marsh to produce relevant claims data to help her manage corporate automobile, general liability, and workers compensation risks. "CSR wanted a decentralized operating structure in the United States linking employee incentive compensation to each location's operating results," Brown says.

"I decided to develop a claims system that would segregate each location's data on a charge back basis—allocating claim losses to each unit and then charging them for those losses. This, in turn, affected a location's budgeting and individual performance appraisals, which determined incentive compensation and bonuses. Not only are workers in charge of their own destiny, we are able to benchmark each of our six locations to keep losses down. I can break down claims information into categories that help me control losses, and then aggregate that data for insurance purposes."

With the disparate claims systems now streamlined into

one purposeful program of collecting and managing loss information, Brown turned her attention next to a particular CSR
trouble spot: workers compensation. "When we launched a return-to-work program here in 1992, we had 122 reportable
lost time injuries," Brown says. "Last year, we reduced that to
twelve."

"Jeanne and CSR are world class when it comes to post-
loss management," says Rick Conner, CSR's broker in the Atlanta office of Marsh. "Over the years, we have tried to find
external benchmarks comparable to what she has accomplished, but there aren't any. CSR is the benchmark in the return-to-work area. Even national organizations like the Bureau
of Labor Statistics and the National Safety Council don't break
down statistics in the sophisticated way that Jeanne and CSR
do."

So what is it that makes CSR's return-to-work program so
successful? It's Brown's philosophy, a no-holds-barred concept
she calls "Everybody Returns to Work." "If someone is injured
and does not require hospitalization, we require them to come
to work," Brown says. "We will provide transport if we have to.
If the worker cannot perform their old job, we'll give them lighter
duties. If they can't do that, then we'll make them comfortable
and provide training, ask them to peruse safety manuals or
watch safety videos. I control their time."

Sounds Machiavellian, but Brown insists the strategy is
win-win for employees and CSR. "According to the Bureau of
Labor Statistics, the average length of time an employee stays
out of work after an injury—in a company without a return-to-
work program—is thirty-three days. Ours is thirteen," she says.
"Employee morale has improved because they're around their
peers doing something other than lying around at home watch-
ing television. They're better off financially, since we pay them
full salaries and benefits, versus the 66.6 percent offered under
workers comp."

Yet, the strategy costs less, says Conner. "People who stay
home after an injury are more apt to stay home," he says.
"Gradually, they develop a negative mindset, and either become a malingerer or call a lawyer. Jeanne has made it so

employees feel needed. The payoff has been reduced lost work-days, lower average costs per claim, and lower average days on restricted duty. Jeanne keeps track of all these statistics and just hammers away at them. Her stats are phenomenal.''

Brown says the work fits her perfectly. ''I simply adore de-tailed stuff,'' she says. ''At home, I pore over my salt-and-pep-per shakers to determine their origins and value. I recently found one that is worth $425. It's a Figaro cat that Disneyland sold for a dollar decades ago. I guard it with my life.''

David Hennes

When the company you work for is in the business of manufac-turing lawnmowers for golf courses, you better learn how to swing an iron. And if the company's financial fortunes are dis-turbed by weather conditions, you better figure out a way to outsmart Mother Nature. David Hennes did both.

As the director of risk management at The Toro Company, a Minneapolis-based manufacturer of irrigation systems, snow-throwing equipment, and lawnmowers, Hennes put together a novel weather insurance program last year that absorbed the cost of customer rebates for Toro's snowthrowing machines. ''In the winter of 1997–1998, we had an El Niño year that caused warmer than usual temperatures and, thus, a lot less snow,'' Hennes recalls.

''When there's no snow, people are less apt to buy a snow-thrower. That caused a huge backlog that affected our summer line of products. When there are a lot of snowthrowers stuck in the distribution chain, there's less room for other stuff.''

Toro needed a way to empty out the snowthrowers blanket-ing its warehouses and dealer outlets. ''We decided to offer con-sumers a refund on the purchase price of a snowthrower that was based on the inches of snowfall in their area,'' Hennes says. ''The rebate would be enticing, up to 50 percent of what they paid. I then looked to lay off the risk of this backfiring on us. We didn't want to give away the store.''

''Dave came to me with the idea of a marketing program that would, in effect, be backed up by insurance,'' says Kevin

Gubrud, a senior vice president with insurance broker Marsh in Minneapolis. "We structured it so that if the snowfall during Toro's critical sales period (from September to December) in a particular region is 40 percent of a pre-agreed average, the consumer would receive 20 percent of the purchase price back. If the snowfall was 20 percent of normal, they got back 50 percent." The insurance, bought from General Star National Insurance Co., cost Toro $425,000 in premium.

The marketing campaign was a huge success. "We emptied our distribution channels," Hennes says. "People gambled that it wouldn't snow and they'd get a snowthrower at half the cost. As a result, we were able to build more products to replenish the pipeline for the coming winter."

Altogether, Toro handed out $250,000 in insured rebates, which turned out to be less than the premium paid—good news for General Star. But Hennes says the strategy was a winner because it achieved the primary purpose of emptying Toro's inventory. "Our consumer division was able to make more aggressive budgets and forecasts because the insurance took the uncertainty out of this business plan," he explains. "Without insurance, I doubt we would have had the confidence to go ahead with the marketing campaign."

The strategy is not something Toro will use each year. "They're passing on it this winter because their pipeline is now clear," Gubrud says. "But when it gets jammed up again because there's no snow, they'll bring it back. When it snows, anybody can sell snowblowers."

Gubrud says Hennes is one of the most skillful risk managers he deals with. "Dave is able to think out of the box," he says. "He's completely original."

Hennes says his expertise is the result of twenty-five years working in risk management for a veritable horde of companies in the Twin Cities. "Let's see, I've been at 3M, Dayton Hudson, Control Data, Diversified Energy Inc., a local utility, and Graco Corp., a pump manufacturer," he says. "I guess you can say I've been around."

As for golf, Hennes says his previous employers didn't put much stock into the game. Toro is another story, altogether.

"More than seventy-five of the top 100 golf courses in the country use our underground sprinkler systems," he says. "Many also use our cutting machines. When I tee off, I do my best not to hit 'em."

Joseph Spencer

Often, when things go bad, they get worse before they get better. Such was the case with FirstEnergy Corporation in June 1998. The Akron, Ohio–based diversified energy company got whacked with what Joe Spencer, its director of risk management, calls a "double whammy." A failure of a transformer at the company's coal-generating plant outside Cleveland knocked out 600 megawatts of power. The next day, the transmission lines stringing into its Toledo-based nuclear plant were torn from the ground by a tornado—another 600 megawatts of power gone.

That's when things got worse. "The temperatures in Ohio and Pennsylvania, our operating region, were stuck in the mid-nineties," Spencer recalls. "Everybody hiked up their air conditioners, creating record demand for electricity. We had to call on our power supply contracts with other generating utilities, but the high demand had outstripped their supply as well, and they defaulted on our contracts. Our only recourse was to buy power on the spot energy market. I absolutely shudder to recall the cost."

Prices on the spot power market had reached ridiculous levels, up to $8,000 per megawatt hour compared with the $50 per FirstEnergy had locked into in its power contracts. The extra expenses—at least $50 million—short-circuited the company's 1998 earnings, down some $104 million. Spencer vowed to find a solution.

He had already begun to venture outside the traditional confines of risk management, working closely with FirstEnergy's trading operation. Like other diversified energy companies, such as Enron, Koch Industries, and Acquila, FirstEnergy trades energy derivatives—a way for it to hedge weather, commodity, and other risks in the capital markets. The experience gave

Spencer, a former accountant with more than twenty years of risk management service, an idea. "I had heard about these double trigger policies that linked uncorrelated exposures together in one insurance policy," he says.

"I thought perhaps it would be possible to link the price of spot power to the loss of our generating capacity, given the rarity of both events occurring simultaneously. If we could put this together, it would provide us with a more predictable earnings stream."

Here's where the bad news finally gets better. Spencer learned about a new line of double trigger policies sold by ACE USA, formerly Cigna Property & Casualty. "I got quotes from three different insurers, but went with the ACE PowerBacker policy, which had the best terms and conditions," he says. "We put together a program that gives us $100 million in coverage if two things happen—a power outage resulting in more than 600 megawatts of lost power, and a spot market power price that exceeds $74 per megawatt hour. Last summer, both triggers actually sprang, but the loss fell below our $25 million retention."

Had the losses exceeded that amount, ACE would have absorbed 90 percent of the cost, up to the full $100 million coverage limit (FirstEnergy has co-insurance, requiring it to pick up 10 percent of the loss after the deductible is breached). Although the cost of the policy is proprietary, other reports indicate it hovers between 4 percent and 8 percent of the coverage limit, roughly $4 million to $8 million.

Spencer also arranged for Energy Insurance Mutual, a Tampa, Florida–based excess general liability insurer, to come into the program as ACE's reinsurer, taking the top layer of risk. "Joe wanted his industry mutual to have the opportunity to be involved with what he felt was a truly innovative strategy," says David Hadler, president of EIM, a mutual insurer with 163 members (including FirstEnergy) formed during the hard market of 1986. "We believe this concept will become more prevalent, and have heard that four or five of our members have already purchased similar programs."

Hadler says Spencer deserves credit for putting together

the new strategy. "He spent months thinking it through and many more placing the actual deal," Hadler adds. "In the rapidly changing utility industry, he is at the forefront of his profession."

Spencer has other ideas up his sleeve, including a possible enterprise risk program blending FirstEnergy's property/casualty exposures with its commodity and finance risks. "People think derivatives will save the world, but there are insurance products out there that are much better—as we have proved," he says. He estimates that FirstEnergy's double trigger policy cost 20 percent less than a comparable derivative put or call hedging the same risks.

As for FirstEnergy's executive management, the double trigger hit the bull's-eye. "Wall Street has given us very positive attention for better quantifying our bottom-line costs and smoothing our revenue stream," Spencer says. So does he still shudder when the temperatures soar beyond capacity levels? "We've put some predictability into our operating costs," he says. "We're covered."

In other words, if things get bad, they won't get worse.

Read More About It

Risk Budgets: Using Your Human Resources

John Mathinsen, Ph.D., John C. Edmunds, and Steven Feinstein
Reprinted with permission from *Risk Management* magazine, April 2000.
Copyright 2000 by Risk Management Society Publishing. All rights reserved.
For more information call 212.286.9364. www.rims.org/rmmag

The ideal risk management system is easy to explain and, in theory, creating and implementing such a system is beguilingly simple. All a business has to do is attack the known risks and maintain the flexibility needed to recognize and adapt to the unknown. But reality does not work out so neatly and ideal systems are rarely achieved.

Nevertheless, it is possible to improve the efficiency and

effectiveness of current risk management systems by examining the lessons of the past and utilizing different perspectives to study the present. The key is using all the resources within the company, from top management to front-line workers. This broad range of input can be summarized and processed in an innovative forum: the risk budget.

Rules of Thumb

Over the past decade, there has been a virtual explosion of theoretical proposals and practical applications in the examination of risk management. We have learned that:

- The ideal risk management system is a moving target that can be easily missed—with often disastrous consequences—by aiming too far behind or too far ahead.
- Risk management systems, approaches, and instruments that claim to convert the risks we have into the risks we want are largely cosmetic. When the cosmetics fade or are inappropriately applied, the faults resurface in poor product selection, pricing, and marketing strategy.
- Covering a complex business organization with a sophisticated risk management system does not eliminate risk; it simply replaces one set of risks with another, which may be more opaque and threatening.
- To combat unforeseen risks, companies need simple, well communicated, and blunt rules of behavior that are indifferent to any particular time, place, or situation. These rules must work on an instinctive rather than cognitive level.
- Risk management is a journey, not a destination.

From these rules we can establish a foundation for a systemwide operational risk management program that touches and is affected by all levels of the organization. But how do we tie all the pieces together?

The annual risk budget addresses each of these risk management lessons and can be easily worked into the framework of the annual financial budgeting process. The risk budget's purpose is to identify the sources of a company's major operating risks, determine which it is willing to face, openly discuss the best way to handle these risks, and assign responsibility for managing and tracking them. It promotes the systematic flow of information from the operating front lines to top management and helps ensure that risk management practices are not wide of the desired mark.

Internal Resources

By respecting the perspective of each level of management and operations, the risk manager develops a better overall picture of the company's health. Gathering information from the operating front lines is important not only for the risks it exposes—the roof seldom collapses without forewarning—but also for what it does not.

For example, take any of the recent disasters, including ValueJet, Chernobyl, Three Mile Island, Barings, P&G, UBS, Solomon Brothers, Orange County, or the *Challenger*. People on the front lines knew what was happening long before each catastrophe. The real issue, after the fact—and what we can learn from—is why the information was not communicated, or if it was, why was it not used? The same analysis can be applied to the loss of national fortunes that resulted from the currency crises in Mexico, Thailand, Indonesia, and Russia.

There are always explanations, but never legitimate excuses. In some cases, it was assumed that top management already knew and approved, or if it did not know, it did not want to know. In other cases, top management was not receptive to hearing bad news. Whistleblowers were seen as loose cannons and not team players. And in the most unfortunate cases, top management knew, but either ignored the warnings or had other priorities. The risk budgeting process examines the vulnerability of the company to similar weaknesses through its utilization of information acquired from all sectors and levels.

Meeting of the Minds

Regardless of a company's goals or stage of development, no risk management system is worth much unless meaningful ways can be found to gather and use the information from the front lines. To this end, an enlightening experience for top management is assembling a group of front-line personnel to discuss the risks the firm faces and to create a risk budget.

The individuals who attend this meeting should be those responsible, in significant ways, for the viability of the company. They should know the business thoroughly and have a full picture of the firm. Participants will vary from company to company, but for large corporations, the risk management department should create a guest list that includes finance managers, marketing managers, and general or affiliate managers. Corporate tax personnel should also be present for advice on taxes and transfer prices. In addition, the CFO and corporate treasury staff can benefit as attentive students.

This meeting should pursue three goals:

1. Identify the major risks facing the company.
2. Get feedback on alternative ways to manage these risks.
3. Uncover the opportunities inherent in the risks.

How many times have changes in external or internal factors put seemingly healthy operations in great peril virtually overnight? External threats have included product liability and antitrust suits, patent rejections, regulatory product denials, discrete technology changes, a negative corporate image, or an economic or natural catastrophe. Internal threats have come from poor product selection, inadequate pipelines, an inability to control costs, or faulty pricing decisions.

Senior management may find examining the company's preparedness for these types of perils both reassuring and frightening. They will be reassured by the fact that most of the risks are known, and risk management subsystems have been put in place to handle nearly all of the most pressing issues. It will be heartening for top management to discover how much they already know (or think they know) and how much has already been done to manage risk.

The frightening part will come into play when management

realizes that, in spite of this, the organization could quickly be brought to its knees by something big, ugly, and life-threatening.

If the company has a long history, a good way to sober the meeting and drive home the message of vulnerability is to reflect on historic events that nearly caused the firm's bankruptcy or led to severe losses. Then, compare today's risks to those past events.

Events so crucial in the past may be nowhere on today's radar screen. If there is any institutional memory of the incidents, it would not be surprising to discover that these past risks were unsuspected by senior management before the events occurred. Twenty-twenty hindsight encourages ridiculing previous management, stating the "obvious" nature of the problem and offering the seemingly simple solution that "ought to have been utilized." This is a dangerous symptom. And even if it is clear that some present company procedures could be improved in light of this comparison, unless there is a significant threat or a huge bottom-line benefit, Pareto's rule (i.e., 80 percent of the time is consumed by the last 20 percent of the work) will stand in the way of any major overhaul.

But in facing these risks, companies may discover more than just the means to mitigate disaster. They may also uncover valuable market opportunities. This is an especially important, but often-overlooked part of these meetings. Because the risks facing a company are likely to be the same ones facing its competitors, the decision to actively manage one or more of the identified risks could be the first step in the development of future core competency.

Effectively utilized, the risk management budgeting process can force the right questions (and answers): What are we blind to today? How can we prepare to face those risks? Can we profit from those risks?

Managing the Resource

The risk budget process illuminates the importance of having a high-quality staff, the basis of every effective risk management system. Those who work for the company are not only its most prolific source of information on potential exposures, they are also its best weapon for prevention.

The common denominator for minimizing virtually all of the internal risks and the effects of many external risks is human resources management. Even for external threats that are clearly out of the control of any person, company or industry (e.g., changes in GDP, exchange or interest rates, or commodity prices), the firm's reaction is based on the decisions of individuals. Putting the right person in the right place at the right time is what makes personnel issues a vital component of risk management.

In fact, one could go so far as to say that the foundation for any cutting-edge risk management system is at the door of the human resources department. Good personnel make first-class decisions about critical issues. What to produce, where and how to produce it, specific markets to target (and avoid), and [an ability to spot] industry trends are keys to the long-term viability of a company, as is having an eye to foresee an impending disaster. These actions must be taken in a corporatewide context and referenced against corporate strategy. And to foster this attitude, top management owes its employees an internal reward system and a clear strategy that provides direction both for the decision making and risk taking that is most valued.

Of course, even if a company invests the time and money to hire the most qualified people, mistakes will still be made and periods of poor performance may still occur. Operating variances will never be reduced to zero, because normal accidents (i.e., accidents due to complexity, as described by Charles Perrow in *Normal Accidents*) and the negative influence of unexpected shocks will always exist. Nevertheless, in such cases, the results will lead to disappointment, but not regret. A risk management system has more to do with the standard deviation of results than with average rates of success. If it reduces downside vulnerability and frees upside potential, it should be considered a success.

Conclusion

Like many insurgencies, the risk management revolution began with thinkers and spread to the masses through simple, commonly understood maxims. Although the most crucial risks must be explicitly managed, risk management must also be made a basic component of the corporate culture, using these practical applications.

To think and act in ways that create the most value, managers and their staff must understand the fundamentals, not the esoterics. To foster this ideal, implementing a risk budgeting process can help companies create a system of thought that encompasses risk management awareness throughout the entity, allows for better risk prevention, and hones a valuable resource of insight into developing exposures.

Read More About It

Vicious Circles: Incubating the Potential for Organizational Failure

By Denis Smith
Reprinted with permission from *Risk Management* magazine, October 1999. Copyright 1999 by Risk Management Society Publishing. All rights reserved. For more information call 212.286.9364. www.rims.org/rmmag

A cursory glance at both the popular and professional press would lead us to believe that most organizations exist on the border of dysfunctionality. The hazards associated with BSE (mad cow disease), genetically modified foods, and the possible contamination of soft drinks have all captured the headlines. Add to this a range of technological failures and transportation accidents, and we see a complex mosaic of problems linked to crisis situations that recognizes few, if any, boundaries.

All organizations have the potential for failure. Just look at the average lifespan of companies, the characteristics of highly visible crisis events, or the range of dysfunctional behaviors—such as harassment, emotional problems and stress, worker safety and health issues, poor communication procedures, and internal conflict—found throughout organizations. How do these issues and the failure potential within organizations escalate into crisis?

While there is little doubt that awareness among managers has increased, there is still considerable ambiguity surrounding the exact nature of crisis. In many respects, crises emerge out of the dysfunctional nature of the organization's very culture, the core beliefs and values of decision makers, and ineffective communication. Irrespective of the causes, it is clear that modern organizations must develop capabilities to cope with these problems.

For many, contingency planning is synonymous with crisis management. At its simplest, crisis management involves the prevention, mitigation, and recovery from those events that can damage the organization's assets. All too often, however, organizations focus on contingency planning without fully considering the incubation of crisis potential; emphasis is placed primarily on issues of corporate recovery in the wake of traumatic events.

Effective crisis management should move beyond contingency planning to deal with the processes of crisis incubation as well as the role of organizational culture in failure. In many cases, traditional approaches to risk neglect these problems, forcing organizations to search for a more strategic and less prescriptive approach to dealing with failure.

Incubating Crisis Potential

Many failures and crises arise from the organization's system of management. By definition, an emerging crisis guarantees that failure modes and pathways will develop for which there is no effective contingency. In fact, the potential for such failures is often built into the system by management practices, protocols, and processes. This creates conditions that may be missed by conventional risk analysis and contingency planning. It is difficult for managers to deal with the limitations of their decisions and the conditions within which decision making occurs. This challenge to the most fundamental of management processes is vexing for organizations.

For example, the early denial of risk to humans from BSE in the United Kingdom led to a control and intervention strategy that failed to acknowledge the root cause of the problem. If BSE presents no risk to humans, then why should we develop a strategy that seeks to prevent it? This state of mind, combined with the multi-agency involvement in the process, served to create an air of complacency among politicians.

Organizations that neglect a complex problem because of a lack of clear proof may seriously degrade their capability to manage the escalation of a crisis by failing to incorporate the unthinkable scenario into their decision making. Even in the face of escalating public fears, the absence of scientific proof prevents organizations from changing their position. Again, in the BSE case, the crisis continued to incubate while the government reassured the public that there was no risk. This vicious circle served to escalate the crisis once it became clear that there was indeed scientific evidence to suggest a link between BSE and new variant Creutzfeldt-Jakob disease.

The concept of crisis incubation owes its origins primarily to the work of the late Barry Turner. In his seminal work, *Man-Made Disasters,* Turner outlines a number of conditions that sit at the heart of the incubation process. The first of these, the notion that the rigid core beliefs and perceptions of managers will inhibit their decision-making capabilities and prevent effective foresight, has been supported by subsequent research.

Turner also notes the importance of organizational culture in helping to set precautionary norms. The idea is that those in management who devise rules and restrictions to prevent a crisis may help to create that very event through their system of beliefs. This condition remains a key source of denial and ensures that controls will be inadequate.

Thus the process of contingency planning can never be adequate in itself—it must always be accompanied by a challenge to the core beliefs and precautionary norms of the organization.

A major step toward this goal is the development of a greater understanding of the nature of crisis incubation and possible intervention strategies. One of the biggest problems for effective crisis prevention, however, centers on the definition of the term itself.

Defining Crisis

Crisis is one of the most misused terms in management literature. Perhaps the best definition is put forward by P. Shrivastava, et al.: "[Crises are] organizationally based disasters which cause extensive damage and social disruption, involve multiple stakeholders, and unfold through complex technological, organizational, and social processes" (*Journal of Management Studies,* 1988).

Elaborating on this, T. Pauchant and I. Mitroff see a crisis as requiring "at least two conditions: first, the whole system needs to be affected to the point of being physically disturbed in its entirety; second, the basic assumptions of the members of that system need to be challenged to the point where they are forced either to realize the faulty foundation of these assumptions, or to develop defense mechanisms against these assumptions" (*The Crisis Prone Organization,* St. Martin's Griffen, 1992).

The distinction needs to be made between a major incident and a crisis, since the terms are often used interchangeably, causing confusion.

While incidents are potentially damaging and need to be managed effectively, they do not threaten the existence of the organization; mitigation strategies in place prevent their escalation. Mitigation is not simply a function of contingency approaches, but also a reflection of the behavioral, emotional, and cultural interventions that have occurred prior to the event. Put another way, it means the organization has learned to a certain extent how to prevent the potential for crisis from incubating. While complete prevention can probably never be achieved, dealing with the issues of incubation will serve to enhance the organization's capabilities in this regard.

Learning Problems

It is argued that the process of learning can help to prevent the incubation of crisis potential and improve corporate response to such threats in terms of containment, control, and recovery.

However, barriers to learning exist which fuel the incubation process. It is this vicious circle that managers need to break into.

Ideally, learning should take place vicariously—organizations should be able to learn from the experiences of others. Unfortunately, many companies show a reluctance to acknowledge that the conditions that preceded a crisis elsewhere could exist within their own organization. Added to this are a series of information-based problems that center on the inability to cull and synthesize the information necessary to learn from an event. Even those organizations faced with a crisis find it hard to draw together its important lessons.

The stigma of association is also an important barrier. Those employees involved in the crisis are often both traumatized and stigmatized by the event. These factors will invariably inhibit the learning process. Those traumatized by the crisis may find it impossible to make sense of the events as the stress of the incident gives rise to confusion, and fear of recrimination leads to a reconstruction of events. The stigma of association may dissuade others from acknowledging that they too may run the risk of a similar fate.

Fueling the Process of Incubation

Turner argues that some organizations show a tendency to deny the warnings of crisis potential when these come from outside the organization. In addition, organizations also tend to deny warnings presented by those deemed not to have legitimate expertise in the area.

For example, with the space shuttle *Challenger* disaster, warnings from NASA's O-Ring contractor about the risks of a low temperature launch were ignored. It could be argued that such outside views challenged the organizational exclusivity of NASA, which coupled disastrously with mounting political pressures to allow the ill-fated launch to go ahead.

Of course, for emergent crises, there is never likely to be any a priori evidence. It is the emergence that managers have to deal with in order to prevent the limitations of their contingency planning from being exposed. This requires much more than simply planning for known events and necessitates that organizations not dismiss the impossible accident. In the BSE case, the credibility of a scientist concerned was called into question in Parliament itself as the government sought to maintain its position that there was no risk from eating British beef. This denial allowed the problem to incubate further and exposed more people to the risks.

The decoy phenomenon also fuels the incubation process. Turner argues that organizations become distracted by those problems that can be easily identified, thereby preventing other problems from receiving attention. This arises from the tendency to break problems down into smaller, easily managed components, without giving sufficient consideration to the wider scope of these aggregated factors.

In the BSE case, government ministers believed that the controls that they had put in place were sufficient to deal with the problem. Many of their assumptions concerning the risks from BSE to humans were based on this certainty in the supremacy of their controls. Combined with the lack of evidence surrounding the possible transfer mechanisms to humans, this assumption created the conditions for crisis. The public health advice on beef was based on reassurances that the controls were working.

Such a reductionist and multi-agency approach to complex problems generally serves to compound communication difficulties. But simply increasing communication within an ill-structured managerial system is no remedy; providing more information when the nature of the problem is still unclear simply results in making the issue more opaque. As a result, the potential victims of the crisis are not fully informed about the hazards.

This raises a further issue in the incubation process, namely the approach taken by the organization toward its corporate responsibility. Ultimately, an organization's crisis management strategy is the result of a number of factors, including the core beliefs and values of managers, the company's view of regulation and compliance, and issues of power and expertise in risk communication and control. The willingness of an organization to acknowledge the limitations of its own knowledge base and to communicate the nature of that uncertainty are important aspects of a responsible approach to crisis incubation. Using precaution in areas of uncertainty, where the potential consequences of the activity are considerable but unproven, may ultimately be considered the best approach to crisis prevention.

The final condition of emergence centers on the role of human error in terms of both operational and latent factors. Human error lies at the heart of many organizational failures. Blaming lower-level operators for errors that are designed into the work system, however, distorts our understanding of causal relationships. In particular, such factors as the compression of decision making (storming), the lack of a sufficiently diverse decision-making body, poor managerial controls, and the lack of foresight on the part of decision makers can all create latent conditions for failure that may become manifest at lower levels of the organization. Our understanding of the cognitive processes by which managers view the world remains a significant and persistent challenge for future research in this area.

Regulations

Much of the incubation process is framed within the regulatory environment in which organizations work. Failure to comply, and the outmoded nature of such regulations, are key components of the process. An early example of poor regulatory controls can be found in the case of the *Titanic*. Here, the U.K. Board of Trade failed to take account of the increased size of ships and the growth in passenger numbers when determining minimum lifeboat requirements. The operating company, White Star Line, while exceeding the regulatory requirements, did not believe that the ship could sink and therefore failed to provide lifeboats for all the passengers and crew onboard.

Turner notes the importance of effective monitoring and control with regard to compliance. After all, if we argue that regulation exists because organizations do not conform to best practices, why should we believe that the same organizations would conform to legislation unless there is an effective policing mechanism? Legislation may provide an illusion of control, but unless its requirements are continually monitored, updated, and policed, it may simply serve to encourage incubation.

Conclusions

The processes by which organizations incubate crisis potential remain some of the most important challenges for management research and practice. Without systematic attempts to address this incubation process, any attempts to develop contingency plans will be based upon the shifting sands of incubation.

But there is no simple diagnostic for the crisis-prone organization. Organizations need to constantly challenge their core assumptions and beliefs concerning the nature of their activities and the potential crises they face. Ultimately, the solutions and causes of crisis incubation are tightly linked and embedded in the psychological and emotional characteristics of the organization. A constant challenge to these factors is perhaps the only way to move beyond contingency planning toward developing a more open culture for dealing with crises.

Suggested Readings

Each of the listed publications was used in preparation of this book. They serve as additional resources for readers looking for more detailed treatment of each of the subjects introduced.

Adams, J. *Risk.* London: UCL Press, 1998.

Arthur Andersen and Risk Books, eds. *Operational Risk and Financial Institutions.* London: Risk Books, 1998.

Barton, L. *Crisis in Organizations: Managing and Communicating in the Heat of Chaos.* Cincinnati: South-Western Publishing Co., 1993.

Beam, B. T., Jr., and J. J. McFadden. *Employee Benefits.* 3rd Edition. Chicago: Dearborn Financial Publishing, Inc., 1992.

Bernstein, P. L. *Against the Gods: The Remarkable Story of Risk.* New York: John Wiley & Sons, Inc., 1996.

Black, K., and H. Skipper, Jr. *Life Insurance.* 12th Edition. Englewood Cliffs, NJ: Prentice Hall, Inc., 1994.

Brealy, R. A., and S. C. Myers. *Principles of Corporate Finance.* 5th Edition. New York: Irwin McGraw-Hill Book Company, 1996.

Brown, G. W., and D. H. Chew, eds. *Corporate Risk: Strategies and Management.* London: Risk Books, 1999.

Doherty, N. A. *Integrated Risk Management: Techniques and Strategies for Reducing Risk.* New York: McGraw-Hill Book Company, 2000.

Dorfman, M. S. *Introduction to Risk Management and Insurance.* Englewood Cliffs, NJ: Prentice Hall, 1997.

Head, G. L. *Essentials of Risk Control.* Vols. I and II. Malvern, PA: Insurance Institute of America, 1995.

Head, G. L., and S. Horn, II. *Essentials of the Risk Management Process.* Vols. I and II. Malvern, PA: Insurance Institute of America, 1997

Head, G. L., M. W. Elliott, and J. D. Blinn. *Essentials of Risk Financing.* Vols. I and II. Malvern, PA: Insurance Institute of America, 1996.

Leverett, E. J., Jr. "Risk Management and Insurance." Athens, GA: University of Georgia, unpublished manuscript, 1992.

Mann, R. A., and B. S. Roberts. *Smith and Roberson's Business Law.* 8th Edition. St. Paul, MN: West Publishing Company, 1991.

Marshall, J. F., and V. K. Bansal. *Financial Engineering: A Complete Guide to Financial Innovation.* New York: Allyn & Bacon, 1992.

Pfaffle, A. E., and S. Nicosia. *Risk Analysis Guide to Insurance and Employee Benefits.* New York: AMACOM, 1999.

Public Risk Management Association (PRIMA). *State of the Profession.* Arlington, VA: PRIMA, forthcoming, June 2000.

Richards, E. *Law for Global Business.* Burr Ridge, IL: Richard D. Irwin, 1994.

Risk and Insurance Management Association, Inc. (RIMS). *Annual State of the Profession Survey.* New York: RIMS, annually.

———. *Cost of Risk Survey.* New York: RIMS, annually.

Towers Perrin. *Captive Insurance Company Reports.* Stamford, CT: Towers Perrin, quarterly.

Trimpop, R. M. *The Psychology of Risk Taking Behavior.* Amsterdam: Morth-Holland Publishing Company, 1994.

Vaughan, E. J. *Essentials of Insurance: A Risk Management Perspective.* New York: John Wiley & Sons, 1995.

Williams, C. A., Jr., M. L. Smith, and P. C. Young, *Risk Management and Insurance.* 8th Edition. New York: Irwin McGraw-Hill, 1998.

Young, P. C. *Managing Risk in Local Government.* Austin, TX: Sheshunoff Information Services, 1999.

Zagaski, C. A., Jr. *Environmental Risk and Insurance.* Chelsea, MI: Lewis Publishers, 1992.

Index